HISTORY

OF

THE IRISH CONFEDERATION

AND

THE WAR IN IRELAND,

1641-1649

AMS PRESS

NEW YORK

T.

HISTORY

OF

THE IRISH CONFEDERATION

AND

THE WAR IN IRELAND.

VOLUME III.—1643-1644:

CONTAINING A NARRATIVE OF AFFAIRS OF IRELAND. BY RICHARD BELLINGS, AUTHOR OF "A SIXTH BOOK OF THE COUNTESS OF PEMBROKE'S ARCADIA," SECRETARY OF THE SUPREME COUNCIL OF THE IRISH CONFEDERATION. WITH CORRESPONDENCE AND DOCUMENTS OF THE CONFEDERATION AND OF THE ADMINISTRATORS OF THE ENGLISH GOVERNMENT IN IRELAND, CONTEMPORARY STATEMENTS, ETC.

NOW FOR THE FIRST TIME PUBLISHED FROM ORIGINAL MANUSCRIPTS.

EDITED BY

JOHN T. GILBERT, F.S.A., M.R.I.A.,

LATE SECRETARY OF THE PUBLIC RECORD OFFICE OF IRELAND;
AUTHOR OF "A HISTORY OF THE CITY OF DUBLIN;" "HISTORY OF VICEROYS OF IRELAND;"
EDITOR OF "FACSIMILES OF NATIONAL MSS. OF IRELAND;" ETC.

ILLUSTRATED WITH FACSIMILES.

DUBLIN:

PRINTED FOR THE EDITOR BY

M. H. GILL & SON, 50 UPPER SACKVILLE-STREET.

1885.

Library of Congress Cataloging in Publication Data

Gilbert, Sir John Thomas, 1829-1898, ed.
    History of the Irish Confederation and the war
of Ireland, 1641ₜ-1649ⱼ.

    Title and imprint vary slightly; on t.p. of
v. 1-2: In two volumes.
    Reprint of the 1882-91 ed.
    1. Irish Confederation, 1642-1648.
2. Ireland—History—Rebellion of 1641.
I. Bellings, Richard, d. 1677. II. Title.
DA943.G462   941.06   72-144616
ISBN 0-404-02840-3

Reprinted with permission from a volume in the George Peabody
Department, Enoch Pratt Free Library, Baltimore, Maryland, 1973.

Reprinted from the edition of 1885, Dublin
First AMS edition published, 1973
Manufactured in the United States of America

International Standard Book Number:
Complete Set: 0-404-02840-3
Volume 3: 0-404-02843-8

AMS PRESS, INC.
New York, N. Y. 10003

PREFACE.

THE present volume commences with an account by Richard Bellings of the affairs of Ireland during the year subsequent to September, 1643. In that month a treaty was executed for a Cessation of hostilities for one year between the Irish and Charles I. This narrative of the period 1643-44 is in sequence to the earlier portion of the history by Bellings, published in our first volume, and, although brief, supplies some details, not elsewhere extant, in relation to important affairs of which he had personal cognizance.

The narrative by Bellings is here supplemented with a series of hitherto unpublished documents extending over the period to which it relates. Of these papers, and the subjects with which they are connected, the following may be mentioned :

Transactions in Ireland arising out of the terms of the treaty of Cessation,[1] and the arrangements for its renewal.[2]

Appointment of and proceedings by agents delegated by the Confederation to attend on Charles I. in England.[3]

Propositions laid before the King on behalf of the Irish Catholics[4] and on the part of Protestants[5] in Ireland.

1. Pages 24-62.   2. Pages 267-273.   3. Pages 65, 85, 136.   4. Page 128.
5. Page 143.

Ordinances by the Confederates relative to the oath of Association,[1] the administration of justice,[2] and the collection of export and import customs duties.[3]

Expulsion of the Irish from Cork and other towns in Munster, by direction of Murragh O'Brien, Baron of Inchiquin,[4] in contravention of the articles of Cessation.

Relations between the Confederation and Queen Henrietta-Maria,[5] Prince Rupert,[6] the Earl of Antrim,[7] and his wife,[8] Katherine, Duchess of Buckingham.

Arrangements for the military expedition, under the command of the Earl of Castlehaven,[9] against the Parliamentarians and Scots in Ulster.

Proclamation by the Confederation against Covenanters,[10] and despatch of troops from Ireland to aid royalists in England and Scotland.[11]

Correspondence, discussions, and negotiations, which, with a view to the establishment of a permanent peace, were carried on between the

1. Page 212. 2. Page 266. 3. Pages 117-120. 4. Pages 221 230, 235-244.
5. Page 271. 6. Page 87. 7, 8. Pages 248-9, 257, 260.

9. Pages 74, 201. In connexion with his appointment, Lord Castlehaven has left the following particulars :—" It coming to the question who should be General of this army, they went to the election after this manner: The [General] Assembly [of the Confederation] sitting. those they thought fit to come in competition, they caused their names, one under another, to be written down, and from each a long line drawn. Then at the table where the Clerk sate, every member of the General Assembly, one after another, with a pen puts a dash on the line of him that he would have to be General. And to the end that none should mark more than once, four or five were chosen out of the Assembly, two of which were Bishops, to overlook this marking, being on their oath. Now, contrary to Owen O'Neal's exspectation, who had designed this generalship for himself, by which he would be Generalissimo, I was chosen."—" Memoirs of James, Lord Audley, Earl of Castlehaven." London : 1680. See also pages 74, 201, 230, and " Contemporary History of Affairs in Ireland, 1641-52." Dublin, 1879-1880.

10. Page 205. 11. Pages 31, 112.

Marquis of Ormonde, as Viceroy,[1] and the Commissioners of the Confederation. The latter documents extend here from page 277 to page 328. They exhibit the views entertained by the Irish Catholics on the constitutional rights to which they were entitled, and the grounds on which they sought them. Among their claims were those for the repeal of all penal acts against Irish Catholics ;[2] the right to a Parliament[3] in Ireland independent of that of England, and constituted solely of resident proprietors ;[4] the erection of Inns of Court,[5] universities and schools[6] in Ireland ; equality for Irish Catholics in the distribution of appointments to offices, places of honour, profit, or trust ;[7] and annulment of statutes passed in England for the confiscation of Irish lands.[8] The Commissioners for the Confederation, in a statement in 1644, observed that there were then in Ireland a hundred Catholics to one of any other religion.[9]

In connection with the foreign relations of the Irish Confederation are the records of the receptions at Kilkenny of the Spanish and French envoys ;[10] correspondence with the King of France, the Queen-Regent, and Mazarin,[11] and letters written from Ireland to that Cardinal by his agent, De la Monnerie.[12] We have here, also, despatches from the Confederation to their agents abroad,[13] as well as letters to the Pope,[14] Cardinals,[15] the Nuncio in France,[16] and the Governor of Spanish Flanders,[17] and a proclamation against interference between Hollanders and the Irish Confederation.[18]

1. Ormonde was appointed Lord Lieutenant of Ireland by patent dated at Oxford, 13th November, 1643, and was sworn into office on the 21st of the following January, at Christ Church, Dublin.
2. Page 128.   3, 4, 5, 6, 7, 8. Pages 128-133.   9. Page 302·   10. Pages 102, 105, 115.   11. Pages 71, 72, 106, 108, 109, 142, 180, 185, 232, 263.   12. Pages 94, 135, 195, 232.   13. Pages 23, 73, 95, 99, 109, 165, 194, 262-265·   14. Pages 21, 186.   15. Page 188·   16. Pages 69, 72, 184, 185.   17. Pages 103, 262.   18. Page 150.

The communications addressed by the Supreme Council of the Irish Confederation to royal and eminent personages on the Continent were in Latin. They are, in the present as in our second volume, accompanied by epitomes in English.[1]

In the Appendix are a recently-found letter from Sir Patrick Wemys, in relation to the engagement at Julianstown, in November, 1641 ; a French manifesto from the Irish Confederates ; and a catalogue of Peers and others in Ireland outlawed for high treason in 1641-43. The latter document furnishes valuable information relative to individuals at the time when officials adverse to the claims of the Irish declared that "the greatest part of the freeholders in Ireland were in actual rebellion."

Among the illustrations in the present volume is a reproduction of Magdalena Passe's engraved portrait of Katherine, Duchess of Buckingham,[2] who took an active interest in the affairs of the Irish, as will

---

1. In relation to letters of the Supreme Council the following appears in the journals of the House of Commons, London, under date of 21st March, 1643-4 :—"Mr. Whittacre presents from the committee a letter intercepted from those who term themselves the Supreme Council of the Confederate Catholicks of Ireland, of February eighteenth, to Monsieur the Cardinal Mazarine, concerning the levying of two thousand foot, besides officers, in the kingdom of Ireland, for the French King's service. And it is ordered that these intercepted letters and papers be referred to the consideration of the committee of both kingdoms to do with them as they shall think fitting."—Commons' Journals, vol. iii. p. 433.

2. Under another rare print of the Duchess by Delarame are the following lines :

"The auncients who three Graces onely knew,
Were rude and ignorant : looke here, and view
Thousandes in this one visage ; yea in this
Which of the living but a shadow is.
If thus her outward graces be refin'd,
What be th' interior bewties of her mind ?"

be seen by her letters, at pp. 249, 260, in the present volume. The historian, Clarendon, described her as a lady of "very great wit and spirit." Facsimiles are given from the writings of Cardinal Mazarin's agent, De la Monnerie; from the letter of the Confederation to Pope Urban VIII.; and of the signatures to the agreement for the renewal of the treaty for a Cessation in September, 1644.

Under the Irish Confederates the press in Ireland was freed from the restrictions imposed on it by the administrators of the English Government there. The Supreme Council of the Irish Confederation at first contemplated the introduction of printers from Flanders.[1] A manifesto issued in France by the Irish Confederates appears in the present volume, together with a reproduction of the title-page of the "Remonstrance of Grievances," published at Waterford by Thomas Bourke, printer to the Irish Confederation. The latter publication is of interest as the first of its class produced in Ireland by a native printer. Another production of the press of Thomas Bourke at Waterford, in 1643, was that entitled "Laws and Orders of War," here printed at pages 74-85, from an unique copy[2] in the archives of the Franciscans of the Irish province. Bourke also printed at Waterford, in that year, "An Argument delivered by Patricke Darcy, Esquire, by the expresse order of the House of Commons in the Parliament of Ireland, 9 Junii, 1641." A treatise styled "Alexipharmacon," which Walter Enos, D.D., dedicated to "The Confederate Catholics of the kingdom of Ireland," was "printed at Waterford by Thomas Bourke, in the months of August and September, 1644."

For the letter[3] addressed by Louis XIV. to the Supreme Council of

1. Vol. i., p. lxx.; ii. p. 126.
2. On the lower part of the title-page is a cross inscribed; "In hoc signo vinces."
3. Page 142.

the Irish Confederation, and hitherto unpublished, the Editor is indebted to the eminent French archivist, M. A. Chéruel, and to M. H. d'Arbois de Jubainville, Professor in the Collège de France, author of "Cours de Littérature Celtique." In connexion with the despatches of De la Monnerie, preserved in the Archives des Affaires Étrangères, Paris, the Editor has to acknowledge his obligations to M. Armand Baschet, Paris, author of important works on French and Venetian archives, and on the history of France.

In the next volume, the history and documents of the Irish Confederation will be continued to the period of the arrival in Ireland of Rinuccini, Nuncio from Pope Innocent X.

JOHN T. GILBERT.

Villa Nova, Blackrock,
Dublin, 1st of June, 1885.

LIST OF ILLUSTRATIONS.

VOL. III.

CONTENTS

OF

THE THIRD VOLUME.

I.—History by Richard Bellings, Secretary of the Irish Confederation.

LETTERS, DOCUMENTS, ETC.

ADDENDA.

HISTORY

OF

THE IRISH CONFEDERATION

AND

THE WAR IN IRELAND

VOL. III.

1643-1644.

HISTORY

OF

THE IRISH CONFEDERATION

AND

THE WAR IN IRELAND.

BY RICHARD BELLINGS.[1]

AFTER concludeing the Cessation [15th September, 1643], the Lord of
Ormonde applied his whole endeavours to make preparations for transporting the army into England, and haveing overcome the many difficulties
which the necessitous times, his proper wants, the generall indigence of
the armie's exhausted quarters, the often renewed pressures of the citty,
and the slow payments made by the Confederates in pursuance of their
offer, had laid in his way, at first made it his design to conduct them in
person. But reflecting what inconveniencies might follow his going with
men whom their wants would make mutinous and disorderly, untill he
were assured that good provision were made for them in England to prevent spoil and rapine, and running away to the contrary party ; he inclined first to make triall of their demeanour, by sending over four thousand foot under the command of Colonel Gibson and Sir Michael Earnely.
Nor did the Lord of Clanricarde spare to lay before him as a further motive
for his stay, that it might give encouragement to the worse affected of the
Irish to overrule those that were well inclined, when his person, power,

---

1. The preceding portion of the History by Bellings, down to the conclusion of the
Cessation, will be found in vol. i., pp. 1-164.

2

and interest should be absent. But the convinceing argument for his iay-
ing aside any thought, even for the future, of leaveing the kingdome, was
the trust his Majestie conferred upon him of commanding it as his Lieutenant-General; and from this time the nation began to fancie to themselves an intire settlement, and most men applied their endeavours to
compasse it. To which end a General Assembly was convened at Waterford, where the chooseing of agents to be imployed to the King, together
with the instructions to be given them, and the designe sett on foot to
carry on the warre powerfully in Ulster, were the principall matters that
came into debate.

The election made of the Lord of Muskery, Mr. Alexander MacDaniel,
brother to the Lord of Antrim, Mr. Nicholas Plunket, Sir Robert Talbott,
Mr. Dermott O'Brien, and Mr. Geoffrey Brown, who were the persons
intrusted for that imployment, took up no time; but the instructions were
long agitated, some thinking that they denyed themselves all they did not
ask, and others being of opinion, that, considering the nature of the times
and the King's present condition, many things were to be omitted, which
in a calmer season were not only fit but necessary to be demanded. At
length they fell to contriving of mediums which had the fortune not to be
intirely satisfactory in Ireland, and were no way acceptable in England.

But we may well say, that if the Confederates framed their Propositions without due regard of the times, the agents from the Protestants of
Ireland, sent at the same time to Court, in drawing up theirs meant rather
to obstruct than lay open any way of accommodation, it being folly (as it
was written from thence by a man of eminent quality) to think that peace
could be procured upon conditions of any affinity with those; whereof the
reader may with more light make a judgment, when he shall have read
the Propositions[1] of all sides printed at Waterford, in the year 1644. But
although those soe great distances were not composed att Oxford, and that
so intricate a work required a longer time to perfect it, yet the King did
then lay a foundation of what after followed, by his Commission to the
Lord Lieutenant, which enabled him to prosecute that affaire.

1. See. *post*, " The Demands of the Roman Catholics of Ireland, 1644."

The service in Ulster against the Scots that had not submitted to the Cessation, came next to be agitated, and neither the moulding of an army out of the forces in the other provinces which the Cessation had rendered useless at home, nor the wayes taken of makeing provisions for it, were so long insisted upon as the naming of a person to command it. The matter at first seemed to be controverted between the Generall of Leinster and the Generall of Ulster. Some were of opinion that Owen O'Neale, who was chief in command for the Confederates in that province, which was to be the seat of the war, should likewise command the auxiliaries. But, although the greater number that stood for the negative, derived arguments from remoter causes, yet the truth is, the apprehensions they had of putting so great a power into the hands of Generall Owen O'Neale, and that antient and everlasting difference between Leagh Cuin and Leagh Mow, which are the tracts of ground lying to the north and south of Ireland, prevailed more with them than his abilities and capacities to undergo that charge, for which in the judgment of all men he apparently meritted to be preferred beyond his competitor. And although Generall Preston seemed, by reason of the number of his friends and allies in the Pale who had votes in that Assembly, to stand fair for carrying it ; yet, when the first heats of discourse were past, and that some of their Supreame Councel (to whose opinion, as being a body grown more knowing by experience, the Assembly deferred much), began to lay before them how improbable it was that such success, as they all wished and all of them were interested in, should attend that choyce of Generall Preston, between whom and Generall Owen O'Neale there was such an antipathy, as, from their first apprentiship in souldiery, which they had past att least thirty years before, notwithstanding their having served for all that time the same Prince, and been imployed in the same actions of war, could not be removed, they were calmed, and they elected the Earl of Castlehaven, a person generally beloved, and so unconcerned in any benefitt or advantage that might be acquired not only by this, but by any of the severall great imployments with which he was intrusted among the Confederates, that no man could tax him of haveing other interest than the publicke, during all the time that he served them ; and Generall Owen O'Neale, in appearance, might perhaps (upon the exclusion of his antient antagonist) at thatt time have been really satisfyed with it. But we shall hereafter finde, that they did not multiply the very few examples of concord between two persons of equall and absolute authority in armes employed upon the same action.

Whilst the Assembly sate at Waterford, the Lord of Antrim that believed there was fitt occasion offered him upon the sending of agents to Oxford from the Confederates, to make known att Court how great his power was in his country, and how usefully he was able to serve the King, entertained thoughts of having himself declared Lieutenant-Generall of the Confederate Catholicks of Ireland; and haveing received incouragement therein from some friends of his that had a part in the government, the designe was framed with much industry, and prosecuted with no little earnestness in his behalf att Councell. It was said that there could be nothing which would more conduce to make the mission into England successfull, than the mediation of powerful friends at Court; and that it was well known what influence the Dutchess of Buckingham had upon the affections of those from whom they were to expect satisfaction in their demands, and what willingness she had already expressed to do them good offices; that to show their gratitude and to oblige her to continue, and (as the present occasion required it) to increase her care in their affaires, it were to be considered whether they ought not to finde out a title with reference to some employment amongst them, that might appeare as the mark of an eminent trust, and to move the Assembly that it might be conferred on the Lord, her husband, and their own countreyman, and whether he might not be fitly named Lieutenant-Generall of the Confederate Catholickes; it was further alledged that the fame of such an employment would strengthen his partie in Scotland, and consequently by diversion free the Confederates from some part of the harme they were to expect from the dayly increaseing power of the Scots in the north. The major part of the Councell, who already found by experience what authority particular Generalls in provinces assumed, had it more in their care to draw the eyes of the souldiers on themselves, and to appropriate the dependance of their affections to the board. Expressing in their countenance their dislike to this motion, the proposer said, that if it were understood, he intended to have him invested in a reall authority to command our armyes or to manage the war, by directing the actions of any of the generalls, his meaneing was mistaken; that for his part the bare title was that which he offered to their considerations, which would get him reputation at Court, and inable him to imploy it for the advantage of the Confederates; that the benefit to be expected by the Lady Duchess's mediation would be worthy the honour done unto her husband in such a name, which, being accompanied with no power, was incapable of prejudiceing their affaires. Although some then att Councell were not ignorant that those were the degrees by which matters of this nature and of less consequence had been formerly introduced; yet, observing how plausibly this offer was made, and being resolved to watch that nothing should creep in which might invallidate the contract, or open a way for this ayery title to become a reall power, the proposition was carryed to the Assembly, and the matter comeing recommended by Councel, it was ordered without debate, that the Supreame Councel should write a letter to the Lord of Antrim, letting him know that the Assembly had chosen him to be Lieutenant-Generall of the Confederate Catholickes.

But when this letter came to be drawn up, the Secretary [Bellings] tould the Councell, that as he was to obey the commands of the House in writing to the Lord of Antrim, which he conceived he ought to doe in such expressions as might best procure him creditt at Court and most oblige the Duchess, which was the principall scope of that letter, so he was likewise to putt them in mind that they ought to provide that it should not lye in the power of the Lord of Antrim to make other use of it, least the Assembly, that granted the request without looking into the grounds, because it moved from them, and they, who made it with reference to an intention that no use, in order to a reall power, should be made of it, might find themselves deceived; and to prevent this, he desired, that since the Lord of Antrim was then absent att Wexford, so as the promises which were made in this behalf could not be authenticated by signature, he might be allowed to write a letter from himself, as by their command, wherein he might informe him to what restrictions their Lordships' ample letter, to be inclosed in that he sent himself, was limited; which being thought reasonable, the Councell haveing seen and approved of what he writte, he made up the dispatch. And this after proved to be a necessary precaution; for the Lord of Antrim comeing to Oxford with so large a trust from the Confederates, he made a double returne, being magnyfied at Court upon the accompt of the Confederates, and att Waterford upon the score of his favour at Court. And being soon dispatched from thence, not onely with large authoritie in relation to the affaires of Scotland, but with a Commission,[1] under the great seal of England, to commande the tenn thousand men, whereof the Confederates by their Remonstrance of the 17th of March, 1642[-3], made offer to the King, when apt remedies were applyed to their grieveances and heavy pressures.[2] And so intent he was upon the execution of what he undertook, that he returned to Kilkenny, where the Councell then sat, att the same time that the agents deputed by the Assembly at Waterford, stayed for a wind att Wexford to transporte them into England; and from thence he dispatched letters to his brother, who was one of the agents, and whom he designed for Scotland, to stay him from his intended voyage, whilst he himself was to attend the charge of tenn thousand men he was to conduct. But his brother prosecuted the trust he had from the Confederates, and himself entered somewhat abruptly upon the management of the power given him. For the Earl of Castlehaven coming to take his leave of the Lord of Antrim a day or two after he came to Kilkenny, and letting him know that he was then goeing to meet the army att the randezvous, the Lord of Antrim asked him what armie; and the Lord of Castlehaven answering it was the armie designed for the expedition of Ulster: Nay, replyed my Lord of Antrim, they are to face about, for I am to carry them to serve the King in England. The Councell was surprized to finde the tenn thousand men, promised by the Confederates upon the conclusion of a settlement in the kingdome, were now in a manner exacted by the Lord of Antrim (who tould them it would be ill taken at Court, if they were not sent before any treaty for applying remedies to their grievances were entered upon),

1. For this document, see, post, under date of 20th January, 1643-4.
2. See vol. ii., p. 241.

and being no way satisfied by his proceedings, commanded the Earl of Castlehaven to continue the design for Ulster.

Whilst the Councell, after the recess of the Assembly, sate at Waterford, Cardinall Mazarine, whom the Queen-Regent of France, after the death of Lewis XIII., had chosen to be first Minister of State, haveing understood that the King of Spaine had, by the friendly reception given the Irish agents imployed to Madrid, and by some moneys for their use put into the hands of Father James Talbott, of which we have formerly made mention, sought to ingratiate himself to the nation, thought it now time for him to look into the affaires of Ireland, and, assuring the Councell by his letters, that he would alwayes endeavour to induce the Queen to assist them with her authority and creditt, and to procure them all the ease and advantage which they could reasonably desire for their consciences and fortunes. He forgott not to putt them in mind that their ancestors[1] had in former times made choyce of contrary remedies to these which onely are allowable in the case of subjects, to witt, prayers and remonstrances from themselves, and intercessions and good offices from other Princes, and had recourse to foreign force, to which God gave not a blessing, and which produced nothing but their oppression, and an incurable distrust in the mind of their Sovereigne, who believed they were therefore only his subjects, because they were not able to be the subjects of that Prince who attempted to force them from his yoak, to put them by a necessary consequence under his owne.

The Councell were not ignorant that he who made no scruple to assist the Catalonians against Spain, had a prospect upon somewhat beyond the soundness of the doctrine and the justice of the principles he recommended to them ; and as they believed that the nature of the governement under which they lived, that was exercised by such persons as they conceived made use of the King's authority intrusted with them, to the distruction of his Majestie's interests, might have excused in some measure the necessite of their takeing armes to prevent the ruine of their countrey, and the extirpation of Catholicke religion, threatened by a Scottish armie,

1. For this letter, *see* page 33 ; also reply, dated 20th November, 1643

so they could not but have observed the admonitions his Eminence gave them, unless they did after the resolution they had already taken themselves, which was to conserve an equall interest in the friendship of those two mighty potentates.   But the apprehension the Cardinall had of their greater inclinations to the House of Austria, made him consider that those advertisements were seasonable, and might, perhaps, be profitable for France.

However, the Councell was not displeased that the people should take notice of the correspondence they held with foraigne Princes, and of the part they took in their affaires.   And as this gave the governement reputation att home, so the Councell were persuaded the noise of such intercourse with France would favour the expectation they had to receive considerable succours by Father James Talbott, the Augustine fryer, who was the second time sent into Spaine[1] with the offer of two thousand men to that Crown, and intrusted to behave himself so as [that] this expression of theirs, although free and far from the nature of a bargaine, should yet produce those liberall effects which this Father gave them encouragement would follow upon it.   But they were much displeased to have found not only this their expectation frustrated by Father Talbott's going to Flanders, and giveing the letters sent by him to the Court of Spaine, to Don Francisco de Mello, the Governour of the Low Countreys; but much more to see him returne from thence, joined in authority with Francisco Foysett,[2] a Burgundian, both of them imployed by that Governour to sollicit the promised levy, assigned (as he writte) by the Catholick King for his service in Flanders.   And although Father Talbott alleadged many reasons to justify the uprightness of his intentions, and that he informed them of the necessity putt upon him to swearve from prosecuteing the literall sence of his instruction, yet he alwayes after remained in their disfavour.

The Councell of the Confederates haveing soon after removed to Gallway, and severall complaints being made to them of the libertie

1. For notices and documents in connection with Talbot and Spain, *see* vol. ii., pp. xxxviii., 278-84.

2. See, *post*, " Memorandum " on audience to Foysett, at Kilkenny, 17th February, 1643-4.

assumed by many to enter into the possession of men's estates, whose ancestours had purchased them for valuable considerations, upon no other pretence than that they were known to have belonged in former times to their family, gave orders to the Earl of Castlehaven, whilst the season of the yeare, and the preparations to be made for the northern expedition, kept him from advanceing into Ulster, to march with part of the armie into Connaught, to prevent the mischief which might arise from an evill already grown to such a height as it was onely remedyable by force. And this the Earl of Castlehaven performed to the generall satisfaction of the province, not onely in the conduct of the action, but likewise in causing his men to live under regular discipline, and to abstain from doing the least injury to the inhabitants,—having sent the Lord Viscount Mayo, and Richard Bourke, of the partie who countenanced this disturbance, with a guard of horse to the Councell at Gallway.

In the meantime, the Earl of Antrim observing that the transporting of the ten thousand men into England was a matter that depended upon more circumstances than the Commission he brought with him to lead them, presst earnestly that he should at least be intrusted in the charge of Lieu-tenant-Generall, which, by direction of the late Assembly at Waterford, the Councell was to confer upon him; but this was grown much more difficult than att first, for the Councell was now better informed of the Lord of Antrim's proceedings in England, and of the use which was made of the letter then sent him; they had likewise been advertised of some expres-sions which the passionate resentment of the delay used in giving his Commission drew from this nobleman: and although they seemed satisfyed with the Lord of Antrim's answers to what was alleadged against him, yet the Secretary [Bellings], who thought himself most concerned in the matter, and alwayes kept in mind the motives alledged for writing that so plausible a letter, which gave a beginning to all those intrigues, was soe jealous that this, which at first was intended for noe other than a bare title, should in time acquire some authority, that when the Commission was ingrossed, and warrant was sent to him to seal it, he for two dayes suspended the doing of it, alledging that although in all other matters he ought to submitt to the major vote of the board; yet, haveing received the public seal in particular trust from the first Assembly, as he had done from those that followed it, he conceived, that in a matter of that importance, and so carryed as this was, he could not justify makeing use of the seale, when himself dissented in opinion, without warrant from those that intrusted him with it. However, he at length, after two dayes' sollicitation, to avoid so new and so nice a contest, haveing satisfyed himself that the end he aymed att, which was no other than to see the intention with which this title was granted duly observed, might be attained by other meanes, he made offer both to signe and seal the Lord of Antrim's Commission, so their Lordships would concurre with him in signeing such instructions as might limitt the execution to the sence the proposer delivered, when suit at first was made for the graunt; and the Councell condescending willingly to this request, the title of Lieutenant-Generall was by an ample Commission conferred upon him, which he thought fitt for the present to accept. But having, at the next Assembly held at Kilkenny, complained of the severe carriage of the Councell towards him, and produced their letters written by command of the Assembly, to aggravate their disobedience he laid down his Commission, thinking it would be restored to him without those clogs and restrictions which accompanied it. And, as there wanted not those who were alwayes apt to fall heavily upon the Councell, and to censure their proceedings, some began to charge them with neglect of their duty, and a design to lay aside any dependance they ought to have upon the House, when the Secretary setting forth att large the circumstances of all that had passed of that matter, and produceing the copy of his own letter to the Earl of Antrim, which was upon record, whereby it appeared what the result was, and how farre from the Councell's intention, and the first request made att the board in the Lord of Antrim's behalf, it was to have him invested in any real power, there was a generall silence; and the Commission resting where himself had placed it, the Assembly entered into the debate of some other motion; and thus an end was put to that pretension, and the Lord of Antrim thence after applied himself to that which he had designed to act in Scotland.

In the mean time, the Earl of Castlehaven haveing appointed the vantguard of the auxiliaries with some field-pieces to meet at Ballinclagh in the countie of Longford, had intelligence by a spy, that the northern armie, consisting of fourteen or fifteen thousand men, haveing twelve dayes provision of oatmeal, with no baggage but what they carryed on horseback, was at Cavan, marching directly to fight him ; and this advertisement likewise comeing to him from a Collonell of that army, who wished well to the King, he instantly retreats to Portleister, where Generall O'Neale with the Creaghts of Ulster then lay, giveing orders to the rest of his armie to come thither to him, and immediately sent Collonell John Butler with four or five hundred horse and foot to defend the bridge of Fina. The enemie, by the Lord of Castlehaven's speedy retreat, being disappointed of their designe to fight him, advanced notwithstanding, burneing and preying the countrey, and chargeing those employed to defend the bridge of Fina, mingling in the rout with them, they gained it, together with the castle of Fina, burneing Carlongstowne and the country about it ; but their provision being spent, they marched back by the way of the county of Louth into Ulster.

After the enemy was retreated, and the whole armie was come to Portleister, the Lord Castlehaven called upon Generall O'Neale for the four thousand foote and four hundred horse, which he had ingaged himself att the Assembly in Waterford to joyn to the auxiliaries upon their advance to Ulster ; his answere was that he would performe his promise when he came thither. The armie moveing from thence by the same way the Scots retreated, came into the countie of Ardmach, where the promised supply was againe demanded by the Earl of Castlehaven ; but the men were more intent upon secureing their Creaghts, now they were gotten into the enemy's countrey, than in joining in a body to strengthen the army. This notwithstanding, the Lord of Castlehaven marched to Tonregie, and there began to build a fort : before this was finished, a strong party of horse and dragoons were commanded to make an inroad into the county of Downe. Those, marching from the camp by night, came to a difficult and narrow pass upon the edge of that countie, called Scarfaile [Scarvagh], guarded with three hundred musketeers and three troopes of horse, commanded by Captain Blaire, which the Lord of Castlehaven (being in the head of the partie) forced, and, falling upon the foote, whom their horse had deserted, very few of them escaped, and their Captain was taken prisoner. Although the Irish had thus with noe great loss gained the pass, yet the party haveing understood that the Scottish armie marched towards them, retired to the camp att Tonregie, where certaine advertisement being brought by noon the next day, that the Scottish army approached, order was presently given to demolish the workes, and Lieutenant-Generall Purcell, with three troops of horse, being left to bring up the rear, the Lord of Castlehaven, (who being disappointed of the Ulster forces, was not able to face them), fell back to Charlemount, and the enemy being come in sight, those left behind drew off.

At Charlemount a councell of warre was called, in which it was carryed by the major vote, that, in regard their provisions were spent, they should retire immediately, and endeavour to be supplyed att a further distance from an enemy that overpowred them. This being concluded, the Earl of Castlehaven sent Hugh M'Phelim, M'Thomas, and Captain Lewis Moor, to advertise Generall Owen O'Neale of the resolution taken, that he might betimes provide for his own, and the safety of his Creaghts. This ould souldier, who was then sick, receiveing this soe sudden and unexpected a message, weak though he was, he sate upp in his bed, and tould them, that without doubt they had lighted on the worst resolution which could be taken in the case ; and if they knew (as he did), that Monroe himself had but a few dayes provision, which being spent, he must of necessitie retire, they would certainely have agreed to attend his motion in a place of safety, whatever extremitie they were compelled to endure, rather than to draw off almost in the sight of an enemy that certainely would overtake and defeat them ; and that the armie should not be exposed to any danger of starving, whilst there were beeves in the Ulster Creaghts.

The Earl of Castlehaven finding so opportune a remedy applied to a disease which was otherwise incurable, visited Generall O'Neale, and having advised with him of what was fit to be done, Lieutenant-Collonell Fennel, with six troopes of horse, was commanded to guard a pass att Binborb, that lay midway between both camps ; and nothing memorable being acted for some dayes that the armyes remained thus poasted, the officers that commanded the auxiliary forces, either finding their men, notwithstanding the care of Generall O'Neale, scanted in their provisions, and grow thin, or being themselves willing to fall back into the provinces from whence they were drawne, began to importune the Lord of Castlehaven to march off with the armie; which being resolved to be performed in the night, Generall O'Neale, foreseeing the confusion that necessarily would have accompanied them, and the eminent danger to which they might be exposed, proposed to the Lord of Castlehaven this expedient to prevent it. There was a passage called Scarfaile, by which Monroe's provisions were brought to his camp, and it lay soe, as, if the Irish armie might pass a great bog that was betwixt that and Charlemount, they would easily seize on it before the Scotch armie would be able to fall back to defend it, and so cutt off all reliefe from them. Wherefore order was given that the armie should imploy themselves in carrying fagots, and making way over the bog, and, in the edge of the evening powder and bullet was distributed among them, which being related to Monroe by a spie then in the Irish camp, he soon gathered what he conceived probably enough to be the design, and marched northward to the passage of Scarvagh, att the same time that the Lord of Castlehaven retreated southward to the countie of Monachan.

This was the success of that enterprize, and no man that knowes how the warre was commonly managed by the Confederates, will wonder to finde it farre different from the generall expectation, and no way suitable to the noise it made when this expedition was resolved upon att Waterford. For we are to consider, that although the countrey was able to maintaine so great numbers of men as were in armes during their being quartered amongst them, whilst day by day they fed on such provisions as they could affoard them, yet there was much difficulty to advance so much as but for a short time would mainetaine them in the field : and although the partes from whence they were drawn accompanied them with fair promises to be constantly supplyed, yet they were scarce ever performed, when they were once ridd of those that compelled them to make the hardest shifts to furnish them.

Whilst it was doubtfull what would be the event of the northern expedition, the English garrisons in Munster and Connaught were content to be thought willing to sitt down satisfyed with the Cessation of arms; but when the success of it had quieted their apprehensions, and that the Scotch armie entered England in favour of the Parliament, under the command of Sir Alexander Lesly, whom the King had made Lord Leven, then they began to cast their eyes upon the growing power of those that stood in opposition to the King's authority, and to decline the Cessation.

The Parliament partie being thus increased in strength, those that adhered to the King were conceived to be in such a state, as they could not make any long resistance; the inequalitie of their condition acquired the stronger party the dependance of many of those whom unalterable principles had not engaged in all events to follow the fortune of the King. In this conjuncture the English garrisons in Connaught, held by the Cootes and Ormsbies, began to exercise acts of hostilitie, first alleadging that the Irish had incroached upon their quarters, and soon after avowing publickly that they adhered to and depended upon the King and Parliament, a forme of expression taken up by those that fought in the King's name against his person. But the armie in Munster, commanded by the Lord of Inchiquin, as it was by much the more powerfull, so it fetched a larger circuit about, and used more industry to joyn interests decently with the prevaileing partie in England; and nothing was thought more justifyable in the case, or likelyer to find creditt with the English in generall, than an apprehension in that party of some notable designe in the Irish to become intire maisters of Ireland, and therefore they reported, and would have it believed, that they had entered into a dangerous conspiracy to betray all the English, and to deliver the kingdome to a foraign Prince. And to prevent a mischief, so ripe and ready to fall as gave them not leasure to consult the King's Lieutenant, whose duty it was to prescribe the remedy, the Lord of Inchiquin immediately did drive all the Catholickes out of Cork, Youghall, Kingsale, and his other garrisons; that, and the suddenness of the action, contributeing somewhat to make the fear seem reall.

This resolution nevertheless was executed after such a manner as gave occasion to the Lord Lieutenant, and the Protestant party that adhered to the King, to suspect that time had ripened it; and although they had by a slow application endeavoured to justify their designes, and invited his Excellency to bear them company; yet they had in all events provided to strengthen their partie, by communicating them to some that depended upon them, before they had acquainted his Excellency with it, which he resents in this his letter to the Lord of Inchiquin; and because it expresses his sense of that matter, I thought fit to insert in this place:

The Lord Lieutenant to my Lord of Inchiquin, July, 1644.

My Lord,—I received lately a letter from Sir Thomas Wharton, by his man, one Jowneston; and by him also, a verbal message, as from your Lordship and his master. The substance of it being of high importance, if true, I caused him to be sworne to, and have sent your Lordship a copie of his examination. I confess, I did much suspect the fellow to have made this tale, and to be sett on so to do, by some one desirous to raise troubles in the mindes of the people here, which abundantly it hath done, to the very great distraction of affairs here; but findeing the man constant in his relation, and willing to abide the triall of the truth of it, I am much staggered; yet it still sticks with me, why Sir Thomas Wharton or your Lordship, if there had been so much danger in writing the matter freely (which I cannot conceive there was, for he came quietly, and safely brought me the letter untouched and unsearched), would not give the man some little word of credence, or, indeed, why in a matter of that consequence, a messenger of better quality and ability was not ventured. I assure your Lordship, the carriage of the matter was, to his Majestie's very great disservice, and not without some blemish to me, which I cannot believe to be any part of your Lordship's, or my friend Sir Thomas Wharton's intention; though it so falls out, by putting me in equal consideration with Piggot,[1] Barrowes, and others, or rather them before me, by first giving them information of it, as if they, and not I, were intrusted with the government of this kingdom. My Lord, I expect with much impatience to be instructed by your Lordship, what the matter is, or whether,

1. For notices of Sir John Piggot, see "Contemporary History of Affairs in Ireland, 1641-52." Dublin: 1879-81, vol. i. pp. 129, 371, 710; iii. 138.

indeed, there be any matter in it, and so I rest, your Lordship's affectionate humble servant,—Ormonde.

Dublin Castle, the — of July, 1644.

At the time when this happened, the Earl of Clanricarde and St. Albans, and the Earl of Thomond, the Viscounts Dillon, Taaffe, Fitz-Williams, and Ranelaugh, and the Lord Baron of Howth, out of a sence of the dayly distraction in which their native country was involved, as good patriotts, desirous of settlement, and willing to set limits to the depredations and spoyles committed by the Scotch Covenanters in Ulster, whom the State att Dublin, although their actions proclaimed their aversion to the Cessation, concluded by the King's authority, was loath to declare Rebells, had drawn and subscribed the ensueing letter :

To the King's most excellent Majesty.

May it please your Majesty,—Though wee believe that the present state and condicion of your Majestie's party and forces in this kingdome is more fully and cleerely represented to your Majesty by the Lord Lieutenant and Councell than can proceed from any knowledge or informacion of ours, yet wee hould it a necessary parte of our duety to your Majesty somewhat to contribute to the general good, and to seek the meanes of our owne preservacion, by humbly representing to your Majestie's gratious consideracion our most unhappy and distracted condicion, and our longe sufferings, even to the ruine of our estates and families, and at this tyme, without any considerable defence, exposed to the mercy of two powerfull armyes nowe in the feild, the one of the Confederate Catholique party, if they were disposed to make any invasion upon us, and the other of the Scotch Covenanters, and such as adhere unto them, who, by burning, spoyling, and the committing of cruell and hostile acts, have broken the Cessacion, and cast off their obedience to your Majestie's Governement here ; which gives us full assurance of our emminent danger, and the necessity of presumeing in this manner to present our humble supplicacions to your Majesty.

Wee humbly offer to your Majestie's gratious consideracion, that dureing all these unhappy distempers and comotions raised in your Majestie's severall dominions, wee have constantly continued most loyall to your Majesty, and obedient to your Royall commaunds; though by reason of the high distracions in England, and the slowe proceedings or suspitions of some that formerly managed the Government heere, many of us have been totally neglected, and without any manner of encuragement or assistance, have exposed our persons to eminent hazard, and our estates to destruction, out of our zeale to your service, and for the preservacion of your Majestie's authority and the defence of your good subjects in the severall places of our residence; and such of us as were best assisted and trusted with imployment and commaund, have beene soe slowly supplyed and releeved, and the dangers and difficulties soe greate, that wee have cause to admire God's infinite mercy towards us, by inhabling us in some sorte to subsist in the midst of soe many tumults and distractions.

Wee must likewise humbly acknowledge your Majestie's greate wisdome and gratious goodnesse towards us, that findeing by the disobedience of many of your Majestie's subjects in these parts, and the sadd distempers of England, your Majesty could not by your owne Royall power seasonably protect and defend us from the dangers wee were in, you were gratiously pleased to admitt of a tymely remedy, by condiscending to a Cessacion of Armes for a yeare, the onely expedient that could then bee found to preserve us, and to which wee doe attribute our safety; and humbly acknowledge your Majestie's greate favor therein, and from thence wee were hopefull that a happy settlement would insue in this kingdome, to the content and satisfacion of all your Majestie's well-affected subjects, soe farr as could bee expected in a contry soe miserably wasted by the cruelties of a civill warr. But the tyme appointed for the continuance of the Cessacion being nowe neere expired, and nothing appeareing to us of supply or necessary defence, nor any thing of peace or settlement concluded, wee cannot but bee very sensible of the generall calamities of this kingdome, and the certaine ruine like to fall uppon us and many other of your Majestie's faithfull subjects, in their persons, fortunes, and families, if a warre bee againe renued in that condicion wee are in, and your Majestie's power soe restrained by the unnaturall continuance and increase of the troubles in England, as that there is litle expectacion of any fitting or tymely assistance for your Majestie's service and your owne preservacions.

Wee most humbly beseech your Majesty to looke upon us with a favorable eye and compassionate reguard of our past sufferings and present danger; and that our loyalty, zeale, and constant faithfull endeavors in your service may bee soe considered, as not to continue us in a more perplexed and distructive estate than any other of your Majestie's subjects, even those whoe have taken armes in opposicion to your Majestie's authority, whoe are upon theire guard and provided for defence, and wee onely exposed to the malice and violence of all insulting enemyes.

Wee humbly propose, that if the Agents for the Confederate Catholique party, out of the opinion of their owne strength, or takeing advantage of the present distracions, have beene high and imoderate in their Proposicions and Demaunds; or if those that went as Agents from your Majestie's Protestant subjects, and theire adherents in this kingdome, through too sharpe a resentment of theire private losses, or for other particular ends, have, under the tytle of Protestant subjects, receyved instructions, or introduced the opinions of others, not well affected, either to the Religion or Government established heere, instead of the intencions and inclinacions of others more moderate and truely faithfull to your Majestie's service, and thereby put unnecessary rubbs and doubts uppon the prosecution of the Treaty, to continue a disturbance, and by a division here hinder your Majesty from the united assistance of your subjects of this kingdome; that your Majesty, by your owne greate wisdome and Royall judgment, will bee pleased to moderate and reconcile those differences, in such a way as may probably produce a speedy and happy agreement; or if that your Majestie's leasure will not soe permitt, that the Lord Lieutenant and Councell heere may have Commission to proceed in the articles and condicions of peace, upon debate and conference with the moderate and well-affected on both sides; and then wee are humbly of opinion, that noe such distance will appeare as is nowe discoursed of, and that your Majesty and your faithful subjects heere will soone finde the benefitt of soe happy a reconciliacion.

Our present danger doth further invite us humbly to propose unto your

Majesty, that in reguard the Scotch Covenanters and their adherents are nowe in armes in this kingdome, violateing and breaking the Cessacion, and doe refuse to pay obedience to your Majestie's Government; and that upon very probable grounds, wee have just cause to beleeve that as they gaine advantage, there will bee litle distinction made betweene us and those whome they nowe assault; that therefore they may bee speedily declared enemyes, and your Majestie's power employed for the suppressing of them; to which the Confederate party whoe keepe the Cessacion, and seeme more ready to returne to their obedience, will doubtlesse give their best assistance: And to subsist in this divided condicion, without joyneing or receaveing the helpe of one party or other, wee conceave utterly impossible. All which wee humbly submitt to your Majestie's gratious consideration, and your speedy resolution is begged by your Majestie's most loyall and faithfull subjects and servants,

Thomonde.	Fitzwilliam.
Clanricarde and St. Albans.	Taaffe.
Ranelaugh.	Howth.[1]
Dillon.	

The Scotch Covenant, about this time, was so much in vogue, and the Presbiterians so successful, that they made proselites of the many. Amongst the rest, there was a lady[2] of quality in Drogheda, so active in debauching the officers, in intelligence with Monroe,[3] and preparatory for admitting a partie from him into the town, that she had provided [false keys] for the ports, and which was much resented by the Lord Lieutenant.[4] Sir Patrick Weams [Wemys], to whom the King had done many favours, and his Excellency many good offices, was considered as faultie in that contrivement; att least, as farre as the concealing of it.

---

1. The original of this letter is extant in Carte Papers, vol. xi., p. 266. Bodleian Library, Oxford.
2. Alice, widow of Charles, Viscount Moore of Drogheda. *See* vol. ii., p. cx.
3. Commander of Scotch troops in Ulster. *See* p. 30.
4. *See* vol. i., pp. 33, 233, ; ii., xxxiii., 266, 364.

Now the fourth year was well advanced, since the beginning of the first commotion in the north, when the Supreame Councell, finding by the constant clamours of the people, by the many insolent delinquents, and the resort of some Catholicke families, to live in the enemies quarters, merely to avoid the impositions and taxes upon them, that the warre was grown insupportable, resolved to be truly informed how farre they might rely on foraign succours; whereof their agents (who were all of them ecclesiasticall persons) often gave them hopes, and which themselves were forward to reckon upon, as an assured support of a warre undergone for so pious and noble a cause. For being all of them men, who, by reason of the constitution of the governement att home, which excluded Catholickes from publicke imployments, were strangers to the management of State affaires, as they are regulated in later ages, by the sole interest of Princes, they intertained themselves with those principles of religion and honour, and the influences they had in those histories which they read, upon the actions of men, in the times of their forefathers. And wondering at the slow effects which their sollicitations abroad produced, they employed one[1] of their number to Innocent X., then newly made Pope, to the Court of France, to the State of Venice, the Duke of Florence, the Republick of Genoa, and the Marquess of Castle-Roderigo, then Governour of the Low Countreys for Phillip IV. King of Spaine : and although many things intervened during the nine moneths he was absent upon that negociation, which we shall have occasion to relate hereafter ; yet I conceived it would be more acceptable to the reader, if he might receive the progress of those forreign affaires, without interruption ; and more proper for one who made it his designe to write a history, not a diary, to present it in this manner.

1. The author, Richard Bellings.

LETTERS, DOCUMENTS, ETC.

I. APPLICATION TO THE POPE FROM IRISH CONFEDERATION FOR APPOINTMENT OF NUNCIO IN IRELAND.

1. LETTER TO URBAN VIII. FROM SUPREME COUNCIL OF CONFEDERATION.

[THE Council state to the Pope that the consideration extended by him to the Irish and their cause, even during war in Italy, emboldens them to apply for a further favour. They beg that the title and powers of a Nuncio may be conferred on the Pope's delegate, Pietro-Francesco Scarampi.[1] Since his arrival in Ireland, Scarampi, they state, has displayed the greatest prudence, and been indefatigable in his exertions on their behalf. By promoting him to the position suggested, many advantages will be secured in the settlement of disputes, and in the reclamation of waverers during this time of Cessation. The Council mention that Father Luke Wadding will communicate to the Pope the reasons for the Cessation, and will inform him that the Confederates have fully restored the Catholic worship throughout the greater part of Ireland, and in many of the cities.—Cashel, 1 October, 1643.]

Beatissime Pater,

Cum is sit Sanctitatis vestræ in nos causamque nostram affectus ut, licet bello in ipsa Italia exorto gravetur, nostris tamen qui tanto terrarum tractu distamus rebus intenso prospiciat studio, nos, eo Sanctissimi Patris nostri favore recreati, non erubescimus illa quibus indigemus a tanto et tam propitio patrono exorare.

Missus est ad nos Sanctitatis vestræ minister, Illustrissimus Dominus

---

I. MS. "Register of Book of Letters" of the Supreme Council of the Irish Confederation. Bodleian Library, Oxford.

1. For notices of Scarampi, see vol. i. p. vii. ; ii. pp. xxxiii.-viii.

Petrus-Franciscus Scarampus, qui indefessa cura et industria se latum in rebus nostris promovendis adhibet : Et quia si quod dissidium aut si quæ controversiæ in clero vel populo exorirentur, Sedis Apostolicæ authoritate facile sopiri possunt, obnixe rogamus ut in tam prudentem virum et tam bene de nobis meritum, Nuncii nomen et potestas conferatur, qua authoritate, si quos hoc induciarum tempore fluctuare contingeret fæliciter in viam possit revocare.

Nobis quis sit ad propagandam fidem Catholicam animi affectus, quantum illam hactenus propagaverimus et in majori regni parte ac plerisque civitatibus in integrum restituerimus, et quo pacto quibusque de causis hanc armorum Cessacionem admiserimus, nostro nomine referet Sanctitati vestræ Reverendus Pater Lucas Waddingus, Ordinis Sancti Francisci, etc., cui ut fides, etc.—Casheliæ, primo Octobris, 1643.

2. Letter to Antonio Barberini, " the Cardinal [Protector for Ireland] at Rome."

[The Council of the Confederation assure the Cardinal that they have daily evidences of their obligations to him. Pietro-Francesco Scarampi, sent to them through the Cardinal's intervention, has devoted himself entirely to the promotion of the interests of the Irish. A Cessation of arms has been concluded for one year. The Council deem it desirable, and, indeed, indispensable, to have in Ireland a Nuncio with full powers, and they have applied to the Pope to confer the office upon Scarampi. They beg of the Cardinal to promote their views, and thus add another to the innumerable benefits which the Irish have already received from him.— Cashel, 1st October, 1643.]

Eminentissime Domine,—Indies occurrunt plurima quæ nos ad agendas Eminentiæ vestræ gratias cogunt et excitant. Ita se gerit Illustrissimus Dominus Petrus-Franciscus Scarampus, Eminentissimæ Dominationis vestræ cura huc ad nos missus, ut in omnem occasionem paratus rebus nostris promovendis totus incumbat et laboret. Conclusis jam unius anni induciis videmus conveniens, imo rebus nostris necessarium esse, ut apud nos sit qui Nuncii nomine et auctoritate polleat ac servatur. Quare a Sanctissimo Patre nostro humiliter petimus ut potestatem illam in optimum hunc suæ Sanctitatis ministrum conferre dignetur, rogamusque ut hoc nostrum postulatum Eminentia vestra benigne promoveat illudque innumeris ante hac beneficiis pro Hibernia prestitis adjiciat. Eminentiæ vestræ manus deosculantur.—Cashelie, prima die Octobris, 1643.

II. Letter to Luke Wadding, Rome, from the Supreme Council.

Reverend Father,—In regarde wee would enable you to satisfie such of our freinds as may, either by practize of the enemye or theire owne inclinacion, be apt to judge suddenly of the Cessacion of armes and all acts of hostilitye which wee have concluded, wee have sent you heere enclosed the reasons and motives which induced us to condiscend unto it; wherein you may see how fitt it is for our freinds, who hitherto have countenanced our actions and given us assistance, to remitt noe parte of theire care of our affaires, for as wee intend inviolablye to observe the promiss wee have made to God of maintaineing the Catholicke religion, soe, in case wee may not prevaile to that end, it is necessarye wee should be in such a posture as wee may resiste violence; lett your endeavors to sollicit be as fervent as heretofore, and any one who rightly apprehends the state wherein wee are will beleeve that the way for us to be considerable and to gaine good condicions is to be prepared.—Cashell, the first of October, 1643.

Reasons for the Cessacion.—Sent to Fr. Waddinge, to Rome.

1.—First, that it was the King's pleasure, whose rights and prerogatives wee have sworne to maintaine, there should be a Cessation of armes.

2.—Secondlie, that those forces which hitherto had fought against us should be carried into England to assiste his Majestie against the Rebbells there who are stronge and powerfull.

3.—Thirdlie, that wee might be the less diverted from prosecuteinge the warr in Ulster against the Scotts who will not submit to the Cessacion.

4.—Fourthlie, that all Catholicke Princes might clerely see for what intent wee tooke armes, if it chance that wee may not obtaine the exercise of our religion in that measure which will be fittinge for a Catholicke nacion, and we shall make that appere to be the ground of our quarrell.

5.—That the possessions wee have of the churches and churche livings doe, by a kinde of implicit allowance and assent, remaine with us for the tyme.

6.—Sixthlie, that, because of the distempers of the tyme, and the continuall preparacions for our armies in soe busie a warr as was on foote in all partes of the kingdome, wee had not leisure to settle the government in soe regular a manner as now wee hope to doe.

III.—CESSATION OF HOSTILITIES, 1643.

DOCUMENTS AND LETTERS FROM VISCOUNT MONTGOMERY, BRITISH KNIGHTS AND COLONELS IN ULSTER, MARQUIS OF ORMONDE, RICHARD BELLINGS, SUPREME COUNCIL OF THE IRISH CONFEDERATION, AND SERGEANT-MAJOR ROBERT MONRO.

1. BRITISH FORCES IN ULSTER, 1643.

To the Right Honorable the Lords Justices and Councell, and unto the Lord Marquess of Ormond, Lieutenant-Generall of his Majestie's armie in this Kingdome of Ireland :

The humble petition of Hugh, Lord Vice-Count Mountgomery, and of Sir William Stewart, Sir James Mountgomery, and Sir Robert Stewart, Knights and Colonells :[1]

Humbly sheweth that the petitioners at the beginning of the rebellion in this kingdome, did, by vertue of a comission from his Majestie, levy the

---

III. The documents in this section—Nos. 1 to 7—are, as follow, from the Carte Papers in the Bodleian Library, Oxford : 1, vol. v. p. 373 ; 2-6, vol. vii. pp. 203, 82, 85, 84 ; 7, vol. lxv. p. 82.

1. Notices of, and documents in connection with, Sir Hugh Montgomery, Viscount Ardes, Sir William Stewart, Sir James Montgomery, Sir Robert Stewart, and their proceedings in Ulster, will be found in "Contemporary History of Affairs in Ireland 1641-1652." Dublin : 1879-80.

severall regiments and troops now under their comand, and, at their own charge, and by the credit of themselves and their frends, provided them with armes and amunition, and have ever since maintained them, and preserved a great part of this kingdome and many thousand Protestant subjects, without any other helpe except some small supplies which they had in victualls and clothes from the Parliament out of England, or by loane from such parts of the cuntrie which they preserved undestroyed by the Rebells (for which the petitioners also stand ingaged), or by what they were able to gaine from the Rebells from time to time.

But now, soe it is, that your suppliants' estates beeing wasted, either by the Rebells' fury or the soldiers' cess, and the rest of the cuntrie where they formerly quartered quite impoverished, soe as they are not able any longer to releeve them; and by reason of the Cessation of armes now concluded in this kingdome, doe doubt that they shall gett noe further supplies from the Parliament out of England, and are also barred from taking anything as formerly from the Rebells; by reason whereof all the said forces under your suppliants' command will disband or starve, your petitioners bee absolutely ruined, and the cuntrie and guarrisons formerly defended and gained by them left to the mercy of the Rebells, except a present course bee taken for the maintenance of your petitioners, and of their severall troopes and regiments aforesaid:

May it, therefore, please your honors to give order for some present supplies unto the petitioners and their said regiments and troopes, and direccions for their future subsistance, and in what manner your suppliants shall dispose of their said regiments and troopes during the said Cessation; and also for the better observation of the Articles of Cessation and the safety of his Majestie's good subjects, that your honors would bee pleased to prescribe such a present course as that the province of Ulster, or so much thereof out of which the Rebells have been driven by the forces under the comand of your petitioners and others of his Majestie's armies in that province, may be freed during the time of the said Cessation from the incroachment or incursions of the Rebells, and the bounds betwixt your petitioners and others his Majestie's good subjects and them knowne and distinguished, soe that his Majestie's good subjects may quietly enjoy the benefitts and profits which can be made out of the said province, or somuch therof as the Rebells have been driven out by his Majestie's armies as aforesaid. And your petitioners as in duty bound shall pray, etc.

2. ORMONDE TO VISCOUNT MUSKERRY.

I understand that som of those of our army who have been taken prisoners by your party are now deteyned for ransome and payment of fees; which is directly oposeing to the Articles of Cessacion. Therefore, I expect that they be released according to agreement as those prisoners who weare with us have beene.

Lieutenant Roaxby and Ensigne Long's commissions beare date the second day of November, 1642.—[ORMONDE.]

Endorsed : Given out the 4th of October, 1643.

3. BELLINGS TO ORMONDE : CONTRIBUTIONS FROM CONFEDERATION.

My Lord,—I am commaunded by the Councell here to advertise your Lordship that the moneys applotted upon this province by them (which amounts to the one half of what in money is to be given in discharge of the first payment) is ready to be sent ; and in regard they understand there may be some hazard in conveying of it through the quarters beyond the Liffy, they desire your Lordship may provide for the safe bringing of it to Dublin ; and upon notice given they will observe such direccions as your Lordship will give therein. The reasons why the remaine of such moneyes as are to bee paid at this present are deferred to be sent, were expressed by a former letter unto your Lordship ; and, as formerly, they now desire the Lords Justices' pleasure may be forthwith made known unto them, whether they have assigned the proporcion due upon the province of Mounster unto the Lord of Insequine to be imployed in his Majestie's service, and their resolucion herein is the onely impediment why the whole summe should not be sent together. They knowe the tyme of payment and would punctually observe it, if they might without hazard or hindrance to his Majestie's service. I am, my lord, your Lordship's humble servant,

RICHARD BELLINGS.

Kilkenny, the 14th of October, 1643.

4. BELLINGS TO ORMONDE.

My Lord,—After dispatching of my former letter, of this daye's date I receaved your Lordship's of the twelfth of this moneth, and, by direccion of the Counsell here, in answere thereunto I am to advertise your Lordship, that, finding your Lordship did daily expect the first payment of those moneys graunted by their Commissioners, they gave direccion £700 sterling should be sent away which wilbe at Ballysonan on Monday at night next, thence to be conveyed upon the first notice from your Lordship to such place as your Lordship shall appointe your convoy to meete it, towards the Liffy, thinking it more convenient and safe of all sydes to try the way with this summe, in regard the expectation of such who may be ill inclined, and might contryve to intercept it, wilbe layed aside by the bruite of the delivery of our moneys safe at Dublin, so as the rest may be conveyed with less hazard. But because they would putt over to fortune as little as they may, they determine not to send the rest all at a tyme, yet with that speede as will render the payment as usefull. What to doe with the moneys in Mounster, which the Lord of Insequine desires, they cannot resolve before they [have] receaved direccions from Dublin.

I am commaunded further to advertise your Lordship that although they may not sett downe the place or tyme, where and when a convoy from your Lordship should attend the delivery of the beeves, having not heard of late from Connaght or Ulster, yet they are confident they are upon their way ; and inasmuch as the Counsell here desire all things should be providently disposed of to the furtherance of his Majestie's service, they doe againe intreate your Lordship to send some knowing man versed in affaires of that kinde to conclude of all matters that shall concerne the preparacion of shipping for transporteing the army there.

Lastly, they assure your Lordship whatsoever is within their power wherwith to serve his Majesty they will contribute it willingly, and endevour that your Lordship be accommodated with such things as may be necessary for the occasion.—I am, my Lord, your Lordship's humble servant,

RICHARD BELLINGS.

Kilkenny, the 14th of October, 1643.

5. LETTER TO LORDS JUSTICES AT DUBLIN FROM SUPREME COUNCIL.

Our very good Lords,—Wee, whom his Majesty's Catholick subjects of this kingdome did intrust with the mannagement of their affaires, have by our publick act ratified and confirmed the Articles of Cessacion concluded upon by our Commissioners, willingly and cheerefully, hopeing in the quiet of that time assigned for it, by the benefitt of the access which his Majesty is graciously pleased to afford us, to free ourselves from those odious callumnies wherewith wee have been branded, and to render ourselves worthy of favour by some acceptable service suiting the expressions wee have often made, and the reall affeccions and zeale wee have to serve his Majesty. And, inasmuch as wee are given to understand that the Scotts, who not long since in great numbers came over into this kingdome and by the slaughter of many innocents, without distinction of age or sex, have possessed themselves of very large territories in the north, and since the notice given them of the Cessacion have not onely continued their former cruelties upon the persons of the weake and unarmed multitude, but have added thereunto the burneinge of the corne belonginge to the natives within that province of Ulster:

Notwithstandinge all which outrages, wee heare that they have (although but faintly, and with relacion to the consent of their Gennerall, after some daies consultacion whether it were convenient for their affaires) desired to partake in the Cessacion, intending, as is evident by their proceedings, soe farr onely to admitt thereof, as it may be beneficiall for their patrons, the Mallignant party now in armes against his Majesty in England, by diverting us from assisting his Majesty, or of advantage to their desire of eating farther into the bowells of our countrey.

Wee, who can accuse ourselves of no one hollow thought, and detest all subtill practices, cannott thinke of serving two masters, or standinge newters where our King is party, and are desirous none should reside in this kingdome but his Majesty's good subjects.

Wee beseech your Lordships, therefor, that those who have other ends than his Majesty's service and interests, and are so farr from permittinge the natives to enjoy three partes of what they have sown, as they may with no security looke upon their former habitacions, and doe absolutely deny to restore their prisoners, contrary to the Articles of Cessacion, may by the jointe power of all his Majesty's good subjects within this kingdome of what nacion soever, be prosecuted, and that, while these succours are in preparacion, our proceedings against them may no way be imputed unto us a desire any way to violate this Cessacion.

And wee doe further pray your Lordships that, for our justification therein, you wilbe pleased to transmitt unto his Majesty these our letters, and to send unto us the copy of those directed unto your Lordships from Serjeant-Major Monroe[1] concearning this matter.

Thus with the remembrance of our hartyest wishes, wee rest your Lordships' loving friends,

Mountgarret.	Hugo Armachanus.[2]	Fr. Thomas Dubliniensis.[3]
Castlehaven, Audley.	Johannes Clonfertensis.[4]	Nicholas Plunket.
Richard Bellings.	Gerald Fennell.	

Kilkenny, 15th October, 1643.

Addressed: For the Lords Justices [Dublin].

1. *See* page 30.
2. Hugh O'Reilly, Archbishop of Armagh. *See* vol. i., pp. xxxvii, 290.
3. Thomas Fleming, Archbishop of Dublin. *See* vol. i., p. xxi.
4. John Bourke, Bishop of Clonfert. *See* vol. ii., p. x.

5 A. [DESPATCH FROM SERGEANT-MAJOR ROBERT MONRO REFERRED TO IN PRECEDING LETTER.]

Right Honourable,—Your Lordships' of the 21, I received at Ardmagh the 29, together with the printed Cessation, which was very displeasing unto this army, who being sent auxiliary for supply of the British forces in distress, were promised by his Majesty and the Parliament of England pay and entertainment from three months to three months; nevertheless, in eighteen months' time, they have endured (both officers and soldiers) unparalleled miseries : And, now, a great part of the service being done, they are rewarded with the conclusion of a Cessation, without assurance of entertainment for the time, or any certainty of the payment of their arrears, and they must conform to the treaty.   This kind of usage and contempt would constrain good servants, though his Majestie's loyal subjects, to think upon some course which may be satisfactory to them, being driven almost to despair, and threatened to be persecuted by the Roman Catholick subjects, as they are now called.   Nevertheless, of the foresaid contempt (for obedience to his Majestie's command) I have moved the army for the time to cease any hostile act against our enemies, till such time as your Lordships will be pleased to consider better of our present condition, and grant us time to acquaint the General, who has onely commission over the army, to advise us how to behave ourselves in this exigency, since I (as Governor of Carigfergus) can give your Lordships no positive answer to this Cessation in the name of our army, having not absolute power over them :   And immediately after receiving the General's resolution, your Lordships shall be acquainted therewith ; which is the least favour your Lordships can vouchsafe upon us, in recompence of our bygone service.

And so I remain, your Lordships' humble and obedient servitor,

ROBERT MONRO.[1]

Ardmagh, 29 Sept., 1643.

To the Right Honourable the Lords Justices and Council [Dublin].

Endorsed : Received the 2nd of October.]

1. " History of Irish Rebellion," London : 1680, p. 136. For further correspondence

6. BELLINGS TO ORMONDE.

My Lord,—I am comaunded by the Councell here to advertise your Lordship that, together with these, the seven hondred pounds sterling mencioned in my letters of yesterdaie's date is sent.   And, inasmuch as they desire the payments which are to be made should be performed with the more certainty and equality, they pray your Lordship the moneys may be receaved there as they pass in sterling money among us, to witt four and nyne pence the patacowne,[1] and the rix-dollar at the same value, and the pistollett in fifteene shillings sterling, which can be no disadvantage to any that receave them there or pay other moneys in exchange of them, seeing they may buy our comodities with them at the same vallue; otherwise wee shall pay them at one rate one day, and receave them at another rate the next day.   They desire, my Lord, that justice may be done them in that particuler.   I am, my Lord, your Lordship's humble servant,

RICHARD BELLINGS.

Kilkenny, the 15th October, 1643.

7. ORMONDE TO BELLINGS: SUPPLY OF SHIPS, ETC.

SIR,—By your letter, dated at Kilkenny, the 1st of October, and written to me, as you therein express, by commande, you did promise to advertise me of the number of vessels which could be procured, and of what burthen and at what rates, and how many frigotts might be had to garde the fleete, and what caution [security] woulde be expected, with an assurance that noe care in expeditinge that worke shoulde be wantinge, which made me rest confident that that shippinge might by this tyme have bene readie to come unto us.   But now, by your letter without date, which I receaved the 14th of this monthe, you give me noe light either of the number of the vessells which may be had, or the burthen, or at what rates they can be procured, or upon what caution, but write unto me (by

with Monro, in September and October, 1643, in reference to Cessation, *see* "Contemporary History of Affairs in Ireland, 1641-1652," Dublin: 1879-80, pp. 550-52.

1. Patacón, Spanish silver coin.

direccion as you express) to imploy some man versed in affairs of that kinde to contract about it.

Beleave me, the greate importance of the business in hand would require more expedition than hitherto hathe bene used, and your demurrage[1] of your shipping (which you mention in that letter), which shalbe borne from the tyme they come hither, is nothinge to the charge of the men who be here on demurrage through the want of that shippinge. And, therefore, I must desire you to represent this unto those by whose comaund you write, as noe ordinarie business, but as one of the waightiest which for the present can fall unto their consideracion. And to the ende I may not be wantinge in what liethe in me, I have entreated the bearer hereof to undertake this jorney of purpose to sollicit this affaire; but for the contractinge, makinge the provision, giving of caution, and what dependethe thereupon, I must of necessitye leave it wholie to you, there beinge upon the place, not knowinge upon the sudden where to finde a man heere fit to be imployed with soe greate and important an affaire.

As for the releasing of your prisoners, I doe assure you that, for soe many of them as were heere in restrainte, and not indited, that order hath bene long since given for theire enlargement; that as many as were indited and found baile have bene likewise set at libertie; and that nothinge dothe stay Collonell Cullon[2] here but his owne slackness in not tendering bayle; but his libertie hee dothe freelie enjoy in this citie [Dublin], and if that he will provide any reasonable baile, which he is now about, it shall be accepted.

[ORMONDE.]

[16 October, 1643.]

1. Compensation for detention.
2. For notices of Colonel Cullen, *see* vol. i., pp. lix., 88, 130; ii., 30, 259; also "Contemporary History of Affairs in Ireland, 1641-1652." Dublin: 1879, vol. i., pp. 41, 62, 74.

IV. LETTER FROM CARDINAL MAZARIN TO SUPREME COUNCIL OF CONFEDERATION, 1643.

[For letters addressed to Cardinal Mazarin by the Supreme Council in December, 1642, see vol. ii., pp. 114-15. The following is the letter from Mazarin mentioned and commented on by Bellings at page 7 of the present volume.]

A MM. du Conseil des Catholiques d'Irlande.

Messieurs,—Comme je compastis generalement au malheur de tous les Catholiques qui 'n'ont pas le libre exercice de leur religion, je vous avoue que je le leur procurerois de tout mon cœur avec mon sang et ma vie, s'il n'estoit question que de les donner pour ce sujet. Mais comme pour cela il faut demeurer dans certains termes, que Dieu et le droit des gens ordonnent, et qu' un tel bien despend de la grace du Prince, qui doit estre seulement recherchée de ses sujets par prières et par remonstrances, et des autres Princes par intercessions et offices, je vous puis asseurer que je m' efforceray tousjours de porter la Reyne à vous assister, de son autorité et de son credit, et à vous moyenner tout le soulagement et tout l'avantage, que vous pouvez raisonablement attendre pour vos consciences et pour vos fortunes.

Vous pères ont voulu autresfois user pour cet effet des remèdes contraires, que Dieu n'a point besnis, et ont eu recours à la force estrangère, qui n'a produit que vostre oppression et une deffiance incurable dans l'esprit du Souverain, qui a creu que vous n'estiez ses sujets qu'a cause que vous ne le pouviez point estre du Prince qui avoit entrepris de vous deslivrer de son joug pour vous mettre sous le sien par une consequence necessaire.

Maintenant que je suppose que vous avez changé de conduite, et que, quittant celle de vos pères pour une meilleure, vous rechercherez, avec la douceur et dans l'usage des devoirs que Dieu commande, ce qu'ils n'ont

IV. Mansc. de la Biblioth. Mazarine, nᵒ 1719, tom. i. fol. 127 verso.—"Lettres du Cardinal Mazarin." Par M. A. Chéruel. Paris: Imprimerie Nationale, 1872, tom. i, p. 420.

peu rencontrer dans la violence, et ce qu'il a reffusé au pratiques et intelligences de dehors, qu'il deffend, je ne fais point difficulté [de croire] que le Prince ne se rende plus traitable qu'il n'a fait à ceux qui donneront de plus grands exemples de l'obeissance qui luy est deue, et qu'il ne se porte à souffrir l'exercice d'une autre religion, comme faisoient les Chrestiens des premiers siècles. Je ne doute point encore que marchant dans ce chemin, Dieu ne fasse reussir vos justes desirs, et que la Reyne n'appuye de son autorité vos interests auprès de vostre Roy, qui vous connoissant pleins de zèle pour son service, trouvera les siens à vous proteger. Pour moy, je vous dis derechef que j'apporteray tousjours ce qui despendra de moy pour une si bonne fin.—[Paris,] 16 Octobre, 1643.

V. Correspondence in connexion with Cessation, October, November, December, 1643.

1. Ormonde to Bellings : Contributions from Confederation, etc.

Sir,—Your last letter of the 14 of this month I receaved yesterday, the 17, and, in answere to both yours of that date, I am to tell you that the Lords Justices have determined not to medle with the £700 you say is ready at Ballysonan untill it bee incresed to such a sume as may bee of use to his Majestie's service, and they expect that the whole sum already payable should bee payed in here by Tuesday next at night ; and to that purpose have comaunded me to send a convoy which shall be at Castlemartin by Monday at tenn of the clock to safeguard the mony and those that are authorised to see it payd and to receave aquitances.

I am further to tell you the Lords Justices are pleased that five hundred pounds of the mony raised in Mounster should bee payed to the Lord Inchiquin, whoe hath authoritie from them to receve and give aquitances for it; and that wee have yeat heard nothing of the beofes whereon wee did soe firmly rely that wee neglected to make seasonable provision to answere his Majestie's pressing ocations : and being now disapoynted, wee are inforced to make very disadvantagious bargains otherways to finde meanes for those ocations.

V. The documents in this section—Nos. 1 to 17—are as follows from the Carte Papers, Bodleian Library, Oxford, vol. vii. pp. 110, 111, 119, 123, 124, 164, 232, 310, 239, 246, 249, 335, 336, 256-9, 363, 366, 375.

And therefore it is expected that not only those beofes bee hastned, but, that, by anticipating the second payment in some good measure repairation bee made to his Majestie for the damage hee will otherwise sustaine by that failer.   To the other particulars of your leter I can give noe other answer than already I have done in my leter dated the seventh of this month.

Lastly, I am to inform you that divers prisoners of ours are still detained in Wicklow and Ulster ; sume, for noe reason, others for excessive fees ; and two vesells at Wexford that were bound hether and taken since the day of Cessation, which is as much ocasion of discontent to the people as the detaining of Collonel Cullin was to those with you, whoe yeat was released as soone as hee had done what by the Articles hee was to doe. Wherefore, I doe expect that present restitution bee made of those vesells and the goods that were taken in them, and liberty given to those prisoners.

I shall further desire you to take some strict course for the satisfaction of Sir William Gilbert,[1] whose case deserveth more than ordinarie consideracion ; and, if that care be taken which you may, I doubt not but most of his goodes may be had in specie.

---

1. William Gilbert, appointed " Constable of the castle and fort of Maryborough, in Leix, in the Queen's County," 10th February, 1622-3.   *See*, also " Contemporary History of Affairs in Ireland, 1641-1652." Dublin : 1879, vol. i. p. 73. In relation to Gilbert, the following letter was addressed by the King to Ormonde :—" Charles Rex,—Right trusty and right entirely beloved cousin and councellor, wee greete you well. Having understood how faithfully Sir William Gilbert, Constable of our fort of Maribrough, in the Queene's County, in our realme of Ireland, hath managed that charge, and how serviceable his son, Lieutenant Henry Gilbert, hath been therein to him, and usefull in other parts of our army in that our kingdom ; wee are graciously inclined to give them both encouragement in an humble suite which the father (now very aged) hath tendered to us, on behalf of his son, that he may be joyned patentee with him. Our will and pleasure, therefore, is that you forthwith give effectuall order for the renewing of that patent, and inserting therein the said Lieutenant Henry Gilbert joynt patentee with his said father to be to them and to the longer liver of them, with all clauses as before, for which these our letters shalbe to you, and to our Lord Chancelor and others in that our kingdom concerned sufficient warrant. Given under our signet at our Court at Oxford, the 17th day of November, 1643.   By his Majestie's comaund.—Edw. Nicholas."—Ms. Carte Papers, vii. p. 314.

I finde that in Wicklow noe greate regarde hath bene given to your order for the restitucion of the cowes taken from hence, which I desire may be forthwith repaired. And, thoose thinges being done of your parte, I shall give present order for the restitucion of all such places as have bene taken by any of our parte sence the day of the Cessation, as far forth as by the Articles is provided. And so I rest your loving frend,

ORMONDE.

Dated at Dublin, 18 Octobris, 1643.

2. ORMONDE TO BELLINGS.

Sir,—I receaved your leter of the 15 of this month, and by my leter of the 18 of this month I signefied unto you the pleasure of the Lords Justices touching the £700 that is at Ballysonan, together with their expectation of a speedy compliance with them on the payment of the rest of the mony here except £500 allotted to the Lord Inchiquin) and the beofs in specie or mony in lieu of them at the rates agreed on; all which, I doubt not, will bee taken into such serious and effectuall consideration there that I shall not neede to say more than that if tymly care bee not taken and a seasonable advance made of the second payment in some considerable proportion his Majestie's service will exceedingly suffer by the tyme that hath bin lost.

Touching the coyne, and the rate you desire it should bee receaved at, I can assure you that those patacownes and rix-dollars being curant heare but at 4s. 8d.; yeat it hath bred much discontent in the armie, and those ministers that brought them over unto us are at this tyme hotly pursued and exclaimed against for bringing the sayd coyne. Soe that you may judge how unreasonable an offer it will bee to have them receave a higher rate than by his Majestie's proclamation they are curant; and what losse it will bee to the King to issue them at lower rates than hee receaves them. Besides that, it will not stand with his Majestie's honour to have coyne within his owne dominions obtruded upon him at higher value than his owne authoritie hath set upon them. Nor can it at all satisfie that your comodities are bought with that coyne, curant at such rates, since his Majestie's ocations will not permit the losse of soe much tyme as the sending into your quarters for the necessarys requisite unto them, and if they could, yeat wee are tought bee experience that the comoditie bought is enhaunsed as the estimate of the coyne that buys it is raysed. But it was hoped that our payments would have bin in English mony (as I beleeve the collections in the country were), whereby this dispute might have bin avoyded, and his Majestie's ocations much better ansuered, and soe I trust the rest will bee. However, it will bee expected that those patacownes, rix-dollers, and pistole bee weight and payd in at the rates curant by his Majestie's authoritie, which only can set values upon coynes.

This I have not acquainted the Justices with, nor devoulged, knoweing well what distaste it would give them, and discontent to all; but have thought fitter by these to desire that any thought of raising the rates of those coynes upon us bee layd asside, and that in all things his endevour bee used clearely and acording to agreement to performe what on that side is to bee done.   Your loving frend,

ORMONDE.

19 Octobris, 1643.

3. LORDS JUSTICES TO ORMONDE.

My Lord,—Concerninge the sendinge downe the beeves to the crane, there shal bee instant orders taken in it.   Your Lordship hathe given a most full and cleere answer to all points of Belling's letter concerninge the coyne, which requires a resolute enforcinnge of it accordinge to your apprehension, otherwise much discontentment will follow (if their vallews be yeelded to) in this army, and they wilbe invited heereby to rayse them higher, if now by your Lordship's provident care not stopt, and they hold to it as you doe.   This is the oppinion [of] your Lordship's humble servants,

John Borlase,
Henry Tichborne.

Dublin, October, 19 [1643].

4. Viscount Muskerry to Ormonde : Question as to Wardships.

My Lord,—I understand that some enquiries are now goeinge forward, to finde the wardshipp of Dominicke Copinger's estate,[1] he beinge lately dead and his estate being in the hands of our Catholicke partie. I presume it was not your Lordship's intention at the percloseinge of the Cessation, that while wee lay downe our armes, advantages of law might be taken against us, or that any the lands in our possession might be made subject to any inconvenience of intrusions, alienations, wardshipps, attainders, or otherwise by means of any offices found dureinge the Cessation, whereas such offices beinge soe found might prove penall, and be produced after the yeare is settled to the noteable prejudice of the sayd partie interested.   Therefore, I desire your Lordship that all inquiries and indictments of what nature whatsoever, concerninge any lands in our possession or any way touching the lives or estates of any of our partie, or any estates wherein they are concerned in reversion or otherwise, may further be forborne, until it be further debated whether any such inquiries may trench uppon or be a breach of the Cessation. I desire to receive your Lordship's answere hearein with speed, least the nation may grow suspitiouse that any designe may be a-foote to involve or subject their lives and estates to any danger duringe the sayd Cessation.   Soe wishinge your Lordship all happinesse, I rest your Lordship's affectionate brother, and most humble servant,   MUSKERY.

Kilcrea, the 19th of October, 1643.

5. Ormonde to Viscount Muskerry.

I receaved your Lordship's letter of the 19th of this month, touchinge some inquiryes goinge forwarde to finde the wardship of the heyre of Dominick Coppinger, beinge lately dead, and his estate beinge in the handes of your partie (as you express it); whereupon I have informed myselfe,

1. The will of Dominick Copinger, of Cork, dated 30th October, 1642, was proved 27th July, 1643.—" History of the Copingers, or Coppingers." By Walter A. Copinger. London : 1884, p. 83.

and doe finde that the sayd Dominick Copinger lived and dyed at Corck, and that the comission of enquirye issued forth under his Majestie's great seale before the Cessation agreed on, and it cannot bee intended by the treatye of Cessation that his Majestie should bee debard duringe the Cessation from inquiringe after the death of his owne tenants, and from seisinge the persons and lands (lyinge within the quarters limited to your partie) belonginge to his Majestie's wards duringe the Cessation, it beinge a principall flower of his Crown, which cannot bee neglected without prejudice to his Majestie's service, and in this particuler without prejudice to the widdowe and heyre of the said Dominick, who are petitioners for the wardship, and beinge proceeded in it cannot (as I conceive) bee any prejudice to your partye.   [ORMONDE].

There is another clause, touchinge indictments, which Mr. Speaker is to consideration. [Undated.]

6. LETTER TO ORMONDE ON GARRISONS AND QUARTERS.

May it please your Lordship,—Wee, the Comissioners of both sydes, haveing this day met to settle and designe the garrizons and quarters controverted, for that your Lordship did not in writing to our former lettres (touching the differences then moved) returne us a resolucion ; soe that, in effect, the contribucion of corne expected to bee had for the Protestant partie cannot bee reconciled by us the Commissioners. Whereupon, by consente of all parties, wee (having admitted the state of the difference to bee as followeth) doe desire your Lordship may bee pleased to send us by the bearer your resolucion therein, viz. : Menn in armes of the Romaine Catholique partie, before and on the 15th of September and untill after the Cessacion accorded, take in and are possessed of this towne and lands of A. B., etc.   The former occupiers and possessors whereof before the said townes were taken in or gained by the said Roman Catholic partie, were protected by the Governor for the tyme beinge of Trym. Question : Whether the parties soe protected, though now residing within the townes and lands aforesaid, soe taken in or possessed by the said Roman Catholic partie in armes, shall now pay the fourth sheafe, etc., beinge on the premises, unto the garrizon of Trym or the Romaine Catholic partie. Soe, expecting your Lordship's resolucion touchinge the premises, wee humbly take leave. Your lordship's most humble servants,

James Fleminge,   Edw. Billingsley,

Luke Fitzgerald,   Thomas Ashe.

Trym, 27th October, 1643.

7. EARL OF CASTLEHAVEN TO ORMONDE.

My Lord,—I came hither employed by the Assembly now held at Waterford, to send you shipping to Dubling; but, according to the waie propounded by my Lord Taaffe and Mr. Plunkett, I doe not thinke fitt to proceede, as well for the imposibility of getting so manie little barkes redie by the time, being the 13 of this month, as allso for the extreme charge of convoying them with frigates of warre who will carie no men, but only goe for defence. Wherefore, I have agreed with one Captin Antonie and the berere, his partner, Mr. Andrew Vanhautt, to attend you with a good shipe both of burden and defence, being nere fower hundred tonn, and carrying sixten peases of ordinance. I am to paie them a pate-coune for eatch man. The bearer hath a copie of our agreement, which he is to shew you; and I desire he may receve favore and your Lordship's assistance during his attendance as ocatione shall require. I entend to send you tow good ships more: the one I have allredie agreed for, her burthen tow hundred tunn, and beres fourteen peesse of ordinance. I hope she will be with you neer by the time apointed. For the third I am labouring harde, and the berer will tell you how the case stands; but, if she failes, I shall endevore to gett another. This course I take as the spediest, safest, and, I am shewre, the cheepest halfe-in-halfe: but, if it be not to your liking, accept the good will of your humble servande,

CASTLEHAVEN AND AUDLEY.

Wexforde, this 7 of November, 1643.

Endorsed: Earl of Castlehaven's. Dated 7, received 11 November, 1643.

8. Letter to Ormonde from the Supreme Council.

Right Honorable,—The enclosed questions and answeres thereupon being delivered by the Lord of Inchiquine to the Viscount Muskry, concerning the baronyes of Barrymore and Imokelly, and the Lord of Inchiquine enforming that those resolutions on the questions came from Dublin, and desiring observance thereof; to avoid any contention that may thereupon happen, wee thought good to lett your Lordship knowe, that, as to the first question in the inclosed, it was not propounded att full. For, though the proprietors of the lands in those baronyes did adhere unto the other partie, and the pretence in the question herein mencioned (for our partie) being onely that our forces marched over the lands, and compelled the undertennants to contribute to our charge; yet the truth is, and is apparantly knowne, that the proprietors and tenants of those baronyes, before the day of the conclusion, did themselves rise in armes, and joyned with our forces, and withall joyned with us in taking of castles and besiedging of Youghall, which is omitted in the case propounded, and may give full satisfaction, that they were noe adherents to his Majesties Protestant subjects, according to the Articles of Cessacion.

As to the second question, in that there should noe resolution be sought for, touching Ahadoe, Coole Ogorry, etc. The competency of wasts thereunto to be applotted, according the articles, are ascertained by Commissioners authorised of our partie and by Commissioners authorised by the Lord of Inchiquine, his Lordship having affirmed, that he had sufficient power to name Comissioners in that behalfe, and to whome, as wee understood att Giggingstowne, that authoritie was transferred.

And, to the third question, there can noe such question fall within this case, for by the first question his Lordship claymeth them as adherents (as indeed they were for a tyme) and never were in the condicion of protected persons or places, whereby a fourth sheafe might be claymed; and if any protection they had taken (which wee are assured they did not), yet their joyning in armes with our partie doth determyn such protections.

Upon consideracion of all which, your Lordship, for prevention of any further contencion in a matter of this cleerenes, (by your Lordship's letters to the Lord of Inchiquine,) may be pleased to give order that noe further dispute be raised therein, which is the desire of your Lordships humble servants,

Muskry.	Lucas Dillon.	Geffr. Browne.
N. Plunkett.	Torl. O'Neill.	John Walshe.

Waterford, the 7th of November, 1643.

To the Right Honorable, our very good Lord, the Lord Marquesse of Ormonde, these present [at] Dublin.

Endorsed : Lord Muskry, cum ceteris. Dated the 7th of November, receaved 20th, 1643. Answeared the 21 Nov., 1643.

9. LETTER TO ORMONDE FROM THE SUPREME COUNCIL.

Right Honnorable,—There is a complaint come to us, concearning Sir Foulke Hunkes his late forces issued to the Illand of Allon[1] by the articles of Cessacion. The said place is within our quarters, and not lyable to any contrybucion of the other parte. Wee cannott find any colour hee had for demaunding any thinge there, other then by pretense of some agreement made by Phillipp Fitz Gerrald, who hath no interest at present in that estate. Neither, as it is averred before us, was any agreement made by him, with the privity of the proprietors or tennants, and if his agreement were any way considerable, yet was it performed, by paying such things as were promised, and soe there remayned no just cause for Sir Foulke Hunkes to seeke any thinge there. Moreover, it is very apparent that, before the conclusion of the late treaty, the forces of our parte were in possession of the Castle of Allon, and the proprietor himselfe in actuall service in the county of Kildare of our parte with forces under his commaunde of our party, as well out of that Illand as from elsewhere in that county, which hath determined any proteccion of the other parte if any himself had taken, and were much more stronger than when a stranger taketh it for lands wherein hee is not interested. My

1. In county of Kildare.

Lord, this particuler appearing thus in the Gennerall Assembly requireth suddaine redress for the wronge done that gentleman, for had Sir Foulkes Hunkes any justifyable demand, as in truth hee had not, yet his sending of forces there, before attendinge the tyme of redress lymited by the articles of Cessacion, may tend to a breach of the articles for which satisfaccion ought to be given and is desired by Your Lordship's humble servants,

Muskry.

N. Plunkett.

Robert Talbott.

Torl. O'Neille.

John Walshe.

Waterford, the 8th of November, 1643.

10.   LETTER TO ORMONDE FROM THE SUPREME COUNCIL.

Right Honorable,—There is noe complaint that cometh to us from your Lordshippe, wherein redresse caun be readilie affoorded, but is accordinglie done, but wee find that your Lordshippe sundrie times hath beene written unto for restitution of Bective, Ardsallagh, and Balsoone, in Meath, and yet those places are not restored, beinge taken after the time to which the Articles of Cessation relate, though Sir William Gilbert's house was restored, beinge a case of the same nature.   It appeareth, likewise, unto us that Lieutenant-Collonell Byroon,[1] assuminge unto himselfe a power not warranted by the Articles of Cessation, doth presse for the customes of the Navan beinge within the quarters of our partie; and the other partie havinge neither garrison therein nor any colour of pretence thereunto, that wee can imagine, the copie of whose warrant for your Lordshippe's better information wee send inclosed.   The garrisons of the other partie in Meath, pretending necessities, doe threaten to be theire owne carvers in takeinge of cattle from our partie for theire reliefe, and have latelie taken some, urginge that allowance should be given for the same out of the moneys payable to his Majestie, wherein wee desire to knowe your Lordshippe's pleasure, and that, in the other particulars herein ex-

---

1. Byron. *See* vol. i., p. 50 ; ii. p. cxi.

pressed, your Lordshippe wilbe pleased warrants be issued for avoidinge such ill consequences as may happen by further delay of those just requests.   And even soe wee remaine your Lordship's humble servants,

Muskry,   N. Plunket,   Torl. O'Neill,
                John Walshe.

Waterford, 8 November, 1643.

11. ORMONDE TO VISCOUNT MUSKERRY, ETC.

Sir,—Diverse complaints have come unto me, from severall parts of the kingdome, that some of your partie, to whom you intrust the government of some places within your quarters, doe give out and publish orders that noe provisions shalbe sould to any of our garrisons. And it is further complained of that those of our partie who have occation to come through your quarters with provisions, or other necessaryes, are forced to pay most excessive and unheard of taxacions; as, for example, at New Castle, which is neare Sir Richard Barnewall's, those garrisoned there by you doe take of every garran which cometh that waie loaden twelve pence, and for everie cow the like some, and so in diverse other places within your comaunde.

By what direccion this is done I know not, but I am sure there may arise very ill consequences from hence; for, besides that it is a breach of that maine and fundamental article of the Cessacion, whereby there is to be free commerce and intercourse and trade betweene all his Majestie's subjects within this kingdome, it doth likewise begett ill blood and continue and increase that strangeness betweene them which theise tymes have occationed, which by all good wayes and meanes ought to be removed.   I desire that this may be taken into present consideracion, and such order taken therein as may prevent those great inconveniences which otherwise undoubtedly will ensue.

I am sorry to understand by the man imployed here by you for payment of the monyes granted uppon the conclusion of the Cessacion, that he

is comanded back for want of work heere. All I can say is, the second
payment is at hand and the last of the first is but newly come in. The
King's service is like to suffer ireparable prejudice by this delay and for
want of the beofs long since due.—[ORMONDE.]

Endorsed : A coppie of my Lord's [letter] to the Lord Muskry or any
of those appointed for the treaty, dated the 10th of November, 1643.

12. LETTER TO ORMONDE FROM THE SUPREME COUNCIL.

Right Honnorable—Your Lordship may perceive by the inclosed,
which is a copie of one Bate his letter, what pretence is made. It is very
cleere by the Articles of Cessation that the sowers and manurers of corne
are to have three parts thereof; yett, contrary to the said Articles, wee
understand that the said Bate, a comaunder of the other party at Crick-
ston, doth detaine from Sir Richard Barnewall three parts of the corne to
him belonging, without any collour of ground that can be warranted by
the Articles. And, therefore, in a matter soe apparant, wee desire present
redresse, the same being formerly written of to your Lordship, and noe
redresse afforded, and the objection by him made is of soe dangerous consequence in gennerall, as it is expected by our party in the Gennerral
Assembly now held at Waterford, that your Lordship give present order
for the restitucion of the said corne unto Sir Richard and his tenants, and
that your Lordship by your direction in writing declare that pretence to
be against the articles, which wee knowe will prevent much mischief. And
soe, praying your speedy aunsweare, wee remayne your Lordship's humble
servants,

| Muskry. | Torl. O'Neill. | John Walshe. |
| N. Plunkett. | Robert Talbott. | Geff. Browne. |

Waterford, 20th November, 1643.

13. LETTER TO ORMONDE FROM THE SUPREME COUNCIL.

Right Honnorable,—Complaynt is made unto us, that forces have
issued out of Trym, to the number of one hundred, and surprized a towne

in Meath within our quarters, called Jordanstowne and cessed themselves there, and in the townes of Possickston, Kilcorn, and Johnston, and many other townes thereabouts in the said county, and likewise within our quarters distroying what corne and other goods our party have there, and doe also plunder the traivailers or passengers who goe the high way in those partes. These particulers, being not onely breaches of the Articles of Cessacion, but in effect acts of hostillity, doe require your Lordship's suddaine direccions, and rebuke to the commaunder there, together with a course for satisfaccion in the losses our party have hereby suffered, which to avoyde all ill consequences that may thereupon happen, is desired by your Lordship's humble servants,

| Muskry. | N. Plunkett. | Geffrey Browne. |
| Robert Talbott. | Torl. O'Neill. | John Walshe. |

Waterford, the 20th of November, 1643.

14. ORMONDE TO MUSKERRY AND SUPREME COUNCIL.

My Lords and Gentlemen,—I received your letter dated the 8th of this moneth the 22d of the same, wherein you say that when any complaint cometh from me to you wherein redress can redily be afforded, that it is accordingly done; but you say I have beene sundry tymes written to for the restitution of Bective, Ardsallagh, and Ballsoone, in Meath, taken since the Cessacion, and yet those places are not restored; you alsoe complaine of some power assumed and customes taken by Lieutenant-Collonell Byron not warranted by the Articles of Cessacion; and, lastly, you say the garrisons of the other party in Meath (whereby, I suppose, you intend ours,) pretending necessity, do threaten to be their owne carvers, in taking of cattle from your party, and that they have lately taken some, urging that if allowance shall be given out of the moneys payable by you to his Majestie; wherein you desire to be resolved by me, and to have warrants for redress in the other particulars.

In answere to all which I must in the first place mind you how many complaints have been made to me, and by me sent to you of thinges taken and done by your party since the conclusion of the Articles of Cessacion, and contrary unto them, whereof as yet there is noe restitution made, nor redress given, nor so much as answere returned to many of my letters. By my letters dated the 28th of September I informed you of the taking from this city [Dublin] on the 18th of September last, 369 head of cattle, or thereabouts (by Barnard Talbot and others of the county of Wicklow) belonging to divers of the inhabitants of the citty, being the greatest part if not the only subsistence the owners had, which cattle Mr. Geoffry Browne undertook at his being here should be restored, and to this day but 40 of them are restored and those of the worst sort, as I am informed, whereas the 300 and odd yet detayned were so good as could hardly be matched in this kingdome, and you may remember how often I have written unto you that restitution of the cattle might be made, whereunto I have beene extreamely importuned by the poore people whose wants are very great, and I have not hitherto received any satisfactory answeare, nor indeed any answeare at all, but long since two letters from Master Richard Bellings, one of which told me that an order was delivered which he said he hoped would free me from further trouble in that particular, and in the other I was tould that the reason why restitution was not made proceeded from those whoe did not solicite their owne cause and aplyed not themselves to such as were authorized there and would see your orders executed, though it bee certaine that severall of the owners of those cattle, and other persons intrusted and expressly sent by them, have to their great charges and losse of tyme and all possible industry to recover what is soe unjustly detained from them. I sent you also letters of the second of October of the surprisall of a pinke[1] within a league of this barre, with her tackling and goods, since the Cessation, and how often I have urged restitution to be made thereof, some of you cannot forget, and yet I am dayly sollicited with fresh complaints for want of performance of the same.

By severall letters (since the Articles of Cessation were published) I have desired that restitution might be made of Sir Edward Povye's house

---

1. A small ship.—Interlineation here: "Restitution is made." *See* letter of Supreme Council, 29th November, 1643.

in the county of Roscommon, taken soone after the Cessacion agreed on, and hitherto I have received no answer from you ; but on the other syde am importuned with complaints of the Generall, who suffers much prejudice by the delay.   On the 10th of this month I directed my letters unto you, signifying that I had then received many complaints that divers of your party had published orders that no provisions should be sold to any of our garrisons, and that those of our party who had occasion to pass through your quarters, were forced to pay most excessive and unheard of taxacion, which Sir Luke Fitz Gerald alledged to be taken by order from thence, and in your letters I instanced unto you Sir Richard Barnewall's new imposition of 12$d.$ on every garran loaden and the like on every cow that passes that way, since which tyme of the two small parcells of cattle that you have sent hither in part of a much greater proporcion, four at one tyme and three at another were taken away by the garison at Newcastle, in lew of your pretended imposicion; and the Preist, Rowen,[1] hath killed some other of the cattle passing that way ; and whether these particulars be not contrary to the intent and effect of the Articles, let any man judge. Severall letters also I sent you about the complaints made of unequall laying out of quarters in Conaght whereupon I never heard that any redress was given nor have I hitherto received any answeare; and about the beginning of this moneth I sent you a fresh complaynt of the detayning of the castle of Mayret in the Queene's County, with the goods thereof taken since the Cessacion, which for ought I can heare to the contrary are not restored, though long sollicited for.   And by Sir Fulke Huncks I am informed that no obedience is yeelded to the Articles of Cessation touching the sheafe of the Iland of Allon protected by the Lords Justices.   So as by all these recited particulars, and divers others, I may justly say that I find not that redress uppon complaints that come from me as by you is intimated, but on the other syde am wearyed with complaints of severall kinds of breaches of the Articles of Cessacion, and of delayes instead of releife applyed, contrary to my expectation, which will make me forbeare further wryting in this kind unless my letters may obtaine right to the partyes

1. *See* " Contemp. Hist. of Affairs in Ireland, 1641-1652." Dublin: 1879. vol. i., pp. 18, 57.

greived; and when I shall understand that the Articles of Cessacion are complyed with by you in restoring the houses and goods by your party taken since the Cessacion, I shall give present order for restoring to your party of all those places which you mention that have been taken by our party since that tyme.

In the next place, I thought good to let you know I have sent order to Lieutenant-Collonel Byron, in answeare to that part of your letter which concernes him, and if he make it not appeare unto me that what he doth is warranted by the Articles of Cessacion I shall give order for his desisting. And, in the last place, touching the necessity which you say is pretended by our garrisons in Meath to take some cattle of yours, I confess I am very sorry that yourselves have occasioned that necessity by your extraordinary delayes used in paying of the 3333 head of cattle payable the last two moneths, whereof the tenth part are not yet payed, notwithstanding my offer laying before you how the delayes was extreamely prejudiciall to his Majesties' service, and would be the causes of very ill consequences to ensue; which to prevent, by my letters of the 18th of the last month, and almost every letter that I sent you since, I have mynded you of. Nevertheless, I have wrytten to the commanders of the garrisons in Meath to require their forbearance of any such courses as might be interpreted to intrench on the Articles of Cessacion, which they can hardly observe unless you do performe your payments imediately that I may supply them. And soe I rest, your very loveing friend,

ORMONDE.

Dublin, 23rd Nov., 1643.

Endorsed: Copy of the letter to the Lord Muskry and the rest, dated the 23rd of November, 1643. Sent away the 24th of November, 1643.

15. LETTER TO ORMONDE FROM THE SUPREME COUNCIL.

Right Honorable,—Wee have receaved your Lordship's letter, dated the 15th of this November, in answere of ours to your Lordship concearning the issueing of forces by Sir Foulke Hunkes to the Ilande of Allon; and, upon the wholle matter, wee are not satisfied that there is any cause wherefore those lands should be lyable to any contrybucion to the adverse party, the proprietor having noe proteccion, nor being privy to any proteccion taken; and if any hee had taken, the agreement whereupon the same was grounded is performed, and by the articles it is plaine that the place soe protected, being within our quarters, is to render no more than the benefitt of such agreement. For which, and other the reasons in our former letter expressed, wee see not what just pretence can be made to that demaunde; yet wee leave the determynacion thereof to the Commissioners of both partes, whereof some are here attending at present in the Generall Assembly, and cannot well be spared; and, therefore, pray your lordship that the said matter be forborne until this Assembly dissolve, which will not now sitte long, or if it should, an authority shalbe issued to others to proceede as Comissioners of our party, and to joyne with the Commissioners of the other parte. Wee remayne your Lordship's humble servants,

| Muskry. | Lucas Dillon. | N. Plunkett. |
| Robert Talbott. | R. Barnewall. | John Walshe. |

Waterford, the 24th of November, 1643.

16. LETTER TO ORMONDE FROM THE SUPREME COUNCIL.

Right Honourable,—Wee have several tymes written to your Honour to have these castles which were taken by your party in the county of Meath, after the Cessacion, with the armes there gained, restored, namely, the Bective, Ardsallagh, Ballsoone, and Assie; and wee doe now earnestly entreate your Honour to send your commaunds to the Governour of Trym to restore them unto Sir Richard Barnewall, whom wee have appointed to dispose thereof. This we expect your Honour will doe, the rather that wee have restored the castles gained by the Earle of Castlehaven. And soe wee reste your Lordship's humble servants,

| Muskry. | R: Barnewall. | N: Plunkett. |
| Lucas Dillon. | John Walshe. | Robert Talbott. |

Waterford, the 24th of November, 1643.

For the Lord Marquesse of Ormonde.

17. ORMONDE TO NICHOLAS PLUNKETT.

Yesterday I receaved from my Lord Taaffe a note of the vessels and their owners to bee contracted with for his Majestie's searvice, and I was directed by him in case the conditions were accepted of to returne my speedy answere to you.

It is true that I conceave the rates demaunded for the hyer of the vessels of force and for the transportation of our men to be very unreasonable, and the scruple unnecessary that is made in receaving our men abord your men of warre, which, if layd aside, would much facillitate the worke and better the bargaine. However, if you can procure it noe better cheape, I must and doe undertake the ships of force shall bee taken into his Majestie's searvice for a month at the rates expressed in the foresayd note, the month to begin from the day of their arrival in this harbour.

I doe alsoe undertake that, for each man that shall bee put aboard, those that have undertaken to receave men there shall bee allowed a patacoune for each man, and to such as have undertaken to bring provisions of any kind for the souldiers acording to what they demaund, and I shall expect the whole fleet should bee in the harbour by the thirtieth of November.

But, according to my first proposition, it is expected that these owners bee contracted with by your partie and by them payed or so satisfied that they expect not payment from hence, and I doe undertake that defalkation shall bee made of what shall bee soe payed or undertaken to bee payed to them for the performance of the searvice aforesayd out of the last payment to bee made by you unto his Majestie, and I desire to bee speedily informed what may be trusted to in this business, their haveing bin already more tyme lost therein than consists with the importance of the searvice.

Touching the pouder which the Lord Taaffe endevoured to contract for and have sent to Bewmaris for his Majestie's searvice, the price demaunded for it is so strangly unreasonable that I will not medle with it, and therefore desire that the severall leters sent by mee to some in

England for the indemnitie of those that should have gone with that or any other provision for warre may bee sent mee if they were left with you as I beleeve they were.—[ORMONDE.]

Endorsed : Letter to Mr. Nicholas Plunkett, concearning shipping, etc.   Dated 27th of November, 1643.

18. PETITION TO SUPREME COUNCIL FROM FRANCIS AND KATHERINE DARCY.

i. To the Right Honorable the Supreame Councell of Confederate
Catholiques of Ireland at Waterford.

The humble petitions of Frauncis Darcy, and Katherine, his wife. In most humble maner declaring that whereas one John Eustace, late of Harristone, within the county of Kildare, gentleman, deceased, was in his lifetime lawfully seised or otherwise intressed for many yeres yett to com and unexpired of and in the rectories and rectoriall tieths of all sorts of corne and graine of Norragh, in the said county of Kildare, and . . . in the countye of Catherlagh, and lickwise of the rectorie of . . . in the countie of Wickloe, and being soe possessed or seised, conveyed by legall assurance four score pounds sterling per annum, to yssue out of the premisses or tithes in kind to the full value thereof yerely to the use of your suppliant, the said Katherin, and her assignees, as a jointour during her life, and departed this transitory life, after whose death your suppliant, the said Katherine, quietly and without any disturbance possessed and enjoyed the same during the time of her viduitye, and your suppliant, the said Frauncis, ever sithenc, in right of the said Katherin, his wife, untill the beginning of theis troublesome times.   Yet now, soe it is, may it please your Honours to be truly informed, that the Countie Councells of the said respective counties' Commissioners lately assigned have, for this three harvests last past, under pretence that the premisses doe of right belong to Sir Morice Eustace Knight, adherent to the adverse partie, collected and disposed of the said rectories without giving your said [suppliants] any accompt or satisfaction for the same, being . . . adherent to the Catholique partie and having [lost all] they had in the defence of the

18. State Papers, Ireland, 1643.—Public Record Office, London.—Ms. damaged.

Catholique cause. [In] tender consideracion whereof, and forasmuch as your supliants have noe other meanes whereby they may subsiste, and that the regulating thereof doth properlye belong to your honors, it may please your honors to give present order that the severall Countye Councells and Commissioners established in the said counties may render an exact accompt for the profitts of the premisses by them receaved to the value of £40 per annum for the in. . . and to continue their payment thereof for the time to come during the life of your suppliant the said Katherin unto your suppliant.

ii. By the Supreame Councell, etc.

Waterford, the 27th of November, 1643.—Forasmuch as it appeareth unto us that the peticioners are, and always have ben of our partie, and never comitted any act (for ought appearinge unto us) against the Confederate Catholicks, and that the peticioners were seised or possessed of two severall anuityes, amountinge unto four scoare pounds per annum, out of the within specified rectories, or soe much of the tyeths as are to the value thereof, at the election of the said Catherin ; wee doe, therefore, order and require the Commissioners for the army in the severall counties of Kildare, Catherlagh, and Wickloe, respectively to permitt the peticioners to receive the said annuitye or tyeths at the election afforesaid for the tyme to come, and to accompt with them for the arrears thereof for the tyme past, or within ten dayes after notice of this our order by their respective agents to show sufficient cause to the contrary before us,

H. Ardmachanus.	Mountgarrett.	N. Plunket.
Emer, Dunensis et	Torlo. O'Neill.	Gerald Fennell.
Conerensis Episcopus.	Patrick Darcy.	

19. LETTER TO ORMONDE FROM THE SUPREME COUNCIL.

Our very good Lord,—The testimony given by your Lordship in your late letters unto us, of the Chauncellor's [Sir Richard Bolton's] designes to advaunce the intrests of this afflicted kingdome, hath beene of such power with the Councell as they were easily drawne to condiscend the Chauncellor might continue the possession of the Bective, notwithstanding it was regained from our party after the Cessation now concluded, so as your Lordship would be a meanes, that in consideration of a place of that consequence and vallue the Lord of Trymlestone may be restored to his castle and lands of Trymleston, desired by his Lordship to no other end than from prevencion onely of the ruine of his said castle, and the destruccion of his orchard, and other husbandry, which will necessarily follow the dayly disorderly wasts committed by the soldyors garrizoned there; and that Assie, a castle also belonging to the Lord of Trymleston, since the Cessacion taken from him, be restored.   And as for anything which wee were by the articles bound, and d [esired] restitucion by any of that party, wee are not conscious [*oblit.*] ourselves that applicacions have beene made unto us by any who have not either gott present restitucion what was detayned from them, or have not beene putt into such a way as was conceived might give them all speedy content and satisfaccion, wee remaine your lordship's humble servants,

Muskry.   R: Barnewall.
N: Plunkett.   Torl: O'Neill.

Waterford, the 29th of November, 1643.

20. LETTER TO ORMONDE FROM THE SUPREME COUNCIL.

Our very good Lord,—Wee have receaved your Lordship's of the 23th of this present, and havinge (by a former letter in favour of the Lord Chancellor Bolton, who bestowes his grateful paines in a very just cause), condiscended the possession of the Bective should be continued in his Lordshipp, desireinge only to have Trimleston restored to the Lord thereof, which is a place of noe great value in itselfe, and very inconsiderable in respect of the other; wee are forced to call uppon your Lordshipp for the

---

19. The documents in this section—Nos. 19-26—are as follows from the Carte Papers: vol. vii. pp. 407-10; vol. viii., pp. 34, 35, 43, 47, 76.

restitucion of Ardsallagh, and Ballsone and of Assye, in the countye of Meath likewise, which by a late complaint made unto us wee doe understand to be detained contrarye to the Articles as beinge taken since the 15th of September.

Wee are spareinge to reiterate unto your Lordshipp any complaint which wee conceive by your Lordshipp's care to have beene putt into a waye of redress, and wee could wish that such as perpetually disquiet your Lordshipp with petitions, tendinge to the same purpose, did first consider how they should rest satisfied by such proceedings of the councell heere, as uppon advertisement from your Lordship are conceived to theire advantadge, whereof the ensuinge answers to the particulars moved from your Lordship will give some light :

Uppon the first notice given by your Lordshipp of the cowes taken into the county of Wickloe, the order, whereof Mr. Bellings writt, was issued, and the want of gaineinge advantadge thereby might well proceed from negligence in the parties concerned (as by a seacond letter from Mr. Bellings your Lordship did understand) ; for, untill Reynolds did appeare in it, noe man was seene to prosecute that cause, by occasion whereof the worke grew more difficult, and now at his request a commission is graunted to men of his owne nameinge, with full power to see him righted.

Concernninge the pincke, direction is given for the restitucion thereof, and uppon questioninge, wherefore the now complaint is made unto your Lordshipp, wee finde that some inconsiderable chardge whereat the captaine whoe tooke the prize hath beene, and which is justly due, as wee are enformed is the occasion of the trouble putt uppon your Lordship in renewinge your letters in that behalfe.

Your Lordshipp makes mention of several letters concerninge Sir Edward Povey's house in the counctye of Roscommon, but wee doe assure your Lordshipp none of them have come into our hands ; soe as to those wee can retourne no other answer than that wee will diligently enquire how that cause stands and see justice donn therein.

For quiet of any complaint which may be made for hindrance of free traficque occasioned by a commaund of the Councell's for furnishing theire severall magazins, although it were improvidence in any that have an army on foote to neglect that care; yet, in as much as the Councell would leave noe cullor to have their actions misconstrued, they have by theire publicke act cleered that doubt; but they hope your Lordshipp will not thinke that those who trafique within our quarters, from what place soever, should be in a better condicion, and have greater imunitye from toule and other imposicions in theire thoroughfare, than such as have borne the burden of the warr with us.   The beeves graunted to his Majestie fall not within this rule, and therefore whatsoever is charged uppon them shall be answered uppon accompt.   Some of the garrisons within your quarters have beene their owne carvers, and for such beeves as are taken by them from any of ours it is reasonable wee should have allowance.

Concerning the laying out of quarters in the province of Connaght, the Councell heere have authoriz'd severall persons within the counctyes of that province to joyne with such Commissioners as are or shall be appointed for quieting of any difference that may arise in that particular.

Your Lordshipp's letter, written about the begininge of this month, concerninge the castle of Marrett in the Queene's Counctye, hath not as yet come into our handes, but wee will uppon advertisement enquire further, and cause justice to be donn.

Concerninge the Island of Allon, findinge the not appeasinge of the difference there arose from the unweldiness of some and carelessness of others appointed to attend the chardge of layinge out the quarters, the Councell heere, at our suite, have renewed the commission and enabled such men for the execucion of it as will give a speedye end to that controversie; soe as uppon the whole matter your Lordshipp may discover how unnecessarye and hastye many of those applicacions were which have been made unto your Lordshipp, and how reddye the Councell heere are to see due satisfaccion made unto such as your Lordshipp doth recommend unto them for redress.

Thus, in answer to your Lordshipp's of the 23th of this instant, havinge retourned speciall answers to your Lordshipp's other letters, and because it is growne to such a lenth, wee have putt over to another letter of ours (and wherein wee hope speedye justice will be donn unto them) the complaintes which are brought unto us touchinge the breache of the Articles whereby many of ours doe suffer.

One thinge, which tendes to the advantage of all sides, wee doe intreate your Lordshipp to provide for, and that is, to hinder by some publicke direction, the destruction and desolacion which is brought uppon the countrye by the libertye the soldiers have assumed to cutt downe woodes and ruine houses within your quarters since this Cessacion, to which evill if there be not a tymely remedie applyed, many will be exasperated to render the same measure of iniquitye to the irreparable prejudice of the kingdome.   Thus we rest Your Lordshipp's humble servants,

Lucas Dillon.   Geffr: Browne.

N: Plunkett.   John Walshe.

Waterford, the 29th of November, 1643.

Upon perclose of this letter, wee finde, conferring with Sir Luke Dillon, that he receaved onely one letter from your Lordship concearninge Sir Edward Povey, whereunto he retourned answere by the messenger that brought it into the county of Roscomman about a moneth since, and more than hee hath signified, as concearning that particuler which he conceived was cleare to your Lordship, wee have not to say.

21. VISCOUNT MUSKERRY TO ORMONDE.

Kilkass [Kilcash], the last of November, 1643.

My Lord,—In answer to your letter of the 22nd of this month, expressing the disservice don his Majestie and the kingdom for want of due performance in the supply promised, the consideration thereof, and of the particular prejudice thereby drawn on your Lordship, induced me to press in the Assembly what evill consequences the faileing thereof may produce in the disadvantage our partie are like to suffer att home by keeping those amongst us that are a burden to both parties, as allsoe how prejudiciall itt may prove to his Majestie's service on the other side.

Itt was soe well understood and recented by the whole House, that strict warrants are issued from hence into all the county's delinquint, for cessing of horse and foote on the defaults for the speedy bringing in of theyre payments, and some particular persons attending in this Assembly imployed purposely for the raising thereof, whereby I hope your Lordship will finde a reall, though (I am sorry to say itt), not soe readdy a performance as was promised.

Tuching aney interruption hapned in matter of free trade and resort to marquetts, I finde that did arise uppon occation of an ordinance made in the Assembly held in May last att Kilkenny, appointinge and comaundinge the storeing of severall magazeanes, and least that might continew a cause of interruption in that behalfe, the Councell have issued directions to remoove all impediments that might happen in that of the commerce. Your Lordship may assuredly believe that the uttermost of my care and best endeavours shall be imployed to serve your Lordship and to prevent aney prejudice that may befall your safetie or reputation, the preservation thereof being not deerer to aney living than, my Lord, your trew, affectionate brother and servant to comaunde,—Muskry.

Endorsed: Lord Muskry, per se. Dated ultimo Novembris, 1643.

22. ORMONDE TO SIR LUCAS DILLON, ETC.

Sir,—I receaved your letter of the 29th of November, wherein you mencion a former letter, not yett come to my hands, whereby you declare your consent that the possession of the Becktiffe should continue in the Lord Chauncellour [Sir Richard Bolton] which is a favour soe well placed as I doe not know how you could bestow it better. But if that you doe expect that Trimlestowne should be givenn upp in exchange thereof, you take away the whole beauty of the former. Neither in truth may I without drawinge much prejudice upon myself assent thereunto; for though Trimleston be, as you write, but a place of noe great value in itselfe, yett, it being the principall seate from whence the Lord hath his title of denomination, it would sound very ill that such a place, and soe long in the possession of our partie, should be delivered up for the Bectiffe, which was scarce held by your partie one day when it was recovered by force from them. Yett hereafter there may be such an accomodacion found out for some of our party as what you desire may be donne without any noise or clamor. And as for the delivering up of Ardsallagh, Balsone, and Assy, you may be pleased to call to minde what I have lately written unto you concerning those places, which I will upon your performance of some thinges expressed in that letter take care shalbe effected.

I am well satisfied touching the pinke which is newly come into this harbor, and in the resolucion taken by you for the removeall of all impediments which should hinder free trafficke; but this much I must intimate unto you as not donne except you take a course that the toles newly raised which are taken within your quarters be forborne; and though you should lay toles upon those of your own partie, yett that ought to be noe rule to charge our partie whoe shall trafficke with you, otherwyse the traffique and commerce is not free as it ought to be by the articles of Cessacion betweene his Majestie's subjects.

I have alreadie declared my sence unto you touching the Iland of Allon and the cowes taken by those of the county of Wickloe, and therefore shall not neede for the present to trouble you any further therewith, but will for some further tyme expect the issue of both. And as for your desire that some tymely provisions should be made for preventing of the destrucion of woods within our quarters, I doe assure you that before I receaved your letter I was contriveing how to put it into such a way as would anticipate your desires, if that you had not at this tyme written about it, and you shall very suddenly finde the fruits thereof; and you may be pleased to remember that upon the late treaty at Sigginstowne this was one of the propositions which moved from me, wherein if you had at that tyme joyned with me all the destruccion which sence hath beene donne might have been prevented.

I have not receaved the answere afirmed by Sir Lucas Dillon to have bin sent mee, touching Sir Edward Povey's howse, by the messenger that delivered mine to him; therefore I desire satisfaction maybee now given mee therein. Touching Morett, in regard you write unto mee that my letter is not come to your hand, I have renued it least it should be miscaryed. And soe I remaine your very loveing frend,—ORMONDE.

Dublin, 6 December, 1643.

Sir Lucas Dillon, etc.—Endorsed: A coppie of my Lord's, in answeare to a letter of the 29th concerning the Bectiffe, and signed by Sir Lucas Dillon and some of the rest. Sent by Hadsor's man, the 7th of Dec: 1643.

23. ORMONDE TO VISCOUNT MUSKERRY, ETC.

Sir,—I find by a complaint exhibited unto me by peticion that the castle of Moyrett in the Queene's County hath beene demaunded by one Leigh, according to the Articles of Cessacion, yet noe restitution is made of the castle or of the armes therein taken, contrary to the quarter which was given by the Earle of Castlehaven. Therefore I expect that the said Leigh be forthwith repossessed of his said castle, and his goods restored unto him, if they may be found in specie, otherwise that such course may be taken as that he may receive damages for his losses sustayned, contrary to the articles of Cessacion. And soe I rest your very loving freind,

[ORMONDE.]

Dublin, 6 Dec. 1643.

Lord Muskry, cum cæteris. Endorsed: A copie of my Lord's to the Viscount Muskry, etc. concearneing the castle of Morett. Sent by Hadsor's man, the 7th of Dec. 1643.

24. ORMONDE TO SIR JAMES DILLON.

Sir,—I have bin divers tymes informed that by your direction there is a gate-house and a wall erected since the Cessation, on this side the river of Shanon and oposite to his Majestie's castle of Athlone, within such distance as may anoy it, whereunto I did not give creditt till I am now againe assured of it.

It is true that by the Articles of Cessation neither side is debard from fortifieing such strengths as are in their hands. But it is as cleere that, under that pretence, neither side ought to raise new fortifications to the anoyance of any fort or castle from whence the same might bee hindered by artillery or small shot if the Cessation were not.

And, therefore, I must desire and expect that if any such gatehouse, wall, or other worke be erected within the reach of the canon of his Majestie's sayd castle of Athlone, that they bee forthwith demolished and slighted, which is so suteable to reason that I noe ways doubt but you will see it performed, whereby you will take away all cause of jelousy which otherwyse may bee justly held of such proceedings.   And soe, in expectation of your answere hereunto, I rest, your very loving friend,

ORMONDE.

Dublin, 9 Dec : 1643.

Sir James Dillon.

Endorsed : Coppy of my Lord's to Sir James Dillon, concerneing fortification.   Sent by my Lord Taafe.

25. Lords Justices and Ormonde to Sir Lucas Dillon, etc.

After our hartie commendations : Wee have received your joint leters of the 29th in answer of ours of the 20th of November, and have perused the note you sent inclosed in your said leters, mentioning what was paid in money as well uppon assignments from us as otherwise, which amounts to three thousand nine hundred and thirtie pounds.   And although the title of your note mentions only payment in money, yet wee finde charged therein one hundred twenty five pounds for the beoves designed for Trim.

Wee have also informed ourselves what beoves have been sent hether, and finde only three hundred and eighteen beoves brought hether, which amounts in money to four hundred three score and seventeene pounds, which being added to the said some of three thousand nine hundred and thirtie pounds, both doe make four thousand four hundred and seven pounds ; soe as of the ten thousand eight hundred pounds, which ought to bee paid by the 15th of November last, there remaines yet unpaid six thousand three hundred four score and thirteene pounds.

And whereas you write that you do not perfectly knowe what other somes have been paid uppon your particular warrants, wee doe lett you knowe, that before the date of your said leters, wee issued noe particular warrants, assigneing any part of the monies or beoves to bee paid, but those charged by you in that note you sent us, excepting two hundred beoves for his Majestie's guarrisons in Connaght, and fourscore beoves for his Majestie's guarrison in Dundalke, both making two hundred and fourscore beoves, but wee understand that none of those two hundred and fourscore beoves are yet paid; soe as though the failer on your parts in those payments to them and in the payments which should be made heere, not only those guarrisons for whom those two hundred and fourscore beoves were designed, are much prejudiced, but also his Majestie's affaires heere are exceedingly disappointed.   And, certainly, the sloeness of your performance, which you confess in your letters, cannot be excused by what you have written to us by your said letters; but, by the neglect of performance on your part, wee have just occasion given us to represent the same to his Majestie.   And, therefore, wee doe now expect that the said six thousand three hundred fourscore and thirteene pound bee immediately paid, according to agreement thereby, if it may be yet, to redeeme the former neglect on your parts, to the highe prejudice of his Majestie's affaires.   And soe wee bid you farewell from his Majestie's Castle of Dublin, 9 December, 1643.—Your loving frends,—John Borlase.—Henry Tichborne.—Ormonde.

To Sir Lucas Dillon, Knight, Nicholas Plunket, Geoffrey Browne, and John Walsh, Esqrs., and to every of them.

26. ORMONDE TO VISCOUNT MUSKERRY, ETC.

My Lords and Gentlemen,—I find by my Lord of Inchiquine that many injuries are and have beene offered by your party to ours in severall parts of the province [of Munster] since the Cessacion agreed on, contrary to the Articles; perticulerly that, under pretence that the army of your party were masters of the feild in the barronyes of Imokilly and Barrimore on the 15th of September last, or that the freeholders or tenants did declare themselves for you, you doe clayme those barronies to be wholy yours, save where wee have particular guarrisons, and doe accordingly take up the corne and other profitts, without answering any part of it to our party, notwithstanding that they paid contribucion these two yeares past unto our party, and had protection from the guarrison of Corke and

Youghall and other guarrisons yet in our hands; whereas it is apparent by the Articles of Cessacion (those guarrisons being in our hands) the places once protected by them are to continue their contribucion unto us, albeit you had beene masters of the feild in those barronies on that day, or that the freeholders or tennants did at or before that day declare themselves to be of your party ; and, therefore, it seemes most straunge unto me, and those who assisted mee upon the treaty, with whome I have consulted touching these particulars, how that contrary to the expresse articles, and to what I formerly writt you should continue that course, and I doe expect present order to be taken by you therein as you tender the performance of the Articles.

His Lordship also alledges that those castles or guarrisons that continue in our hands in those baronies within your quarters are not permitted by your party to enjoy the lands belonging to them, nor any lands but some small inconsiderable quantities, and are so circumscribed by narrow limits that our men are not able to subsist therein, and yet that your party doe take to the guarrisons or castles lately fallen unto them as is above expressed, not only the lands belonging unto them, but lands that they neither did or could before the Cessacion come at as lands in the great island and other lands neere Corke; that your party keepes all Roche's Country, where, on the 15th of Sept. you had neither guarrison nor force, that barronie being not only within our quarters, but also cleerely within our power at that tyme, and yielding contribucion to our party and all the strengthes there deserted, some few only of your party being in a sculking, private way not observed on some part of those lands at that tyme. And herein also I desire speedy redresse.

His Lordship doth further alledge that you pretend by the Articles noe restitution ought to be made of any goods taken by your party from any of ours after the Cessacion, unless particular notice were first given to them that tooke the same; whereas you knowe that restitution by the Articles ought to be made in specie of any thinge taken before publicacion of the Articles, if the same could be found, and, after publicacion, the goods with damages; and that publicacion was made of the Articles on the 15th of September, and that if perticular notice ought in that case to be given, the difference would be endless. And where it is affirmed by some of you, as the Lord of Inchiquine informed mee, that our party gained a barrony called Bremigham's Country in the county of Kildare (as you did Roche's Country) I thought good to let you knowe that that barrony was a long tyme under our power and protection before the Cessacion agreed on, and that Sir John Gifford had guarrisons there at the tyme of the conclusion of the Articles and that the same ought by the Articles cleerely to contribute only to our party during the Cessation.

These and such like disputes raised for private ends I desire may receive such a satisfactory end by your moderate complyinge with what may conduce to the preservation and the publicke peace of the kingdome as neither you nor I maybe any more troubled with any complaints of this kind.

About the 17th of the last moneth, I wrote you a letter and enclosed an abstract of severall injuries done unto Sir Phillip Percevall in gaininge of some castles and lands out of his hands since the Articles of Cessation, and contrary to the same, as was informed, whereof I have not heard of any redress, nor have I receaved any answeare. And soe I remain, your very loveing frend,—[ORMONDE.]

Endorsed : A coppy of the letter to the Lord Muskry, etc. concearneing the Lord Inchiquin. Dated the 14th Dec. 1643. Sent by the Lord Inchiquin's man the same day.

VI. PAYMENT TO GENERAL THOMAS PRESTON BY SUPREME COUNCIL.

14 Dec. 1643.—It is ordered that the Supreame Counsell shall consider of the reporte made by the Comittee concerneing the payment of one thousand pounds unto the Lord Generall of Leinster, expended by himself, and how far his Lordshipe may be accommodated with the same, either in his lady and famyly in theire commeing to the country ; and further consider of the proposicions made by his Lordshipe concearening Enishcorthy,

VI. State Papers, Ireland, 1643. Public Record Office, London.

part or payment of the reserved rent therout unto him; and to doe herein as to them shalbe thought fitt.

Exam: per Phill: Kearneye.

VII. LETTERS ON APPOINTMENT OF COMMISSIONERS OF CONFEDERATION.

1. BELLINGS TO ORMONDE.

MY LORD,—The Councell heere by the commaund of the Assemblye of the Confederate Catholickes of Ireland, by theire letters bearinge date the 19th of November, did advertise your Lordship that they had chosen the Lord Viscount Muskerye, Mr. Alexander McDonnell, Mr. Nicholas Plunket, Sir Robert Talbot, Baronet, Dermot O'Brien, Richard Martin, and Geoffrye Browne, Esquires, to be theire Commissioners[1] and to present theire greevances unto his Majestie; and they desire your Lordship would procure a safe-conduct, both heere and from his Majestie, and such further meanes as should be thought necessarye might be in a reddiness for secureinge them and theire retinue in theire repaire to his Majestie, duringe theire aboade at Court, and theire retourne into this kingdome; and havinge not received an answer to theire said letters, they have commaunded me to renew theire former request, which your Lordship wilbe pleased to give answer unto uppon this advertisement of, my Lord, your Lordship's most humble servant,

Richard Bellings.

Waterford, the 19th of December, 1643.

2. ORMONDE TO VISCOUNT MUSKERRY.

My Lord,—I have indeed by two of yours been informed, that choise is made of you to be one of those that shall attend his Majestie from your party of the kingdome, and in both you desire my advise, as I thinke, touching your deportment in that weighty imployment. But since I am only acquainted in the generall, that your errand is for a settlement to this kingdome, and that I am utterly ignorant what you will propose, and

VII. 1, 2, Carte Papers, viii., pp. 102, 104.   1. *See* p. 2.

how farre you have power to assent to what his Majestie shall propose in behalfe of his owne interests, and those of his other subjects; I say, this my ignorance considered, I can only in generall advise you to remember:

First, with whome it is you are to treate; not with your equall, but with your King; and therefore your negotiation must be qualifyed with those due respects both in formes and substance, as is needfull and usuall from subjects to their Princes.

Secondly, to consider, that as you come intrusted to desire benefitts and graces from the King; soe one part of your businesse there may be to give satisfaction as farre as may be to the injurees susteyned by the King and his English and Protestant subjects (as will be alleadged) by the causelesse and unnecessary takeing of armes: And therefore you are not to expect such a reception as at other tymes Agents have had, which would not suite with the King's honor, or with his affaires to give.

Lastly, consider what a good exchange peace will be for warre, the name of loyall subject for that of a Rebell, and hapinesse for devastacion and misery. And then, I doubt not, though you make such demands as you are appointed, you will satisfy yourselves with what the King shall think fitt for you; which is my advise, and (I protest before God) should be my practice, if I weare in your place.

Haveing given you this short view of my sence, I must tell you plainely that I hould it noe wayes fitt for you nor the rest of the Agents to stirr hence, till you have caused his Majestie's occasions (which now presse very sorely uppon him) to be complyed with in some better measure, by paying the great areare is uppon you: For if you doe goe before that is don, your entertainement will be the worse, and whereever you promise aught, your publique faith, soe fowly violated in this, will be rejected as a foyld and worthlesse assurance. I am, etc.

[ORMONDE.]

Dublin, 19th Dec., 1643.

Endorsed: 19 Dec., 1643. A coppy of a letter to the Lord Muskry. Advice given him how to deporte himself before the King; he being chosen one of those that are to attend the King from the Confederate party.

VIII. Letter to Ormonde from the Supreme Council.

Right Honorable,—After the conclusion of the Articles of Cessation, and publishing thereof in the countie and cittye of Corke, our forces in obedience thereunto (being then in the fyld in that countie) did withdrawe themselves to their owne quarters, expecting that there would be the like observance of the other parte.   But, contrarywise, the regements of the Lord of Insiquine and of Collonell Myn, and the Lord of Insiquine his troope, did issue oute into Rosse in the barronye of Carbrye in that countie, and continued there for three weekes, and in that tyme possessed themselves of all the corne in the barronye of Ibane, and of a greate parte of the barronye of Carbrye, to the value of tenn thousand pounds att least, notice of the Articles of Cessation being brought to them before, by a trumpett of their owne from Sigginstowne, and tooke nott onely the fourth sheafe whereunto anye pretence might be made by their partye, butt tooke allsoe the other three partes of that corne which, by the Articles, doth cleerelye belong to the sowers and manurers withoute exception.   Wee must likewise informe your Lordship that one Thomas Bennett, commaunder of the garison of Ballymore did, aboute the twentye-sixt of September last, enter and possess himselfe of the castle of Dunnalonge in the barronye of Carbrye, beinge untill then in the possession of our partye, and within the lymitts of their quarters.   This complayntt is soe manifest, and of soe greate consequence that wee expect a present course to be prescrybed for satisfaction therein, agreeable to the Articles of Cessation.   Soe wee remayne your Lordship's humble servants,

Muskry.—N: Plunkett.—R: Barnewall.—Robert Talbott.— Torl: O'Neill.—John Walshe.—Geffrey Browne.

Waterford, the 20th of December, 1643.

For the Right Honnorable the Lord Marquesse of Ormonde.

Endorsed : Lord Muskry, etc.   Dated the 20th of Dec., 1643.

VIII. Carte Papers, viii. p. 110.

IX. Letters and Despatches to France from the Irish Confederation, in November and December, 1643.

1. To Cardinal Mazarin.

[The Council thank the Cardinal for the good offices he has rendered them with the Queen-Regent of France. They would deem themselves unworthy of such patronage, if they had in any way failed in their loyalty to King Charles, to defend whose prerogatives they had bound themselves by solemn oath. Nothing could be more glorious for the Queen-Regent than to be known to posterity as having aided a grateful people contending for their religion, the rights of Kings, and the liberties of their country. Some of the Irish, in past generations, pursued devious courses, with which, however, the kingdom at large was not identified.[1] All Catholics in Ireland are unanimously engaged in the present war. They desire that the Queen-Regent and the Cardinal may continue to favour them only so long as they labour to advance their most just cause by the most legitimate means. The state of their affairs will be communicated by Father Mathew O'Hartegan.—Waterford, 20 November, 1643.]

Pro vestro in nos causamque nostram propenso animi affectu, et apud Serenissimam Galliæ Reginam præstitis beneficiis, gratias habemus maximas ; neque certe nos ipsi Hiberniam tali patrocinio aut Eminentissimæ Dominationis vestræ favore dignam existimaremus, si in fidem optimo Principi Carolo, Regi nostro, datam peccasset ; sed cum solemni sacramento illi nos fideles esse illius prærogativa defendere adstricti simus, quid gloriosius a potentissima Galliarum Regina posteris poterit commendari, quam quod gentem nunquam ingratam, pro Catholica fide, pro Regum indubito jure, pro libertate patriæ pugnanti, subvenerit. Ex patribus nostris quosdam deviasse confiteri necesse est, et quod regnum adeo innocens

IX. MS. "Register Book of Letters" of Supreme Council of Irish Confederation.—Bodleian Library, Oxford. *See* vol. i. p. lxx.
1. *See* p. 7, in relation to letter from Mazarin, which will be found at p. 33.

fuit ut pro cujuslibet indigenæ delicto se in judicium trahi velle non vere-
retur. Jam tota gens quot sunt in Hibernia Catholici unanimi consensu
iisdem studiis bellum inierunt nec diutius potentissimam Reginam pro-
pitiam nec Eminentiam vestram intercessorem petimus quam justissimam
causam justissimis mediis prosecuti fuerimus. De reliquo, etc. aperiet
Reverendus Pater, Pater Matheus O'Hartegan, etc.

    Eminentissimæ Dominationis vestræ observantissimi servi.

Waterfordiæ, 20 Novembris, 1643.

2. To the Nuncio in France.

[The Council congratulate the Nuncio on his elevation to the Cardinalate. The promotion of so good a friend to the Irish is regarded by
them as contributing to advance their cause, in which he has been most
indefatigable. They give him the greatest thanks for his aid, and, if the
expected end be attained, the memory of his Eminence will descend with
honour to posterity. The state of the affairs of the Council will be
explained by Father Mathew O'Hartegan.—Waterford, 20 November,
1643.]

    Gratulamur certe Sanctissimum Patrem nostrum Eminentiam vestram
Cardinalium Collegio adscripsisse; nec quicquam honoris aut potestatis
tanto rerum nostrarum patrono potest accedere quin eodem gradu causam
nostram evehi credimus. Non tepide, nec pro forma, Hiberniæ pro Catholica fide pugnanti subvenisti, indefessa cura hinc illinc in illius subsi-
dium omnem movit lapidem. Eminentiæ vestræ, gratias quæ debemus
habemus maximas, et si benignissimus Dominus cujus hactenus auxilio
stetit res nostra ad illum quem speramus opus perducet finem, meritorum
Eminentiæ vestræ larga ad posteros deveniet memoria. Quis vero rerum
nostrarum presens status sit aperiet Reverendus Pater, Pater Matheus
O'Hartegan, Societatis Jesu Sacerdos, cui ut indubitata fides adhibeatur,
Eminentissimæ Dominationis vestræ observantissimi, rogamus.

Waterfordiæ, 20 Novembris, 1643.

3. To MATHEW O'HARTEGAN.

Reverend Father,—You are to render in our behalfe humble and hearty thankes unto her Majestie, the Queene-Regent of France, who hath beene pleasd to lay a marke of her favor uppon our cause and may be wonn to advance it by her gratious mediacion to our Soveraigne. Wee have alreddy concluded uppon a Cessacion of Armes for a yeere, and have appointed agents by whom our greevances are to be presented unto our Kinge, soe as you must make it now your cheefe care to have directions sent from thence to the embassadour of Fraunce now in the courte of England to interpose the Queene his mistresse her authoritie and inter-cession for obtaining just and wholesome remedys to bee applyed to our greevances. You are likewise to presente our lettres to his Eminencie the Cardinall Mazerin and to express unto him the hearty affections wee beare unto him ; and that wee hope the advantage our religion and nation shall receave by the happie conclusion of theise commotions wilbee a benefitt wee shall owe to his furtherance.

You cannot render too many thanks in our behalfe to his Hollines' Nuntio, Cardinall Grimaldi, who since the first houre hath laboured with unwearied care to promote our affayres.

Our condicion as to the warr is little altered, the Puritant part in the North being powerfull, and wee enforced to raise an army against them, soe as you are to remitt noe parte of your endeavours to provide all assistance for that service which out of the experience and proofe wee have had of your zeale and diligence wee are confident you will performe. Thus, with our heartiest wishes, we rest.

Waterford, 20 November, 1643.

4. To GASTON, DUKE OF ORLEANS.

[The Council trust that the Duke will excuse Colonel Cullen for having stayed for a time under their command. Cullen has fought bravely in Ireland for religion, the undoubted rights of Kings, and the liberty of his country. Having deserved well of his countrymen, he now returns

to the Duke, whom he specially honours. The Council, grateful for
Cullen's services, recommend him to the favour of the Duke.—Waterford,
20 December, 1643.]

Serenissime Princeps,—Facilem apud tantum principem et tam propi-
tium rebus nostris inveniet veniam Dominus Cullon, quod nostro obtemperans mandato, hic moram traxerit; fortiter enim pro Catholica fide,
pro Regum indubitato jure, et libertate patriæ pugnavit, et jam, optime
meritus de nobis, redit ut Serenitatis vestræ aspectu fruatur, quem unice
veneratur. Illum itaque ne pro præstitis officiis ingrati essemus Serenitatis vestræ favori commendamus.—Serenissimæ Dominationis vestræ
observantissimi servi.

Waterfordiæ, 20 Decembris, 1643.

5-7. To the Queen Regent of France, Cardinal Mazarin, and the Nuncio in France in relation to Colonel Cullen.

[The Council state that Colonel Cullen, now about to return to France,
has served during eighteen months with great bravery in the war in
Ireland for religion, King, and country, against the Puritans. They commend Cullen to the Queen's favour, and to the patronage of the Cardinal
and the Nuncio, as an officer who has deserved well of his own countrymen, and has already served for many years under the banner of the King
of France.—Waterford, 20 December, 1643.]

5. To the Queen-Regent of France.

Serenissima Regina,—Ignoscat nobis vestra Majestas, precamur, quod
Dominum Cullon, Christianissimi Regis in exercitu Collonellum, gravissimi mole belli laborantes hactenus detinuimus. Fortiter contra Ecclesiæ
et omnis regiæ potestatis hostes Puritanos pugnavit, et nunc, bene de
nobis meritus magna cum laude redit; scimus eo Majestatem vestram vir-
tuti patrocinari affectu ut illius recommendacionem Majestati vestræ
ingratam fore non vereamur.—Majestatis vestræ humillimi servi.

Waterfordiæ, 20 Decembris, 1643.

6. To Cardinal Mazarin.

Eminentissime Domine,—Dominus Cullon, qui per opportune octodecim retro mensibus huc appulit et, exinde nostro imperio obtemperans, contra Puritanos hostes strenue pugnavit, jam Galliam repetit. Bene meritus de nobis in illa quam illi commisimus cura, nec magis fortiter quisquam, nec prudentius, officii munia in nostro exercitu peregit. Quapropter justum duximus illum istuc redeuntem Eminentiæ vestræ pro eo quo virtutem prosequitur affectu commendare ut, qui multis jam annis sub potentissimi Galliarum Regis vexillis merebat, sentiat hæc illius in patriam officia ulteriorem Eminentissimæ Dominationis vestræ favorem sibi conciliasse.— Eminentiæ vestræ observantissimi servi.

Waterfordiæ, 20 Decembris, 1643.

7. To the Nuncio in France.

Eminentissime Domine,—Redit in Galliam Dominus Cullon,[1] qui nostro mandato hactenus detentus, strenue pro Catholica fide pugnanti adfuit patriæ. Meruit certe a nobis coli, et multa fecit et passus est in hoc quod gerimus bello; et, cum pro singulari in causam nostram studio dignetur Eminentia vestra communi nobiscum affectu res nostras prosequi haud ingratum fore duximus virum de nobis bene meritum favori vestro commendare, ut virtutem ubique posse sentiat.—Eminentiæ vestræ manus deosculantur Eminentiæ vestræ observantissimi servi.

Waterfordiæ, 20 die Decembris, 1643.

8. Passport for Monsieur De La Brosse.

[The Council certify that Monsieur De La Brosse, who now returns to France, his own country, had, attracted by the justice of their cause, relinquished the care of his affairs at home, and seized every opportunity to be present at battles, in several of which he fought for the Irish with courage and success. For these services he was advanced to the post of Lieutenant of the body-guard of horse.—Waterford, 20 December, 1643.]

1. In relation to Colonel Cullen, see p. 32.

Cum jam habita venia in Galliam patriam suam revertere decrevit Dominus De La Brosse, ne quæ apud nos strenue gessit incertæ famæ nuncianda relinqueremus, æquum visum est attestari illum, causæ nostræ justicia allectum, cura rei familiaris postposita, e Gallia venisse et omnem arripuisse occasionem qua pugnæ adesset et in multis congressibus fortiter et fœliciter dimicasse. Quapropter in officium Locum-tenentis turmæ equitum de custodia evehi meruit.

Datum Waterfordiæ, vicesima die Decembris, 1643.

9. To Mathew O'Hartegan, at Paris.

Reverend Father,—Wee have understood, by Mr. Geoffrey Baron,[1] that the payment of £2,000 of the moneys which wee were to receive by the order of the Courte of France was suspended by a seacond direccion. Wee shall therefore pray you to sollicit the remove of any impediment that may hinder the obtaininge of it, wherein you will be assisted by the bearer, Liftenant-Generall Cullon, a gentleman who hath layd many obligacions of gratitude, both by his gallant carriadge in the warr and the provision he made uppon his privatt fortune to releeve his countrye, uppon us and this kingdome.

When you shall get this money you are to deliver seaven hundred and fortye pounds sterling to the Liftenant-Generall, who is to dispose thereof accordinge such instruccions as he hath receaved from us. The remaine you are to send over to supply our occasions heere, and to continue your care to enable us by the assistance of our freinds to goe through this great worke wee have in hand.

Dated Waterford, the 21 of December, 1643.

1. Delegate to France from the Supreme Council of the Irish Confederation. *See* vol. ii., p. 390.

X. EXPEDITION TO ULSTER, 1643.

LAWES AND ORDERS OF WARRE, MDCXLIII. ESTABLISHED [BY LORD CASTLE-
HAVEN] FOR THE CONDUCT OF THE ARMIE DESIGNED FOR THE EXPEDITION
OF ULSTER.[1]

By the Generall.

James, Earle of Castlehaven and Lord Audley, Generall[2] of the Army
for the Ulster expedition : To the Lieutenant-Generall, Sergeant-Maior-
Generall, the Colonells, Lieutenant-Colonells, Sergeant-Maiors, Captaines,
and all other officers and souldiers of horse and foote in the army, and to
all the Confederate Catholicks and others whom these lawes and orders
ensuing shall concerne, which lawes and orders hereby published under
my hand, I require all the said persons respectively and severally in this
army, or quarters of the Confederate Catholickes of this kingdome, to
observe and keepe, on the paines and penalties, as by these presents are
expressed.

Prayers to be frequented.

First, I doe straitly charge and command all commanders and officers
of the army, to see that Almighty God be duely and reverently served, by
often frequenting the sacraments and daily hearing of Masse. And those
that often and wilfully neglect this great good be duely punished.

Blasphemy, Heresie.

2. Let no man speake impiously and maliciously against the Holy and
Blessed Trinity, or any of the Three Persons, God the Father, God the
Sonne, and God the Holy Ghost, or against the knowne articles of the
Catholicke Faith, upon paine of death.

Profanation.

3. No man shall take God's holy name in vaine, or use unlawfull oaths
or execrations, or commit any scandalous act, to the derogation of God's

---

1. Printed at Waterford by Thomas Bourke, Printer to the Confederate Catholicks
of Ireland, 1643.

2. For notice of election of Castlehaven as General, *see* Preface and p. 3.

honour, upon paine of the losse of his pay, imprisonment, and such further punishment as a marshall-court shall thinke his offence deserves.

Trayterous words.

4. No man shall use any trayterous words against his Maiestie's sacred person or royal authority, upon paine of death.

Disobedience to commanders.

5. No man shall speake, or practise anything to the dishonour or destruction of the Supreme Councell of the Confederate Catholickes of Ireland, on paine of death.

Disobedience to commanders. Mutiny.

6. No man shall offer any violence against, or contemptuously disobey his commander, or doe any act, or speak any words which are like to breed any mutiny in the army or garrison, or impeach the Generall, Lieutenant-Generall, or principall officers' directions, on paine of death.

Not repairing to the rendezvous.

7. No man shall wilfully, or thorow grosse ignorance, fayle in coming to the rendezvous or garrison assigned to him by the Generall or other principall officer that commands the army, upon paine of death.

Extortion, etc., upon a march.

8. No Captaine, Officer, or souldier of troope or company, on their march thorow any country within our quarters, or which shall be in peace or Cessation with us, going to any garrison or place of service, shall, upon any pretence of want whatsoever, commit any waste, spoyle, or violence, or extort any victuals, money, or pawne in lieu of victuals, from any good subject whatsoever, but shall content themselves with meat and drinke competent, paying the usual and accustomed rates for the same, upon paine of death. But if in time of open action, by occasion of any march through the country, the souldier shalbe in want, then the officer shall seeke and provide such diet and lodging for them as shalbe thought fit,

at reasonable rates heretofore accustomed, for the which the Captaine or officer shall give ready money, or for want thereof deliver his ticket to be satisfied upon his entertaynment.

Persons not inrolled in the army.

9. No man that carries armes, or pretends to be a souldier, shall remayne three dayes in the army after it is on foote, except he be inrolled in some company, on paine of death.

Not repairing to the colours.

10. No man shall fayle immediately to repayre unto his colours (except upon evident necessity), when an alarme is given, upon paine of death.

Holding intelligence with, or relieving the enemy.

11. No officer or souldier whatsoever shall have conference or intelligence with any enemy or rebell that is in open action against his Maiesty, or the Confederate Catholickes, or harbour or receive any such within the campe, or in any towne, fort, castle, or garrison, or shall send, or procure to be sent any victuall, ammunition, or other reliefe to any enemy or rebell in action. Neyther shall doe any other thing to the danger or prejudice of the armie, or being acquainted therewith, shall conceale the same from the chiefe officer, upon paine of death. Onely such as shall be avowed and warranted thereunto by me, or those that command the army in my absence, may speake, confer, have intelligence, or converse with the enemy or rebell, for the advantage of his Maiestie's service.

Revolting to the enemy.

12. No man shall runne to the enemy or rebell that is in action, or depart the army, from the garrison or colours, without licence, upon paine of death.

Departing from Captaine.

13. No souldier shall depart from his Captaine without licence, though he serve still in the army, upon paine of death.

Entering or going out of the campe by unusual ways.

14. No man shall enter or goe out of the army or garrison, but by ordinary ways, upon paine of death.

Watchword.

15. No man shall make knowne the watchword to the enemie or any other, but by order, nor give any word other than is given by the officer, on paine of death.

Sentinell and watch.

16. No man being set sentinell by his officer, shall sleepe, depart, or forsake his place without being relieved or drawne off by the officer that placed him. Nor any other person, being placed upon his watch, shall neglect his duty commanded by his officer, upon paine of death.

Drawing sword after the watch set.

17. No man shall presume to draw his sword without order after the watch is set, upon paine of death.

False alarm or noyse in the night.

18. No man shall give a false alarm, or discharge a piece in the night, or make any noise, without lawfull cause, upon paine of death.

Murther, or private quarrel.

19. No man shall commit any murther, or kill any person, or draw blood of any, or draw sword in private quarrell, with intent to offer violence within the camp or garrison, upon paine of death.

Officers of the watch suffering duells.

20. No corporal, or other officer commanding the watch shall wittingly suffer a souldier to go forth to private fight, upon paine of death.

Seditious words.

21. No person shall rehearse seditious words, in the presence of private souldiers, without order, upon paine of death.

Unlawful assembly.

22. No person shall make any unlawfull assembly, or be present or assisting thereunto, upon paine of death.

Mutinous demand of pay.

23. No man shall demand money with an unlawfull assembly, or by other way, tending to mutiny, more especially upon marching towards an enemy, or upon the execution of any enterprize, upon paine of death.

Abuse to bringers in of victuall.

24. No man shall outrage or doe any violence to any that come to bring victuals to the army or garrison, upon paine of death.

Deceit in victuall or ammunition.

25. No providor, keeper, or officer of the Confederate Catholickes victuall or ammunition shall wilfully corrupt or imbeazell any part thereof, or give any false account to the Generall, with a purpose to deceive the Confederate Catholickes, or to hinder the service, upon paine of death.

False muster.

26. No souldier in musters shall answer for another, or take two payes, or muster in a false name, to defraude his Maiesty, upon paine of death.

Spoyle or sale of ammunition.

27. No person shall sell, spoyle, or carry away any ammunition, upon paine of death.

Selling or pawning of armes.

28. No souldier shall sell, or lay to pawne, his horse or hackney, or any part of his furniture, armes, or apparel, for any respect, or pretence of want whatsoever, upon paine of death.

Robbery or stealth.

29. No man shall steal, or take by force, any treasure, victuall, or ammunition of his Maiestie's, or take by force, or steale from any person any

money, armes, apparell, or other goods, being above the value of xii. *d.* in marching, camp, or garrison, upon paine of death.

Betraying castles, forts, etc.

30. No man shall deliver any towne, castle, fort, or sconce, without warrant, or depart from any strait or passage which he is commanded to make good, or take passport of the enemy or any rebell in action, or make any ignominious composition with the enemy or rebell in action, upon paine of death.

Flying from colours, etc.

31. No man shall throw away his armes, or abandon his ensign, cornet, or guidon, or fly away in any battaile or skirmish, upon paine of death.

Departing a mile from the army.

32. No man shall depart a mile out of the army or campe without licence, upon paine of death.

Breach of order in chase, etc.

33. No souldier shall breake his order to follow rout, or chase or to seek any prey or spoyle except he be commanded by such as have authority, or further when he is so commanded, upon paine of death.

Purloyning of prey or spoyle.

34. No officer or souldier, whensoever any prey or spoyle shall be taken from the enemy, either when the army is in the field or by any residing in the garrison, shall attempt to imbeazell or purloyne any part thereof, but shall endeavour themselves to the uttermost of their powers to keepe the same together to be disposed of at the direction of me, the Generall, or any other by me thereunto authorized, upon paine of death.

Ransoming of prisoners.

35. No Captaine, officer, or souldier, or any other that shall take any prisoner, shall presume to deliver him upon any ransome, or conceale him,

but within foure and twenty houres he shall make the same knowne unto me, or other chiefe commander, and deliver the same prisoner under the charge of the provost-marshall, upon paine of death.

Rape.

36. No man shall ravish or force any woman, upon paine of death.

Burning of houses, corne, etc.

37. No souldier shall burne any house or lodging, or burne or wilfully spoyle any corne, ship, or boate, or carriage, or any other thing that may serve for the provision of the army, or his garrison, without he be commanded so to do by me, or some principal officer of the army, upon paine of death.

Resisting Provost-Marshalls or other officers.

38. No man shall resist or offend any Provost-Marshall, or other officer in the execution of his office, by rescuing offenders, upon paine of death.

Breaking of Prison.

39. No man that is committed shall break prison, upon paine of death.

Adultery.

40. No man shall commit adultery or fornication, upon paine of imprisonment, banishment from the army, or such other penalty as by the marshall's court it shall be thought meete.

Violence.

41. No man shall beate, threaten, or dishonestly touch any man, woman, or child, upon paine of punishment, according to the qualitie of the offence.

Boyes or Women.

42. No soldier serving on foot shall carry any boy, nor any woman shall be suffered to follow the army, upon paine of such punishment as shall be inflicted by me the Lieutenant-Generall, or other officer.

Drunkennesse.

43. Every souldier or officer that shall be found drunk, shall be committed to prison for the first offence, and if he fall into it the second time, being a private souldier, he shall, besides his imprisonment, forfeyte two months' pay: If he be an officer, he shall loose his place. The third time a common souldier shall have such greater punishment as a marshall-court shall order.

Affronts and challenges.

44. No man shall give any disgraceful words or commit any act to the disgrace of any person in the army, garrison, or any part thereof, upon paine of imprisonment, public disarming, and banishment from the army, as men for ever disabled to carry any armes. And as I do forbid all men under my command to renew any old quarrels or to begin any new, so I doe acquite and discharge all men that have quarrels offered or challenge made to them of all disgrace or opinion of any disadvantage, since they do but the duties of souldiers, which ought to subject themselves to marshall discipline. And they that provoke them shall be proceeded withall as breakers of all good discipline and enemies to the good success of the service.

Weake Companies.

45. No captain shall, through corruption, or wilful or gross negligence, suffer his company to grow weake, upon paine of imprisonment, loss of his place, and ignominious banishment from the army.

Deceit in muster.

46. No Captain, Lieutenant, or other officer ot the army shall, in the tender or presentment of their musters, use any fraud, practise, or deceit, whereby the Muster-Master, his deputies, or the Commissaries may be misled, mistaken, or prevented of the due understanding of the true estate of that company, upon paine of loss of his place, and such other ignominious punishment as by a marshal's court shall be thought meete.

Unequal Cheques. —Cheques without view.

47. No Muster-Master shall either for favour, friendship, or other

by-respect whatsoever, impose a less or greater checke upon any Captaine
or officer than his default shall justly merit, or any check at all where no
defect or default shall appeare, upon due view taken of the company, and
that no check shall be imposed by discretion, without view, upon paine
that every offender who shall be found to transgresse in all or any part of
this article, shall forfeyte his place which he holdeth, and be further subject to such corporal or pecuniary punishment as by the discretion of a
marshall court shall be thought convenient.

Defects certifyed, not supplyed.

48. Every Captaine shall have a list of all the defaults in apparel,
arms, or trayning, certified by the Muster-Master or the Commissaries
authorised for musters sent unto him, attested under their hands, whereupon the said Captaine shall presently take order that the same be fully
supplied before the muster then next ensuing such notice given him thereof,
and every Captaine failing in his duty therein shall for the first neglect
have one month's pay defalked out of his entertaynment. And if he continue the said neglect without amending and supplying the same, he shall
be discharged of his place and command.

Neglect in Trayning.

49. All Captaines shall be diligent in trayning their companies, and
shall be carefull in governing them well, and in providing for them according to the orders published for the musters; and also shall see in all services that they doe the duties of souldiers, as they will hope for favour or
advancement, or escape ignominious discharge from their charges.

Armes unfixt.

50. No souldier shall appeare with his armes un-fixt or undecently
kept, upon paine of punishment, according to the officer's good discretion.

Defect of armes.

51. No souldier shall come not fully armed to his colours, being to
watch, or to be exercised, upon paine of being punished according to discretion.

Non-residence in garrison.

52. No Captaine or officer shall, without expressed licence in that behalf signified, remayne or abide forth of his place assigned unto him by me for his garrison, upon paine of death.

Orderly quarters.

53. All Captaines or other officers that for the time shall have command of troope or company, shall see them orderly quartered, as they are appointed and as they are commanded, upon paine of the loss of their places.

Silence.

54. Every private man and souldier, upon paine of imprisonment, shall keep silence when the army is to take lodging, or when it is marching, or imbattailling, so as the officers may be heard, and their commandments executed.

Goods of the dead.

55. No man shall spoil or take the goods of any that dieth or is killed in the service, upon paine of restoring double the value, but the goods of such as die in the army or garrison, if they make any will by word or writing, shall be disposed of according to their will; if they make no will, shall be distributed to the hurt, sick and poor of the company where the souldier was, or shall go to the hospital of the army.

Buying or taking to pawne of armes.

56. No inhabitants in towne or countrey shall presume to buy or take to pawne any horse or hackney of any souldier, or any part of his furniture, armes, or apparell, for any respect or pretence whatsoever, upon paine of forfeyting the double value thereof, and to suffer imprisonment untill he shall restore the goods so unduely bought or taken to pawne.

Loosing of armes by negligence.

57. If any horseman shall lose his horse or hackney, or footman any part of his armes, by negligence or lewdnesse, whereby he shall be un-

able to discharge the duty of his place ; then, untill he shall recover the
same or furnish himself with as good, he shall remayne in the state and
condition of a pioner, or sustaine further punishment at my discretion, or
other officer thereunto authorized.

Unwholesome victuals.

58. No victualler shall presume to issue or sell unto any of the army
unsound, unsavoury, or unwholesome victuals, upon paine of imprisonment and such other punishment as by a marshall court shall be thought
fit to be imposed on him or them that shall so offend.

Unseasonable hours at victualling houses.

59. No victualler shall entertayne souldiers at unseasonable hours,
upon paine of being severely punished.

Souldiers not to be victuallers.

60. No souldier shall be a victualler without the consent of the chiefe
of the army, on paine of punishment according to discretion.

Captains not to give passport.

61. No Captaine shall give passport to any officer or souldier under
his command without my leave.

Casheering of souldiers.

62. No Captaine or other officer of the army shall discharge or Casheer
any souldier entered in his Maiestie's list of this his army, without my
privity and allowance, and my special warrant in that behalfe, unless it be
by the privitie and allowance of the officers of the musters, upon the
publike days of muster.

Entertaining runaways.

63. No inhabitant of citie, towne, or countrey shall presume to receive
any souldier into their service not having a sufficient authority ; neither
shall any conceale or hide any such runaway, or use meanes to convey
them out of the kingdom, or to any other secret place, but shall apprehend

all such and deliver them over to the provost-marshal, upon paine of imprisonment, as shall be thought fit by the chief commander to be inflicted.

Detecting, etc., of offenders.

64. All Captaines, officers, and souldiers shall doe their endeavours to detect, apprehend, and bring to punishment all offenders, and shall assist the officers of the army for that purpose, as they will answer their slackness and be censured in the marshal's court.

Faults in gen·rall provided against.

65. All other faults, disorders, and offences that are not mentioned in these articles, shall be punished according to the general customes and lawes of war; and therefore it is by me commanded, that all men looke to their charge, and he that hath no charge to look to his own carriage, as he will answer the contrary.

66. Finally, the Lieutenant-Generall of the army, Sergeant-Major-Generall, the Colonells, Captaines, and all other officers of the Confederate Catholicks within this kingdome, whom it may concerne, are hereby required to observe these lawes, and to see them put in due execution from time to time.

These lawes and orders I require every Captaine in the army to cause to be read in the head of their severall companies forthwith, and the chiefe officers of every regiment are required to see to the careful performance and observation as well of this direction as of all the said laws and orders. CASTLEHAVEN AUDLY.

XI. SAFE-CONDUCT TO ENGLAND FOR COMMISSIONERS FROM IRISH CONFEDERATION, 1643-4.

By the Lords Justices : John Borlase—Henry Tichborne.

In pursuite of the articles of Cessaccion of armes, agreed and concluded on at Sigginstowne in the countie of Kildare, the fifteenth day of

XI. Carte Papers, viii. p. 273.

September, in the nineteenth yeare of his Majestie's raigne, wee doe heereby give full and free safe-conduct to the Lord Viscount Muskery, Alexander M'Daniell or M'Donell, Nicholas Plunkett, Sir Robert Talbott, Dermot O'Bryen, Richard Martin, and Geoffry Browne, and theire servants goeing along with them, that they shalbee safe and free from all danger, molestacion, restraint, or detention, in theire repaire to his Majestie during the the said Cessacion of armes. And, therefore, wee command you and every of you that you doe permitt and suffer the said Lord Vice-Count Muskery, Alexander M'Daneill or M'Donell, Nicholas Plunkett, Sir Robert Talbott, Dermot O'Brien, Richard Martin, and Geoffry Browne, and every of them and theire servants going along with them, as aforesaid, during the said Cessacion, freely to passe to Court, without any let, restraint, or molestacion. Heereof any of you may not faile, as you tender his Majestie's service and will answeare the contrary at your perils.—Given at his Majestie's Castle of Dublin, the fourth day of January, 1643[-4].

To all comanders, officers, and soldiers of his Majestie's army, and guarrisons, and to all Mayors, Sheriffes, and Balives, and allsoe to all Customers, Comptrollers, and Searchers of portes and harbours, and to all other his Majestie's officers, ministers, and loving subjects whatsoever to whom these presents shall come, or whom they shall or may concerne, and to every of them.

XII. LETTER TO ORMONDE FROM BELLINGS.

My Lord,—I write by the commaunde of the Councell here, who (upon reading of the inclosed copie of an authority given by the Lords Justices and Councell to one Jaise to commaunde the castle of Wickloe) did with a great deal of sence, and disquiet of minde, take notice of the word Rebells, which attrybutt they doe soe farr detest[1] that they could not passe it by, without acquainteing your Lordship therewith, and makeing it their suite, that justice may be don unto them, in the punishment of the clearck, who of his owne head might incerte that worde, for they can hardly beleeve, that, after the conclusion of the Cessacion, the Lords Justices and Councell would fix upon the party of the Confederat Catholicks,

XII. Carte Papers, viii. p. 284.   1. On this subject see vol. ii. p. lxxxii.

of Ireland, soe odious a name, and doe conceave it was onely prepared for their signature, and past without reading, upon the skore of that trust which necessarily must be reposed in a sworne minister to the Boorde.   I am commaunded further, my Lord, to informe your Lordship that many soldyers, both horse and foote, serveing in the army of his Majestie's Catholick subjects, have bene procured by som officers under your Lordship's commaunde to leave their collors and to list themselves as men serveing in their troope or company, by whose practice they were withdrawen, and they desire your Lordship that the Articles of Cessacion, which are directly opposite to such proceedings, may be better observed in that particuler.

I am, my Lord, your Lordship's humble servant,—RICHARD BELLINGS. Waterford, the 5th day of January, 1643[-4].

Endorsed: Richard Bellings. [Dated] 5, received 28 January, 1643[-4]

XIII. LETTER FROM PRINCE RUPERT TO SUPREME COUNCIL OF CONFEDERATION.

My Lords and Gentlemen,—The Kinge is pleased to command me to take the care and conduct of the army in Cheshire and the partes thereabouts, with power to recruite and raise all possible forces for the repulsing of the Skots, who are now marcthing, and reddye to invade this kingdom.   In which undertakinge, I am very much encouraged by the hope of your good kindness to the Kinge's affaires in furnishinge me with five thousand musketts, and three hundred barrailes of powder,[1] and

XIII. Carte Papers, viii. p. 344.

1. In connection with the above. the following was addressed by Ormonde to Geoffrey Browne, on 28th Nov., 1644: "Sir,—You may remember that uppon my compleating the powder sent by your party to Prince Rupert, to the number of twenty barrells (theire share being but seaven barrels and a halfe) you engaged yourselfe by your promise that I should be repayed in the same kinde to the full valew of what I then sent, being effectively twelve hundred and fiftye waight, whereof I thought good hereby to minde you.   I rest, to the end you may cause the said quantity to be forthwith sent unto, Sir, your very lovinge friend,—ORMONDE." The copy of this letter contained the following passages (which Ormonde subsequently struck out), after the words "minde you:" "by this convenience, to the

match proporcionable, to Chester-Water, or any other porte in North Wales; for which I desire only creditt with your Lordships, and a day of payment and retourne of the commoditie in kinde, or the value, as the armes and ammunicion shall be valued by your bills of stoare.

This I rather press to you, and am the more instante with your Assemblye and Councell therein, as in that from whence this present Rebellion tooke footing in this kingdome, and wherein I am hopefull, by God's blessinge, and your good assistance to me in this favour, to see it fall and dye.

This Knight, Sir Edmund Butler, who hath borne himselfe very eminently in his Majestie's affaires here, is particularly addressed to you for this service. I pray you looke upon him as a person that your Lordships, and the Knights and gentlemen of your Convocacion and Councell will finde industrious in his Majestie's service, and for whom I have this further suite to you, that you will please to dispatch him away to me againe with all convenient speed, the present condicion of his Majestie's affaires engadginge him to make provisions by sea in winter, when the weather fights for him.

My Lords, I expect very greedely a good success of this my first suite unto your Lordship's, and shall for ever rest, your very affectionate freind, RUPERT.

Oxon, this 18th of January, 1643 [-4].

XIV. CHARLES I. AND THE EARL OF ANTRIM.

INSTRUCTIONS TO RANDAL [MACDONNELL], EARL OF ANTRIM, GIVEN AT OUR COURT AT OXFORD, THE TWENTIETH DAY OF JANUARY, 1643[-4].

CHARLES REX.—Your first work, after your coming into Ireland, must be to persuade our Catholick subjects there to lend us ten thousand men, well armed, to be transported hither unto England with all possible expe-

end you make good your promise in the returne of soe much, which is but just and reasonable, seeing the whole was sent, as if it weare from those who weare least contributory to his Majesty's service in that particuler. And soe, expecting your speedy returne heereunto."—Carte Papers, xii. p. 651.

XIV. Clarendon State Papers, 1643 4, No. 1745.—Bodleian Library, Oxford.

dition; whereby we may be the better enabled to resist the Scotch invasion. You are likewise to solicit them for the loan of ammunition and
artillery for such an army, as also of ships to transport the same.

In case that their agents shall contain themselves within [such] reasonable bounds in their demands as we can with justice, prudence, or conscience condescend unto, we make no question but they will then very
freely afford us the aid desired.

But in case they shall insist upon such things as we cannot, without
great inconvenience and danger to the whole frame of our other affairs,
grant, and that their agents shall, contrary to our resolutions (if reason
will content them) part unsatisfied, so as that you shall find difficulty to
obtain by their consent the assistance desired; you are then upon the
stock of your own interest, and of such others as shall be faithful unto us,
and be willing to engage themselves in our service, to endeavour, by
virtue of your commission to that purpose, to draw as many as you can to
take service under you, and to transport them over unto us here under
your command; and for so doing we shall give you all assistance possible
by shipping to be sent from our ports of England for that purpose. You
are also, in that case, to endeavour the procuring underhand upon credit,
we assisting you with the best security we can, such quantities of arms
and ammunition as shall be necessary for the arming and setting forth
such men as you shall be able to draw unto your party. For that purpose
you are further to persuade our Catholick subjects to lend for our service
two thousand men well armed, to be transported by yourself, if your
other service can permit you the time, or, if not, by your brother, into
the islands of Scotland and the Highlands; where you are to excite your
party to rise with you to fall upon the Marquis of Argyle's country;
wherein we make no doubt but you will find ready assistance from the
Earl of Seaforth and Sir James M'Donald, the said Earl being joint Justi-
ciary with you, and Sir James, Colonel of our forces under you, for the
transporting of the said two thousand [men] into the islands, as also of
those who shall conjoin with them there, into Scotland. You are to solicit
our Catholick subjects for shipping, as also to provide what flat-bottomed
boats may be; and we shall likewise assist you from our ports with what

shipping we can in this business of the islands and Highlands. You or your brother are to hold frequent and careful correspondency with the Earl of Montrose, our Lieutenant-General of all our forces in Scotland; who will advertise and advise in the ways and times of proceeding, as may best correspond with the motions and undertakings of the rest of our party there. You are likewise to treat with Monro, and to see whether you can draw him over, with the forces under his command, unto our service; in which case, we shall make good unto him what you in your discretion shall agree with him for, so far forth as to make the said Monro an Earl of Scotland, and to grant him a pension of £2,000 sterling per annum.

XV. Ormonde to Viscount Muskerry and Supreme Council.

1. After our hearty commendacions to your Lordship and the rest with whome wee lately treated: You will understand by his Majestie's letters of the 27th of December to us directed, a coppy[1] whereof wee send you heere inclosed, the good esteeme wherein Sir Robert Walsh is with his Majestie, and what his Majestie doth expect from us to be done for him; wherein wee shall not be wanting, but will, according his Majestie's earnest recommendacions to us in his behalfe give him our best further-ance and assistance. Which because wee cannot performe better than by recommending him to your care who can best serve him in those partes where he doth intend to rayse his regiment, wee doe earnestly desire you by these our letters, as you tender his Majestie's service, to afford him your best furtherance and assistance in the rayseing and transporting

XV. Carte Papers, ix. pp. 15-16.
1. "Charles Rex.—Right trusty and entirely beloved cousin and counsellour, wee greete you well. Whereas wee have graunted our Commission to our trusty and wel-beloved Sir Robert Welch, Knight, for the leavying of one regiment of foote within our kingdome for our service in this kingdome, wee doe hereby earnestly recommend him to your care as being a person of whose worth and good affection to us we have a very good esteeme, and shall therefore expect your best furtherance and assistance of him in the leavying of his men, and in all other things that may conduce to the advance of that service, wherein our present condition renders us soe much concerned. And soe wee bid you heartily farewell. Given att our Court att Oxford, the 27th of December, 1643."—Carte Papers, viii. p. 138.

of his regiment. Whereof if that he shall find reall and good effects, wee doubt not but his Majestie will take it in good part, and so wee bid you hartyly farewell from his Majestie's Castle of Dublin, 23 January, 1643[-4]. Your loveing frend,—[ORMONDE.]

2. After our harty comendacions to your Lordship and the rest with whom wee lately treated: You cannot forgett how earnest you weare with us uppon the late treaty in the point of sending of agents unto his Majestie, which made us think that your agents needed not to bee quickened in their goeing thither, but that they would have wayted on his Majestie long before this tyme.

What was undertaken by us in that treaty, touching that particuler, is fully performed by the sending of our [safe] conduct from hence unto you, and by his Majestie's safe-conduct which you receaved out of England. Both which being donne, you must thinke that you have been before this tyme expected there. Which because you have hitherto delayed, his Majestie hath commanded us by late letters to hasten you thither. Wee need say noe more but bid you hartyly farewell. And remaine, from his Majestie's Castle of Dublin, the 23rd day of January, 1643[-4]. Your loveing frend,—[ORMONDE.]

XVI. LETTER TO LORDS JUSTICES, DUBLIN, FROM SUPREME COUNCIL.

Our very good Lords,—Wee have seene your Lordships' of the 14th of January, concerning the advertisements received of the daylie encroachments of our partie uppon the quarters designed for his Majestie's Protestant subjects in Ulster ; and wee doe little wonder that those whose disaffections to his Majestie's service are notorious should suggest anythinge that might lessen the opinion of our desires to serve his Majestie faithfullie, and as we are well assured that none of our partie will presume soe highly to violat the Cessation agreed uppon of all sides, for the benefitt of us and the rest of his Majestie's good subjects, soe wee hope your Lordships will not afforde that name to such of the Skotts in those partes, as doe disavowe the Cessacion, and after they had notice of the conclusion of

XVI. Carte Papers, ix. p. 18.

it, did kill man, woeman, and child indifferently, burned the corne and howses of our partie and have in favor of the Rebbells now in armes in England against his Majestie, sworne a Covenant destructive to religion and monarchye, contrary to your Lordships' proclamacion inhibitinge the same.

By our letters bearinge date the 6th. of November (which wee humbly entreated your Lordships should be transmitted unto his Majestie) wee did desire your Lordships' assistance and succor against those, and wee doe crave your Lordships' resolucion thereuppon.   For the rest who have submitted to the Cessacion, and beene obedient to his Majestie's commaunds, since the conclusion of it, wee shall apply our best endeavors that noe wronge be done them by any of our partie. The armye wee raise cannot affright any, but such whose consciences may accuse them of disaffecion to his Majestie's service, and [we] doe hope that all his Majestie's good subjects will be commaunded to joyne with us in any designe against them, who will appeare to be men that have soe bad inclinacions.   Wee rest your Lordships' humble servants,

Mountgarret.—Castlehaven, Audley.—Fr. Thomas Dublyn.[1]—Netterville.—John   Clonfert.[2]—Richard   Bellings.—Torlogh O'Neill.— Thomas Preston.—George Commyn.—Thomas Fleming.

For the Right Honnorable, the Lords Justices.

Endorsed : Lord Mountgaret, and others, to the Lords Justices. Dated 23, received 28 January, 1643[-4].

XVII. Sir Lucas Dillon to Ormonde.

Right Honorable,—Your Lordship's letters of the 6th of this month, with the copies of a letter and certaine greevances represented to your Lordships from divers officers and others of pretended garrisons in the countye of Roscommon, came to my handes butt a few days since, which then I transmitted to the Commissioners appointed of our partye for setting out of quarters in the said countye, then sitting upon that settlement with the

1. Thomas Fleming, Archbishop of Dublin.   2. John Bourke, Bishop of Clonfert.
XVII. Carte Papers, ix., p. 25.

other Commissioners, and for many dayes before, especiallye aboute the tyme that those complaintes were sent up ; whereupon I had this generall returne, that it wilbe justified the said complaintes are in the greater parte most maliciously false, and some of those who subscribed unto them are the onely disturbers of a much longed for and desired peace, which her- after wilbe more particularly made manifest by the certificatt of the Com- missioners.   The lymits and condicions for quarters to the castles of Athlone and Roscommon, the twoe places of the countye wherein his Majestie's service is most concerned, of that side, are set out and agreed upon, and, as is conceived, more plentifully accomodated than could be looked for by vertue of the articles, there being given to Athlone £200 in money, fifty barrells of wheate, fifty of oates, and fortye beeves, with the precinct of land called the Monkes' land, and provision for fireing ; to Roscommon castle all the lordship thereof and possessions of the Lord of Ranellagh within the countye, as well inhabited as wast, except a few wast quarters, remote and ten myles distant from it, with which quarters Sir Robert Newcomen seemes to be well satisfied, being the most indif- ferent and best affected to settle and preserve the quiet of the countrye that appeares amongst them ; to the Boyle was offered all the lands of Sir Robert King within the countye [of Roscommon], with the territoryes called the Ranns and severall possessions of other freehoulders, being in the whole of large extent, best inhabited, and for soe much the most pro- fitable parte of the countye.

To Castlecoote, Tulske, Elphin, and other places, were likewise offered very competent quarters, and more than by the articles they ought to have or could expect.   But Captain Robert Ormsby, those of the Boyle and Castlecoote, are not to be satisfied with reason, whose immoderate wilfull- nes if not overruled and themselves governed otherwise than they are (for as now it appeares not that they will obey any authoritye) there can be noe hope of peace or prosperitye in the province ; wherof it is most humbly desired your Lordships wilbe pleased to take speciall notice in prevention of the ruine of the contrye, and the greate prejudice it maye bring upon his Majestie's service, in the furtherance wherof my particular indeavours shalbe faithfully applyed, and in my weake power shall not faile to approve myselfe your Lordship's most humble servant,

LUCAS DILLON.

24 January, 1643-[4].

I will give notice to the severall countyes of the directions come downe for payment of beeves and money to the garrisons, and labour performance therin the best I maye.   Capten Robert Ormsby obeyes not the order graunted in the behalfe of Mr. Thomas Dillon for restitution of his goods, nor doth the commander of the Boyle garrison cause satisfaction to be made for the £6 and twoe horses taken from Joseph Hollis, a servant of myne, contrary to the articles, and heretofore complained of, wherin redress is againe humbly desired.

Endorsed : Sir Lucas Dillon's, dated 24 January, received 3 February, 1643[-4].

XVIII. LETTER TO CARDINAL MAZARIN FROM MONSIEUR DE LA MONNERIE, ENVOY FROM KING OF FRANCE TO SUPREME COUNCIL OF THE IRISH CONFEDERATION.

Kilkennin, 25 [Janvier], 4 Fevrier, 164[3-]4.

Monseigneur,—J' attendois tousjours la response de Messieurs du Conseil d'Irlande pour la faire sçavoir à votre Eminence ; mais, voyant qu'ils me remettent de jour à aultre, J'ay pris la liberté de luy escripre la presente pour l'asseurer que je presse la plus qu'il m'est possible l'effect des choses pour lesquelles Je suis envoyé et croy que si on peult juger de l'événement par les apparences, que je doibs espérer qu'ils me donneront contentement et que le retardement ne procéde que de l'arrivée d'un Flamand que Dom Francisco de Meslos [Mello] a envoyé icy vers ces Messieurs pour leur demander la permission de pareille levée.

Ce qui les embarrasse fort, estans résolus de le renvoyer sans aucun contentement, mesmes, un Chevalier Anglois[1] qui leur a fait la mesme demande pour le Roy d'Angleterre.   Tous ces accidens joinct avec la nécessité qu'ils ont de mettre une armée sur pied pour repousser les Escossois,

XVIII. Archives des Affaires Etrangères, Paris. Série Angleterre, vol. li. p. 12.
1. *See* p. 90.

qui viennent sur leurs terres, me font beaucoup appréhender. Néant-moins, ils me font dire soubz main qu'ils travaillent pour contenter la France au prejudice des autres : cela me donne courage, mais l'apprehension que j'ay que ces troupes ne soient pas assez à temps en France pour estre au commencement de la campagne, m'afflige beaucoup : et comme je prèvoy qu'ils manqueront de vaisseaux pour le passage des troupes qu'ilz pourront m'accorder, Je supplie votre Eminence, Monseigneur, de vouloir commander que l'on y donne ordre, affin que cela ne puisse apporter aucun retardement.

Sytost qu'ils m'auront faict response, Je ne manqueray d'en informer exactement vostre Eminence pour qu'elle m'ordonne les choses que j'auray à faire, si ils m'apportoient quelques difficultez ausquelles Je ne peusse respondre sans ses ordres, désirant, en tout et partout, faire veoir à votre Eminence, que je n'auray jamais plus de satisfaction que de paroistre, Monseigneur, de votre Eminence le très-humble, très-obeissant, et très fidèle serviteur et creature,   MONNERIE.

A Kilkennin, ce 25 Janvier, 4 Fevrier, en France, 1644.

XIX. LETTER TO FATHER HUGH BOURKE, FLANDERS, FROM SUPREME COUNCIL.

Reverend Father,—Wee have received your severall letters concern-inge your employment into Holland, and the diary of the accidents which befell you, wherein wee finde you have acquitt the trust reposed in you with that care and judgment that meritts thankes at our hands, which wee heartely retourne unto you ; and, in as much as it was thought fitt that to conclude uppon soe weighty a busines as is the manner how wee shall behave ourselves towardes the Hollander, uppon this occasion the rest of the Coun-cell now absent should be now cald uppon. Wee have, in the meane tyme, while you are expectinge of answer to the other particulars of your letters, sent you these to lett you knowe the motives which did induce us to treate of a Cessacion of armes, and wee doe assure you wee doe but re-peate those things whereof by our former from Cashell, presently uppon

XIX. Ms. "Register Book of Letters" of Supreme Council.

the conclusion of the Cessacion, wee did advertise you. However our letters did miscarry, our motives were thos wee send you heere enclosd,[1] which, together with the carelessnes wee observed in these Catholicke Princes, who would find (if God had not beene pleased to patronise our cause) that the Catholicke religion had suffred irreparably in the loss of this kingdome, will be sufficient to satisfye any man of the necessitye imposd uppon us to goe through with it.   And wee doe feare that those who should assist us (if wee should againe be forced to armes) would, with the same regarde, looke uppon our affaires, which even at this tyme may justly call uppon theire assistance, for wee are now sendinge of an armye of six thousand foote, and six hundred horse, into Ulster against the Puritants there, who will not submitt to the Cessacion.   Wee pray yow continue your care and sollicitacion in our behalfe.—Dated, Kilkenny, the 26th of January, 1643[-4], stilo veteri.

XX. Certificate from Supreme Council.

[The Supreme Council certify, in relation to contract between Fr. James Talbot and Walter Robbins, merchant, of Antwerp, for the sum of one thousand pounds and upwards, that the amount is amply secured by the following persons: Sir Robert Talbot, Baronet; John Talbot; Henry Burnell, of Castle Rickard; Sir Lucas Dillon; Viscount Netterville; Walter Bagnal;

1. No copy of the enclosure here referred to appears in the " Register Book." At p. 23, *ante*, will be found " Reasons for the Cessation," as sent to Wadding, at Rome, by the Supreme Council. The " Register Book " contains the following from the Supreme Council, dated in January, 1643-4, but without any mention of the name of the Cardinal for whom the original was intended: " Eminentissime Domine,—Ingrati essemus si, pro præstitis officiis et sincero Eminentiæ vestræ in causam nostram affectu, non haberemus gratias. Certe agimus maximas Hiberniæ nomine, quæ rerum suarum summam apud nos esse voluit, et speramus illum Omnipotentem causæ nostræ patronum, cujus auspiciis hactenus stetit res nostra, eum in finem quem agimus perducturum, ut afflictæ Catholicæ in Hibernia Ecclesiæ statui amicorum ope succurere possimus,quod, Eminentissimæ Dominationi vestræ maximæ remuneracionis loco fore scimus. Quo vero in statu, etc., aperiet Reverendus Pater Hugo de Burgo.—Datum Kilkeniæ, 26 Januarii, 1643[-4] stilo veteri."

XX. Ms. " Register Book of Letters " of Supreme Council.

Ambrose Plunket; Nicholas Darcy, of Plattin; Edward Plunket; James Plunket, ; and Patrick Scurlock. These persons have, during two years, through the calamities of the war, been so harassed, in lands and property, that they are unable at present to pay the money.—Undated.]

Per Supremum Concilium, etc.

Cum Reverendus Dominus Pater Jacobus Talbotus, a nobis supplex, petierit ut quia status contractus cujusdam inter ipsum Jacobum et Gouterum Robbins, Antuerpiæ mercatorem, initi, clarior redderetur quid sentiamus de sufficientia infrascriptorum virorum quorum chartas obligatorias pro mille et amplius libris se tradidisse Petro Wybrants, mercatori Dublinii, factori ejusdem Goteri Robins, idem Jacobus asserit, scriptis mandaremus nos: Et illius supplicacione et patefaciendæ veritatis desiderio moti, attestamur Robertum Talbott, Baronettum, et Johannem Talbott, Armigerum, Henricum Burnell de Castle Rickard, Armigerum, Lucam Dillon, Militem, Dominum Vice-comitem Newtervill, Walterum Bagnall, et Ambrosium Plunket, Armigeros, Nicholaum Darcy, de Platten, Armigerum, et Edwardum et Jacobum Plunkett, Armigeros, et Patritium Scurlock, Armigerum, pro multo majori pecuniarum summa sufficientes fuisse vades, licet jam per belli calamitates hoc biennium bonis et terris exturbati sic vivant ut presenti solucionis impares habeantur.

XXI. Letters to Ormonde from Supreme Council.

1. Our very good Lord,—The barke, whereof his Majesty makes mencion in his letters directed to your Lordship, is the same that did in hostill manner make severall shot at his Majestie's towne of Ross, and was taken by our own men much about the tyme that Paul Duffe of the same towne, marchant, his ship of three hondred tun, loaden with commodities bound for Wexford, was made a prize upon this coast, by one imployed with letters of marte to distress our party, and sould at a high rate at Kinsale. The accompt wee can give your Lordship of that

XXI. Carte Papers, ix. pp. 69, 79.

barke is this, that she hath beene bought by many poore marchants at Ross, who have spent much to fitt her for a voyadge, upon which she is now sent, and that wee are confident if she doe retourne safe, she may be had for the fourth parte of what those who bought her lost in that ship belonging to Paule Duffe. Thus humbly takeing leave, wee rest, your lordship's humble servants,

                    Muskry.—Nicholas Plunkett.—Torlogh O'Neill.

Kilkenny, the sixt of February, 1643[-4].

To the Right Honnorable the Lord Lieutenant-Generall of Ireland.

Endorsed: Lord of Muskry, etc., Dated 6, received 8 Feb., 1643[-4].

2. Our very good Lord,—The Counsel here have a deepe sence of their failer, who long since should have brought in the beeves, applotted upon the provinces of Connaght and Ulster; and although they be advertised that several payments are made upon warrants and assignments graunted unto several garrizons in the countrey, whereof your Lordship hath not as yet receaved an accompt, yet, because they would be certaine to have due satisfaccion made, and be able to informe your Lordship truely of the number of cattle which have bene disposed of by order from thence, they doe now imploy two trustie and carefull men into those provinces, who shall constantly attend that charge.

Concearening the third payment of the moneys (for already the two first are satisfied) your Lordship shall within a few dayes find that noe care hath beene omitted to disengage the obligacion layd upon our party by the free offer and graunt made unto his Majesty by us and the rest of the Comissioners that treated upon the Cessacion, and that this may be don in that way which may best please your Lordship and further his Majestie's service. Wee desire to be speedily advertised whether the five hondred pounds sterling graunted by the late Lords Justices their warrant, of the twelth of January last, unto the Lord of Insequine, or the hondred pounds graunted to the Lord Esmond, much about the same tyme, and by the same authority, shall be paid, as in those warrants is directed, or whether your Lordship be pleased, according the contents of your Lordship's letters in November last, to have some of the moneys paid to the Dutchman in Lymerick to be retourned to Dublin. And thus humbly takinge leave, wee rest your Lordship's humble servants,

Muskry.—Torl : O'Neill.

Kilkenny, the 7th of February, 1643[-4].

To the Right Honnorable the Lord Lieutenant-Gennerall of Ireland.

Endorsed : Lord of Muskry and Torlogh O'Neill's.—Dated 7, received 8 Feb., 1643[-4].

XXII. ALBERTUS O'BRIEN, PROVINCIAL OF IRISH DOMINICANS.

1. LETTER TO FR. LUKE WADDING, ROME, FROM SUPREME COUNCIL OF THE CONFEDERATION.

Reverend Father,—The bearer, Father Albertus O'Brien, Provinciall of the Friars Preachers in this kingdome, beinge sent for to the Generall Chapter of his Order to be held at Rome, hath merited soe well of us and our cause, and hath beene soe zealous in furtheringe of it both by himselfe and those subject to his authoritye that wee may not omitt to recommend him unto you as a man who hath made it his studye to advance our designes as well by cherrishinge and encouradginge those who did assist us as by chastisinge some who thought to disquiet our proceedings. Wee pray you therefore to further and to give all due countenance to his affaires.—Kilkenny, the 9th of Februarie, 1643 [-4].

2. A pass for Father Albertus O'Brien.

Quandoquidem ad Capitulum Generale Ordinis Prædicatorum, auctoritate Sanctissimi Patris Nostri, Urbani VIII., Romæ mense Maii proximo celebrandum, Admodum Reverendus Pater, Pater Albertus O'Brien, ex officio vocatus pergat, æquum duximus illum, nobili e stirpe ortum, integerrima vita et doctrina insignem, sui ordinis in Hibernia Provincialem,

XXII. Ms. "Register Book of Letters" of Supreme Council.

omnibus Catholicis has litteras inspecturis commendare, ut qui in promovenda Catholica Hiberniæ causa omnes labores omne studium impendit. Omnibus eidem causæ nostræ faventibus gratus accedat et Christiana humanitate ac charitate (ut par est) excipiatur.—Datum Kilkeniæ, 10 die Februarii, 1643[-4], stilo veteri.

XXIII. LETTERS FROM VISCOUNT MUSKERRY AND ORMONDE.

1. May it please your Lordship,—An office hath beene latelie found in the cittie of Corcke post mortem Dominicke Coppinger,[1] Esq., whose estate is within the Catholique quarter. The widdowe of the said Dominicke Coppinger sent her several letters to Sir Philip Percivall, Knight (the passage beinge not then free for her or her agent to goe thither) and prayed him, by her said letters, to certifie the Master of the [Court of] Wardes of her readines in that particular, when the tymes had proved better, and that, in the meane time, the wardship of her sonn might not otherwise be disposed of ; and the partie to whome the bringing of her letters to Dublin was intrusted, beinge Serjent-Major Thomas Piggott did not deliver the said letters accordinge the trust in him imposed but (as I am informed) procured a commission to inquire after the death of the sayd Dominicke Coppinger, and a promise of the wardship of the bodie and lands of the saide Dominicke Coppinger's son and heyre. By vertue of which comission, the office is found by the widdowe's prosecucion, and now returned to Dublin by her agent. And the widdowe by her agent, sudainlie after the publishinge of the Cessacion peticioned to the Master of the Wardes for the said wardship to the use of the sayd ward, and one son more, and eight daughters, left by the said Dominicke Coppinger unprovided for, and upon the said peticion obtained a fayre promise of the said wardship ; yet the widdowe is verie fearful the wardship of her son should be comitted to the hands of a stranger, and prove distructive to his estate, or that she should be denyed the benefit of the lawe and the practice of that courte, to be preferred to the sayd wardship before anie stranger.

XXIII. Carte Papers, ix. pp. 109, 129.　　1. *See* p. 38.

My Lord, Mr. Coppinger and his poore widdowe had relacion to mee before these troubles, soe far that I have a good desire to preserve his children in their due rights and estate and owne theire just grievances as my particular entrest. Therefore I presume to pray your Lordship upon the poore widowe's peticion, to require the Master of the Wardes, whether the tymes will admitt the present fileinge of the sayd office, or not, to conceive an order for the assureinge of the sayd wardship to the widdowe to the use of the sayd ward, and the rest of her children and therein your Lordship will oblidge your Lordship's most affecionate brother and humble servant,   MUSKRY.

Kilkenny, 14 Feb., 1643[-4].

2. After our hearty comendacions : Upon consideracion of the season of the yeare for sending in of beofes by your agreement for his Majestie's use nowe past, and of the extreame failers of your parte in sending the proporcions promised, and of the greate disservice which arises to his Majestie in the affaires of his army and otherwise thereby, and alsoe of the extreame vexation fallen on us meerely by your failers and to the end that some course may yet bee taken which may in some sorte answer his Majestie's occasions, and prevent further discontents to fall on us, wee have thought good to let you knowe that if you shall take present order for sending unto us 1,500 barrells of herrings (whereof wee are informed there are good store in Wexford and other places within your quarters) wee shall take order for sending you a sufficient discharge for 1,000 of the beofes yet remayning due by your agreement, which is a farr greater price then wee could procure such a quantity for, if those 1,000 beofes or the value of them expressed in your agreement had beene paid in accordingly. And wee have thought fitt alsoe to let you knowe that if you faile herein, or in answering the beofes or the value of them without any manner of further delay, greate prejudice must unavoidably fall on his Majestie's service, which you onely are to bee answerable for, wee having from tyme to tyme taken hould of all occasions and opportunities to acquainte you howe his Majestie's occasions called upon your performance both uppon the conclusion of our treaty and since. Wee remaine, from

his Majestie's Castle of Dublin, the 17th day of February, 1643 [-4], your very loving friend,—ORMONDE.

Wee alsoe let you know that if you shall send us good wheate or meslin,[1] wee shall see a beofe allowed you for each barrell, yet soe as we may without any delay bee receaveing from the parts of Wickloe or hereabouts untill you may send greater proporcions by sea and that you ascertaine us what wee may depend uppon.

Lord Muskery.

XXIV. NEGOTIATIONS BETWEEN SPAIN AND THE IRISH CONFEDERATION, 1643-4.

1. RECEPTION OF SPANISH ENVOY AT KILKENNY.

Memorandum : That uppon the [17th] day of [February,] one thowsand six hundred and forty-three, Don Francisco de Fosset,[2] employd to the Right Honnorable the Supreame Councell of the Confederat Catholickes of Ireland, by his Excellence, Don Francisco de Melos, Governor and Commander-Generall of the Low Countries, had audience before the said Councell.

2. The answer to the Agent from the Lowe Countries, given the forenoone of the day followinge, beinge Monday :

Kilkenny, the 18th of February, 1643[-4].

By the Supreame Councell of the Confederat Catholickes of Ireland :

It is this day ordred by the unanimous vote of the said Councell (nullo contradicente) that Don Francisco de Fosset, employed unto us by his Excellence, Don Francisco de Melos, Governor and Commaunder-Generall of the Low Countries, should receive this answer, viz. :

That, if our government doe continue, and wee shall not conclude a peace, that his Catholicke Majestie of Spaine, accordinge the promiss and offer wee have made unto him, may, by our licence and assistance, after the five and twentieth of June next, have a levye within this kingdome of

XXIV. Ms. "Register Book of Letters." 1. Mixed corn. 2. *See* p. 8.

two thousand foote, with their officers, for his Catholicke Majestie's service, to be transported from hence into Spaine uppon such capitulacions as shall be agreed uppon.   And that, in case a peace shall be concluded, wee have alreddye given instructions to our Commissioners to press that the said two thousand foote may be raysed in the like manner for his Catholick Majestie's service, and wee shall further, to the best of our endevours, seeke to assist his Catholicke Majestie.—Mountgarett.—Thomas [Walsh, Archbishop of] Cashell.—Castlehaven and Audley.—Netterville.—John [Bourke, Bishop of] Clonfert.—Thomas Fleming.—Patrick Darcy.—Torlogh O'Neill.—Gerald Fenell.—George Commyn.

3. Letter to Don Francisco de Mello, Governor of Flanders.

[The Council state to De Mello the causes which, against their will, oblige them to defer sending the troops promised to the King of Spain. They declare their attachment to the House of Austria, and detail the difficulties of their position in terms similar to those in their letter in English, page 104, addressed on the same day to Father Hugh Bourke.—Kilkenny, 22 February, 1643-4].

Illustrissime ac Excellentissime Domine,—Literas ad nos per Dominum Franciscum de Fosset missas accepimus, et sicut nihil magis gratum potuit accidere quam quod occasio oblata fuerit qua possemus indubitatum gentis nostræ in Catholicum Regem affectum aliqualiter exprimere, ita supra modum dolemus illam nobis impositam esse necessitatem, qua cogimur promissos suæ Majestati milites in tempus aliquod differre.   Siquidem habemus Scotos, infestissimos semper hostes, qui novo milite stipendiis Parliamenti Angliæ conscripto exercitum suum in nos adaugent et Ultoniæ fines excedere in dies minitantur.   Supervenit etiam aliud longe magis timendum.   Comperimus Parliamentarios cum Hollandis agere, de invadendis et occupandis occidentalibus hujus regni partibus, ubi e regione Holandiæ commodissimi sunt portus quod si illis ita succederet, et portum aut stationem ullam inibi occuparent, transvectis auxiliis propriores sibi regni partes paulatim invaderent et tam commodas nacti stationes mare navibus infestarent, non sine Catholicæ religionis periculo et Christiani orbis perturbatione. Cui tam ingenti malo ut strenue occurratur, vires omnes intendimus, et ne imparatis nobis superveniatur milites in illum usum destinatos semper in promptu habere, necesse esse ducimus. Præterea Colonellis quibusdam commissione Regis nostri milites in Hibernia conscripturis id concedere haud visum est commodum quam vero indigne ferret sua Majestas id alteri concedere prudentissimus et excellentissimus Dominus facile judicabit. Hac igitur, undequaque urgente necessitate, Excellentiam vestram obnixe obtestamur, ut pro suo ingentem et causam nostram affectu dignetur intueri et considerare rerum nostrum statum, et velit uti illa qua apud Catholicum Regem tantus et tam bene meritus minister pollet auctoritate, unde intelligat adimplendi promisse dilationem hisce quibus opprimimur angustiis adscribendam esse, cum nihil interim remiserimus de satis noto et semper testato in domum Austriacam affectu et desiderio inserviendi Regi Catholico cui nostrum in hac parte promissum prima data commoditate executioni mandabimus et ulterius illi inservire si pro rerum nostrarum statu licuerit proponimus. Excellentiæ vestræ manus deosculantur Excellentissimæ Dominationis vestræ studiosissimi.—Kilkeniæ, 22 Februarii, 1643[-4].

Domino Francisco de Melos, Gubernatori Belgii.

4. LETTER TO FATHER HUGH BOURKE, FLANDERS, FROM SUPREME COUNCIL.

Wee have this day given the agent sent hither by Don Francisco De Melos his answer, and in regard the necessitye of our affaires did enforce us to deffer the performance of our promiss, least any misrepresentacion or misconstrucion should be made thereof, wee have thought fitt to acquaint you with the motives which hard against our will did compell us thereunto. First, althoe wee had a Cessacion of armes with those that side with his Majestic, yet the Skotts and Parliament partye, which of late have receivd a vast sume of money from the Parliament of England, are preparinge against us both in Skotland and in Ulster. Against those wee send an army under the command of the Earle of Castlehaven, which, of all likelyhood, will be in constant action and therefore will need a great reserve of men for theire supplye. Seacondly wee are assured, from good and faithfull hands, that the Parliament and Hollanders have joyned in some designe for takinge in some portes on the westerne coastes, which if they may compass they will become a terror to all the princes in Christiandome. Wee pray you to labor with all earnestness and secresie to finde out the particulars of this designe, if any such there be. Thirdly, some Colonells, who had commission from our King and were recommended unto us by the Marquess of Ormond, Lord Lieftenant of this kingdome, have, notwithstandinge, beene denied of men, and with what indignacion thinke you would his Majestie looke uppon our Commissioners now treatinge for a peace if wee did suffer for the present any men to leave this kingdome to serve elsewhere, when they were stoppd from his assistance. Wee know that all men who looke indifferently uppon our occasions will finde by those reasons that, without the ruine of the kingdome, wee could not for the present parte with our men, but wee will soe provide that however it falls out with us, wee will performe our promiss with the Kinge of Spaine. In the meanetyme, wee pray you, that as our affections continue the same they alwayes were, soe that none may take advantadge of this occasion, whereby wee are enforced much to our disquiet to deffer expressing of our desire for some tyme to serve his Catholicke Majestie in that particular. Wee have given a further and more certaine answer to Don Francisco de Fosset, touchinge the sendinge of those men to his Majestie of Spain, as you will perceive by the enclosed[r] beinge an authenticke coppie of the order or vote containeinge the answer made him at full. Thus, with our hearty wishes, etc.—Kilkenny, the 22 of February, 1643 [-4].

XXV. Negotiations between France and the Confederation, 1643-4.

1. Reception of French Envoy at Kilkenny.

Memorandum : That, uppon the [17th] day of [February] anno Domini one thowsand six hundred forty-three, Monsieur de Moynerie, Gentleman-in-ordinary of his Chamber to the Most Christian Kinge, employed to the Right Honnorable the Supreame Councell of the Confederate Catholickes of Ireland by his said Most Christian Majestie, had audience before the said Councell.

XXVII. 1-4. Ms. " Register Book of Letters." 1. *See* p. 106.

2. The answer to the French Agent, given the afternoone of the day followinge, being Monday :

Kilkenny, the 18th of February, 1643 [-4].

By the Supreame Councell of the Confederat Catholickes of Ireland :

It is this day ordered by the unanimous vote of the said Councell (nullo contradicente) that Monsieur de Moinerye, Gentleman-in-ordinary of his Chamber to the Most Christian Kinge, employed unto us from his Majestie, should receive the ensuinge answer, viz. :

That, if our government doe continue, and wee shall not conclude a peace, wee will, by the five and twentieth of June next, give licence that two thowsand foote, with theire officers, for the service of the Most Christian King, shall be levyed within this kingdome and transported from hence uppon such capitulacions as shall be agreed uppon ; and that in case a peace shall be concluded wee have alreddy given instruccions to our Commissioners to press that the said two thowsand men may be raysed in the like manner for his most Christian Majestie his service : and wee shall further to the best of our endeavors seeke to assist his Most Christian Majestie.—Mountgarrett.—Thomas [Walsh, Archbishop of] Cashel.—Castlehaven and Audley.—Netterville.—John [Bourke, Bishop of] Clonfert.—Thomas Fleminge.—Torlogh O'Neill.—Patrick Darcy.—Gerald Fenell.—George Commyn.

3. LETTERS TO LOUIS XIV., ANNE, QUEEN-REGENT OF FRANCE, AND CAR-
DINAL MAZARIN, FROM THE SUPREME COUNCIL OF THE CONFEDERATION.

[In these documents the Council acknowledge receipt of the letters delivered to them by Monsieur De La Monnerie. The Council state the necessities which enforced them to defer sending the two thousand men which had been desired from them by the King of France for his German army. They express their affection to the Crown of France, and their grief at their present inability to comply with the application received through De La Monnerie. They beg that the Ambassador of France may be instructed to afford all reasonable aid to the Commissioners of the Confederation

now engaged in treating for a peace with the King of England.   The
Council's account of their position corresponds with that given by them
in their letter in English, page 109, written on the same day to Mathew
O'Hartegan, S. J.—Kilkenny, 22 February, 1643-4].

i. To Louis XIV., King of France.

Potentissime Rex,

Majestatis vestræ per Dominum de Moynerie, Majestati vestræ a Cubiculo Ordinarium, literas accepimus, in quibus regium vestrum in Ecclesiam
Dei zelum et summum in gentem nostram favorem abunde perspeximus.   In
illis duo militum millia pro Germanico suo exercitu conscribi in Hibernia
et ad se mitti desideravit.   Gratissima certe accidit occasio qua indubitatum gentis nostræ in Coronam vestram affectum exprimere possemus,
sed supramodum dolemus tantam nobis impositam esse necessitatem, ut
hoc presenti tempore nostrum Majestati vestræ inserviendi desiderium ad-
implere non possimus.   Habemus Puritanos plurimos, Parliamento Angliæ
adhærentes, nostræ armorum Cessacionis contemptores qui novum militem
stipendiis Parliamenti Angliæ indies conscribunt.   Exercitum suum in Ultonia ex Hiberniæ provinciis una in nos adaugent, et Ultoniæ fines excedere
parant.   Supervenit aliud longe magis timendum.   Compertum nobis est a
Parliamentariis parari et adornari classem ad invadendas occidentales hujus
regni partes, ubi commodissimi portus, quos si occupare illis contigeret
invectis auxiliis et copiis totum regnum paulatim invaderent et tam commodas nacti stationes mare navibus infestarent non sine Ecclesiæ Dei
et Christiani orbis perturbacione et periculo; cui summo malo ut fortiter
occurratur vires omnes adhibemus, et ne imparatis nobis superveniatur,
milites hunc in usum destinatos semper impromptu habere necesse esse
ducimus.   Præterea Colonellis quibusdam auctoritate Regis nostri militem in Hibernia conscripturis id concedere haud visum est commodum
quam vero ægre ferret sua Majestas nunc cum de pace per Commissarios
agimus, id alteri Regi concedere dignetur considerare Serenissima sua
Majestas.   His igitur undequaque pressi angustiis, humiliter rogamus
vestram Majestatem ut nostrarum rerum statum intueri dignetur, sibique

persuadeat nos Coronæ suæ addictissimos prima data commoditate affectum et inserviendi desiderium libere monstraturos nihilque prætermissuros quo Christianissimæ Coronæ, tam bene de nobis meritæ, gratificari aut inservire possimus. Unum restat, quod obnixe imploramus ut Majestatis vestræ apud Regem nostrum Legato detur in mandatis, Commissariis nostris de pace inuenda tractaturis favere, et causam nostram, interposita Majestatis vestræ auctoritate, in quantum justa videbitur promovere.—Majestatis vestræ observantissimi servi.—Kilkeniæ, 22 die Februarii, 1643[-4].

ii. To the Queen-Regent of France.

Potentissima Regina,—Per Dominum de Monerye, Regi Galliarum a Cubiculo Ordinarium, Majestatis vestræ literæ regii favoris et studii in gentem nostram plenæ ad nos sunt allatæ. Hisce militum duo millia ad inserviendum Christianissimo Regi in Germanico suo exercitu conscribi in Hibernia desiderat. Dolemus vehementer eo in statu res nostras esse ut pro præsenti nostro desiderio et debitis Coronæ Galliæ officiis deesse inviti cogamur. Undequaque nos premunt angustiæ. Puritani, Parliamento Angliæ faventes, et nostram armorum Cessacionem nequaquam admittentes, adaugent exercitus sui numerum in Ultonia, quæ ex provinciis Hiberniæ una est. Quem in finem ingens pecuniæ summa, armatis ad promovendum in nos bellum ab Angliæ Parliamento contributa est; sed et intelligimus in occidentales hujus Regni partes ab eodem Parliamento parari et destinari classem cum summo religionis Catholicæ et Christiani orbis periculo. Præterea Colonellis quibusdam ex Regis nostri auctoritate milites conscripturis, veniam dare haud visum est commodum, quam vero ægre ferret sua Majestas, nunc cum per Commissarios de pace agimus, id alteri Regi concedere judicare dignetur Potentissima Regina. Quare obnixe et humiliter rogamus ut arcta hæc qua premimur necessitas occasionem nullam præbeat in Christianissimam Galliæ Coronam studia et affectus in dubium apud vos vocandi quem a Majestatis vestræ clementia speramus favorem, cum nobis conscii simus paratos nos esse omni zelo et industria quævis aggredi et subire ut tam bene meritæ rerum nostrarum patronæ aliquomodo gratos nos exhibeamus. Unum restat quod obnixe imploramus ut

Christianissimi Regis et Majestatis vestræ apud Regem nostrum Legato
dctur in mandatis, Commissariis nostris de pace ineunda tractaturis favere,
et causam nostram, interposita Majestatum vestrarum auctoritate, in quantum justa videbitur promovere—Majestatis vestræ observantissimi servi.—
Kilkeniæ, 22 Februarii, 1643[-4].

iii. To CARDINAL MAZARIN.

Eminentissime Domine,—Quandoquidem res nostræ eo in loco sint ut
milites pro præsenti hinc auferri grave nobis incommodum futurum sit
cum in Ultonia, quæ ex nostris provinciis una est, Parliamentarii exercitum
suum adaugeant et novum aliquod classe jam parata in occidentales hujus
regni partes machinentur, sed et Colonellis quibusdam commissione Regis
nostri milites hic conscripturis venia concessa non sit.   Ne illa quâ premimur necessitas Christianissimi Regis et potentissimæ Galliarum Reginæ
ullo modo in nos causamque nostram affectum minueret, ad Eminentiam
vestram recurrimus quæ tam pie ac juste pugnantes auctoritate qua merito
pollet fovit sæpius et fovere non cessat.   Idem certe nobis est qui semper
fuit animus Galliæ Coronæ inserviendi, sed prudentissima sua Eminentia
dignabitur intueri angustias ad quas redacti sumus.   Porro responsum
nostrum in particulari, missum a Domino de Moynerie, qui omnibus apud
nos gratissimus est, Eminentiæ vestræ cognoscet, et Reverendus Pater,
Pater Matheus O'Hartegan fusius omnia exponet.   Unum restat, quod
ab Eminentia vestra obnixe petimus ut Commissariis nostris de pace
agentibus Christianissimi Regis Legatus apud Regem nostrum et mandato
suarum Majestatum faventer adsit et illorum justas promoveat peticiones.
Eminentiæ vestræ manus deosculantur Eminentissimæ Dominationis
vestræ observantissimi servi.—Kilkeniæ, 22 die Februarii, 1643[-4].

4. LETTER TO MATHEW O'HARTEGAN, S.J., PARIS, FROM SUPREME COUNCIL.

Reverend Father,—Wee have this day given the agent sent hither by
his Most Christian Majestie his answer ; and, in regarde the necessityes of
our affaires did enforce us to deffer the sending of men thither for the
present, least any misrepresentacion or misconstruccion should be made

thereof wee have thought fitt to acquaint you with the motives which, hard against our will, did compell us thereto. First, although wee have a Cessacion of armes with those that side with his Majestie, yet the Skotts and Parliament partye, which of late have received a vast summe of money from the Parliament of England, are prepareinge against us both in Skotland and in Ulster. Against those wee send an army under the commaund of the Earle of Castlehaven, which of all likelyhood will be in constant action and therefore will need a great reserve of men for theire supplie.

Secondlie, wee are assured from good and faithfull hands that the Parliament and Hollanders have joyned in some designe for takinge in some portes uppon our westerne coastes; which if they may compass, they will be a terror to all the Princes in Christiandome. Wee pray you labor with all earnestness and secresye to finde out the particulars of this designe, if any such there be.

Thirdlie, some Collonells, that had commission from our Kinge and were recommended unto us by the Marquess of Ormond, Lord Lieftenant of this kingdome, have, notwithstanding, beene denied of men, and with what indignacion, thinke you, would his Majestie looke uppon our Commissioners, now treatinge for a peace, if wee did suffer any men to leave this kingdome to serve elsewhere, when they were stopped from his assistance?

Wee know that all men who looke indifferently uppon our occasions will finde by those reasons that without the ruine of the kingdome, wee could not, for the present, parte with our men. In the meane tyme, wee pray you that as our affections continue the same they alwayes were, soe that none may take advantadge of this occasion wherby wee are enforced, much to our disquiet, to deffer expressinge of our desire to serve his Most Christian Majestie in that particular. Wee have given a further and more certaine answer to Monsieur de Moynerye touchinge the sendinge of those men to his Majestie of France, as you will perceive by the enclosed[1] beinge an authenticke coppie of the order and vote containeinge the answer made him at full. Thus, etc.—Kilkenny, 22 Febr., 1643 [-4].

1. *See* p. 106.

XXVI. Letter to Ormonde from Supreme Council.

Our very good Lord,—Wee have receaved your Lordship's of the 12th of this instant, directed to me, the Lord Viscount Mountgarrett, and others, whereby wee find those letters of ours, which were sent in answere to those of the fowrth of January directed to the Lord Viscount Muskery, or other of those who treated with your Lordship, hath been less satisfactory than wee hoped they would have proved, although wee conceive that both in our answer to the particulers of that letter, and the effectuall pursuance of our resolucions thereupon, wee did what became us, first to the incroachment of our partie, and the acts alleaged to have beene done by them, wee said wee were well assured, that none of our partie would presume soe highly to violat the Cessacion agreed upon of all sides, for the benefitt of us and the rest of his Majestie's good subjects; and this confidence of ours was grounded upon the advertisements wee daily receave of the punctuall observance of the strict charge wee had given to have those partes settled in that particular. Yet, least wee should be misinformed, it was intimated that wee should apply our best endevours no wrong should be don to any of your partie, and accordingly wee have intrusted some able, discreete men, who will joyne with others of your partie, authorized in that behalfe, to examyn and quiett those differences.

And where it is said that exception is taken by us, in the letter of the fowrth of January, as if you had given the tytle of good subject to such as disavow the Cessacion, and have sworne a Covenant destructive to monarchy, wee conceive this is an inference too positive out of those words, [*oblit.*] wee hope your Lordship would not afford them that name, and as wee are assured you will countenance and protect all such as do embrace the Cessacion, so wee des[ire, as] wee formerly did, to be assisted by your Lordship in punishing such as doe disobey his Majestie's authority, and doe refuse to submitt unto it. Thus wee humbly take leave and rest, your Lordship's humble servants,—Mountgarrett.—Fr. Thomas

Dublyn.—Castlehaven, Audley.—Netterville.—John Clonfert.—R. Bellings.—Gerald Fenell.—George Commyn.—Patrick Darcy.

Kilkenny, the 27th of February, 1643[-4].

For the Right Honnorable, the Lord Liftenant of Ireland.

Endorsed: Lord Mountgarret, etc. Dated 27 Feb., received 2 Mar. 1643. Concerning breaches of the Cessation.

XXVII. Negotiations for Irish forces for England and Scotland, 1643-4.

1. Letter to Ormonde from Supreme Council.

Our very good Lord,—Wee have receaved a letter, directed to Richard Lord Viscount Mountgarrett, and others the Lords and gentlemen, assembled at Kilkenny in Ireland, bearing date the 18th day of January last, from Prince Rupart,[1] wherein hee desires wee should convey to Chester water, or any other perte in North Wales five thowsand musketts, three hondred barrailes of powder, and match proporcionable. Now, in asmuch as wee have understood formerly from Collonell John Barry, that your Lordship, out of your great care to see those partes furnished for his Majestie's service with armes and ammunicion, allowing the payments for them out of such moneys as by our Commissioners who concluded upon the Cessacion, in the behalfe of the Confederat Catholickes of Ireland, were graunted unto his Majestie, wee have thought fitt, before we retourne a positive answere to Prince Rupart to that particular, to beseech your Lordship to advertise us, how farr wee may comply with your Lordship's first desire and his Majestie's engagement upon us, in endevouring by all possible meanes, to provide such armes, and ammunicion, in discharge of som parte of our arreares, as may be spared from such necessary preparacions as at this tyme wee do make for his Majestie's service. Thus wee humbly take leave, and rest, your Lordship's humble servants, Mountgarrett.—Fr. Thomas Dublyn.—T: Preston.—Patr: Darcy.—Gerald

XXVII. 1, 2. Carte Papers, vol. ix. pp. 206-7; 3, vol. xiv. p. 108; 4, vol. ix. p. 206, pp. 214, 224.   1. See p. 87.

Fennell.—R. Bellings.—Ever Magines.—Castlehaven and Audley.—Netterville.—John Clonfert.—Torl: O'Neill.

Kilkenny, the 28th of Febr., 1643 [-4.]

To the Right Honnorable, the Lord Lieuetennant of Ireland.

2. By the Supreame Councell of the Confederat Catholickes of Ireland.

Uppon conference had with our very good Lord, Randle M'Donnell,
Earle of Antrim,[1] wee find that his Lordshipp's designe for rayseinge forces
in the Iles of Scotland to infest the adverse partie in that kingdome, and
divert theire incursions into England, doth very much conduce to his
Majesties service : For the furtherance whereof, wee are resolved to
assist his Lordshipp with two thousand musketts, two thousand foure
hundred weight of powder, proportionable match, two hundred barrailes
of oatemeale, by the first day of May next, uppon knowledge first had
that all other accomodations be concurringe, and a safe and convenient
porte provided in Ulster for receivinge the said armes, amunition, and
victuall : provided the said porte be commanded by Walter Bagnall, and
the men there to be by him appointed such as in his judgment shall be
thought faithfull and observant of just commaunds.—Given at Kilkenny, the 29th of February, 1643[-4].

3. It is this day ordered that the Right Honorable Earle of Antrim,
and Daniell O'Neill,[2] Esquire, one of his Majestie's Bed-Chamber, to
theire proposition of sending into England ten thousand men well armed,
with ordnance and munition fitt for an army, and shipping to transport
them, should receive the ensueing answeare :

And, uppon advertysement thereof from our Commissioners, wee will
with all possible expedition not only be redy to serve his Majestie with
ten thousand men, but, further, to employ our uttmost endeavours to
advaunce his Majestie's interests in the condition and quallity of loyall
subjects.—[February, 1643-4.]

By command of the Supreame Councell.—RICHARD BELLINGS.

1. For instructions from Charles I. to Earl of Antrim, *see* page 88.

2. Letters of Daniel O'Neille, in connection with these negotiations, will be found
in "Contemporary History of Affairs in Ireland, A.D. 1641-52." Dublin: 1879-80,
vol. i. p. 569.

4. Letters from Earl of Antrim to Ormonde.

i.—My Lord,—I can never too often present you with my service, haveinge so good a messinger to deliver it. I have done small dispatches heare with the Supreme Counsell, but the principall busines is left undone, which shall yet be performed, if I may have your Lordship's assistance; but I hope you will keepe that to yourself. I will by Daniel O'Neile acquaint you with more particulers, but this onelie thinge I beseech you beleeve that I shall for your one person, and the King's service, joyne with you in anie thinge that may better expresse me to be your Lordship's most affectionat servant,—Antrim.

Kilkenie, 29 Feb, 1643[-4].

ii.—My Lord,—This morning I receaved your Lordship's letter which gives me a great deale of joye to find that I shall not faile of your assistance to accomplish his Majestie's desires, wherein your Lordship is equallie concerned. I have obtained part of my desires, and part is delayed, though not denied, but delays are as equallie dangerous to the Kinge. The sum of the proceedings my cossen, Daniel O'Neile, will enforme you, and what other wayes of accomplishinge his Majestie's service, I shall referre to his relation. I desire by him to receave your directions and commands how to proceed for the King's advantadge, and I shall verie puntuallie observe them. I have by him likewise sent you the King's letter, by which you will find that this imployment was not undertaken without hopes of your concurrance. I am verie confident you have not, nor will not, make anie promise, but what you intend to performe; therefore I am easilie induced to beleeve that you have done this for my nephew of Slane, which indeed is a verie great obligation upon your Lordship's most humble servant,—Antrim.

Kilkenie, 2 March [1643-4].

XXVIII. Supreme Council's Answer to Agent of the King of Spain.

1 March, 1643[-4].—It is ordered that Mr. Secretary shall retourne this further answer to the proposicions made by Don Francisco de Fosset att his first audience,[1] and againe renewed by him this day, concerninge the leavy of some men in this kingdom to be imployd in his Catholique Majestie's service in Flanders, viz. : That they have already, in the end of theyr former answer, touching the leavy of two thowsand men to be sent into Spaine, answered this proposicion.

Mountgarett. T. Preston.—Patrick Darcy.—Gerald Fenell.—Thomas Fleming.—Torlogh O'Neill.— Ever Magines.

XXIX. Letter to Nicholas Everard [Flanders,[2]] from Supreme Council.

Mr. Everard,—Wee heare you have lent Monsieur Lalloe[3] fifteene hundred florence, to furnish him into this countrye, which shall be repayd unto you out of the customes growinge due uppon any commodityes which shall be either exported or imported uppon your accompt, and beinge assured you will be therewith satisfied, wee have sent to Mr. [blank] to have the said Lalloe's instruments delivered unto him for the present service. Thus, etc.

Kilkenny, 1 Martii, 1643[-4].

XXX. Ormonde to Commissioners for Quarters in Kildare.

After our hearty comendacions : Wee send you heere inclosed a coppy of a letter written by us in the behalfe of Gerald FitzGerald of the Nurny, in the county of Kildare, and the answere thereunto. And for as much as

---

XXVIII-IX. Ms. "Register Book of Letters" of Supreme Council.

1. *See* page 102.   2. *See* vol. ii., p. 341.

3. Lalue, "a Frenchman, ingenier for the Irish." *See* "Contemporary History of Affairs in Ireland, 1641-52." Dublin : 1879, vol. i., p. 102.

XXX. Carte Papers, ix., p. 231.

wee conceave the matter complayned of most fitt to be determined by you who are appoynted Commissioners for the settleinge of the quarters in that county, wee doe hereby pray you to take the same into consideracion, and eyther to settle the same or to certify us with all convenient speede the true state thereof; and that you doe in the meane tyme take order that Mr. FitzGerrald may not bee forced to pay any cess to eyther syde till it doe appeare to whome hee ought to pay his contribucion. And soe wee bid you farewell. From, etc., 2 Martii, 1643[-4].

Your very loveing frend,—ORMONDE.

Commissioners of the county of Kildare for the quarters.

XXXI. ORMONDE TO GERALD FENELL, M.D.

Dr. Fenell,—Since the remembrances I gave Mr. Saul, and since my last letter unto you, wherein I advised a speedy and punctuall complyance from your party with the Earle of Antrym's desires, I have seen soe much of his Majestie's authority to countenance his Lordship's negotiation, and am so well acquainted with the pressing necessity that his Majestie should be powerfully and seasonably assisted hence, that I must recomend it to your judgement and care to dispose those in authority with you to that worke, wherein their owne interest is so farr concearned, that wee thinke it is evidently the most probable way to gaine those good conditions unto them, when his Majestie shall not only be engaged in honnor (which is the strongest tye uppon a Prince), but inabled to performe that ingagement by an opertune and considerable assistance.

The particulers desired I find have been alreedy made knowen to you, and are no more than by your publick Remonstrance,[1] by many and frequent professions, by your owne interest, if rightly considered, and by your duty to the King, you are obleeged unto. And therfore I shall not doubt but that, adding to all this your affection to mee, who am particulerly and strictly comanded to contribute my assistance to the performance of the Earle of Antrym's charge, you will put your whole strength to obteyne for him a speedy and satisfactory dispatch.

XXXI. Carte Papers, ix., p. 439.   1. See vol. ii., p. 226.

As to that part of his Lordship's negotiation, whereunto (as I am informed) you have assented, I presume you will consider how precious tyme is, soe much that the losse of a few weeks will render the designe ineffectuall and irrecoverable.

When you shall advertise mee that your armes, amunition, provisions of victuall and shipping for the conveyance of it is redy, and whither it is held most convenient to have them sent, there shall not be wanting a place to receive and secure them to your satisfaction, if reason and evident demonstracion in that point shall satisfy you.

Of these particulers I desire a very speedy accoumpt, as things wherein the King's service, the safety of this kingdome, and my particuler satisfaction are infinitely concearned.   And soe I rest, your very assured frend,

ORMONDE.

Dublin Castle, 6 March, 1643 [-4].

Endorsed : Coppy of the letter to D[octor] F[enell], dated 6 Martii., 1643[-4].   Concerning the negotiation of the Lord Antrim with the Supreme Councill at Kilkenny, in behalfe of the King.

XXXII. CLAIM OF CONFEDERATION TO RECEIVE CUSTOMS, 1643-4.

1. CERTIFICATE OF LORD CHANCELLOR AND JUDGES AT DUBLIN.

May it please your Lordship,—Wee have, according to your Lordship's reference of the 8th of this instant March, considered the lettre dated the first therof from Terlagh O'Neile[1] and Ever Magenis,[2] wherein the ground formerly laid by us in our former certificat dated the 15th of February is admitted, viz. : That the Customes doe belong unto those within whose power, command, or possession, the ports leading to Waterford and Rosse were at the time of concluding the Cessation.[3]   But in

XXXII. 1. Clarendon Papers, 1643, No. 1749.—Bodleian Library, Oxford.

1. 2. Members of Supreme Council of the Irish Confederation and Commissioners to treat for and conclude a Cessation of hostilities, 1643. *See* vol. ii., pp. 86, 366.

3. For Articles of Cessation, 15th September, 1643, *see* vol. ii., p. 365.

that lettre there is noe answere given to the other ground laid by us in that certificat, viz., that his Majestie's port of Duncanon is soe scituated that it hath the power and comand over the said port or haven leading from the sea to Waterford and Rosse, as in truth it then and yet hath. And although that severall vessells might come in and goe forth, without the permission of the said forte, which is not acknowledged, yet that doth not prove the port leading to Waterford and Rosse to bee within their comand, power, or possession. Which if it were, why did the merchantes of Waterford and Rosse before the Cessacion decline the said port or haven leading to Waterford and Rosse for Tramore bay and the haven of Dungarvan, to utter or receive the commodities brought thither from Waterford and Rosse, whereas Dungarvan is a dangerous haven and twenty miles by land from Waterford, and neither of them soe comodious or safe for ships to ride in as the port or haven leading to Rosse and Waterford ? Which doth further appeere in that, since the concluding of the Cessation, the said port or haven leading to Waterford and Rosse hath been altogether used by their merchantes, all which doth appeere by the said lettre of the first of Marche.

And for that which is urged that the Customes have been allwaies paid at Waterford and Rosse, it is not to the question,—the true state thereof not beeing of the place where the Customes are or were paid, but within whose power, command, or possession the port or haven leading to Rosse and Waterford is and was at the concluding of the Cessation, which is the only point which doth determin the matter in question. And though the country adjacent there unto the said port or haven bee in their possession, yet that doth not prove that the port or haven is within their quarters, for they want the forte which doth comand it. Neither is it matteriall what is said of Ballyhack[1] and the forte of Passage,[2] for that noe shipp can come thither or goe from thence but by the permission and allowance of the said forte of Duncanon.

Soe as, uppon consideracion had of the whole matter, wee are of the

1. In county of Wexford.
2. In county of Waterford.

same opinion that wee formerly certified your Lordship, which wee humbly certify and submit to your Lordship's consideracion.

Richard Bolton, C[hancellor] —Gerrard Lowther.[1]—Samuel Mayart.[2] —William Ryves.[3]—James Donellan.[4]—William Hilton.[5]—Maurice Eustace.[6]

Dated 10th Marche, 1643[-4].—Examined per Paul Davys.— Endorsed : x. Martii, 1643[-4]. Coppie of second certificat from the Lord Chancellor and Judges, etc., concerning customes at Waterford, etc.

2. LETTER FROM CHARLES I. TO MAYOR, SHERIFFS, AND CITIZENS OF WATERFORD, IN RELATION TO CUSTOMS.

Charles Rex.—Whereas we are informed that when the officers intrusted by us, in the tyme of peace, to receave our customes in the porte of our citty of Waterford, could not, by reason of the violence used towards them, collect our customes there, that you in your tyme and those who were before you in office, did take care to receave and preserve the same for us untill our pleasure were knowne concerning the same ; wee now thought fitt to declare unto you that it is our will and pleasure, and wee doe hereby require and authorise you to pay soe much of our said customes as have been receaved by you or any other person thereunto authorised or allowed in that our port, and such as shall hereafter accrew unto us there, unto our right trusty and entirely beloved cousin and councellor, James, Marques of Ormonde, our Lieutenant-Generall of that our kingdome, or to such as hee shall appoint. The same is to bee imployed by him in our service, and the acquittance of our said Lieutenant, or of any other whome hee shall authorise in that behalf, shalbee unto you and all others whome it may concerne a sufficient acquital and discharge for soe much.

Given at our Court at Oxford, the 23th of March, 1643[-4].—By his Majestie's comaund,—EDW : NICHOLAS.

1. Chief Justice, Common Pleas.   2. Justice, Common Pleas.   3. Justice, King's Bench.   4. Justice, Common Pleas.   5. Baron of the Exchequer.   6. Prime Sergeant.

XXXII. 2. Carte Papers, ix. p. 354.

XXXIII. Custom-House Regulations and Rates under the Irish Confederation.

i. Fees to be taken of the Custome House of the Porte of New Rosse, and other portes within the quarters of the Confederate Catholiques, as followeth:

	Customer. d.	Surveyor. d.	Comptrowler d.
First, for the entrye of all shipps or barques from England, by English or Irish	iiii	iiii	iiii
For entrie of goods in the same shipps or barques, by English or Irish	iiii	iiii	iiii
For the entrie of all shipps and barques from foraine countries, by English or Irish	viii	viii	viii
For entrie of all goods in foraigne shipps or barques, by English or Irish	viii	viii	viii
For makeinge of bonds to the use of the publique, by English or Irish	xii	nichil	nichil
For every entry into the certificate booke	ii	nichil	nichil
For every endorcment	iiii	iiii	iiii
For takeinge bond, to his Majestie's use, or the use of the publique, to permit the officer to goe aboorde at all times, and not to departe away before they be cleered by the officers and theire bookes examyned	xii	nichil	nichil
For entry of all shipps and barques to England, by English or Irish	iiii	iiii	iiii
For entry of all goods in the same shipps or barques, by English or Irish	iiii	iiii	iiii
For every cocquett,[1] by English or Irish	xii	ix	ix

XXXIII. State Papers, Ireland, Charles I., No. 287.—Public Record Office, London.
1. Cocket, or coket, a scroll of parchment, sealed and delivered by the officers of the Custom House to merchants, as a warrant that their merchandise was entered.

	Customer. d.	Surveyor. d.	Comptrowler. d.
For entry of every ship, barque, or boate, alongest the coast	ii	i	i
For makeinge every certificatte for goods which paid custome, poundage, or imposicion, inwards, and paieth none out	xiiii	vii	vii
For every certificatt uppon warrant from the Lord Deputy, or other Cheefe Governor	xviii	ix	ix
For endorceinge all warrants and lycences ...	iiii	nichil	nichil
For forraigne bills	vi	vi	vi
For every coaste certificate with tymber or boords	iiii	ii	ii
For every coaste certificatt, and for entry into his Majestie's bookes	xii	viii	viii
For dischardginge of bonds and fileinge the certificate	vi	nichil	nichil
For makeinge certificates of retorne in the King's booke, wax, and parchment	xii	iiii	iiii
For cleeringe of shipps and barques and examineinge bookes from England	vi	iii	iii
For cleeringe of shipps and barques, and exameneinge bookes from forraigne partes	xii	vi	vi
For entry of shipps and barques from England, or anny other parte beyonde the seas, by strangers ...	xii	xii	xii
For entry of goods in the said shipps or barques, by strangers	viii	viii	viii
For cleeringe of shipps and exameninge of bookes from England or anny other parte, by strangers...	xvi	viii	viii
For makeinge of bonds to his Majestie's use for imployments or otherwise, by strangers ...	xviii	nichil	nichil
For entry of all shipps and barques to England, or anny other parte beyonde the seas, by strangers ...	xii	xii	xii

Mountgarrett.—Thomas [Archbishop of] Cashell.—Netterville.—John [Burke, Bishop of] Clonefert.—R. Bellings.—Thomas Fleming.—Patrick

Darcy.—Gerrald Fennell.—Malachias [O'Queely, Archbishop of] Tuam.—Geffery Browne.

ii. Fees and perquissitts to be recaved and taken by his Majestie's Searcher of the Porte of Waterford.

	s.	d.
Inprimis, for every shipp or barque arriveinge from forraigne partes, either by natives or strangers, for ingate[1]	1	6
Item, for the like, for out-gate[2]	1	6
Item, for every shipp, barcque, or boate aloungest the coaste, with anny goods brought in or transported out, by natives or strangers	0	3
Item, for every shipp, barcque, or boate out of England or Scotland, by natives or strangers	0	9
Item, for every billet or warrant for dischardginge of goods inward, by natives, directed to the Searcher	0	4 ob.
Item, for every dischardge or warrant for goods comminge in by porte-coccquett, by natives or strangers	0	4 ob.
Item, for every certificate alongest the coast, by natives or strangers, of the dischardge of goods which come by porte-coccquett	0 ·	4 ob.
Item, for every dischardge or warrant for goods in or out by lett pass	0	4 ob.
Item, for every bill of view, by natives	0	4 ob.
Item, for every bill of view, by strangers ...	0	9 ob.
Item, for every coccquett, by natives, outward bound	0	4 ob.
Item, for every coccquett, by strangers, outward bound	0	9
Item, for every coccquett of anny great shipp laden with corne, outward bound	5	0
Item, for every coccquett of anny small barque loaden with corne, outward bound	2	6
Item, for every barrell of tallowe or butter exported by native or stranger, payeinge custome ...	0	2

1. Entrance, passage inwards.   2. Passage outwards.

		d.
Item, for gadginge of every tonn of wyne, oyle, vinegar, or beere, imported by native or stranger ...	nichil	0
Item, for every tonn of beere exported by native or stranger	-	3
Item, for every warrant at lardge for dischardginge of goods and merchandizes retourned, upon bill of viewe, by natives	-	6
Item, for every billet or warrant for the dischardginge of goods uppon the retourne uppon bill of view, by strangers	-	9
Item, for every bill of store or an allowance for provision to natives as well inserted in billets, warrants, or coccquetts, as by itselfe aloane for dischardge of goods inwarde or outwarde	-	4 ob.
Item, for such bill of store or allowance for provision for strangers	-	9
Item, for every packe of yearne by native or stranger	-	6
Item, for every packe, bagg, or fardell of woll, wollfell, sheepskins and lambskins, beinge packed in packes, baggs, or fardells	-	3
Item, for every barrayle of hearings exported by natives	-	0¼
Item, for every barrayle of hearings exported by strangers	-	0 ob.
Item, for every barrayle of beefe exported by natives	-	0¼
Item, for every barrell of beefe exported by strangers	-	0 ob.
Item, for every barrell of beefe exported by strangers (*sic*)	-	1
Item, for every dicker of tanned hides exported by natives or strangers	-	1 ob.
Item, for every passenger or souldier to goe for forraigne partes, le peece	-	3

Mountgarrett.—Thomas [Archbishop of] Cashell.—Malachias [O'Queely] Tuamensis.—Nettervill.—Emerus [Mac Mahon] Clogherensis.—Nicholas Plunkett.—Gerrald Fennell.—Geffery Brown.

iii. Fees and perquissitts to be receaved and taken by his Majestie's Searcher of the porte: Established by the Right Honorable the Supreame Councell :

	s.	d.
Imprimis, for every shipp or barque arryveinge from forraigne partes either by natives or strangers for ingate	1	6
Item, for the like, for outgate	1	6
Item, for every shipp, barque, or boate alongest the coast, with anny goods brought in or transported out by natives or strangers	0	3
Item, for every shipp, barque, or boate out of England or Scotland, by natives or strangers	0	9
Item, for every billet or warrant for dischardginge of goods inward by natives, directed to the Searcher	0	4 ob.
Item, for every dischardge or warrant for goods cominge in by porte-cocquett, by native or stranger	0	4 ob.
Item, for every certificatt alongest the coast by natives or strangers of the dischardge of goods which come by porte cocquett	0	4 ob.
Item, for every dischardge or warrant for goods in or out by lett pass	0	4 ob.
Item, for every bill of viewe, by natives	0	4 ob.
Item, for every bill of viewe, by strangers ...	0	9
Item, for every coccquett, by natives, outward bound	0	4 ob.

XXXIV. Letters to Ormonde from Supreme Council.

1. Our very good Lord,—Wee received your Lordship's of the 21st concerninge the supplye for Scotland. Wee thanke your Lordshipp for presentinge our proposicions to his Majestie. The consequence of the designe wee apprehend to be very great, both in relation to his Majestie's service and the safetye of this kingdome, accordinge your Lordshipp's expression, your Lordshipp's undertaking to provide shippinge, and his Majestie's royall worde passed for the safety of our men, armes, and amunicion, are good inducements to us to consider, of further resolucions uppon that expedicion. Our boarde is now somewhat thin, some princi- pall members of it beinge now uppon important employments. Where- fore, wee hold it not convenient for us to alter, what a full Councell con- ceived, without much deliberacion. Within a few dayes they all meete, and by our Commissioners appointed for the treatye, who are to be at Dublin the 10th of the next month, wee will acquaint your Lordshipp with our full resolucions uppon this affaire, the advancement whereof is heartely desired by your Lordshipp's very lovinge freinds,

Emerus Clogherensis.—Daniel O'Bryen.—Edmund Fitz Morice.— Patrick Darcy.—Thomas Flemyng.—Gerald Fenell.—Rob. Lynch.

Clonmell, 26 Martii, 1644.

For his Excellencie the Marquess of Ormonde, Lord Lieutennant of Ireland.

2. Our very good Lord,—Because wee find, by your Lordship's letters of the eighteenth of this instant, a jealousie to be conceived that some forces of ours are thus earely, and in such number drawne into the field, wee thought fitt to give your Lordship this assurance, that they have not beene rais'd, neither are they to be imployed upon any service, which in the least circumstance may violatt the articles of Cessation. Wee have within our quarters, within the province of Connaght, a few ill-disposed persons, who made use of the distempers of the tymes to their privat

XXXIV. Carte Papers, x. pp. 12, 14.

advantage, by dispossessing the right owners of estates legally acquired, and haveing for some tyme reaped the benefitt of their injustice, must have more powerfull arguments than their conscience can suggest made against them, before they doe relinquish such their acquisicions.[1] And as we will make their punishment our first worke, so in the rest of the occasions whereupon that army is to be imployed, none shall find themselves aggreived, but such as are his Majestie's professed enemyes, or have contemned his royall authority entrusted with your Lordship when you treated upon and concluded a Cessacion of armes with the Confederate Catholickes of Ireland. And although the garrisons of Castle Coote, Tulske, Boyle, Elfinn, and other garrisons in the county of Roscomman, have misdemeaned themselves so farr as to an evident breach of the Cessacion, and that complainte thereof hath beene made unto your Lordship, whereupon wee doe expect redress, yet wee doe not intend to proceede against them, without haveing first acquainted your Lordship therewith, and satisfied all the circumstances and provisions concluded upon to that purpose in the articles of Cessacion. Thus, with the remembrance of our hartyest wishes unto your Lordship, wee rest, your Lordship's humble servants,—Thomas [Walsh, Archbishop of] Cashel.—Malachias [O'Queely] Tuamensis.—Netterville.—Torlogh O'Neill.—George Commyn.—Johannes [Bourke] Clonfertensis.—Thomas Preston.—Lucas Dillon.—Gerald Fenell. —Daniel O'Bryen.—Rob : Lynch.

Gallway, the 26th of March, 1644.

XXXV. Letter to Fr. Hugh Bourke, Flanders, from the Supreme Council.

Reverend Father,—By the enclosed peticion, preferred to us by some marchants of this towne, you may observe how hardly they are dealt with by those of Dunkerke. These manner of proceedinges were not expected and especially from them, which gives our marchants very great discouradgment and is to be feard, if tymely satisfaccion be not made them, will bringe much prejudice uppon our cause. Wee doe, therefore, re-

---

1. *See* notice by Bellings, p. 9.   XXXV. Ms. "Register Book of Letters."

commend this matter unto your care and earnest sollicitacion with those in authoritye there, as well in the behalfe of the marchants who have suffered exceedinglye in their owne particular, as of the kingdome, who are highly intrested in the consequence of it, if tymely redress be not procured, and some course taken for prevencion of the like inconveniency. Thus, etc.—Dated [at] Galway, the 27th of March, 1644.

XXXVI. LETTER TO ORMONDE FROM VISCOUNT MUSKERRY AT OXFORD.

My Lord,—We have this afternoone presented our Demaunds to his Majestie, which wee studied to make soe moderate and reasonable, as wee know not how it may be hoped that the nation may subsist in the condition of free subjects, if our deseyres be not granted. Neyther is the heighest of them such a rock, but that the King may finde a way to satisfie his people in that kingdome, without prejudice to his partie heare. And the reall advantage of the assurance of our kingdome, and of a nation soe faithfully affected to his service, is much more considerable than the feares and jealousies to discontent a partie.

My Lord, I believe a copie of our Demaunds[1] are now sent you, and you may be soe farr intrusted by his Majestie therein, as itt may ley in your way either there, or by your advise hither, to give verey great furtherance to the present settlment of the affaires of that kingdome. I doe not hope to perswade you to this, not by aney good that may redounde to your selfe, posteritie, kinred, or nation, for I know in the place you hould, you regard not theise: But as you know the state of that kingdome, and the strong disease that raignes heare, specially in the Commons generally over all the kingdome, you shall finde the peace of that kingdome to be of extreame great consequence to his Majestie['s] service. All which I submitt to your Lordship's better consideration, and remaine your Lordship's most affectionat brother, and most humble servant,   MUSKERY.

Oxford, the 29th of March, 1644.

P.S.—My Lord, to compley with the King's necessities, wee have falen to the very lowest that wee could devise, and there is noe hopes wee shall decleyne aney thinge of what wee have given in.

XXXVI. Carte Papers, x., p. 32.   1. *See* p. 128.

XXXVII. The Demands[1] of the Roman Catholics of Ireland.

Humbly presented to his Sacred Majestie [Charles I.] in pursuance of their Remonstrance[2] of Grievances, and to be annexed to the said Remonstrance.

1. That all Acts made against the professors of the Roman Catholique fayth, whereby any restraint, penalty, mulct, or incapacity may be layd upon any Roman Catholique within the kingdome of Ireland may be repealed, and the sayd Catholiques to be allowed the freedome of the Roman Catholique religion.

2. That your Majesty be pleased to call a free Parliament in the sayd kingdome, to be held and continued as in the sayd Remonstrance is expressed, and the statute of the tenth yeare of the raigne of King Henry the Seaventh, called Poynings' Act, and all Acts explaining or enlarging the same, be suspended during that Parliament, for the speedy settlement of the present affayres, and the repeale thereof to be there further considered of.

3. That all Acts and Ordinances made and past in the now pretended Parliament in that kingdome, since the seaventh day of August, 1641, be cleerly annulled, declared voyd, and taken off the file.

4. That all indictments, attainders, outlawries in the King's Bench, or elsewhere, since the sayd seaveanth day of August, 1641, and all letters patents, graunts, leases, custodiums, bonds, recognizances, and all other records, Act or Acts dependinge thereupon, or in prejudice of the sayd Catholiques, or any of them, be taken off the files, annulled and declared voyd, first by your Majestie's publique proclamation, and after by Act to be passed in the sayd free Parliament.

5. That, inasmuch as under colour of such outlawries, and attainders,

XXXVII. Carte Papers, x., p. 46.
1. See p. 2.
2. See vol. ii. p. 226, " A Remonstrance of Grievances, in the behalf of the Catholics of Ireland," 17th March, 1642-3.

debts due to the sayd Catholiques haue been graunted, levyed and disposed of, and, of the other syde, that debts due upon the sayd Catholiques to those of the other party have been levyed and disposed to publique uses, that therefore all debts be by Act of Parliament mutually released or all to stand in statu quo, notwithstanding any graunt or disposition.

6. [That,[1] whereas your Majestie's subjects of that kingdome have and doe suffer extremely by the offices found, since the first yeare of Queene Elizabeth, of many countries and territories, upon no reall title, or upon fayned or old titles of two hundred, three hundred, four hundred yeares, and by many illegall, and unjust attainders, by Acts of Parliament or otherwise, since the tyme aforesayd, unto which hetherto no travers, monstrans de droyt, or Peticion of Right could be admitted, it is therefore humbly desyred that the sayd offices, and attainders, and all grants, leases, and estates thereupon derived from the Crowne be reviewed in free Parliament according to justice and conscience; still reserving to your Majesty the rents and proffits thereout answered before the late Commission of Defective Titles; and speciall care to be therein likewise had of purchases made for valuable consideration by your Majestie's faythfull subjects. And] That the late offices, taken or found upon fayned or old titles since the yeare 1634, to intitle your Majesty to severall countries in Connaght, Thomond, and in the counties of Tiperary, Lymerick, and Wickloe, be vacated and taken off the file, the possessors settled and secured in their auncient estates by Act of Parliament, and that the lyke Act of Limitation of your Majestie's titles for the security of the estates of your subjects of that kingdome be passed in the sayd Parliament, as was enacted in [1623-24] the 21th yeare of his late Majestie's raigne in this kingdome.

7. That all markes of incapacity imposed upon the natives of that kingdome to purchase or acquire leases, offices, lands, or hereditaments, be taken away by Act of Parliament, and the same to extend to the securing of purchases, leases, or graunts already made; and that for the

1. In margin: "Omitted in the second Propositions, April 2, 1644." This refers to the matter within brackets.

education of youth, an Act be passed in the next Parliament for the erecting of one or more Innes of Court, Universities, free and common schooles.

8. That the offices and places of command, honour, proffit and trust within that kingdome be conferred upon Roman Catholiques natives of that kingdome, in equality and indifference with your Majestie's other subjects.

9. That the insupportable oppression of your Majestie's subjects by reason of the Court of Wards, and respite of hommage, be taken away, and a certaine revenewe in liew thereof settled upon your Majesty without diminution of your Majestie's proffit.

10. That no Lord not estated in that kingdome, or estated and not resident, shall have vote in the sayd Parliament by proxie or otherwise, and none [be] admitted to the House of Commons but such as shall be estated and resident within the kingdome.

11. That an Act shall be passed in the next Parliament, declaratorie that the Parliament of Ireland is a free Parliament of itselfe, indepen-dant of, and not subordinate to, the Parliament of England; and that the subjects of Ireland are immediately subject to your Majesty as in right of your Crowne ; and that the members of the sayd Parliament of Ireland, and all other the subjects of Ireland are independant, and no way to be ordered or concluded by the Parliament of England, and are onely to be ordered and governed within that kingdome by your Majesty and such Governors as are or shall be there appointed, and by the Parliament of that kingdome according to the lawes of the land.

12. [That[1] two Acts[2] past in the Parliament of this kingdome of Eng-land, the one intituled An Act for the speedy and effectual reducing of the Rebells in his Majestie's kingdome of Ireland to theyr due obedience to his Majesty and the Crowne of England, and another Act entituled An Act for adding unto and explaning the same, shall be declared voyd; and that all graunts and assignements, under such graunts or any other Acts or estates whatsoever made in pursuance of them, or otherwise, or

1. Matter within brackets omitted in the second or revised " Propositions."
2 See vol. i. Preface, p. xxxv., and p. 259; also vol. ii., pp. 238-9.

in pursuance of the Act or Acts of Subscriptions, or any other Act or proclamation, and all other Acts and ordinances made in the Parliament of England in prejudice of the sayd Catholiques, shall be declared voyd.]

13. That the assumed power or jurisdiction in the Councell Board, of determining all manner of causes, be limited to matters of State, and all patents, estates, and graunts illegally and extrajudicially avoyded, there or elsewhere, be left in state as before, and the parties grieved, their heires or assignes, till legall eviction.[1]

14. That the statutes of the eleventh, twelfth, and thirteenth yeare of the raigne of Queene Elizabeth concerning staple commodities be repealed, reserving to his Majesty lawfull and just poundage, and a book of rates to be settled by an indifferent committee of both Houses for all commodities.

15. That, in as much as the long continuance of the cheefe governor or governors of that kingdome, in that place of soe great eminencie and power, hath been a principall occasion that much tyranny and oppression hath been exercised upon the subjects of that kingdome, that your Majesty will be pleased to continue such Governors hereafter but for three yeares; and that none once employed therein be appointed for the same again untill the expiration of six yeares next after the end of the sayd three yeares; and that an Act passe to disable such Governor, or Governors, during theyr government, directly or indirectly, in use, trust, or otherwise, to make any manner of purchase, or acquisition of any mannors, lands, tenements, or hereditaments within that kingdome, other than from your Majesty, your heyres, or successors.

16. [That,[2] whereas your Majestie's standing army formerly in that kingdome, was of so small and inconsiderable a number, that they rather appeared a marke of suspition and jealousie on the nation, and rendered them to all other nations as a people not to be trusted, than any strength for the defence of the kingdome, and yet exhausted a great part of your

---

1. Owing to the omission above indicated this section is numbered 12 in the revised " Propositions."

2. Matter within brackets omitted in revised " Propositions."

Majestie's revenue, which the severall officers converted to their private use, having few or no souldiours, but such as they collected of their tenants and servants, at dayes of musters and pay ; to remove therefore that badge of distrust from your sayd subjects, it is humbly desyred that no such army be any longer maintained in that kingdome, whereby much of your Majestie's revenue will be hereafter saved for better uses, and your subjects there, with your Majestie's consent, will take such course for the safety of that kingdome, by way of trayned-bands or otherwise as shallbe most serviceable to your Majesty, and satisfactory to your sayd subjects.

17. That the present Government of the sayd Catholiques may continue within theyr quarters and jurisdictions untill the Parliament, and after untill theyr grievances be redressed by Acts of Parliament, and for a convenient tyme for the execution thereof.[1]]

18. That an Act of Oblivion[2] be passed in the next free Parliament, to extend to all your Majestie's sayd Catholique subjects of that kingdome, for all manner of offences, capitall, criminall, and personall, [with[3] a saving and reservation to both Houses within six moneths next after the passing of the sayd Act, to question any person or persons of any syde for any no-

1. The portions above within brackets are omitted in the revised " Propositions," in which section 15 is as follows : " That an Act be passed in the next Parliament, for the raising and settling of trained-bands within the severall counties of that kingdome, as well to prevent forreigne invasions as to render them the more serviceable and ready for your Majestie's occasions, as causes shall require."

2. Sections 16 and 17 are as follow in revised " Propositions " :—

" 16. That an Act of Oblivion be passed in the next free Parliament to extend to all your Majestie's Catholique subjects, and their adherents, for all manner of offences, capitall, criminall, and personall, and the said Act to extend to all goods, and chattles, customes, measne profits, prises, areares of rents taken, received, or incurred since these troubles.

" 17. Forasmuch as your Majestie's said Catholique subjects have been taxed with many inhumane cruelties which they never committed, your Majestie's said supplicants, therefore, for their vindication, and to manifest to all the world their desire to have such heinous offences punished, and the offenders brought to justice, do desire that in the next Parliament all notorious murthers, breaches of quarter, and inhumane cruelties, committed of either side, may be questioned in the said Parliament (if your Majesty so thinke fit), and such as shall appeare to be guilty to be excepted out of the Act of Oblivion, and punished according to their deserts."

3. Matter within brackets omitted in revised " Propositions."

torious murders, cruelties, rapines, and robberies against publique fayth, and such persons as have privately or publiquely in theyr councells or actions joyned against your Majesty with the Rebells at Westminster, and the same to heare and determine according to lawe, honour, and justice ;] and the sayd Act to extend to all goods and chattells, customes, maisne proffits, and prizes, arreares of rents, received or incurred since these troubles.

Forasmuch, dread Soveraigne, as the wayes of our addresse unto your Majesty for apt remedyes unto our greevances was hitherto debarred us, but now at length through your benigne grace and favour layd open, wee therefore,[1] in pursuance of our Remonstrance formerly presented, doe humbly offer these, which graunted, your sayd subjects will readily contribute the ten thousand men, as in the sayd Remonstrance is specifyed, towards the suppressing the unnaturall Rebellion now in this kingdome, and will further expose theyr lives and fortunes to serve your Majesty as occasion shall require.

Endorsed : Irish Agents' Propositions, March the 28, 1644.

XXXVIII. Letter to Ormonde from Supreme Council.

Our very good Lord,—Wee doe not conceive that wee may discharge the trust reposed in us by the Confederat Catholickes, if besides confirming the people of our party in their loyalty and good affeccions to his Majestie's service, wee did not advertise your Lordship how great our feares are, and how just the grounds of them, that many who pretend to serve the King of your party, and have places of high trust and consequence in their commaund, have hollow heartes, and may, to his Majestie's unspeakeable disservice and the ruin of this kingdome, receive the Rebbells now in armes against his Majesty in England into the marittime townes and fortes which they have in their hands.

---

1. In the revised " Propositions," the matter is as follows: " wee doe humbly present these, in pursuance of the said Remonstrance, which granted, your said subjects are ready to contribute the 10,000 men (as in their Remonstrance is specified) towards," etc.

XXXVIII. Carte Papers, x. p. 33.

In the first place, wee do pray your Lordship to have a care of the forte of Doncannon, where the Lord Esmond, whom we suspect to be ready to adheare to the Malignant party of the Parlyament in England, commaunds, and two or three Roundheads, who are gratious with him, are in office.

To confirme this, wee have heard that in discourse with a gentleman, who said it was reported your Lordship had his Majestie's letter to appoint him a successor, he said, that must not be, until hee were paid of all his arreares.

Concearneing Youghall, wee are given to understand that upon reporte of that parte of the Parlyament's fleete, which is under the commaund of the Lord Lile[1] and Grinville[2], their being in Milfordhaven, the towne is devided, som ready to defend it for his Majesty, others to receive the forces prepared for an invasion, and in what condicion the young Earl's[3] affeccions to his Majestie's service do stand, your Lordship best knowes; but wee allway suspected the father and the sonn to be well-wishers to those Rebbells in England.

Corck was, in the absence of the Lord of Insequin, putt into the hands of Sir Hardres Waller, whom most men doe beleeve to be a Roundhead; and the governement of that parte of the province which lyes within your quarters, was intrusted with Sir William Fenton, one of the same cutt. And now the Lord of Insequin is retourned, wee feare the power of Corck and Kinsale may be in a worse hand, for it is reported hee came discontented from Courte. Wee do beseech your Lordship to reflect upon the importance of the places, and to prevent a mischiefe which may be fatall to this kingdome.

Wee understand further, that letters have beene procured out of England, by which one of the Creaghes is appointed Collectour of the Customes within the porte of Lymerick, and that som other (they say the Lord of Broghill) is nomynated Governour of the castle there.

It appeares by the Articles of Cessacion,[4] that the citty of Lymerick

---

1. Lisle. *See* vol. ii. p. 400.   2. Grenville. *See* vol. ii. p. 398.
3. Richard Boyle succeeded his father as Earl of Cork in September, 1643.
4. *See* vol. ii. p. 371, "Articles of Cessation," 1643.

and the county of it are within our quarters; and therefore we pray your Lordship, that way be given to noe act which may violatt the Cessacion. Thus, with our heartyest wishes, wee rest, your Lordshipp's humble servants,

Daniell O'Bryen.—Torl. O'Neille.—Netterville.—Lucas Dillon.— Thomas Cashell.—T. Preston.—Rob. Lynch.—Malachias Tuamensis.— Patr. Darcy.—Geo. Commyn.

Gallway, the 29th of March, 1644.

Endorsed: Lord Ne[tterville],—Supreame Councell att Galway. Dated 29 March, received 14 April, 1644.—Concearning Duncannon, Yeoghall, and Lymbrick, and on Creagh's being made Customer of Lymbrick, etc.

XXXIX. LETTER TO CARDINAL MAZARIN FROM DE LA MONNERIE AT LIMERICK.

Monseigneur,—Ayant receu une lettre de Monsieur le Tellier, dattée du 25e Fevrier, par laquelle il m'accuse du peu de soing que j'ay eu, de ne l'informer pas de toutes les choses que j'avançois dans l'affaire qui m'a este commise, j'ay creu que votre Eminence, Monseigneur, aura peu cognoistre par celles que j'ay pris la liberté de luy escripre, que je n'ay laissé passer aucune occasion sans l'informer de tout ce que j'ay fait, depuis mon arrivée icy. C'est ce qui m'oblige encore à present d'user en celle-cy de redites dans l'appréhension que j'ay que les miennes ne soient pas tombées entre les mains de votre Eminence.

J'ay faict ce qui m'a esté possible pour avoir response de ces Messieurs, lesquels, après beaucoup de remises, m'ont enfin dict qu'ils ne pouvoient permettre la levée que dans le 15ème de Juing,[1] m'allèguant pour leurs raisons qu'ils désiroient sçavoir auparavant de me rien accorder, s'ils seroient en paix ou en guerre avecq leur Roy : et que pour cet effect, ils envoyoient des Agens vers luy, desquels ils ne pouvoient avoir response

XXXIX. Archives des Affaires Étrangères, Paris. Série Angleterre, vol. 51, p. 41.

1. The 25th of June, 1644, was the date mentioned in the order by the Supreme Council in the preceding February. *See* p. 106.

qu'en ce temps là : et qu' aussy ils m'asseuroient que soit qu'ils eussent paix ou guerre, que pour lors, ils m'accorderoient la levée m'ayant donné, pour plus grand asseurance de leur parole, une promesse escripte et signée de leurs mains, de laquelle j'en ay envoyé coppie à votre Eminence par le gentilhomme que Monsieur le Comte d'Harcourt m'avoit envoié avecq la permission du Roy pour la levée de 3000 hommes, ce qui me fait croire que votre Eminence aura receu infailliblement ce pacquet, et qu'elle aura esté pleinement informée de tout ce que j'ay faict.

J'espère aussy qu'en bref j'auray les ordres qu'il luy plaira que j'exécute, remerciant cependant votre Eminence de la bonté qu'elle a eue de commander que l'argent ne me manquast pas. Aussy je la puis asseurer que je ne l'emploieray que fort à propos, vous asseurant, Monseigneur, que s'il y a jour de pouvoir espérer de faire davantage de monde que ce que j'ay demandé au Conseil, j'y travailleray si puissamment que votre Eminence en sera contente. C'est le seul but que je veux avoir, estant, Monseigneur, de votre Eminence le très-humble, très-obeissant, et très-fidèle serviteur et créature,—MONNERIE.

Limeric, 8 Avril, 18 Avril (en France), 1644.

XL. LETTERS FROM AGENTS OF CONFEDERATION AT OXFORD TO RICHARD BELLINGS AND SUPREME COUNCIL, APRIL, 1644.

1. TO THE SUPREME COUNCIL.

Right Honorable,—Our Propositions have been delivered to his Majestie ten dayes since. This day was the first day that wee weare called to any debate concerning them, and wee find that a Comittee of the Board is appointed to heere and debate with us, viz., the Lord Threasurer Cottington, the Earl of Bristoll, the Earl of Portland, the Lord Digby, Secretary Nicholas, and the Master of the Rolls, Sir John Culpeper.

Uppon our coming before them, wee sate with them uppon nine points in particular; and perchance there is a resolution to dispatch mee (sic) speedyly, for they tould mee they would sitt every day at three of the cloack in the afternoone, untill the businesse weare finished. Wee had sent your Lordship a coppy of the Propositions, but that there is much to be said concearning them which [is] not fitt to be written, and which in effect will be properer[1] to come to by one of your number, if this shall come to you by one of our number. If they shall come to you from any of their hands, I presse noe judgement on them untill you see one of us, or heere from us.

Mr. Christopher Bryan, who caryeth this dispatch with him, did accompany mee in our journey hether, and in this place, and did, within the quallity of the imployment wherewith wee weare instructed, all the honnor hee could, for which he doth justly deserve your Lordship thanks and for that, and there is defects best knowne to your Lordship in the publique service of this kingdom, that wee hould him worthy of your favour as your Lordship may conferre on him.

Wee beleeve that very soone your Lordship will have one of our number, and, the meane and allwaies, wee are your Lordship's humble servants,

Muskry.—Nicholas Plunkett.—Geffr. Browne.—Alex.[2] M'Donell.—Robert Talbott.—Dermot[3] O'Brien.

Oxford, April 7th, 1644.

To the Honorable Councell of the Confederate Catholiques.

2. To RICHARD BELLINGS.

Browne and Nick Plunckett setts forth uppon the 7th of Aprill, 1644, that the Earle of Antrim is to be Lieutenant-Generall of ten thousand men to be raysed in Ireland to be sent for England to supresse of Robert, late Earle of Essex, and of other the Rebells in London, though wee had noe notice from thence of any such Commission,[4] or how farr it was with their allowance, them (sic) yett coming of it heere wee thought fitt

---

1. " propurne " in Ms.

2, 3. In the contemporary copies (Carte Papers, x. pp. 100-1) these names are erroneously given as " Henry " and " Petro," instead of Alexander and Dermot. See pp. 65, 86.

4. See page 88.

to signify thither, that you may imploy all your care to prevent the coming of any men from thence untill there be such settlement as you intend to relye on. The Councell was written to formerly as [to] a design the Lord Inchiquin had alsoe to bring men, and hope you will frustrate his purpose therein, for it is that that will give life to your affaires, that your men com not without your consents. Wee have been promised by some of the Earle of Antrim's frends heere that hee will not make use of that Commission untill your occasions heere be concluded.

Wee understand that the Marquis of Ormonde hath written hither to the Lord Digby to advertise him tymely into Ireland if wee shall not agree heere and to send to him a Commission to inable him to warrant the submission of such as will desire it, and to pass them pardons. This is a dangerous way to break our Association.

The last news heere is that Prince Rupert[1] hath raysed the seedge of Newark and gott 4,000 arms; I mentioned that tyme [Sir Ralph] Hopton[2] had a defeat by [Sir William] Waller. His Majestie is now purposeing an army to incounter Waller. This bee all. Wee remaine your affectionate frends and servants,—Nicholas Plunckett.—Geffry Browne.

Oxford, 7th April, 1644.

3. To Richard Bellings.

Sir,—The bearer, Captaine Bryan, will relate unto you all the newse from hence. What concearne our businesse you shall see by our own letters, which is little of any certainety, yet your caracters had been good or my uncle's, any of them, yett not of any certainety, only this, that I can see but little expectacion to come to the heigh of the 5^3 : 6 : 7 : 8 : 9 : 10 : C : 12 x f 3 d : M 2 d 3 95 and therefore consider what is to be don of your side, by way of preparacion against the next dispatch, my uncle

---

1. Newark, in county of Nottingham, relieved by Prince Rupert on 22nd March, 1643-4.—"History of Rebellion and Civil Wars in England." By Edward, Earl of Clarendon. Oxford, 1843, vol. i., p. 476.

2. Clarendon, id. ib. p. 478.

3. The ciphers in this letter have not been interpreted in the Ms.

will teach you to read what followes : Take heed of 15 ; you have reason alredy given to you, and the prosecuteing of an enormous war is worse than the falling into it.   He is frend to f 2, as I heare ; his frends are with 38.   What they doe there I know not, ventt ill stuffe, 18 may give 2 a caution.   The servants of 50 doe all sing one tune in a good consort, and will doe their indeavours to helpe upp 51, but it is hard to doe all at wance. Comend mee and this to the Doctor, my uncle, and your selfe.   Soe I rest, yours etc.—GEFFRY BROWNE.

Oxford, the 10th April, 1644.

Endorsed : 10 April, 1644. Copys of letters to Beling, etc. Brought by Captain Bryan and opened.

XLI. LORD TAAFFE TO ORMONDE.

My Lord,—I knowe you have receaved an accompt from my Lord of Clanriccarde and Jacke Barry what was effected at Gallway concearning my Lord of Antrim.   Since then, I mett his Lordship in the county of Roscomman, where he tould me his resolucion was to poste imediately towardes the north, haveing appointed a randevouse neere Greencastle or Carlingford, about the twentieth of this moneth, for four thousand men intended for Scotland, all necessaryes being prepared for their accomodation but shippeing, which he expects wilbe (by your Lordship's meanes) readdy at those places to receave them, and if there be a fayler, he is confident 'twill not appeare of his parte.   I knowe not what assurance your Lordship might give him for shippeing, but if there be none in a readines (and that your Lordship might procure them) 'tis intended to be represented to his Majestie as a neglect of very great consequence, which I thought myselfe obliged (being solely at your disposall) to signify.   He hath receaved late letters of high expressions of affection and trust both from the King and Queene, which he shewes to all men of considerable condition, and uppon my word, my Lord, that, with his wayes, gaines him noe small opinion amongst the people, he being of theire Counsell and

Association. He tould me he was conjured to comply with your Lordship in all thinges, soe far as the oath was reciprocall, and soe farr as your intentions are bent that way, did I knowe it, my course should stirr noe farther. He was pleased to dirrect fifteen hundred of his men to march through this county, who in my absence destroyed all my tenants, I suppose with permission.

The Scots of Iniskillin and Legan, to the number of six hundred, marched two dayes agon to the borders of this county, and tooke out of the barronyes of Carbrye and Tirerill above two thousand cowes. I receaved a letter this day that Montroe is nowe uppon his march with eight thousand men and Sir Fredericke Hamilton with two thousand. Theire randevous is at Iniskellin, about the twentieth of this moneth, and resolve to march towards Gallway. Owen O'Neyle is come to Clooneis.[1]

My Lord, whether this be trueth or noe, I cannot affirme; yet am certayne the country wilbe destroyed by the very next garrisons of Mannor Hamilton and Ballyshany, if your Lordship prevent it not by proclaymeing them enemyes. 'Tis soe necessary an act, as if neglected, it will be justly supposed your Lordship justifyes theire actions, and if I be not misinformed from my Lord Digby, your Lordship is desired to hinder their proceedings. For my owne parte, my condition is very sadd, being resolved to goe noe wayes, but such as your Lordship will dictate to me : and at this distance, knoweing nothing materiall of your resolucions and howe to be neerer at the present is impossible, haveing noe way of subsistance there, and what I have remayneing here certaynly lost in my absence ; soe as I can determine nothing of myselfe untill I receave your Lordship's advise.

I was yesterday at the Boyle, and haveing sent to Captain Robert Kinge to meete me with his troope, a myle from the towne, he came himselfe alone, and tould me that he could not commande one man of his troope, his brother, Captain Francis Kinge, and Captain Ormsby, haveing seduced them all, by assureing them all of the immediate advance of the Scots, who weare (as they affirme) the only presarvars of honesty and religion. Uppon this scare, most of the garrisons of that county expect

1. Clones, in county of Monaghan. *See* "Contemporary History of Affairs in Ireland, 1641-1652." Dublin : 1879, vol. iii. p. 202.

but an opportunitie to declare themselves.   All this was confirmed to me by Capten Robert Kinge, and desired me to intimate it to your Lordship with all expedition, with protestacions that he means nothing by it, but his Majestie's service, and disavowes all malice to the persons of the people.

I receaved a letter from Prince Rupert[1] to solicitt the Counsell at Gallway for the sending him four thousand musketts and two hundred barrells of powder, which I could not obtaine, nor any part thereof, though earnestly indevored by offering my estate for repayment.   A letter from them to him, signifying my willingnes to procure those armes and an excuse from myselfe, I herewith send your Lordship, which I begg you will transmitt to his Highnes with the first conveniency.

I have writt to Mr. Lane concearneing some injuryes donn me in the county of Lowth by my Lord Moore and one Sheriffe Townsly, for which I expect present reparacion from your Lordship.

I sentt your Lordship, by a servant of myne, a letter and severall complaintes from the Commissioners of the county of Roscomman, and though your Lordship sent downe instructions for reformacion, they are not put in execution.   Your Lordship omitted the giveing any answeare to the Commissioners, which is consterred [construed] as a neglect of them.   I pray, my Lord, to satisfy them, (if you thinke it fitt,) give them some accompt of it, for too much reservednes lessens the people's affections.

I am nowe come home,[2] and though I doe not drinke, yet am madder than ever I was, and shall continue soe untill I kiss your Lordship's handes as your humblest and most faithfull servant,—[TAAFFE].—13 April, 1644.

My Lord, since the writeing of this letter, Sir Fredericke Hamilton[3] is certainely come with two thousand foote to Manor Hamilton, with resolucion to destroy all that comes in his way : and your Lordship's assurance of theire not attempting this mischiefe is the occation of much hazard to the kingdome generally, who supposed your Lordship as much or more concearned in the presarvation of it than all the kingdome besides, and

1. *See* p. 87.
2. This letter bears no note of the place where it was written, which was probably Lord Taaffe's castle at Ballymote, co. Sligo.
3. *See* vol. ii. p. lxvii.

that occationed most men to neglect theire owne securityes, and me soe much, as, at this present, though I expect an assault every hower, I am not very well provided of anythinge, but will maintaine this place for three months against all Rebells in Christendom.

Endorsed : A coppie of my Lord Taaffe's letter to my Lord Liuetenant, the 13th of Aprill, 1644.

XLII. Letter from Louis XIV. to Supreme Council of Irish Confederation.

Lettre du Roy au Sieurs du Conseil d'Irlande, du xviiime Avril, 1644.

Tres-chers et bons amis,—Nous avons appris avec beaucoup de contentement les bonnes paroles que vous avez données au Sieur de Moynerie sur la permission que il vous a demandée en nostre nom pour la levée de deux mille hommes de pied en Irlande ; mais comme Nous voyons par sa lettre que vous avez remit[1] à luy donner ladite permission au 15 du mois de Juin prochain, Nous avons esté obligez de vous faire cette seconde lettre, par l'advis de la Reyne Regente, nostre tres-honorée Dame et Mère, [pour vous prier] de ne la pas differer davantage, d'autant que, si elle n'est faicte dans peu de temps, Nous ne pouvons pas esperer d'en recevoir, de toute cette année, aucun service, et que aussy il n'y a pas d'apparence que l'advance d'un mois de temps puisse causer aucun prejudice à vos affaires, pour le bien desquelles Nous vous asseurerons que nous contribuerons tousjours de bon cœur tout ce qui sera en nostre pouvoir, attendant de vous l'effect des bonnes dispositions que vous Nous avez tesmoigné en cette occasion, dont nous avons beaucoup de ressentiment avec la Reyne, nostre Dame et Mère, sur quoy nous remettons au dit Sieur de Moynerie de ce que Nous pourrions vous dire de plus particulier. Nous m'adjousterons ren à cette lettre que pour prier Dieu que il vous ayt, tres-chers et bons amis, en sa sainte garde.

Escrit à Paris, le xviiime Avril, 1644.   Louis.

Le Tellier.

XLII. Papiers de Michel Le Tellier.—Bibliothèque Nationale, Paris. Ms. No. 4,179, fol. 101.   1. *See* p. 135.

XLIII. Propositions to Charles I. from Agents at Oxford for Protestants in Ireland, April, 1644.

1. Wee humbly desire the establishment of the true Protestant religion in Ireland, according to the Lawes and Statutes in the said kingdom now in force.

2. That the Popish titular archbishops, bishops, Jesuites, fryers, and priests, and all others of the Roman clergy bee banished out of Ireland, because they have ever been the stirrers of all rebellions, and while they continue there, there can be no hope of safety for your Majestie's Protestant subjects; and that all the Lawes and Statutes established in that kingdome against Popery and Popish recusants may continue in force, and be put in execution.

3. That restitution may bee made of all our churches and church rights and revenues, and all our churches and chappels reedified, and put in as good estate as they were at the breaking out of the Rebellion, and as they ought to be, at the charge of the Confederate Roman Catholiques (as they call themselves) who have been the occasion of the destruction of the said churches, and possessed themselves of the profits and revenues thereof.

4. That the Parliament now sitting in Ireland, may bee continued there for the better settlement of the kingdome, and that all persons duly indicted in the said kingdome, of treason, felony, or other heynous crimes, may be duly and legally proceeded against, outlawed, tryed, and adjudged according to law, and that all persons lawfully convicted and attainted, or so to be convicted or attainted for the same, may receive due punishment accordingly.

5. That no man may take upon him or execute the office of Mayor or Magistrate in any Corporation, or the office of a Sheriffe, or Justice of

---

XLIII. "The Humble Propositions of the Agents for the Protestants in Ireland (residing at Oxford) presented to his Majesty the 18 of April, 1644, in pursuance of the petition of the Protestant subjects in Ireland. London: 1644.—Published according to order."

Peace, in any city or county in the said kingdome, untill he hath first taken the oathes of supremacie and allegiance.

6. That all Popish lawyers who refuse to take the oaths of supremacie and allegiance, may be suppressed and restrained from practise in that kingdome, the rather because the lawyers in England doe not here practise untill they take the oath of supremacie: and it hath been found by wofull experience, that the advise of the Popish lawyers to the people of Ireland hath been a great cause of their continued disobedience.

7. That there may bee a present absolute suppression and dissolution of all the assumed arbitrary and tyrannicall power, which the said Confederates exercise over your Majestie's subjects, both in causes ecclesiasticall and temporall.

8. That all armes and ammunition of the said Confederates, be speedily brought into your Majestie's stoares.

9. That your Majestie's Protestant subjects, ruined and destroyed by the said Confederates, may be repayred for their great losses, out of the estates of the said Confederates, not formerly by any Acts of this present Parliament in England otherwise disposed of, whereby they may be the better enabled to reinhabit and defend the said kingdome of Ireland.

10. That the Confederates may rebuild the severall Plantations, houses and castles, destroyed in Ireland, in as good estate as they were at the breaking out of this Rebellion, which your Majestie's Protestant subjects have been bound by their severall patents to build and maintaine for your Majestie's service.

11. That the great arreares of rents due to your Majestie out of the estates of your Majestie's Protestant subjects, at and since Michaelmasse 1641, may bee payd unto your Majesty by such of the said Confederates, who have either received the said rents to the uses of the said Confederates, or destroyed the same by disabling your Majestie's Protestant subjects to pay the same, and have also destroyed all, or the most part of all other rents and meanes of support belonging to your said Protestant subjects, may be discharged of all such arreares of rents to your Majestie.

12. That the said Confederates may give satisfaction to the army of the great arrerages due unto them since the Rebellion, and that such

commanders as have raised forces at their owne charges, and layd forth great summes of ready money out of their owne purses, and engaged themselves for money and provisions, to keepe themselves, their houlds, and souldiers under their command in the due and necessary defence of your Majestie's rights and lawes, may be in due sort satisfied, to the encouragement of others in like times and cases which may happen.

13. That touching such part of the said Confederates estates as being forfeited for their treasons, and come, or shall come into your Majestie's hands and possession by that title, your Majestie, after due satisfaction made to such as claime by former Acts of Parliament, would be pleased to take the same into your own hands and possession, and for the necessary increase of your Majestie's revenue, and better security of your said kingdome of Ireland, and Protestant subjects living under your gracious government there, to plant the same with Brittish and Protestants upon reasonable and honourable terms.

14. That one good walled towne may bee built and kept repayred in every county of the said kingdome of Ireland, and endowed and furnished with necessary and sufficient meanes of legall and just government and defence, for the better security of your Majestie's lawes and rights, more especially the Protestant religion, in times of danger; in any of which townes no Papist may be permitted to dwell or inhabit.

15. That for the better satisfaction of justice, and your Majestie's honour, and for the further security of the said kingdome, and your Majestie's Protestant subjects there, exemplary punishment according to law, may be inflicted upon such as have there traiterously levied warre, and taken up armes against your Majestie's Protestant subjects and lawes, and therein against your Majestie, and especially upon such as have had their hands in the shedding of innocent blood, or had to doe with the first plot or conspiracy, or since that time have done any notorious murther, or overt acts of treason.

16. That all your Majestie's townes, forts, and places of strength destroyed by the said Confederates since the said Rebellion, may be by them, and at their charges, reedefied and delivered up into your Majestie's hands, to be duly put into the government (under your Majestie and your lawes)

of good Protestants, and that all strengths and fortifications made and set up by the said Confederates since the said Rebellion, may be sleighted and throwne down, or else delivered up and disposed of for Protestant government and security, as aforesaid.

17. That according to the presidents of former times in cases of generall Rebellion in Ireland, the attainders which have been duly had by outlawry for treason done in this Rebellion, may be established and confirmed by Act of Parliament, to be in due forme of law transmitted and passed in Ireland ; and that such traytours as, for want of Protestant and indifferent jurors to indict them in the proper counties, are not yet indicted nor convicted or attainted by outlawry or otherwise, may upon due proofe of their offences, be by like Act of Parliament convicted and attainted, and all such offendors to forfeit their estates as to law appertaineth ; and your Majesty to be adjudged and put in possession without any office or inquisition to be had.

18. That your Majestie's Protestant subjects may be restored to the quick possession of all their castles, houses, mannors, lands, tenements, hereditaments and leases, and to the quick possession of the rents therof, as they had the same before and at the time of the breaking forth of this Rebellion, and from whence, without due processe and judgement of law, they have since then bin put out or kept out, and may be answered of and for all the meane profits of the same in the interim ; and for all the time untill they shall be so restored.

19. That your Majestie's Protestant subjects may also be restored to all their moneys, plate, jewels, household stuffe, goods, and chattles whatsoever, which without due processe or judgement in law, have by the said Confederates bin taken or detayned from them since the contriving of the said Rebellion, which may be gayned in kinde or the full value thereof, if the same may not be had in kinde, the like restitution to be made for all such things which during the said time have beene delivered to any person or persons of the said Confederates in trust to be kept and preserved, but are by colour thereof still withholden.

20. That the establishment and maintenance of a competent Protestant army, and sufficient Protestant souldiers and forces, for the time to come, in

Ireland, be speedily taken into your Majestie's prudent, just and gracious consideration, and such course layd down and continued therin, according to the rules of good government, that your Majestie's rights and laws, and the Protestant religion and peace of that kingdome be no more endangered by the like Rebellions in time to come.

21. That whereas it appeareth in print that the said Confederats amongst other things aime at the repealing of Poynings' Law, thereby to open an easy and ready way for the passing of Acts of Parliament in Ireland, without having them first well considered in England, which may produce many dangerous consequents both to that kingdome, and to your Majestie's other dominions ; your Majesty would be pleased to resent and reject all propositions tending to introduce so great a diminution of your royall and necessary power for the confirmation of your royall estate and protection of your good Protestant subjects both there and elsewhere.

22. That your Majesty, out of your grace and favour to your Protestant subjects of Ireland, will be pleased to consider effectually of assuring them, that you will not give order for, or allow of transmitting into Ireland any Act of generall oblivion, release or discharge of actions or suits whereby your Majestie's said Protestant subjects there may be barred or deprived of any of those legall remedies which by your Majestie's lawes and statutes of that kingdome, they may have against the said Confederates or any of them, or any of their party, for, or in respect of any wrongs done unto them, or any of their ancestors or predecessors, in or concerning their lives, liberties, persons, goods, or estates, since the contriving or breaking forth of the said Rebellion.

23. That some fit course may be considered of to prevent the filling or overlaying of the Commons House of Parliament in Ireland, with Popish Recusants being ill affected members, and that provision may be duly made that none shall vote or sit therein, but such as shall first take the oathes of allegiance and supremacy.

24. That the prooffes and manifestations of the truth of the severall matters conteyned in the petition of your Majestie's Protestant subjects of Ireland, lately presented to your Majesty, may be duly examined and

discussed, and in that respect the finall conclusion of things respited for a convenient time, their agents being ready to attend with their prooffes in that behalfe as your Majestie shall appoint.

XLIV. LETTER TO ORMONDE FROM COLONEL JOHN BARRY.

My very good Lord,—These inclosed papers will give your Lordships the best accoumpt of what I have don at Gallwaye ; more I could not doe thoughe I wanted neither importunitie or impudence, and towards beinge soe (it may be) drinke was sometymes necessarie, as it was to molifie and incline to kindnes the hard hartes of some of the members of the greate Councell.

I am nowe upon my journie to Kilkennye to observe the necessarie instructions aunciently prescribed by honnest Iago. Some newe (and, as they call it, more probable) directions, I have to prevaile for the thous[1] . . I formerly write to your Lordship, James Gale . . . convaye to Dublin, but he fayled, and soe did advertise me at Gallwaye, which, upon sechound solicitation, produced this newe order from the Councell.

I have alsoe obtayned two thousand pounds weight of powder more, in addition to what M'Gragh had, but they are very scruplous it should be knowen that they have assented unto it, whether because they have dennyed Prince Ruperte, or in respect of some of theire owne partie, I knowe not ; but they have injoyned me secrecie, and desire your Lordship to appointe some one of theire party to recave it and to convaye it privately to you, which the sooner it is don the better, for, as it was well observed by a good authore not longe since, Councells may alter, and soe may this, as often withoute as with reason. Remember Oportunitie has but one locke. These men's magazines are not well stored as the world beleeves ; though dispersed and confused upp and downe the kingedome there is great plenty of all kinde of armes and amunicion but not all together within thire powre. I have caused Belinge by order from the Councell to contracte with a marchante that was then goeinge to sea with two friggatts loaden from hence to bring in five thousand armes, and five hundred bar-

XLIV. Carte Papers, x. p. 181.   1. Defects in Ms. indicated thus . . .

rells of powder, and have ingaged myselfe that your Lordshipe would take off all that they would not make use of for ready monny or good comodities at reasonable or moderate rates. The assignement for my Lord Esmonde is satisfied, and your bonde for the powder to the Dutchman taken, in bothe which I am promised as soone as I come to Killkenny.   I doubt the monny designed for Sir Phillipe Percivall is all gon to satisfie some of them, soe as your Lordshipe moust thinke of some other waye of paymente for him.

I have heere togither with the reste sente your Lordshipe the Confederate Secretarie's letter to me receaved this morninge, by which you maye see howe much the Scotch advancement is apprehended by them, and where they would conceave partly the blame should lye, but that is without reason, as I beleeve for my parte much of their feares to be without grounde, thoughe it may be the beinge of my Lord of Castlehaven heere with a peece of an armie maye occasion the Scotes to drawe to a bodie fearing an attempt upon them and soe advance to the borders of thire owne confines with a purpose to defend themselves rather then with any intention to invade them soe early in the yeare, when all thinges are soe unseasonable in this country for marches especyally with the body of a greate armie, as they conceave them to be.   But what may be don either for the safety of the kingdom or for the fittinge satisfaction and preservation of these people I knowe (soe far as it stands with judgment and providence) will not be by your Lordship neglected therefore I will press it noe further thoughe I am importuned by diverse to doe it only thus much I humbly conceave maye be don, in case the Scotes should advance into this province those of the king's partie maye have comision to joyne with the other in the common deffence of the countrie; and without som . . . or such comision from your Lordship I doe not finde . . . will stirr, thoughe thire owne particulare suffer in it without distinction except such as joyne with the Scotes, soe as a conditionall comision maye be given, which will very much unite the province togither, for I finde my Lord of Clanrickarde has a greater influence upon the people heere then any body, and did he appeare in any quarrell wherin they are soe farr ingaged they would moste of them all unanimously flocke to him and serve under him sooner then any other; I will not trouble you with the relation of the Marques (as he is called heere) of Antrim's proceedinges, only tell you that a good peece of battery is much more powerfull to take in a castle than is his Lordshipe's oratorie, for it was one of his undertakeings to the Councell upon the signinge of his commision, that he would take in or would be yeelded at first sight unto him, all the refractorie castles in this province for that they were all held for him and by such as in obedience to him would surrender them. But the truth is, upon his Lordshipe's summons, noe one castle would surrender, thoughe he attempted divers, so as in conclusion he was forced to write to the Councell to prosecute them for enymies for he could doe noe good upon them. Litle Castle-Haven has since taken three or four of the most considerable of them. My Lord of Mayo absentes himselfe from the Councell, and is thought to run to the Scotes, or at least to be conspireinge theire draweinge in to this province ; Castlehaven will leave him never a house to entertayne his guests . . . he be not diverted by them. My Lord, my Lord of Clanrickard will informe you more particularly of much of this busines, soe as it will be tyme for me to conclude myselfe, my Lord, your Lordship's moste faythfull and most humble servant,—John Barry.

Portumna, the 18th of Apprill, 1644.

XLV. PROCLAMATION BY SUPREME COUNCIL OF CONFEDERATION ON LEAGUE WITH HOLLAND, APRIL, 1644.

A Proclamacion against such as would breake the League betweene the Hollander and the Confederate Catholickes.

By the Supreame Councell, etc.

Whereas divers persons, either out of ignorance of the condicion wee stand in with forraigne States in amity with his Majestie, or out of privat ends to advance theire proper benefitt and lucre, without respect to the common good, doe whisper and give out that the States of Hol-

XL. Ms. " Register Book of Letters " of Supreme Council of Confederation.

land are declared enemyes of the Confederat Catholickes of Ireland, thereby to incouradge desperat and disaffected persons to attempt some act that might decline the good correspondencye hitherto entertained amonge us, to the great and universall prejudice of the trafique and navigacion of this kingdome. To prevent, therefore, the mischeefes which might arise from the want of a right understandinge of our sence heereof, wee thought fitt to establish and declare, and by these presents doe publish and declare, that the States of Holland are now in league and amitye with our Sovereigne Lord the Kinge, and us, his most faithfull subjects, and, therefore, wee doe expressly forbidd all his Majestie's subjects of the Confederat Catholickes of Ireland from attemptinge anythinge or useinge any act of hostilitye against any of the faithfull subjects of the said State that doe or will trafique amonge us in any of the portes of our partie, under paine of the penaltye encurred by the lawes and statutes of this kingdome uppon the infringers and disturbers of the publicke peace.—Given at Galway, the 20th of April, 1644.

XLVI. Correspondence between Ormonde, Supreme Council of Confederation, Richard Bellings, etc., April, 1644.

1. Letter to Ormonde from Supreme Council.

Our very good Lord,—Wee have, since the conclusion of the Cessacion, behaved ourselves with that regarde and observance of the Articles of Cessacion that nothinge of moment can be alleadged wherein our partie hath transgressed. But, of the other side, wee have suffred soe much by the hostile actions of some garrisons in Connaght, that wee cannot say they ever intended to have submitted to that Cessacion. Heereof many complaints hath beene made unto your Lordship, and the redress hath neither answered your Lordship's desire nor ours. And, to add to our partie's daylie sufferings by them, upon the 25th of March last, the garrison of Iniskillin preyed Manus M'Donnell, James Mergagh, Bernard M'Ward, Coole M'Cahir, and Hugh Buy, and all theire tenants and followers; tooke away two thowsand foureskore and tenn cowes, three hundred horses and mares ; stript three thowsand men, woemen, and children, tooke away such armes and pilladge as they had, and retourned in triumph ; soe as now soe many Christians have nothinge to live upon but grass, and nothinge to cloath them but hay. Those are the wordes of the intelligence wee received from a shure hand.

Wee did, by our letters to the Lords Justices in December last, desire not only theire countenance but the assistance of his Majestie's forces, against such as wanted but an oportunitye to declare themselves publicklye against his Majestie, and to doe us a mischeefe ; and wee further prayed that our said letters might be transmitted unto his Majestie, but wee found noe benefitt by that sollicitacion, by meane whereof soe many Christians are like to perish with famine.

Wee knowe your Lordship, who, by his Majestie's authoritye, did conclude uppon the Cessacion, will endevour to preserve it inviolable, and commaund that restitucion be made of the cattle, and the people satisfied for their other losses. But wee beleeve those who did adventure uppon soe publicke and high a breach of the Cessacion, did it not with intencion to submitt themselves to your Lordship's directions ; and, therefore, wee pray your Lordship, as you tender the good of his Majestie's service, to thinke of a way how these men's bad intencions may be best mett with, and his Majestie's good subjects preserved from theire mallice, wherein none shall shew themselves more forward in defence of his Majestie's interests, nor none more reddy to concurr with your Lordship in resolucions that tend thereunto than your Lordship's most humble servants,

Thomas [Walsh, Archbishop of] Cashel.—Malachias [O'Queely] Tuamensis.—Nettervill—John [Bourke, Bishop of] Clonfert.—T. Preston.—Daniel O'Brien.—Rob. Lynch.—Torlogh O'Neill.— Patrick Darcy.—Gerald Fenell.—George Commyn.

Galway, the 5th of Aprill, 1644.

For his Excellence, the Marquess of Ormonde, Lord Liftenant of Ireland. Haste.

2. Bellings to Ormonde.

i. My Lord,—By commaunde of the Councell heere, I doe send unto your Lordship the inclosed,[1] which came unto them from those gentlemen who are intrusted with the mannadgment of the affaires of the county of Cork. They have heretofore advertised your Lordship of their suspition that the Mallignant party had correspondence with some men of power in Mounster, and they desired the townes, and strong holts within your quarters there, might be putt into men's hands of undoubted good affeccions to his Majestie's service. Now their feares do multiply upon them, by this intelligence, comeing from those men whom they have good reason to beleeve, in a matter that most concearnes that parte of the province, where their charge lyes. The Counsell, therefore, do pray your Lordship to apply a tymely remedy to a disease of so dangerous consequence, and that the sooner, because thirty sayles of the Parlyament shipping, as they are informed, do hover about that coast. I am, my Lord, your Lordship's most humble servant,—R. Bellings.

Gallway, the 10th of Aprill, 1644.

ii. My Lord—Havinge performed my duty, in obeying the commands of the Counsell heer, and written theyre sence of the state of that parte of the province of Mounster which lies within your quarters, I have presumed (first, making use of the Articles of Cessation, and letting your Lordship know I am Dick Bellings still) to tell your Lordship from him that I apprehend the haughtiness and ambition of the Lord of Insequin, who hath continually before his eyes those services of his in Mounster, which as he values to that height that he thinkes theer scarse can be a rewarde found for him, which may save you from the blemishe of ingratitude, so he hath a various unsettled witt, that easely will carry him upon any designe, which may give his hoopes roome to play in, and open a way to the naturall but ungratious sweetness of revendg ; and he hath a spiritt that will not intangell itself with the thooght of danger. This nobleman, as

1. Not in Ms.

well by the cheyf commaund you have given him within your quarters in Mounster, as by the leisure he hath had to place such men in the forts of Coorke, Kinsall, and other maritime places, as will runn the same fortune with him, hath made himself considerable unto, and to be looked upon by the Parlament as a man in whoos hands it lies to facilitate their designs. Besides, my Lord, I am not satisfied with my Lord of Keerie's stay in London. Keery is a country full of harbors and havens, and towards the land fortified with rocks and mountaines, and thees two Lords may have or may be invited to have, the same thooghts and booth concurr to be adverse to his Majestie's intrests. And further, my Lord, in a man not unmindfull of his discent, and full of the thooght of his owne merits, as my Lord of Insequin, theer may be some smacke of envy at your Lordship's advancement, and a deep sence of the sloe pase he followes you.

Thus, my Lord, your Lordship sees I have written my mind with that freedom which your Lordship's allowance and approbation for many years did habituat in me. The enclosed was given me by an understanding gentleman, and versed in the affayres of Mounster, which for your further information I send unto your Lordship.

Yesterday the Counsell heer receaved a certaine notice that upon the arivall of seaven ships with arms, amunition, and victuall, sent by the Parlamentaries of London, at Carrigfergus, the Scots weer appointed a generall randevouse, and that since they have past the Band [Bann], in a body. The truth is, my Lord, you may make accoumpt your Lordship cannot lay your finger upon four sound men of thoos that pretended to be of your party in Ulster; so as your Lordship hath on all sides much to provide for in the execution, whereof I pray God in Heaven to assist you and preserve your Lordship and my Lord to be a comfort to each other and thoos very hoopfull blessings the ties of the affection between you. I am, My Lord, your Lordship's most humble servant,— R. BELLINGS.

Galway, this 10 of Aprill, 1644.

3. Letter to Ormonde from Supreme Council.

Our very good Lord,—By our letters of the 7th of March last, wee did acquaint your Lordship how much wee were greeved that it lay not in our power to gratifie Prince Rupert,[1] with those armes and amunicion which his Highnes desired of us, and for which your Lordship did make offer of payment out of the moneys graunted to his Majestie by our Commissioners that treated uppon the Cessation. Soe as wee have cause to feare those letters òf ours came not into your Lordship's hands, and beinge not able now to retourne your Lordship any other answer ; wee pray your Lordship to rest assured, that if it lay within our power to satisfye Prince Rupert's desire in this, wee would reddely have donn it, beinge sure thereby as well to pleasure his Highness, who hath donn very good offices in behalfe of this nation, as to dischardge parte of the remaine of the moneys due to his Majestie. Thus, with our hearty wishes unto your Lordship, wee rest your Lordship's servants,

Thomas [Walsh, Archbishop of] Cashel.—Netterville.—Rob : Lynch. —Gerald Fenell.—George Commyn.—Daniel O'Brien.—Torlogh O'Neill.— Patrick Darcy.

Galway, the 15th of Aprill, 1644.

4. Ormonde to Bellings.

After our harty commendacions : Wheras we have heretofore understood that Captain Daniell Treswell, being before the late Cessation taken prisoner by Lawrence Shurlock, was, upon bond of £2,000 given by Phillip Fitz Garrold, set at liberty upon condition that if the said Treswell were not redeemed by exchange or ransome before the first of August last, then the said bond to be in force. And wheras not only one Crips, then prisoner in this Castle of Dublin, was (as we have been informed) upon like bond sett at liberty in exchange for the said Treswell before the said first of August last, but allsoe that after the tyme of the said Treswell's being taken prisoner, amongst other Articles of the late Cessation, it was concluded and accorded that all prisoners and hostages of both sides in all

1. *See* p. 87, letter from Prince Rupert.

parts of this kingdome (except such as were then indicted of any capitall offence) should be mutually released and sett at liberty within seaven dayes after publication of the said Cessation : Now ther haveing been humble complaint made unto us by the said Captain Treswell that notwithstanding both the said exchange perfected as aforesaid, and notwithstanding allsoe the cleare intention of the said Article of Cessation, yet the said Fitz Garrald hath not his said bond cancelled, or delivered unto him as we conceive very reasonable and just that he should.   Wee doe therfore hereby thinke fitt to recommend the redress of this complaint unto you, that, for the reasons aforesaid, the said Fitz Garrald may receive noe prejudices by colour or pretence of the said bond, nor have any suit commenced against him there in that behalf, he being of our party and within our quarters, but may have the same forthwith cancelled or returned unto him as is desired. And soe wee rest, from his Majestie's Castle of Dublin, 15 April, 1644, your very loveing freind,—ORMONDE.

5. BELLINGS TO ORMONDE.

My Lord,—Yours of the second of Apriell I receaved, wherby I finde that the answere to your Lordship's letters of the fift of March, signed by the Councell here, came not into your Lordship's hands that day, but I am confident it hath beene since that tyme presented unto you by the conveyance of Mr. James Salle, who promised me both to have it speedily sent, and by his owne letters to sett forth the particulers of the course was taken for a speedy supply to your Lordship.   What I am directed to give in answere to your Lordship's letter of the second of Apriell, is no other, than what the Councell have formerly written, in their letters upon that subject and will appeare more particularly by the answeres given to some proposicions in your Lordship's behalfe made, by Collonell John Barry, wherein they sett forth that the Earle of Castlehaven hath in charge from them to compell the refractories of this province to bring in the moneys due for the beoves ; that Collonell John Butler, in Leinster, and Lieutenante-Gennerall Purcell, in Mounster, are comaunded by cess of horse and foote upon the delinquents to force them to pay the remayne of what is due upon them ;

and that they have further given order to Mr. Piers Roothe of Kilkenny appointed receavor of the moneys levyed for the extraordinary charges of the army designed for the Ulster expedicion, to lett Mr. Henry Archer have one thousand pounds sterling of the moneys which shall come into his hands to be sent unto your Lordship.

This, my Lord, is the accompt I can give your Lordship of that matter by which the great care of the Councell here, and their willingness to do what possibly they may to furnish his Majestie's occasions, is manifest, and they desire your Lordship wilbe pleased to consider favourably thereof. I am, my Lord, your Lordship's most humble servant,—R. BELLINGS.

Gallway, the 15th of Aprill, 1644.

6. LETTERS TO ORMONDE FROM SUPREME COUNCIL.

i. Our very good Lord,—Collonell John Barry, hath in your Lordship's name beene very earnest with us[1] to furnish speedily the Earle of Antrym with the armes, ammunicion, and oatemeale promised for the furtherance of a designe in the Isles of Scotland tending much to the advauncement of his Majestie's service. And wee, who in the graunt of them, laid aside the consideracion of our wants, when his Majestie's interests were so highly concearned in so small a supply, do still with the same fervour endeavour there should be no failer on our partes, as wee presume there will not, and wee desire your Lordship that, according the offer made by the Earle of Antrym and his accord with us, a convenient place may be provided for the receaveing and safe keeping of them, and speedy notice sent unto us, what that place is, and how secured. Thus, with our hartyest wishes unto your Lordship, we rest, your Lordship's humble servants,

1. This letter is endorsed : " Earle of Castlehaven and others. Dated 17 Aprill, received 4 May, 1644. By a footman."—In the same Ms. (Carte Papers, vol. x. p. 249) is a contemporary copy of this letter, in which the signature of Thomas, Archbishop of Cashel, appears instead of that of the Archbishop of Tuam ; Lord Netterville's for that of Lord Castlehaven and Audley ; and George Commyn's for that of Patrick Darcy. The endorsement is as follows : " Copy of the letter of the Lord Netterville and others, which was torne and sent back to Colonel Barry in his letter, the 26th of Aprill, 1644."

Malachias [O'Queely] Tuamensis. — Castlehaven, Audley. — John [Bourke, Bishop of] Clonfert.—Daniel O'Brien.—Rob. Lynch.—Richard Bellings.—Torlogh O'Neill.—Patrick Darcy.—Gerald Fenell.

Gallway, the 17th of Aprill, 1644.

Lord Lieutenante.

ii. My Lord,—I write by commaund of the Counsell here, who, haveing understood by Collonell John Barry how desirous your Lordship was to have two thousand weight of powder, to be imployed upon some present and pressing occasion in his Majestie's service, have given way that your Lordship should be supplyed with that quantity of powder out of their magazin at Waterford, to be allowed in parte payment of such moneys as do remaine due upon them, although they might retourne a just excuse, that their store for the present doth not equall their occasions. I am, my Lord, your Lordship's humble servant,—R. BELLINGS.

Gallway, the 17th of Apriell, 1644.

iii. Our very good Lord,—What at all tymes wee did apprehend to be the greatest danger which might befall the kingdome, in this tyme of Cessation, is now come to pass, and your Lordship hath beene abused by trecherous people, who made use of your desire to serve his Majestie by keepinge them within those bounds of loyaltye, which they would perswade your Lordship they had sett to themselves, athough those of our partie, in manifest breach of the Cessacion, did often feele the sadd beginings of these theire malitious attempts, and that many complayments have beene made thereof. While wee stood in suspence, and durst not adventure uppon them because they were still kept within the protection of the Articles of Cessacion, they have had leisure to growe uppon us, and now, being releivd from the Rebbells in England, Sir Fredericke Hamilton is advanced with two thowsand foote and some horse as farr as Mannor Hamilton, and Monroe is to martch with his armye, as wee finde by certaine intelligence, whereof wee thought fitt to give your Lordship tymelye notice, to the end wee may knowe in what condicion they stand in your Lordshipp's esteeme, and whether his Majestie's Protestant subjects, be not in the same danger with us and what ayde wee may expect from your Lordship, at what tyme and in what place.

Wee conceive them to be our common enemyes, and doe desire they should be repelled with our joynt endeavours. Wee expect your Lordshipp's speedy answer, and doe rest your Lordship's servants,

Netterville.—John [Bourke, Bishop of] Clonfert) —Daniel O'Brien.— Rob. Lynch.—George Commyn.—R. Bellings.—Torlogh O'Neill.—Gerald Fenell.

Galway, the 17th of Aprill, 1644.

For his Excellency the Marquess of Ormonde, Lord Liftenant of Ireland. Haste, haste, haste.

7. ORMONDE TO BELLINGS.

i. After our hearty commendacions: Wee have thought fitt to send you this inclosed peticion to peruse, which doth express the greevance of of Mr. William Buckley, Clerke, and shall desire that a present course may bee taken whereby hee may reape the benefitt of the articles of Cessacion in the quiet enjoyment of his lands mencioned in his petition, of which wee expect due performance. And soe wee remayne from his Majestie's Castle of Dublin, the 18th of April, 1644, your loveing frend,

ORMONDE.

ii. The peticion of William Buckely, Clerke : That your peticioner, conceiveing his lands of Donlavan to be wholy or most parte of it in the county of Dublin, and keeping continuall possession thereof by some of his tenants and servants, under your Honour's protecccion peticioned your Honour that some course might be taken to free his lands and tenants from all exaccions and payments to the Irish. Whereupon your Honour was pleased first to wryte to Collonell Hugh M'Phelim Byrne, and afterwards in January last (because there was noe Commissioners for the county ot Wickloe, and that there was noe other cause but this requireing Commissioners) to direct your order to the Commissioners of the county of Kildare, to consider of your suppliant's peticion, and to give such order for his releife as as should bee just and according to the Articles of Cessacion. Yet, so it is, may it please your Honour, that though Sir John Hay and Mr. Henry Warren, Commissioners for the English, waited often att the place and tymes appointed, yet the Irish Commissioners would not meete, but sent your petitioner word that they could not meddle with this business without a spetiall direccion from theyr Councell. By which delay your petitioner's whole land lyeth wast and is lyke soe to doe, noe tenant dareinge to venture uppon it, by reasons of such exaccions and arreares which the Irish clayme thereout. May it, therefore please your Honour to direct your Honour's letters to the Grand Councell of the Irish att Kilkenny to take examinacion of the petitioner's cause, and to yeeld him such releife as the articles of Cessacion require, that his land may bee manured, to the benefitt of the common weale. And, etc.

8. ORMONDE TO BELLINGS AND FENELL.

Sir,—You may perceive by this inclosed[1] how shipping which was like to bee the greatest want for the Iland expedicion doth most opportunely offer itselfe, and may bee now had upon the certainety, expressed in the letter which you are instantly to procure, if provisions and armes bee ready, and I shall bee content that out of the moneyes alredy due, the fraight which shall be agreed to bee paide, bee satisfied, or if any other security or bond shall be desired from mee, eyther by engaginge his Majestie's Customes or any lands, or frends of mine in the contry for the securinge of those who shall bee bound, I will most redyly doe it. I doe presse this the more earnestly at this tyme, because the Marquess Huntley, and a strong partie in Scottland, are allready risen for the King, who have taken Aberdine, and some other places of importance; which hath already wrought that good effect, that the Marquess of Argile is sent from the Scottish army, which marched towards Newcastle, to raise forces to make head against the Marquess. If those men who are now in preparacion, and wilbe ready, as the Earle of Antrim writeth, by the last of this moneth

---

1. Not in Ms.

to bee shipped, beyond which hee saith, hee shall not bee able to keepe them, bee sent away in tyme, it may occasion diversions of the Scottish forces out of England, and from hence more than if you could imploy 10,000 men in this kingdome against them ; and nothing that you can thinke of will advance your agents' busines more in England, and work more security for yourselves at home, than this service, soe it be done in tyme. But if the party now in armes should be suppressed before those men were sent, the hope of that service is blasted. I can say noe more, but that I am your very loveing frend,—ORMONDE.

Dublin Castle, 22 April, 1644.

Postscript.—I have written this morninge backe to Mr. Powre that I approved well of the course which hee was takeinge about the three shipps, and comaunded him to proceede therein, and to stay there untill that hee had received orders and directions from you concerning the business, which I pray you to dispatch unto him, and that the armes and provisions bee in a readiness by the tyme appoynted by the Earle of Antrim. You are alsoe to consider the proposition for the fraught sent mee by Mr. Powre, and for how longe they shalbe contracted with. The surest way is to agree for the longer tyme, which will not much increase the charge, and may bee of very greate use and importance for that and other services. But two moneths, I suppose, is the least tyme for which they are to bee contracted with. But of this consider, and resolve as you see cause.

XLVII. ORMONDE TO VISCOUNT MUSKERRY.

My Lord,—I am very glad to hear from you, that you tooke pains to make your Propositions moderate : but they weare given soe lately before my dispatches came, that I know not whether they be soe esteemed by his Majestie or noe ; soe that I can say nothing of them, save that if they be not, I wish you would make them soe.

I apprehend very well what advantage it may be to his Majestie to make an honorable and just peace with his subjects, and I am confident

XLVII. " Carte Papers," x. p. 262.

if there weare no other, the saveing of a kingdom from desolation, and many innocent people (who must fall with the guilty in a war) from destruction, are motives sufficient to incline his royal heart to receave the humble submissions of his people. My labour, therefore, on that part is needlesse; but if I had confidence that my advise had any esteeme with you, who are imployed from your party in this kingdome, and must give a strict accoumpt of every drop of blood that shall be shed in case a breach insue the unreasonable[ness] of your demands; I say, if I weare perswaded my words bore any waight with you, I should advise you to preferr (like those good subjects you say you are) his Majestie's honor and safety, much wounded and threatened by false rumors raysed of him touching the businesse of Ireland, before the present satisfaction of such of your desires, as may perhaps in themselves be soe just, that his Majestie may heereafter with more safety grant, than he can yett heere them propounded.

For my part, I shall give all the furtherance I can to the just settlement of this broaken kingdom; wherein few have more interest, and in the growing up whereof noe man shall more rejoyce than your Lordship's affectionate brother and servant,—ORMONDE.

Dublin Castle, 29 April, 1644.

Endorsed by Ormonde: Coppy of my letter to Lord Muskry, dated 29 Aprill, 1644. Lord Digbye's pacquett.

XLVIII. MEMORANDA FOR SERVICE OF CHARLES I. FROM AGENTS OF CONFEDERATION AT OXFORD CONCERNING AFFAIRS OF IRELAND.[1]

1. The Citie of Corke, commaunded by Sir Hardress Waller, cousingerman to Sir William Waller, and alwayes devoted and affected to the Parliament.

2. The fort of Corke, commaunded by Captaine Muschamp, a man of

1. This document was transmitted to Ormonde in a letter from George Digby, dated at Oxford, 6 May, 1644, in which he wrote, in reference to it: "The advertisements of the Irish Agents here inclosed, I desire your Excellence to consider of, and to return me your opinion, as soon as may be."— Carte Papers, vol. x., p. 311.

XLVIII. Carte Papers, x. p. 316.

noe estate, and [whose] father, brother, and friends are in actuall service of the Parliament, with whome he keepeth correspondence, and is himselfe totally affected to that partye.

3. The fort of Duncannon, commaunded by the Lord Esmond, extreamly decayed with age, very ill affected to your Majestie since the Earle of Strafford's time, much favoured and obleidged by the Parliament duringe these warrs, and most of his officers and soldiers sent thither by the Parliament, and whoe hath lately broaken the Cessation.

4. The fort of Kinsale, commaunded by Captaine William Brockett, by the apointment of the Parliament in the place of Captaine Kettellby, whoe was displact and imprissoned for his loyalty to your Majestie; which Broiekett might surprize sixteene of your Majestie's royall ships in the service of the Parliament, as was designed by the Marquis of Ormond; but instead of soe doinge, feasted the captaines, and warned them of the danger, and soe all scaped.

5. The castle comanding the harbour of Baltemore, beinge a place of greate consequence and well planted with ordnance, is in the handes and under the commaund of Thomas Benet, a man appointed by the Parliament, of noe estate in England or Ireland, and one that received sevenn months provisions of late since the Cessation from the Parliament, and withall one that (knowing Forbesse proclaimed for traytor by your Majestie) enterteyned and feasted him for twoe or three dayes together.

6. The castle of Castlehaven, a place of greate consequence, well planted with ordnance, commaundinge that harbour, is in the handes of Robert Salman, a man havinge not a foote of estate in England or Ireland, and whoe (by his owne confession) was att London since the Cessation, and severall times duringe the commotion; which argueth the greater feare of suspition, it beinge to be feared his repaire soe often to the Parliament was in assureance of these forementioned harbours, and withall to be suspected. He was imployed as agent from the rest to assure their fidelitye to them and their cause; and this the rather, because that hee and the rest receaved the provisions aforesaid, procured by this man's sollicitation.

7. The residence of the Lord Kerry at London, and the report of his acceptance there, breeds a feare that being in ellection to bee imployed in

Forbesse[1] his place the last voyage, he will be now imployed ; and this the rather, for that his eldest sonne being at schoole at Bristoll, was by him sent for to London; which giveth more cause of suspition, it being feared his father being an Irish [Peer] may faile trust unto them, and therefore for assureance of his fidelity to the Parliament, hee should have his eldest sonne and heire with them as a pledge or hostage of his fidelitye towards them.

8. The arivall of Daniell MacCarthy, sonne and heire of Florence MacCarthy,[2] whoe was committed in the Tower, and there continued upwards of forty years, and a man that sustained sundry other crosses by the King (as he conceives), and being a powerfull man in alliance and dependance in the counties[1] of Kerye and Corke, and a man haveinge a claim to the Earledome of Desmond and Valentia, and very intimate with the Lord of Kerye by alliance, and otherwise, and withall matched to a neere coosin to the Marquis Hamilton, may be suspected and feared ; and this the rather, because it is not full three monthes sithence he left London, haveinge his passe from the Parliament ; wherefore [the] Marquis Hamiltòn [being] taken, and Kerye in London, and hee heere, and a fleet, as they say, in preparation for that kingdome, and these forts and castles in the hands of such suspected persons, speedy prevention is to bee used.

9. Roscomon, Boyle, Elphin, Tulsk, Castle-Coote, and James-Towne, garrisons of the county of Rosscomon belonging to Sir Charles Coote, Sir Robert King, and the Lord Ranellagh, and at this time commaunded by their servants and officers, doe dayly committ acts of hostilitye, and obeye noe commaund of your Majestie's officers, either the Lord Lieutenant or the Governour of Athlone, and att this present by the meanes of Sir Frederick Hamilton, and Sir William [Cole], with whome they are joyned in an assotiation to draw the Scots to the province of Conaght.

10. These informations received by us from Ireland wee humbly present out of the duty wee owe to your Majestie's service, that, by putting these commands into faithfull hands in your Majestie's [use, the] places may bee secured, and the dessignes of your [enemies] prevented.

1. *See* vol. pp. 137-148; ii. p lxxxvi.
2. For account of Florence Mac Carthy, *see* " Facsimiles of National Mss. of Ireland," Part IV. 1. London: 1882.

11. Wee have beene written unto by those, from whome wee are entrusted hither, that they are informed that severall men, whoe would engratiate themselves to your Majestie, and magnifye themselves in your esteeme, endeavour to perswade your Majestie that they have that power either by their allyance or dependance, that they are able to bring you men. Wee desire that your Majestie may be informed how vaine those suggestions are, and how unsafe it will be to graft any designe upon such expectations; those entrusted by the Confederate Catholikes to manage their affayres are only able to performe what such men doe promisse; though to draw men to their desires, they promise treble pay to that which they are to expect, which may prove inconvenient to your Majestie's service, and therefore wee desire such particular applycations be not listened unto.

It is come to us likewise from thence, that your Majestie hath lately since the Cessation appoynted a governour of the castle of Limmerick, and a collector of the customes in that citty, the same beinge within our quarters, wee hope that therein, and in all other places within the quarters of the Confederate Catholikes, untill a settlement, your Majestie will please to continue the same as now they are, and not disable yourselfe by such graunts to conferr the places of trust or proffitt accordinge to our desires in the Propositions presented, with indifferency on your subjects of that kingdome; and that if any letters or other engagements be graunted to that purpose, they may be stopt and recalled.

Endorsed : Advertisements concerning Ireland, 16.7. 74. 4. 64. 80. 30. 57. 3.26. 4. 50. 78. 60. 11. 44. 49. 12.3. 65. 48. 31. 49. 20. 225. by the Irish Agents. a 5. n. 3. 226. 102. 60.

XLIX. Letter to Luke Wadding, S.J., Spain, from Supreme Council.

Reverend Father,—Wee are advertised that some stopp hath beene given to Luke White, of Waterford, marchant, his factor in Bilboe, to sell some calfe-skins of great value taken in a vessell loaden in Chester, the 13th day of January, 1642[3], and bound after her retourne made at

XLIX. Ms. "Register Book of Letters" of Supreme Council.

Bilboe to London, as by the charter-partie and the certificat.   Uppon view whereof, as alsoe uppon reading of the judgment given in the Admiralty Court of Dongarvan, to which wee have affixed our seale, may appere : wee pray you procure from Courte a direction to such as are interested in Bilboe in the determinacion of things of this kinde to doe that justice unto our marchant which his cause meritts, and not give way that he may suffer by the earnest prosecucion of some Puritants factors there, whoe, as wee are enformed, have beene admitted to speake bitterlye of our cause without any notice taken of theire language.—Kilkenny, the 26 May, 1644.

L. Correspondence between Ormonde, Supreme Council of Confederation, Richard Bellings, etc., May, 1644.

1. Ormonde to Bellings.

Sir,—I beleeve you have heard how an outragious munky defaced a dispatch directed to mee from those you obey. I am not yet fully informed in the businesse of those letters; when I am, I shall returne a befitting answeare. In the meane tyme, I am to let you know of a like mishap, occasioned by the curiosity of one heere, and by the negligence of Mr. Christopher Bryan. The story is thus tould me.

Upon Munday last, at night, Mr. Bryan being in companie with halfe a dozen (I beleeve) good fellowes, having occasion to withdraw himselfe to some other roome, left some pacquetts, where one of the companie came at the enclosed, and, with the help of a hot knife, opened the seale, and tooke coppys of the several letters under the cover, and made up the letter againe, as you see (for since the seale hath not been touched) with intent to convey it into its place. But Mr. Bryan returning sooner than he looked for him, he was prevented. On the morrow, he acquainted a gentleman that hath relation to me with this passadge, and by him sent me first the inclosed copy,[1] and after (upon my demand) the pacquett, affirming that all he found was in it, and that no other copy than this[2]

L. 1, 2, 3, 4, 5, 6. Carte Papers, x. pp. 294, 387, 398, 435, 473, 474; 7, 8, 9. Carte Papers, xi. pp. 27, 33, 40.   1, 2. Not in Ms.

now sent you was taken. Whether that be true or noe, I cannot say; this I can, that since they came to my hands, they have not at all been altered.

I must confesse, I have read the coppy, with approbation of the dexterity of your agents, who can already give you accoumpt of my dispatches to the Lord Digby. And though their intelligencer should give them truth for their money, I shall yet hould on my way, and that the best I can light on, to bring this kingdom to his Majestie's perfect obedience, and soe to the blessings of peace and plenty; these are the principal ends of all my endevoirs. Sir, I rest, your affectionate cousin,   ORMONDE.

Dublin Castle, 2 May, 1644.

2. SUPREME COUNCIL TO ORMONDE.

Our very good Lord,—Wee have seene your Lordship's concearning the transportacion of three hundred men by Wexford into North Wales, as also the speedy payment of the supply graunted unto his Majesty by our Commissioners, that treated with your Lordship upon a Cessacion of Armes.

Wee are exceeding sorry for the occasion which necessitates your Lordship to diverte your resolucion of sending them from the port of Dublin, where provision is made for them, and from whence they may be transported with more conveniency; and, immediatly upon receipt of those letters, wee sent to Wexford to see what shipping may be had there, for that purpose, and upon notice retourned that shipping can be had, order shalbe given for fouer daies victuall to be layd aboard, and your Lordship shalbe advertised thereof. Coneearneing the remayne of what our Commissioners did fix upon for a supply to his Majesty, whatsoever is in arreare shalbe provided speedily. The advertisement wee receave of the Parlyament shipps lying before Dublin putts us in doubt what to doe concearning our shipping, which now upon the matter are ready to sett saile, and although that finding your Lordship sent no countermaund to your former direction for haveing them sent to Bullock, wee did not give any stopp to the course they were in, yet wee shalbe glad while the wynd stopps them to have further notice of your Lordship's resolucion therein.   Wee doe likewise desire to know how the three hundred men, in case they come to Wexford and that the winde shall not serve, shalbe provided for, while they remayne there.

Thus, with our hartyest wishes unto your Lordship, wee rest your Lordship's humble servants,

Mountgarret.—Fr. Thomas [Fleming, Archbishop of] Dublyn.— Thomas [Walsh, Archbishop of] Cashel.—Emer [Mac Mahon], Dunensis et Conorensis.—Thomas Preston.— Edmund Fitz Morice, Richard Bellings.

For his Excellency the Lord Marques of Ormonde, Lord Lieuetenante of Ireland.

Endorsed : Lord Mountgaret and others, dated 16th, received 20 May, 1644.

3. ORMONDE TO BELLINGS.

Sir,—In my last letter I acquainted you with the streights and exigencies we are put into by reason of the Parliament ships which have blocked up this harbour.   And now I thought fit to let you know further that, upon Tuesday last, Monroe, with 2,000 men, surprised Belfast;[1] and the same time sent 2,000 more to Lisnegarvey [Lisburn], whereof the soldiers, now in garrison there, having notice, betook themselves to their armes and kept them out.   But they still lye before the town, with a resolution to take it by force, if they cannot otherwise prevaile.   It is said that Owen Rce O'Neile hath been sent unto by the Lord Blayney, who is within the town, to come to their relief, and that he is preparing to go to raise the siege : But whether this be so or no is more than I can assure you.   It is rather thought that such an opportunity (if offered) is more like to be neglected than laid hold on ; for it is observed that much time is lost, and little done by some, whom it doth concerne to be most active.

And now it behoveth me to let you know how much it concerneth his

1. *See* p. 178.

Majestie's service, my own honour, dearer to me than my life, and the preservation of the kingdom, that I be forthwith supplyed with meanes, according to the agreement upon the Articles of the Cessation, to keep those men I have here in a posture to oppose the Scots, who certainly will advance into the bowels of the kingdom, if some stop be not given them. The wants of the common soldier at Belfast was the cause of the loss of that place, and I may as well feare the like or worse (there being the same cause) if I be not timely supplied by you, from whom only I can now expect it; whereof, if you faile me, the loss may be more than is fit for me to express, which I pray you to make known to those who have the managing of your affaires; wherein, if they be careless, let the blame fall upon them : I am free thereof, and so I rest, your loving friend,—

ORMONDE.

Dublin Castle, 17 May, 1644.

4. BELLINGS TO ORMONDE.

My Lord,—Wee understand from Wexforde that Captaine Doran[1] arrived theer the twentieth of this instant (he is an Irishman, commaundinge a frigott in the service of our Counsell) and that since his going to sea last he tooke three prises in the northern seas, the one bound from one port to another in Scotland to loadge herrings; annother loden with corne, both left at sea to follow him ; the thirde was a Londoner, come out of Amsterdame and bound for London, of four hundred tunn, with four and twenty peeces of ordenance, loaden with amunition, and in hir good store of silver, of which they have brought to shoare three thousand pounds by their owne confession. This prise, having in her four-and-twenty Wexforde men and two Flemings, was pursued by four Parlement men-of-warr, and it is feared she is recovered by them. The Captaine tooke likewise another shipp between Wexford and Dubline, loaden with corne for the accompt of

1. The number of vessels captured by the Irish, and brought into Wexford as prizes at this time, is noticed by the author of the "Aphorismical Discovery," who mentions that Captain Doran (O'Deorain) was an "Irishman by birth, but bred in Flanders since a child."—"Contemporary History of Affairs in Ireland, A.D. 1641-1652." Dublin : 1879, vol. i., p. 54.

Vanhoult. She comes from Amsterdame, and by one of hir cocketts was bound for Knockfergus ;[1] another makes mention of Dubline. Out of the London prise theer is one prisoner brought a-shoare, who, being examined, declares that there are bound for this coast forty men-of-warr. The prisoner is sent for hether, and when he comes, I shalbe able to give your Lordship a more full accompt of this particular.

My Lord, since my last, it is resolved that two thousand foote and three hundred horse, of the army designd for the Ulster expedition, should be drawen forth as the vangarde to meet at Granarde in the county of Longforde, the 12 of June, and the whole army is to bee drawen to some place theerabouts the fifteen of July. They bringe three months provision, two parts in victuall and the third in moony. Your Lordship may be pleased to listen to thoos that will multiply our forces, opinion carries somwhat of terror with it.

My Lord, I am much disquieted at the unsafe condition whearin you live at Dubline, amonge a sort of raskally Roundheads, whearof the Devill may make some one so zealous as to be ambitious of beinge an assassinat. God in heaven preserve you and your family. I am, my Lord, your Excellencie's most humble servant,—RICHARD BELLINGS.

Kilkenny, this 22 of May, 1644.

Endorsed: Mr. Belings. Received 26 May, 1644.

5. BELLINGS AND DR. FENELL TO ORMONDE.

My Lord,—Mr. Daniell O'Neale[2] and the Bishop of Downe [Emer MacMahon] did conferr with us seriously last night concerninge a proposition nue unto us, as having not at any time either by messadg or letter had any light from your Lordship thereof. The entrance into it was the consideration of the state of the kingdome, and the distractions which, by the competition of the Earle of Antrime and the Earle of Castelhaven, might be introduced, to the great disquiett of our affayres ; and that theer-

1. Carrickfergus.

2. *See* "Contemporary History of Affairs in Ireland, 1641-1652. Dublin : 1879, vol. i., p. 585.

for, a hand must be sought whearunto the military parte of commaunde should be putt, to whom they might boothe submitt, and this could be no other than your Lordship. Littell was replied by us, wee being resolved to keep ourselves at a distance in a matter of that weight which came upon us on the suddaine. And now, my Lord, wee have recourse to your Lordship to knowe whether this be as new to you; if not, how your Lordship did entertayne it when it was moved unto you, and what judgments you made upon it; for even the offer of such a commaunde, unless you might accept of it, might bring some prejudice upon you; and if your Lordship have any such inclination, wee conceave ourselves intrested in the knowledge of it, because wee are your Lordship's faithfull and humble servants,—RICHARD BELLINGS.—GERALD FENELL.

Kilkenny, this 25 of May, 1644.

Wee send your Lordship heerwith two letters taken at sea, that your Lordship may not be careless of your particular safty when the danger towards you is spooken of in places so farr distant, and perhaps may be within your famely.

Concerning this proposition, wee desire to receave your Lordship's express pleasure, that wee may be provided how to behave ourselves; for moved it wilbe, and wee doe suspend it because wee would be first informed.

For his Excellency the Marques of Ormonde, Lord Liftenant-Generall of Ireland, Dublin.

6. ORMONDE TO BELLINGS.

After our hearty commendacions: Wee have receaved informacion from Captaine Theodore Schout, Mr. Frederick Panckard, Mr. Garrett Vanhovan, and others, merchants of this city, that the good shipp called 'The Swan' of Dublin, whereof is Master Peeter Corneliusson Yongboore, being consigned with her goods and ladeing to them and this port by certaine merchants in Amsterdam, was surprised by one Captaine Dowran, of Wexford, uppon this pretence, that the said shipp was bound for Scottland, or some port of this kingdom, not obeying the Cessacion. Now, you will find by the inclosed instruement, signed by the Judge of the Vice-Admiralty of this province, that it is deposed uppon oath that the said shipp was realy bound for this place and noe other ; which wee are by many pregnant and urgent proofes induced to give creditt unto ; and therefore wee have thought good to pray you to move effectually unto those of your party that the said shipp, ladeing, and goods may be forthwith restored unto the true proprietors and owners, wherein they shall performe but what in right of the Articles of Cessacion wee may justly claime at their hands. And soe wee bid, etc. Your loveing frend,—ORMONDE.

25 May, 1644.

7. ORMONDE TO BELLINGS.

i. After our hearty comendacions : By this inclosed peticion, you may discerne the hard measure affoorded the peticioner (by those of your party in the county of Kildare) as being an adherent to his Majestie's Protestant subjects. Wee shall desire you to move it to those of your party, that a present course bee taken for reparacion of his sufferings for the tyme past, and that hee may bee freed for the future from the cesses and imposicions layde on him by them, which is noe more than is justly due by the Articles of Cessacion to bee granted him. And soe, not doubting of your performance herein, wee remayne, etc., your loveing frend,—ORMONDE.

29 May, 1644.

[Enclosure].

ii. To the Most Honorable James, Marquess of Ormonde, Lord Lieutenant-Generall of Ireland.

The humble peticion of Gerrott Wall, of Promplestowne, in the county of Kildare :

Most humbly shewinge that your peticioner hath beene protected by your Excellency from the begininge of the late insurrecion, and sithence that tyme hath bein at excessive great charge, severall tymes in lodginge his Majesty's army, and contributed to the mayntenance of Catherlagh, and payd the fourth sheafe of all his cropp of corne to the sayd guarrison. Now, soe it is that notwithstandinge your peticioner was never out of the possession of his owne house and lands, nor contributed to any Irish tax or imposicion, yet the Irish cessors for the county of Kildare (contrary to the intent and meaninge of the Articles of Cessacion), doe daily assess and impose uppon your peticioner such heavy taxes that he wilbee utterly undon unless speedily relieved by your honnor. The premisses considered, may it please your Excellency to settle a course, eyther by your honnor's letter directed to the Irish Commissioners in your suppliant's behalfe, or otherwise as your Excellency shall think fitt, whereby your orator may bee eased of his unjust vexacion, freed out of the Irish quarters, and remayne as formerly under the English. And hee shall pray, etc.

8. LETTER TO ORMONDE FROM SUPREME COUNCIL.

Our very good Lord,—Being wee have determined those men which are designed for the expedicion into the Isles should be shipped at Passage and Ballehack the sixt of June, we have thought fitt for prevencion of the intelligence, which may be brought unto our enemyes, of their setting to sea, to give order that no vessel within the portes in our partes should weigh anchor upon pretence of any voyadge, untill they shall know our further pleasure, and wee desire your Lordship would be pleased to provide, that what wee doe endevour to conceale here be not made knowen from any the havens or creekes in Mounster, or by the boates which as wee heare do daily resort from Dublin to the Parlyament shipps lying before the harbour. Thus, with our hartyest wishes, wee rest, your Lordship's humble servants,

Mountgarret.—Malachias [O'Queely] Tuamensis.—John [Bourke, Bishop of] Clonfert—Emer [Mac Mahon] Dunensis et Conorensis.—Arthur Iveaghe,—Thomas Preston.—Patrick Darcy.— Edmund Fitz Morice.—Gerald Fennell.—R. Bellings.

00*

9. Letter from Bellings to Ormonde.

My Lord—I write by commaund of thoos who have observed your zeale to his Majestie's service, and your endevours to preserve the kingdome since you weer intrusted with the government of it, and howbeit they may not yet enjoy the full effects of a happy peece, yet they desire the distance should not be such as, for want of a perfect understandinge, the safety of the kingdome might be brought in question. After notice receaved from your Lordship that Belfast[1] was surprised by the Scots, they gave order for drawing ther army into the field, the vantgard, consistinge of two thousand foote and two hundred horse, to Granarde, the 12 of June, and the rest, being four thousand foote and four hundred horse, to the same place, the first of July next. The list[2] of the officers is sent to the end your Lordship (faling into consideration of the forces you are able to bring into the field) may forecast what may be exspected to be performed in this summer's service, and what accomodations the army may be supplyed with, either in their march or duringe the service in the northe. And, inasmuch as busines cannot be so well debated nor drawen to conclusion so spedely by intercourse of letters as by the discourse and person of one versed in our affayrs, they have determined to send either Dr. Fennell, Mr. John Walsh, or Mr. Edward Commerfoorde, to confer with your Lordship concerninge all matter that may tend to the well disposinge of the army, and the managinge of the warr, leaving the person, the place, and such other circumstances as your Lordship shall think necessary, to be choosen and regulated as to your Lordship shall seem meet. I am, my Lord, your Excelence's most humble servant,

RICHARD BELLINGS.

Kilkenie, this 30 of May, 1644.

Endorsed: Mr. Bellings. Dated 30 May; received 1 Junii, 1644.

1. *See* p. 178.
2. *See* p. 201: "A list of the officers designed for the expedition into Ulster."

LI. Answer of Charles I. to the Demands of Irish Confederation.

1. Concerninge any thinge in religion, his Majestie's answer is that as the lawes against those of the Romish religion within that his kingdome of Ireland have never beene executed with any rigor or severitye : soe, if such his subjects shall, by returninge to their dutye and loyalty, merit his Majestie's favour and protection, they shall not for the future have cause to complaine that lesse moderation is used towards than hath beene in the most favourable of Queene Elizabeth and King James his times, provided that under pretence of conscience they doe not stirr upp sedition, but live quiettly and peaceably according to their allegeance.

2. Touchinge the callinge a free Parliament (by which his Majestie supposes the proposers intend a new Parliament) his Majestie sayes hee could wish that all the particulars might be fully agreed upon, and ratifyed this Parliament, his Majestie well understandinge that his Protestant subjects maybee in farr greater danger in a new Parliament than the proposers and their party can bee in this, his Majestie being willing to give them any securitye that can be desired against their apprehensions. However, since some objections and doubts are raysed of the legall continuance of this Parliament since the death of the Lord Deputy Wan[de]sford,[1] and by the late arrivall of his Majestie's commission after the day of meeting upon the proroguation[2] (though those doubts may bee easily solved), his Majestie is content to call a new Parliament, upon condition that all particulars bee first agreed on, and the Acts to be past be first transmitted, accordinge to custome (for his Majestie will by noe meanes consent to the suspension of Poynings' Act): and the proposers givinge his Majestie securitye that there shall bee noe attempt in that Parliament to passe any other Act than what is agreed on, and first transmitted, or to bringe any other prejudice to any of his Majestie's Protestant subjects there.

LI. Carte Papers, x. ,pp. 171-3.—For the " Demands " *see* p. 128.

1. Sir Christopher Wandesforde, Lord-Deputy, Ireland, died 3rd December, 1640.

2. *See* vol. i., pp. 20, 24, 27.

3. His Majestie neither can nor will declare Acts in themselves law-full to bee voyde, but is well content that neither the proposers nor their party shall suffer any prejudice by any Acts or ordinances passed since the time in that Proposition mentioned, by reason of this commotion, and for that end shall give his full concurrence.

4. The matters of the 4, 5, and 16 Propositions are to bee disgested into an Act of Oblivion, in which his Majestie will admitt any clauses to inlarge his mercy, but will not, by declaringe indictments legally taken and regu-larly prosecuted to bee voyde, give any countenance to, or make any ex-cuse, for the present Rebellion, which would bee a great prejudice to truth, and to the future security of that kingdome ; and, therefore, his Majestie is content to graunt a full and generall pardon to all persons whatsoever within that his kingdome (except for all treasons, rebellions, or crimes whatsoever, growing and arising from or by reason of the said Rebellion), and will likewise give his consent to such an Act of Oblivion as shall be prepared and transmitted to him by the advise of his Lord Lieutenant and Counsell of Ireland, who are fittest to consider in what state debts are to bee left, and particular actions and remedyes to be waved, in which his Majestie, for the peace of the kingdome, will bee content to release what concernes himselfe.

6. When all other particulars shall bee agreed on and faithfully exe-cuted on the parts of the proposers, his Majesty (expecting a just acknow-ledgement of his bounty, as well knowing that hee parts with very much to which he hath a legall and undoubted title) is content to release and quitt his right to all such lands in the countyes mentioned (except within the countyes of Kilkenny and Wickloe) upon the termes formerly assented to by his Majestie in his answere[1] to the greevances in the 17th yeare[2] of his raigne [1641-42], and will consent to such an Act of Limitations as is desired.

7. When all other thinges shall be concluded, his Majestie will con-

1. In margin : " And quarto Caroli," in reference to the "Graces," A.D. 1628.

2. *See* vol. i., p. 27 ; and "Contemporary History of Affairs in Ireland, 1641-52." Dublin : 1879, vol. i., p. 11.

sent to an Act for the taking away any incapacity as natives either to lands or offices, if any such there bee, and will willingly consent to the erectinge an Innes of Court, University, or Free Schooles, provided that they be governed by such statutes, rules, and orders, as his Majestie shall approve, and agreeable to the custome of this kingdome.

8. Such of his Majestie's subjects of the Romish religion within that kingdome as shall manifest their dutye and affection to his Majestie shall receive such markes of his Majestie's favour, in offices and places of trust, as shall manifest his Majestie's good acceptance and regard of them.

9. His Majestie will take care that his good subjects of that kingdome shall not be oppressed by his Court of Wards; and if oppressions of that kinde have beene, upon good and due information, his Majestie will cause justice to be done for the time past, and for the future will prevent the like by instructions, but for the taking away of the Court, his Majestie can make noe answere till the particulars for his satisfaction bee sett downe, and presented to him.

10. His Majestie consented, as farr as is fitt for him in this poinct, in his answere to the 25th grevance, in [the] 17th yeare of his raigne, the which hee is still willinge shall be enacted, looking forward still to the five yeares to begin after the Peace [is] concluded.

11. His Majestie conceives the substance of this Proposition (which concernes the fundamentall rights of both kingdomes) fitt to be referred to the free debate and expostulation of the twoe Parliaments, when it shall please God that they may freely and safely sitt, his Majestie beinge soe equally concerned in the priviledges of either that hee will take care to the utmost of his power that they shall both contayne themselves within their proper limitts, his Majestie beinge the head and equally interested in the rights of both Parliaments.

12. This is sufficiently provided for in his Majestie's answere to the 10th greivance, which hee is content shall passe.

13. Since it appeares by long experience that these lawes have not produced that good effect for which they were made, his Majestie was graciously pleased, by his late Graces, that those statutes should be repealed, save only for wooles and woolfells, and will observe the same

resolution; and a booke of rates shall be settled by indifferent Commissioners.

14. His Majestie doth not admitt that the longe continuance of the Cheife Governours of that kingdome in that place hath beene an occasion of much tyranny and oppression, or that any tiranny or oppression hath beene exercised upon his subjects of that kingdome. However, his Majestie will take good care that such governours shall not continue longer in those places than hee shall finde for the good of his people there, and is content that they shall bee inhibited to make any purchase (other than by lease, for the provision of their howses) during the time of their government in such manner as is desired.

15. This Proposition is to bee explained, and some particular wayes to be proposed to his Majestie for the doinge thereof, and then his Majestie, upon due consideration of the safety and security of his Protestant subjects, will returne his answer.

16. Answered in the 4 and 5. Such persons whoe shall be excepted out of the Act of Oblivion, shall be tryed by the knowne lawes of the land.

Endorsed : His Majestie's answer to the Irish Agents' Propositions.

LII. Letter to Ormonde from Supreme Council.

Our very good Lord,—Notice being sent unto us by Gennerall Owen O'Neille of the surprizall of Belfast,[1] and the beseedging of the garrizon of Lisnegarvy by Major-Gennerall Monroe, and the forces under his commaund, and wee being informed of his and their resolucion to breake the Cessacion established by his Majestie's royall authority, and to fall upon us in our owne quarters, whereunto the said trecherous actions are but a preparacion, as appeares more manifestly unto us by the provisions sent unto them and declared to be for that purpose; wee thought fitt to signifie unto your Lordship that wee have, as well for our owne defence as the preservacion of others, his Majestie's good subjects in this

---

LII. Carte Papers, xi., p. 62.

1. For "Account of surprizal of Belfast," 1644, *see* "Contemporary History of Affairs in Ireland, 1641-1652," Dublin: 1879, vol. i, p. 586.

kingdome, who shall adheare unto his Majesty and observe the Cessacion, given direction for the drawing of our forces together; and least this preparacion of ours during the Cessacion should be so farr mistaken as to begett terror in such his Majestie's subjects, wee doe hereby declare and protest before God and to your Lordship (which wee do humbly desire may be published, and made knowen unto his Majestie's good subjects) that all our ayme and scope herein is to give a stopp unto the said trecherous proceedings, and their further intencions against us, which, if not tymely looked unto, and prevented may be as well destructive to your Lordship and to your partie as unto us; and wee doe further assure your Lordship that wee will attempt nothing (except it be in our owne just defence or the preservacion of the kingdome from ruine and destruction), whereunto nature, and our allegeance unto his Majestie doe binde us, but by your Lordship's good allowance during the Cessacion. And least that, through want of knowledge, any of his Majestie's good subjects should receive prejudice by our army intended for their preservacion, wee doe desire your Lordship that you wilbe pleased by some publick act to declare what citties, townes, garrizons, or other places within your quarters you conceive fitt to be protected, and what not; for, as wee are informed, very many within your quarters, and specially where these trecherous accions have beene committed, have of late, by the incitement of fower ministers sent out of Scotland, taken an oath or covenant full of treason and sedicion, which is destructive to his Majestie's royall authority and the freedome and lybertie of his Majestie's good subjects in this kingdome, which is likewise sett forward by the said Major Monroe, and Sir Frederick Hamilton, fiery instruments of sedicion amongst his Majestie's good people. But as they who have either taken the said oath, or drawen any of his Majestie's good people to take the same, have thereby fallen from their loyalty, so wee did hope that long before this tyme they should have beene declared by your Lordship to have soe done unnaturally and ungratefully to our gratious Soveraigne, whereby they being thus marked wee might the better knowe and so reduce them to due obedience or condigne punishment, as wee do now desire wee may, with your Lordship's good leave and allowance, be permitted to doe. And soe desiring your Lordship's direction herein, wee rest, your Lordship's humble servants,

Mountgarrett.—Fr. Thomas [Fleming, Archbishop of], Dublyn.—Thomas [Walsh, Archbishop of] Cashel.—Malachias [O'Queely] Tuamensis.—Emer [MacMahon] Dunensis et Conorensis.—John [Bourke, Bishop of] Clonfert.—Castlehaven and Audley.—Netterville.—Richard Bellings.—Ever Magines.—Edmund Fitz Morice.—Thomas Flemyng.—Patrick Darcy.—Gerald Fenell.—George Commyn.

Kilkenny, the third of June, 1644.

Endorsed : Lord Mountgarret and others.   Dated 3, received 7 June, 1644.

LIII. Letter to Cardinal Mazarin from De La Monnerie, at Kilkenny.

Monseigneur,—Pour obeir aux commandemens que votre Eminence m'a faict faire par Monsieur de Lionne, je n'ay manqué de représenter à Messieurs dú Conseil d'Irlande le tort qu'ils avoient d'avoir faict esperér à leurs Majestez, la permission d'une levée de 2,000 hommes sans aucune difficulté, et en avoir, après cela, faict naistre: mesmes que l'on s'estoit tellement attendu à cela que l'on en avoit fait fonds pour la campagne présente, et par conséquent que ce nombre se trouveroit à redire dans l'armée, n'ayant pas donné ordre qu'il se levast ailleurs, sur l'asseurance qu'ils avoient faict donner, de le donner sans difficulté.

A quoy, ils m'ont respondu que je les aurois trouvé prests de satisfaire aux asseurances qu'ils avoient faict donner, s'ils n'en avoient esté empeschez par les raisons qu'ils ont alléguées à votre Eminence dans la lettre qu'ils luy ont escripte, m'ayant protesté que le monde seroit desjà en France sans cela, et qu'ils seront tousjours mémoratifs et recognoissans des obligations qu'ils ont à la France.

Monsieur Collon [Cullen[1]] est arrivé icy, il y a huict jours, lequel ne

LVIII. Archives des Affaires Étrangères, Paris. Série Angleterre, vol. 51, pp. 79, 84.

1. *See* page 72.

demeure pas d'accord de tenir le traitte que son frère a faict avecq Monsieur le Tellier, le désavouant tout à fait, et m'a dit de ne vouloir entendre à aucun autre traitte s'il n'est pareil à ce luy que l'on a faict dernièrement avecq les Escossois, avecq le mesme nom de Régiment des Gardes Irlandois : à quoy je n'ay point voulu entendre, n'ayant point pouvoir de traitter autrement que conformément à mes instructions : et ce qui me met beaucoup en peine, c'est que, par le traitte que son frère a signé avecq Monsieur le Tellier, il luy a esté promis huict escus pour soldat ; et on ne m'ordonne d'en donner que quatre, et encores met on dans ce dict traitté qu'en cas que j'en accorde davantage à celuy qui entreprendra la levée des deux mille hommes que l'on leur baillera le surplus.

Ils ne manqueront pour ceste raison à publier partout que l'on leur a accordé en France huict escus pour la levée de chasque soldat, et que, si on veult tenir bon, ils en auront davantage de moy. Cela me met beaucoup en peyne ; toutes fois puis qu'il ne veut pas tenir le traitte que son frère a faict, je croy que votre Eminence ne trouvera pas mauvois si je le retiens de peur qu'il ne le fasse voir à quelqu'un, j'usques à ce que M. le Tellier luy ayt faict response à une lettre qu'il luy escript sur ce désadveu et sur la résolution qu'il a de ne vouloir traitter que sur le mesme pied des Escossois.

Je sollicite d'ailleurs le plus diligemment qu'il m'est possible pour avoir la permission de la levée plustost que le temps auquel ils m'ont remis, mais je n'y advance rien, me remettant tousjours au retour de leurs Agens d'Angleterre qu'ils attendent tous les jours.

Mais si, par quelque accident que l'on ne peult prévoir ils n'estoient de retour au temps qu'ils m'ont promis la permission, et qu'ils voulussent les attendre, je supplie très humblement votre Eminence de me faire sçavoir ce qu'elle aura agréable que je fasse, ne souhaittant rien faire que par ses commandemens, ayant l'honneur d'estre, Monseigneur, de vostre Eminence, le très-humble, très-obeissant, et très-fidèle serviteur et créature,

MONNERIE.

Quilquennin, ce 1ᵉ Juin, 10ᵉ Juin (en France), 1644.

LIV. Letter to Luke Wadding, Rome, with credentials for Edmund O'Dwyre, D.D., from the Supreme Council.

Reverend Father,—Havinge received advertisment from you of your desire to have the assistance of Dr. Dwyre, or some other whom wee should thinke fitt for the employment, to assist you in promotinge our affaires in the Courte of Rome, wee have not putt ourselves to any doubtfull election, but have sent you the same man whom you did name and recommend unto us. It hath pleased his Holliness, at your instance in our behalfe, to suspend the grant of any spirituall promocion or benefice within this kingdome other than to such persons as should be retourned unto him with the marke of our recommendacion. This was a resolucion very avayleable for us, and of great quiet to his Holliness, to whom doubtless many supplicacions would be presented for graunts of benefices, which yet are to be fought for, and in the behalfe of such as had little other meritt than some powerfull patronadge. For the present, wee have thought fitt, out of the certaine knowledge wee have of the good life and abilityes, well befittinge a pastorall chardge, of the under named persons, to recommend them by you to his Holliness that they be preferred respectively to the ensuinge miters and benefices :

Father Hugo de Burgo,[1] of the Order of St. Francis, now in Flanders, to the see of Aconrye [Achonry] ;

Father Joseph Everard, Religious of the same Order, to the see of Fearnes ;[2]

Doctor Edmond Dwyre, who is employed with these, to be co-adjutor to the Bishopp of Limericke[3] (who is now very unweldye), and to be his successor ; and

LIV. Ms. " Register Book of Letters " of Supreme Council.

1. Delegate to Flanders from the Confederation. *See* pp. 95, 104, 126. De Burgo was appointed Bishop of Kilmacduagh in 1647.

2. Ferns. John Roche was appointed to the see of Ferns in 1645.

3. Richard Arthur. O'Dwyre was appointed, in 1645, as co-adjutor to Arthur, with right of succession.

Father Nicholas Shee,[1] to the parsonadge of Callen, in pursuance of a presentacion made to that effect by the lay patron heere.[2]

Wee shall not need to particularize the state of our affaires. Doctor Dwyre, who hath taken care to enforme himselfe, will relate them and our necessityes to you at full; and if ever any releife be intended for us, wee stand in need of it at this present.—Dated [at] Kilkenny, the 13th of June, 1644.

COMMISSION FROM CONFEDERATION FOR EDMUND O'DWYRE, D.D.

[The Supreme Council notify that Father Luke Wadding, of the Order of St. Francis, has frequently expressed to them his desire to have an assistant at the Court of Rome for promoting the interests of the Confederation. The Council have consequently appointed for that office Edmund O'Dwyre, Doctor of Divinity, in whose integrity, solicitude, and prudence they fully confide.—Kilkenny, 13 June, 1644.]

Per Supremum Concilium, etc..

Reverendo Domino, Domino Edmundo O'Dwyre, Sacræ Theologiæ Doctori, salutem: Cum Reverendus Admodum Pater, Frater Lucas Waddingus, Ordinis Sancti Francisci Religiosus, a nobis sæpius obnixe postulasset ut mitteremus qui illi in promovendo causam nostram apud Suam

1. *See* vol. i. lxix., 118; ii. xciii-vi., 108-12, 202-3.
2. The following, in connection with sees in Ireland, was, later in the same month, addressed to Wadding, at Rome, by the Supreme Council:—" Reverend Father,—After wee had closed upp our dispatch of an elder date, which Doctor Dwyre likewise carryes, wee did, at the instance of the illustrious Petrus Franciscus Scarampus, his Holliness' Minister employed into this kingdome, take a resolucion to supplye some other vacant sees and therefore wee pray you that you doe sollicit the promocion of Father Robert Barrye, Doctor of Divinity, to the see of Ross, alias Rossensis, in Mounster; and Father Francis Kirevan to the see of Aconrye, alias Accadensis, in Connaght. Thus committinge what wee have further to write, since the arrivall of our Commissioners, to the bearer's relacion, with the remembrance of our heartyest wishes, wee rest,—Kilkenny, 26 June, 1644."—Ms. " Register Book of Letters " of Supreme Council.

Robert Barry was appointed to the see of Cork and Cloyne, in 1647, and Francis Kirevan to that of Killala, 1645.

Sanctitatem assisteret, nos de integritate, sollicitudine, et prudentia tua plurimum confidentes, eo te fungi munere et eidem Patri Lucæ Wadding in peragendis negociis nostris assistere volumus et mandamus.—Datum Kilkenniæ, decimo tertio die Junii, anno Domini, 1644 :

> Mountgarrett.—Fr. Thomas [Fleming, Archbishop of] Dublin.— Malachias [O'Queely], Archiepiscopus Tuamensis.—Castlehaven, Audley.—Netterville.—Edmund Fitz Morrice.—Richard Bellings.—Patrick Darcy.—Gerald Fennell.—George Commyn.

LV. Letter to Cardinal Grimaldi from the Supreme Council.

[The writers state that they are unable fully to express their deep sense of the singular zeal and paternal care evinced by the Cardinal towards the cause of their nation. His acts will be long remembered with gratitude by the Irish. The Cardinal's departure from France is regretted by the writers, who now congratulate him on his arrival at Rome. They doubt not that he will there promote the cause of Ireland. Of their affairs accounts will be given by Father Luke Wadding and Edmund O'Dwyre, D.D.—Kilkenny, 14th June, 1644.]

Eminentissime Domine,— Quantum Eminentiæ vestræ debeat Hibernia pro vestro singulari in causam nostram zelo, paterna charitate, curis, molestiis, consiliis nunquam satis exprimet, condignas nunquam aget gratias. Rependet, qui bene cœpit, Deus Optimus Maximus, et eximia vestra de Ecclesia Dei et nostra natione bene meritis dignis compensabit præmiis. Tua officia, beneficia, fama, apud nos in æternum vivent, et ad omnem posteritatem grata Eminentissimi Grimaldi transmittetur memoria. Doluimus vestro a Galliis discessu et absentia desiderium sensimus; sed cum Dei Providentia omnia regi sciamus, acquiescimus Divinæ in hoc voluntati, et fœlici vestro in Urbem adventu et honore quem tibi fortunatum optamus gratulamur ac lætamur, nec dubitamus nostram Ecclesiæ Dei et Hiberniæ causam ab Eminentia vestra eximie hactenus promotam semper deinceps

LV. Ms. "Register Book of Letters" of Supreme Council.

fore commendatissimam.   Quis vero sit præsens rerum nostrarum status
Eminentiæ vestræ exponet Reverendus Pater Lucas Waddingus, cui, ut
in causa nostra promovenda assisteret, misimus Admodum Reverendum
Dominum, Dominum Edmundum O'Dwyre, Sacræ Theologiæ Doctorem,
rerum nostrarum testem oculatum.   Eminentiæ vestræ observantissimi :

Mountgarett.—Fr. Thomas [Fleming] Dublin.—Malachias [O'Queely]
Archiepiscopus Tuamensis.—Emer [Mac Mahon] Dunensis et Cone-
rensis.—Castlehaven, Audley.—Edmund Fitz Morrice.—Thomas
Fleminge.—Richard Bellings.—Gerald Fenell.—Patrick Darcy.—
George Comyn.—Kilkenniæ, 14 Junii, 1644.

LVI. LETTER FROM THE SUPREME COUNCIL TO THE NUNCIO IN FRANCE.

[The Council state that they were deeply grieved when Cardinal
Grimaldi, the friend and patron of their nation, departed from France. They
are, however, consoled by the arrival there of the present Nuncio, whose
zeal and attachment to their cause have been notified to them by their
countrymen at Rome.   They doubt not of being favoured by him as they
were by his predecessor, Cardinal Grimaldi.—Kilkenny, 14 June, 1644.]

Illustrissime ac Reverendissime Domine,—Non exiguo nos mœrore
affecit, Eminentissimi Domini Cardinalis Grimaldi, viri optimi et gentis
nostræ patroni amantissimi e Galliis discessus ; sed illum subito dolorem
minuit nosque recreavit Illustrissimæ Dominationis vestræ adventus, et
Apostolici Nuncii in Galliis munus a Sancta Sede vobis commissum.   Siquidem a nostratibus, qui Romæ sunt, de vestro in causam hanc nostram
zelo, studio, affectu satis intelleximus, nobisque gratulamur Illustrissimam
Dominationem vestram eo fungi munere ubi Eminentissimi Cardinalis vicem
et paternam in nos benevolentiam supplere possit, suumque una de quo
optime speramus affectum ad Dei gloriam et Ecclesiæ profectum exprimere.   Quis sit rerum nostrarum præsens status Eminentiæ vestræ Pater

LVI. Ms. " Register Book of Letters," of Supreme Council.

Matheus O'Hartegan exponet, cui ut indubitata fides adhibeatur rogamus. Illustrissimæ, Dominationi vestræ addictissimi :

Mountgarett.—Thomas [Fleming] Dublin.—Malachias [O'Queely], Archiepiscopus Tuamensis.—Emerus [MacMahon] Dunensis et Conerensis.—Castlehaven, Audley.—Netterville.—Thomas Fleminge.—Edmund Fitz Morrice.—George Commyn.—Patrick Darcy.— Richard Bellings.—Gerald Fennell.—Kilkenniæ, 14 Junii, 1644.

LVII. Letter to Pope Urban VIII. from Supreme Council of Confederation.

[The writers state that the whole world knows that the Irish encountered most severe trials, even death itself, rather than abandon the Catholic faith ; that, under great disadvantages, they engaged in, and have hitherto carried on successfully, a war against those who had determined to eradicate the Catholic religion. God is now publicly worshipped in Ireland, according to the Catholic rites, several Catholic bishops and rectors possess their cathedrals and parish churches. Many Religious Orders also enjoy their houses. These boons to the people of Ireland were reserved by God for the time of the present Pope, under whose auspices the Catholic religion, so long oppressed in that island, now raises its head with becoming dignity, and the Irish people trust eventually to win the reward of their courage and patience. With a view to further advance the Catholic faith, the writers implore that the dignity of the Cardinalate may be conferred on Father Luke Wadding, an Irishman of noble descent, whose other qualifications and merits are not unknown to the Holy See. The writers acknowledge that they are conscious that they ask for a great and an unusual favour, but they also know the character of the Pontiff from whom they seek it. He has ever cherished the Irish with paternal affection, conferred the greatest benefits upon them, and has, with singular zeal, aided them in their present struggles. The gracious concession of their petition, and the fulfilment of their desire, would add effectively to

LVII. Ms. "Register Book of Letters" of Supreme Council.

the many favours already received by their country from Pope Urban VIII., and cause Ireland to be eternally mindful of him.   To promote the object of their petition to the Pope they have sent to Rome Edmund O'Dwyre, Doctor of Divinity, an eye-witness of their proceedings. They implore the Apostolical benediction for themselves, for the other Confederate Catholics, and for the whole kingdom of Ireland.—Kilkenny, 14 June, 1644.]

Beatissime Pater.

Satis superque Christiano orbi innotuit quam invicta hactenus patientia hereticorum insolentiam, proscriptiones, bonorum jacturam, mortemque ipsam, Catholicæ fidei causa contempserint Hiberni, ac pertulerint, quam alacriter, constanterque, inermes licet, in aciem irruerint, sacrum bellum susceperint, sustinuerintque, quo successu bellatoribus suis divina indulserit clementia cum Apostolicæ Sedis jurati hostes de Catholica fide radicitus evellenda nefarium et impium iniissent consilium. Jam Deus Optimus Maximus Catholico ritu palam colitur, dum Cathedrales pleræque suis Antistibus, parochiales parochis, Religiosorum multa cœnobia propriis gaudent alumnis. Et hæc tanta Omnipotentis Dei in nostram gentem beneficia, in vestri, Beatissime Pater, Pontificatus tempora sunt reservata; cujus auspiciis Religio Catholica, in hac insula jamdudum jacens et afflicta gloriose caput erigit, seque varietatibus circumdatam, et ornatam, sponso suo Christo visendam exhibet; cujus favoribus animata et promota gens nostra patientiæ et fortitudinis lauream sperat se tandem reportaturam : Cum vero Catholicæ fidei splendidius excitandæ præcipua nobis supersit ambitio, supplices petimus, ut Sanctissimus Pater dignetur condescendere ad ascribendum Sacro Cardinalium Collegio, Patrem Lucam Waddingum, natione Hibernum, nobili oriundum familia, cujus aliæ commendationes et merita Apostolicæ sedi non sunt incognita. Magnum quidem et rarum est quod petimus, sed et scimus a quo Pontifice illud petamus ; ab illo certe qui Apostolico, paterno nos nostramque gentem semper hactenus fovit affectu summa in nos beneficia conferendo et præsentes nostros conatus singulariter promovendo. Hujus nostræ supplicationis gratiosa acceptatio et votorum obtentio reliqua Sanctitatis Vestræ in nos beneficia abunde cumulabit, et Hiberniam Urbani Octavi Pontificis

Maximi æternùm memorem illique obæratam et devotam servabit. Hanc nostram ut promoveret supplicationem apud Sanctitatem Vestram misimus Reverendum Admodum Dominum Edmundum O'Duire, Sacræ Theologiæ Doctorem, rerum nostrarum oculatum testem. Nos vero nobis ipsis, et reliquis Hiberniæ Confœderatis Catholicis, regnoque universo Apostolicam Vestram benedictionem demisse petimus, Sanctitati Vestræ ad pedum oscula provoluti:

Kilkenniæ, 14 Junii, 1644:

Mountgarret.—Fr. Thomas [Fleming], Dublinensis.—Thomas [Walsh], Archiepiscopus Casilensis.—Malachias [O'Queely], Archiepiscopus Tua-mensis.—Emer [MacMahon], Dunensis et Conorensis.—Castlehaven, Audley.—Edmund FitzMorrice.—Gerald Fenell.—George Commyn.—Thomas Fleming.—Netterville.—Richard Bellings.—Patrick Darcy.[1]

Addressed: Sanctissimo Domino Nostro Urbano Octavo.

LVIII. LETTERS TO CARDINALS AT ROME IN REFERENCE TO LUKE WADDING, 14TH JUNE, 1644.

[1-3.—In these communications, addressed respectively to Francesco Barberini and Antonio Barberini, the writers express their gratitude to those Cardinals for the aid given by them to the cause of the Irish Con-federates. They further beg them to use their influence to obtain the Pope's consent to the application addressed to him in relation to the ad-vancement of Father Luke Wadding to the Cardinalate.—Kilkenny, 14 June, 1644.]

1-2. To CARDINAL FRANCESCO BARBERINI, ROME.

1. Eminentissime Domine,—Commune nostrum votum et desiderium

1. These signatures, not in the copy in the Ms. "Register Book of Letters," are here given from the original in the archives of the Franciscans of the Irish Province. The document is reproduced in "Facsimiles of National MSS. of Ireland," Part IV.-2, Plate LIV. London: 1884.

LVIII. 1-3. Ms. "Register Book of Letters" of Supreme Council.

est, pro totius gentis solatio, pro Ecclesiæ hic resurgentis splendore, ut Reverendus Pater Lucas Waddingus, natione Hibernus, natalium splendore et virtutum meritis conspicuus, de Ecclesia Dei et hoc regno optime meritus, Sacro Cardinalium Collegio ascribatur, quod expressis literis a Beatissimo Patre suppliciter rogavimus. Cum vero sciamus Eminentiam vestram apud Suam Sanctitatem plurimum posse pro singulari vestro in causam et gentem nostram affectu ut hoc nostrum postulatum promovere velit confidenter rogant Eminentiæ vestræ observantissimi.—Kilkenniæ, 14 Junii, 1644.

2. Eminentissime Domine,—Pro communi gentis nostræ solatio, pro Ecclesiæ hic renascentis splendore, jam expressis literis a Sanctissimo Domino nostro rogavimus ut Reverendum Patrem Lucam Waddingum, natione Hibernum, natalium splendore et virtutum meritis illustrem virum, de Ecclesia Dei et regno hoc bene meritum, Sacro Cardinalium numero dignetur ascribere. Quod ipsum Eminentiæ vestræ commendamus ut pro ea qua apud Sanctissimum Dominum pollet auctoritate, pro vestro singulari in causam et gentem nostram affectu, negotium hoc apud Sanctissimum Dominum promovere velit. Vestras manus deosculantur Eminentiæ vestræ observantissimi.—Kilkenniæ, 14 Junii, 1644.

Addressed: Eminentissimo et Reverendissimo Francesco Cardinali Barberino, Sanctissimi Domini Nostri nepoti.

3. To Antonio Barberini, Cardinal Protector of Ireland, at Rome.

Eminentissime Domine,—Suppliciter a Sua Sanctitate per literas petimus ut in nostræ gentis, pro Catholica fide bellantis, commune solatium dignetur Reverendum Patrem Lucam Waddingum, nacione Hibernum, generis nobilitate et virtutum meritis conspicuum virum, Sacro Cardinalium ascribere Collegio. Quod nostrum postulatum ut Eminentia vestra, pro ea qua apud Beatissimum Patrem pollet auctoritate, pro singulari suo in

---

2, 3. The originals of these documents, preserved in the Archives of the Franciscans of the Irish Province, bear the autographs of Lord Mountgarret, and of those who signed the application to Pope Urban, printed at page 188.

patriam et causam nostram affectu, promovere velit obnixe rogant Eminentiæ vestræ observantissimi.—Kilkenniæ, 14 Junii, 1644.

Addressed: Eminentissimo et Reverendissimo Domino Antonio Cardinali Barberino, Sanctissimi Domini Nostri nepoti.

LIX. LETTERS TO ROME, ETC., FROM THE SUPREME COUNCIL.

[1-4.—In these documents the Council mention the great and perilous war in which they are engaged against the Puritans, from whom they expect nothing but perpetual enmity. The Puritans, they state, are combined with the London Parliamentarians, the avowed enemies of the King and of the Irish, and have obtained abundant supplies of every kind. While the Confederates carry on the war on land, the ships of the Scotch and Parliamentarians infest the coasts and cut off supplies. The writers declare that they are not deficient either in perseverance or in men, but that they urgently need military equipments, money, and other necessaries for war. They appeal to the friends of religion and of the Church to aid them with supplies, without which they may be unable to maintain the contest. Edmund O'Dwyre, D.D., and Father Luke Wadding will furnish full information as to the state of the affairs of the Irish.—Kilkenny, 14 June, 1644.]

1. The Dispatch sent to Rome, the 14 of June, 1644.

Suscepimus grande periculosumque bellum et, Deo potenter gloriose nobis succurrente, sustinemus pro Deo ejusque Ecclesia, quæ ruinæ apud nos proxima fuit (*sic*) nobis bellum, et pugnæ contra Puritanos, Catholicæ religionis infensissimos hostes. Cum his nulla nobis armorum Cessatio, neque porro erit, dum Deo Optimo Maximo, uti semper hactenus nobis bene propitio, perduellionis et impietatis pœnas luent. Inierunt illi cum Londinensibus Parlyamentariis, Regis nostri acerrimis hostibus, impium et nefandum fœdus, et solemne votum de Catholica religione penitus ex_

LIX. 1-4. Ms. "Register Book of Letters" of Supreme Council.—The names of the personages to whom Nos. 2, 3, and 4 were addressed do not appear in the Ms.

tirpanda susceperunt. Illis Parliamentarii, arma, commeatum, stipendia, reliquaque ad bellum in nos gerenda necessaria, abunde suppeditant. Unde insolentiores facti in Ultonia virus et vires omnes exerunt et magno numero patriam vastantes ulterius regnum penetrare conantur. Cum his terra pugnamus; dum interim Scoti et Parliamentarii navibus instructissimi mare circa infestantes commercium omne impediunt et annonam, ac subsidia a nobis avertunt. Ita hæc insula, pro Ecclesia pugnans, potentissimis acerrimisque undique obsidetur hostibus, Dei pene solius potenti brachio hactenus invicta, constans et triumphans. Verum ne Deum continuo tentare videamur, et Ecclesiæ quam sustinemus causa taciturnitate et incuria nostra periclitetur aut pereat, pecuniam, arma, aliaque sine quibus bellum foveri non potest, nobis deesse confidenter exponimus, vestramque in hac Ecclesiæ causa benevolentiam et subsidia rogamus et speramus, cum major debeat esse inter genuinos veræ Romanæ Ecclesiæ filios et alumnos pro Ecclesiæ defensione charitas et mutua subsidiorum communicatio, quam quæ nunc, ad Catholicorum confusionem, inter ipsos hæreticos est ad perdendam Ecclesiam bonorum et rerum omnium profusio. Quis vero rerum apud nos præsens sit status exponet Reverendus Admodum Dominus, Dominus Edmundus O'Duire, Sacræ Theologiæ Doctor, rerum nostrarum testis oculatus, cui ut certa et indubitata fides adhibeatur hisce rogamus:

Mountgarett.—Fr. Thomas [Fleming], Dublin.—Malachias [O'Queely], Archiepiscopus Tuamensis.—Emerus [Mac Mahon] Dunensis et Conerensis.—Castlehaven, Audley. — Netterville. — Edmund Fitz Morrice.— Richard Bellings.—Patrick Darcy.—Thomas Fleminge.

2. Eminentissime Domine,—Hactenus omnia quæ Puritani, infestissimi Ecclesiæ hostes, aut vi, aut fraude, in nostram machinati sunt perniciem, indefessis pertulimus animis, Deo nobis adeo propitio ut rebelles in Ultonia Puritanos ex insula ejecissemus, nisi illis Londinenses Parliamentarii, qui Regem nostrum armis infestare non cessant, copiosa subministrassent subsidia. Jam vero illi, frumento, armis, et militum stipendiis suffulti, non solum in regno hærent, sed et bellum in nos parant eo magis timendum

quod execrando fœdere cum Parliamentariis inito, solenne votum et juramentum de Catholica religione radicitus extirpanda susceperint. Cum his nulla nobis armorum cessatio, induciæ nullæ ; speramus fore ut Deo (cujus causam sustinemus) promovente impietatis et perjurii pœnas luant condignas. Deterret nos tamen utcumque status nostri consideratio. Suppetunt animi, suppetunt manus ; alia tamen ad bellum necessaria subsidia (ne Ecclesiæ, pro qua pugnamus, causa silentio nostro prodi perdive videatur) nobis deesse fateamur necesse est. Et hæc inopia partim bello quod sustinemus, maxime vero gubernatorum, cujus hactenus subjacuimus, insolentiæ et iniquitati tribuenda est. Unde fidenter speramus rogamusque ut Eminentia Vestra, in quam Catholicæ religionis hoc in regno protegendæ proprior cura incumbit, suo nos patrocinio adjuvet et nostris paterne succurrat necessitatibus. Quis vero præsens rerum nostrarum sit status Eminentiæ vestræ exponet Reverendus Pater Lucas Waddingus, Ordinis Sancti Francisci Religiosus, cui, ut in causa nostra promovenda assisteret, misimus Admodum Reverendum Dominum, Dominum Edmundum O'Duire, Sacræ Theologiæ Doctorem, rerum nostrarum oculatum testem. Eminentiæ vestræ observantissimi.—Kilkenniæ, 14 Junii, 1644.

3. Eminentissime Domine,—Pro eo quo causam nostram fovet affectu et promovet apud Suam Sanctitatem ne ingrati essemus profitemur nos devinctos, et rerum nostrarum status is est ut tali indigemus patrocinio. Errant qui dicunt nos ab armis a bello cessare. Habemus in ipsis regni visceribus hostes magno numero Puritanos qui, inito cum Angliæ Parlyamentariis execrando fœdere, solemne votum et juramentum de extirpanda apud nos Catholica religione susceperunt. Illis Parliamentarii stipendia arma reliquaque ad bellum necessaria abunde subministrant, unde insolentiores facti, campo se inferunt qui dudum redditum in Scotiam meditabantur. Nos hactenus potenter Deus, et deinceps speramus, adjuvabit. Verum, ne, Dei potentiæ solum confidentes et humana media negligentes, Deum tentare videamur et hanc Ecclesiæ causam periclitari patiamur, arma, stipendia, reliquaque ad bellum necessaria nobis deesse ingenue fatemur. Quis vero sit præsens rerum nostrarum status Eminentiæ vestræ exponet Reverendus Pater Lucas Waddingus, Ordinis Sancti Francisci

Religiosus, cui ut in causa nostra promovenda assisteret misimus Admodum Reverendum Dominum, Dominum Edmundum O'Duire, Sacræ Theologiæ Doctorem, rerum nostrarum oculatum testem.—Kilkenniæ, 14 Junii, 1644.

4. Potentissime Princeps,—Jam, per biennium et ultra, gravissimi mole belli laborantes, Puritanorum, Ecclesiæ Dei infensissimorum hostium, furorem pertulimus et vesaniam, et Deo ubique potenter succurente nostrosque conatus promovente, ita partes nostras egimus, ut, nisi amplissimis ab Angliæ Parliamento subsidiis continuo fuissent instructi, jamdudum ex Hibernia Puritanos omnes ejecissemus. Jam vero illi, conflato exercitu, armis, stipendiis, rebusque omnibus ad bellum necessariis abunde receptis (tanta est hæreticorum inter se ad Dei Ecclesiam perdendam unio) bellum in nos parant, certe periculosum, eoque magis timendum quod solenni sacramento sese obstrinxerint, et juramentum ac fœdus unanimiter susceperint, de Catholica religione radicitus inter nos evellenda et Catholicis omnibus perdendis atque delendis. Illa ipsa fides et religio, qua Deum Optimum Maximum colis, Princeps potentissime, hic pellitur et periclitatur. Ecclesia Christi, cujus Catholici omnes Principes sunt filii, indigne violatur et opprimitur: neque limites sibi ullos statuit Puritanorum hæreticorum ambitio; unde tutius est grassantem a longe hæresim obterere quam in visceribus receptam fovere; habent ubi a nobis exemplum sumant et cautiores fiant Catholici Principes. Non desunt nobis animi, non desunt manus, desunt tamen militaria stipendia, reliquaque ad bellum sustentandum necessaria; quod vobis, Potentissime Princeps, confidenter exponimus ne Ecclesiæ pro qua pugnamus causa nostro silentio aut injuria prodi videatur, simulque a vobis rogamus et speramus necessitatum nostrarum levamen et opportuna ad Ecclesiæ Dei defensionem subsidia. Quis vero rerum apud nos præsens sit status exponet Reverendus Admodum Dominus, Dominus Edmundus O'Duire, Sacræ Theologiæ Doctor, rerum nostrarum testis oculatus, cui ut certa et indubitata fides adhibeatur hisce rogamus.

Mountgarett.—Fr. Thomas [Fleming], Dublin.—Malachias [O'Queely], Archiepiscopus Tuamensis.—Emerus [Mac Mahon] Dunensis et Conerensis.—Castlehaven, Audley.—Netterville.—Edmund Fitz Morrice.—Richard Bellings.—Patrick Darcy.—Thomas Fleminge.

Kilkenniæ, 14 Junii, 1644.

LX. LETTER TO LUKE WADDING, ROME, FROM SUPREME COUNCIL.

Reverend Father,—Takinge into consideracion the estate of your countrye, and how much it wants of that countenance which other king-domes doe enjoye in the Courte of Rome, by meane none of our nacion hath beene preferred to that degree of eminence in the Church of God which would render them in any high measure usefull to theire countrye by their power and perswasion, and knowinge how acceptable your partes, your constant attendance in the Cittye [Rome], and your experience of affaires hath rendred you to his Holiness and the whole Courte, wee have thought fitt, after mature deliberacion thereuppon, to become humble suitors in your behalfe that you might be made a Cardinall;[1] and as in soe doinge wee were not ledd by privatt affeccion or particular regarde of your advancement, soe wee desire you that your modestye, or your with-drawinge yourselfe from promotinge our request by our freinds, doe not bringe a prejudice uppon your countrye, which is to receive benefitt by this preferrment. And although this act be soe intirely ours, that, for aught wee knowe, this place, or the way to it, hath not before this tyme come within your thought, yet because wee would not precipitatlye, or without your owne privity engadge you further in it, wee have directed our letters[2] uppon the subject should be delivered open unto you, and have sent you here enclosed[3] all the difficultyes which wee could gather might arise in prosecucion of our desire therein, to the end your freinds may be provided to answer them in our behalfe.—Dated [at] Kilkennye, the 15th of June, 1644.—Sent with the ensuinge dispatch[4] to Rome.

LX. Ms. " Register Book of Letters " of Supreme Council.
1. *See* p. 186.   2. *See* p. 188.   3. Not in Ms.   4. *See* p. 190.

LXI. Letter to Cardinal Mazarin from De La Monnerie, at Kilkenny.

Monseigneur,—Je croy que votre Eminence aura esté advertie par ma dernière de l'arrivée du Colonel Collon [Cullen] en ce royaulme et aussy des difficultez qu'il apportoit à traitter avecq moy, si je ne luy accordois les mesmes capitulations que l'on a accordées aux Escossois.

Maintenant, je vous apprendray, Monseigneur, qu'il est mort d'une apoplexie qui l'a estouffé depuis quatre jours : ce qui est cause que son frère, vous escrit pour vous supplier de luy conserver le régiment de feu son frère, promettant de satisfaire au traitté qu'il a faict avecq Monsieur le Tellier, et de mener de fort bons hommes en France : pour moy, je n'ay point voulu l'empescher de travailler à sa levée, m'estant imaginé que s'il peult venir à bout de son enterprise, que votre Eminence ne trouvera pas mauvois qu'il les transporte en France en qualité de Colonel : que si vous ne souhaittiez pas, Monseigneur, qu'il eust le régiment, votre Eminence prendra, s'il luy plaist, la peyne de me le faire sçavoir, affin que je trouve les moyens de retirer l'argent de feu son frère qu'il a desjà touche pour ceste levée.

Il n'y a donc plus que la seule promesse de huict escus pour soldat que Monsieur le Tellier luy a faicte qui m'embarrasse pour le regard de ma levée, d'aultant qu'il a dit à ung chascun qu'il avoit accordé à cela, et que s'ils y tenoient bon avecq moy, qu'ils en auroient davantage. Je croy pourtant que ce seroit meilleur marché de leur donner huict escus pour soldat s'ils vouloient entreprendre de les passer à leurs despens en France, que de ne leur en donner que quatre, et s'obliger à les passer la mer, d'aultant qu'il y a fort peu de navires en ces ports, et qu'il cousteroit beaucoup davantage.

Votre Eminence aura, s'il luy plaist, la bonté de me faire sçavoir sa volonté sur ce subject. Cependant, si ces Messieurs viennent à m'accorder la permission de la levée auparavant que j'aye receu ses ordres, j'y travailleray de sorte qu'elle ne trouvera point á redire à ce que j'auray conclud, estant résolu de suivre de point en point mes instructions.

J'appréhende que ces Messieurs n'usent encores de remises, attendu que le temps auquel ils m'ont remis est proche, et leurs Agens ne sont point de retour et n'en ont aucunes nouvelles.   Cela n'empeschera pas que je ne leur demande l'exécution de leur parole au jour porté par leur promesse et escoutteray leur responce pour la faire sçavoir à votre Eminence, ne souhaittant rien faire sans luy en donner advis, estant, Monseigneur, de votre Eminence le très-humble, très-obeissant, et très-fidèle serviteur et créature,—MONNERIE.

Quilquenny [Kilkenny], 15 Juin (25 en France), 1644.

LXII. LETTER TO ORMONDE FROM SUPREME COUNCIL.

Our very good Lord,—Haveing already promised for supply of the forces under your Lordship's commaund six hondred barrailes of corne and fower hondred beoves and being now prest not onely to send in that supply speedily, but to augment it, wee thought fitt to give your Lordship a cleere light of our present condicion, whereupon your Lordship may ground a resolucion.   Wee confess plenty of provision for maintaineing the army may be had within our quarters, and although the imposicions be heavy, yet there is money sufficient in the countrey to answere the occasion. But the people have not given us that power over them, which may be exercised without yeilding an accompt of our accions and a reason for any new tax; so as wee, who to procure the last supply, did (as a motive for it) perswade them your Lordship was intended to appeare against the Covenanting Scotts, shall but irritate them by renewing that argument, whereof no ground appeares unto them as yet, besides that they knowe not in what condicion to esteeme themselves, when those men, whom by our frequent declaracions and remonstrances wee have published to the world to be traytors to his Majestie and to have sought the ruine of the kingdome, are as yet, for aught appearing unto them, reputed loyall subjects.

This is the necessity imposed upon us not to adventure to draw a further charge upon them, and wee shall thinke ourselves well dealt with, if wee may be admitted to excuse the former. But if your Lordship should once declare [against] the Covenanters, or appeare by your accions against them, then wee might confidently assure your Lordship of this people's cheerfulnes and reddinnes to supply the forces under your comaunde, whereas without it wee have no hope to prevaile with them. And therefore wee beseech your Lordship, while his Majestie hath the continuance and power of an army sent by his loyall subjects, the Confederat Catholickes of Ireland, into the field, right use may be made of this oportunity to the advantage of his Majestie's service. And in the first place wee desire your Lordship would be pleased, in answere to our former many requests of this kinde, to give us tymely notice, what townes and garrisons in Ulster are in the hands of such as are true unto his Majesty, and who are those upon whom wee may serve his Majesty. For although wee can distinguish those who in contempt of his Majestie's authority have in hostile manner violated the Cessacion, yet wee are willing to comaund our army should be led against all those within the kingdome indifferently that are disaffected to his Majestie's intrests, or associated to the Rebbells in England, and in this matter wee doe againe earnestly pray your Lordship to direct us.

Concearening the speedy bringing in of the corne and beoves, wee do yeild your Lordship this accompt thereof, that three hondred barrailes of corne are now putt into the magazin at Wexford for that use, and that wee do intend they should be conveyed by sea to Wickloe, if so your Lordship thinkes fitt, that wee are informed the other three hondred barrailes of corne applotted upon the county of Kilkenny are ready to be sent to Catherlagh; that the beoves to be levyed in the county of Tipperary had beene sooner brought in than any parte of the corne, but that the northern men who yet lye upon them, take up their wholl thoughts and care, yet wee are assured they will shortly be driven to Catherlagh. Thus, with our hartyest wishes, wee rest your Lordship's humble servants,

Mountgarett.—Fr. Thomas [Fleming] Dublyn.—Emerus [MacMahon]

Dunensis et Conorensis.—Castlehaven, Audley. — Patrick Darcy.—
Edmund Fitz Morrice.—Gerald Fenell.—George Commyn.—Thomas
Fleming.—R. Bellings.

Kilkenny, 21 Junii, 1644.

Endorsed : Lord Mountgarrett, Lord Castlehaven, and others. Dated
21 ; received 24 Junii, 1644.

LXIII. Commission from Charles I. to Marquis of Ormonde, Lord
Lieutenant of Ireland, to treat for Peace with Agents of Irish
Confederation, June, 1644.

Charles, by the grace of God, Kinge of England, Scotland, France,
and Ireland, Defendor of the Fayth etc. To our right trusty and right-
entirely beloved cousin and counsellor, James, Marquesse of Ormond, our
Lieutenant-Generall of our kingdome of Ireland, greetinge :

Whereas, since the Cessacion of Armes agreed and concluded on within
that our kingdome, the Agents imployed from thence have presented unto
us severall Proposicions in order to a firme and setled peace, which wee are
obliged to desire if the same may be had with our honnor and the safety
and security of our Protestant and other good subjects within that
kingdome:

And because many of the particulers proposed by them cannott be
soe well weighed, considered and judged of as by those whose experience
and knowledge of the constitucion and affaires of that kingdome inables
them to judge, as well of matters of circumstance as substance: And for
that what agreement and conclusion soever shalbe made for peace must
be prepared and digested for Act of Parliament which must be penned and
debated by our Councell there and transmitted from thence to us here :

Knowe you therefore that wee, reposeinge especiall trust and confidence in your courage, wisedome, fidelitie, and circumspection, of which
you have given us greate and eminent testimony and assurance, have
constituted, ordayned, and appointed, and by these presents doe consti-

tute, ordayne, assigne, and appointe you, the said James, Marquesse of Ormond. our Lieutenant-Generall of our said kingdome of Ireland, to be our Commissioner to treate concerninge the setlinge and establishinge a firme and perfect peace within that our kingdome; and doe hereby give unto you full power, warrant, and authoritie for us and in our name to treate, conclude, and agree with any person or persons whatsoever deputed or to be deputed by our subjectes of Ireland nowe or late in armes, or nominated or to be nominated on theire behalfe, or with any other person or persons whatsoever, as you in your judgment shall think fitt for the setlinge and concludeinge of a firme and lastinge peace in that kingdome; and to take into your serious consideracion the demaunde and Proposicions which have been made unto us, or shalbe made or tendred unto you, touchinge or concerneinge the premisses or any of them; and to compose and end all differences 'ariseinge thereuppon; and likewise for us and on our behalfe to offer and propound what you in your wisdome shall thinke just and honorable and may conduce moste to the speedy and effectuall obtaineinge of the ends and purposes aforesaid, or any of them, and to conclude and agree therupon, and in and concerneinge the said premisses, or any of them, as you in your judgment shall thinke convenient; and to call and take into your assistance in the premisses such other person or persons as you shall finde usefull, or which may contribute helpe and furtherance thereunto.

And, if you finde it not reasonable to consent to such proposicions as shalbe made for a full peace, then to conclude of a further Cessacion of Armes in such maner as you shall thinke most behoofefull for our service and the good of that our kingdome.

And whatsoever you, our said Commissioner, shall doe, conclude, or agree uppon in the premisses, or any or either of them, wee doe by these presents ratifie and confirme the same.

In wittnes whereof, wee have caused theise our lettres to be made patents. Witness ourselfe, att Buckingham, the fower and twentieth day of June, in the twentieth yeare of our raigne.   Per ipsum Regem.—
WILLYS.

LXIV. Letters from Ormonde and Supreme Council of Confederation.

1. Ormonde to Mountgarret and Supreme Council.

After our hearty comendacions : Yesternight, the 27th of this moneth, wee received a letter subscribed by you and others, dated the 25 of the same, expressing that you understand by your Comissioners imployed into England that his Majestie hath by severall dispatches, advertised us that it is his pleasure wee should joyne in the service against the Covenanting Scotts, and you doe pray us to lett you know what wee have resolved therein. Whereunto wee returne you this answeare, that if his Majestie hath been pleased to send any such dispatches, they nor any of them are yett come to our hands, and that whensoever his Majestie's pleasure shall be signifyed unto us in that particular, wee shall returne you such further answeare unto your said letter of the 25th of this moneth as becometh us. Soe wee rest, your very loveing frend,—[Ormonde].

Dublin Castle, 28 Junii, 1644.

2. Letter to Ormonde from Supreme Council.

Our very good Lord—Being doubtfull what to ground a resolucion upon, when wee receaved your Lordship's letter of the eight and twentith of this instant, by which wee understood that such comaunds as his Majesty and the Chiefe Secretary, the Lord Digby, did often intimat unto our Comissioners, to have beene sent unto your Lordship for joyneing with us against the Covenanting Scotts, are not yet receaved by you, wee have thought fitt to imploy unto your Lordship our very good Lord, the Lord Viscount Muskery, Nicholas Plunkett, and Geoffery Browne, Esqrs., who lately came from Court, and can fully acquaint your Lordship with his Majestie's expressions touching that particuler, and Doctor Gerrott Fennell, one other of our Counsell, who being constantly present with us, at all our debates, will informe your Lordship how great a prejudice your Lordship's backwardnes in this occasion drawes upon his Majestie's service, and what uncertainty of resolucion wee are driven unto thereby, to the end nothing may be left unattempted or unimportuned by us, which may promote his Majestie's interests and the welfare of this his kingdome of Ireland, and in reporteing of such things as they have in charge from us, wee pray your Lordship to give them credence. Thus, with our hartyest wishes unto your Lordship, wee rest your Lordship's humble servants,

Fr. Thomas [Fleming, Archbishop of] Dublyn.—Netterville.— Arthur [Magennis, Viscount of] Iveaghe.—Edmund Fitz Morice.—Malachias [O'Queely] Tuamensis.—George Commyn.— Richard Bellings.—Thomas Preston.—Torlogh O'Neill.

Addressed : For his Excellency the Marquess of Ormonde, Lord Lieutenant of Ireland, Dublin.

Endorsed : Lord Nettervill and others, [dated] 1, received July 6, 1644.

LXV. Expedition to Ulster, under Earl of Castlehaven, General for the Irish Confederation, 1644.

1. A list of the officers designed for the expedition into Ulster : [1]

The Right Honnourable the Earl of Castlehaven, Generall.
Patrick Purcell, Lieutennant-Generall.
Lucas Taaffe, Serjeant-Major Generall.
Thomas Dongan, Quarter-Master Generall.
James Butler, of Callen, Provost-Martiall Generall.

Richard Buttler, sonn unto the Lord Viscount Mountgarrett, Collonell of a regiment of	1,000	foote.
The said Richard Buttler, Collonell,	100	,,
—— Browne, Liftennant-Collonell,	100	,,
James Buttler, Sarjeant-Major,	100	,,
—— Grace, Captain,	100	,,
—— Kavenagh, Captain,	100	,,

LXV. 1. Ormonde Archives, Kilkenny Castle.
1. See pp. 3, 74, 174.

Michael Synnott, Captain,	100 foote.
Pierce Brereton, Captain,	100 ,,
Edmond Birne, Captain,	100 ,,
Olliver Dongan, Captain,	100 ,,
Phelym Tooll, Captain,	100 ,,

Sir James Dillon, Collonell of a regiment of	1,000 foote.
The said Sir James Dillon, Collonell,	100 ,,
William Warren, Lieutennant-Collonell,	100 ,,
Gerrott Fitz Symons, Sarjeant-Major,	100 ,,
Bryen Geoghegan, Captain,	100 ,,
Robert Dillon, Captain,	100 ,,
Edward oge Farrall, Captain,	100 ,,
Brandon Cusack, Captain,	100 ,,
—— Connor, Captain,	100 ,,
—— Fitz Patrick, Captain,	100 ,,

The Lord Barron of Castle-Connell,[1] Collonell of a regiment of	1,000 foote.
The Lord Barron of Castle-Connell,	100 ,,
Walter Walsh, Captain,	100 ,,
Rory Mac Shihy, Captain,	100 ,,
Lieutennant-Collonell Donnagh Mac Nemarra,	100 ,,
Tirlagh O'Brien, Captain,	100 ,,
Shide Mac Nemarra,	100 ,,
Serjeant-Major William Buttler,	100 ,,
James Birne, Captain,	100 ,,
John Buttler, Captain,	100 ,,
Piers Buttler, Captain,	100 ,,

Phillipp O'Sullevan, Collonell of a regiment of	1,000 foote.
Phillipp O'Sullevan, Collonell,	100 ,,
Tiege McCarty, Lieutennant-Collonell,	100 ,,
Edmond Wall, Sarjeant-Major,	100 ,,

---

1. *See* vol. ii. pp. 52, 214.

Fynnyn McCarty, Captain,	100	foote.

Fynnyn McCarty, Captain,   100 foote.
Donnogh McDermody, Captain,   100 ,,
Nicholas Barry, Captain,   100 ,,
Maurice Fitz Gerrald, Captain,   100 ,,
Stephen White, Captain,   100 ,,
Frauncis Wise, Captain,   100 ,,
Bran Birne, Captain,   100 ,,

Sarjeant-Major Generall Taaffe, Collonell,   100 ,,
Morrogh ne Doe O'Flaherty, Liftennant-Collonell,   100 ,,
Richard Bourke, Sarjeant-Major,   100 ,,
Edward Tirrell, Captain,   100 ,,
Maurice Lynch, Captain,   100 ,,
Donnogh Reagh Kelly, Captain,   100 ,,
Gerrald Dillon, Captain,   100 ,,
Daniell O'Connor, Captain,   100 ,,
Edmond Farrall, Captain,   100 ,,
John O'Gara, Captain,   100 ,,

John Moore, Collonell,   100 ,,
Laughlin Moore, Lieutennant-Collonell,   100 ,,
Walter Bourke, Sarjeant-Major,   100 ,,
John Browne, Captain,   100 ,,
The foote company formerly commanded by Lieutennant-
     Generall Bourke,   100 ,,
Theobald Dillon, Captain,   100 ,,
Roger O'Connor, Captain,   100 ,,
Teige Rourck, Captain,   100 ,,
Bryen Reynolds, Captain,   100 ,,
David Bourke, Captain,   100 ,,

Collonell John Buttler, Commander of the Horse for that expedicion.
   The said John Buttler, brother unto the Lord Viscount
     Mountgarrett, Collonell,   50 horse.

Lewes Moore,[1] Captain,	49 horsc.
David Chorne,[2] Captain,	51 ,,
The Gennerall's troope,	50 ,,
James Browne, Captain,	50 ,,
David Roch, Captain,	50 ,,
Edmond Fennell, Captain,	50 ,,
Patrick Purcell, Lieutennant-Generall,	50 ,,
Robert Dillon, Captain,	50 ,,
James Barnewall, Captain,	50 ,,
John Finglas, Captain,	50 ,,
And the other troope left to my Lord of Castlehaven's nameing a Captain,	50 ,,

Endorsed: 1644. List of officers: Expedition into Ulster.

LXV. 2. EARL OF CASTLEHAVEN[3] TO ORMONDE.

My Lord,—The taking in of Belfast[4] by the Scotts, and their appearing before Lisnegarvie [Lisburn], was the chiefe cause of the drawing mee and the armie I have now heere unto the field, at this tyme.[5] I have just now certaine intelligence that the Scotts of Tyrconill[6] have made one boddie with those of the Route,[7] and Munroe, which though I did not expecte from the old Scotts, being allwaies as I conceaved under your Lordship's obedience, yet it does not much trouble mee; but a parte of my armie, which I expected out of Conaght, I am forced to leave to waite uppon the English garrisons of the counties of Roscoman and Leatrim, which, without distinction, as they finde their opportunities, doe not faile

1. Brother of Roger Moore or O'More. *See* vol. ii., p. 403; also "Contemporary History of Affairs in Ireland, 1641-1652." Dublin: 1879, vol. iii. p. 436.

2. Styled "Shorne, a German," in the "Aphorismical Discovery." *See* "Contemporary History," vol. iii. p. 443.

3. *See* p. 10.   4. *See* p. 187.

5. *See* "Memoirs of James, Lord Audley, Earl of Castlehaven." London: 1680, p. 44.   6. Donegal.   7. In the county of Antrim.

LXV. 2. Carte Papers, xi. p. 205.

to kill, prey and pilladge in all partes. I must out of these except the two garrisons of Athlone and Roscoman, who of late have conformed themselves to the Cessation. My Lord, wee cannot any longer, either in honnor or conscience, suffer the poore people of that province to groane under those calamities, soe much destructive to the great occasions wee have now in hand, for his Majestie's service, and the settlement of peace in this kingdome. My Lord, heere are now with mee Sir Lucas Dillon, Sir Ullicke Burke, and severall of the chiefe gentrie of that province who have lively set forth the miserable sufferings of that province. The particulars I neede not set downe, they being severall waies made knowne unto your Excellency. But, not to trouble you long, my Lord, I finde an absolute necessitie of sending an armie to reduce those garrisons to somm better obedience; which I have this day done. But such is the desire I have to observe your Excellency, as they shall not lay siedge to any of those garrisons, till your pleasure bee knowne either by leaving of them to us, that wee may vindicate our selves, or your Lordship undertake to give us justice for what's past, and securitie for the future. The speedie dispatch of the berrer wilbe an obligacion uppon your Excellency's most humble servant,—CASTLEHAVEN AND AUDLEY.

From the Camp at Ballenelee, 3 Julii, 1644.

LXVI. PROCLAMATION AGAINST COVENANTERS, JULY, 1644.

God save the Kinge.

By the Supreame Councell of the Confederate Catholicks of Ireland.

Whereas the Scottish armie in the province of Ulster, and other their adherents in the said province, and in other parts of this kingdome, have of late, as often before, taken a trayterous oath of Covenant against his sacred Majestie, his crowne, and dignitie, and made an unchristian and prophane vowe for the utter extirpacion of the Irish nation and totall supression of the Catholicke Roman religion, subversion of Monarchicke Government,

LXVI. Carte Papers, xi. p. 217. Under the head-line are " The King's armes."

and introduction of confused anarchy within this realme, and not contented with the inumerable inhumane, and unparralleled massacres by them comitted on poore labourers, woemen, children, and many thowsands of other innocents of our nacion, without distinction of age, sexe, or condicion, before the conclusion of the Cessacion at Sigginstowne, on the 15 day of September last [1643]; nor with continuall depradacions, robberies, thefts, burnings, and destruccion of all the corne and habitacions in many counties, and territories within the said province and elsewhere by them enacted before the said Cessacion. The said trayterous Covenanters, receiveing their maintenance, support, and orders from the Rebells, now in armes against his Majestie in England and Scotland, have augmented, and doe daily rather multiply and increase than diminish their said exorbitant courses; and whereas the said Rebells have joyned in a stricte union and confederation, to destroy Monarchie, and to abolish all order and Governement in Church and Commonwealth in his Majestie's three kingdomes, and more particulerly to destroy the Irish nacion (both roote and branch, as they tearme it), and their ministers and adherents by their direccions, by sea as well as by lande, doe exercise no lesse cruelty; for as oft as theire shippinge doe meete any weaker vessell, at sea, transporting men from this kingdome for his Majestie's service in England, if Irishmen, though Protestants, and valiant and usefull servitors against the Confederate Catholicks in this warre, the Irish are throwne overboard, as doth appeare by the late throwing into the sea, and drowning of an Irish company of foote of Collonell Willoughbie's regiment, all Protestants and servitors as aforesaid, and many woemen in their passadge from Dublin to Bristoll, by one of the pretended Parliament shipps, and sundry other examples of that kinde against the lawes of warre and nations : And whereas the said Scottish army, all composed of Rebells and assassinates, are now in their march in great numbers towards the other three provinces of this kingdome, to accomplish the plotts and machinations aforesaid : And whereas the said Rebells in England have provided a great navy (a considerable part whereof surround the sea-coaste of this kingdome), and are resolved this summer (if it rest in their power, which God defend) to

land great forces in the provinces of Mounster and Leinster, and the said
Rebells of Scotland have the like designe of landing forces in the parts of
Ulster next unto the province of Connaght : And whereas the auxiliary
forces of the said three provinces, designed and raised for the necessary
defence of our religion, King, and nation are now marched to the province
of Ulster under the comaund of our very good Lord, the Earle of Castlehaven, Generall appointed by the last Generall Assembly for the expedicion of Ulster, to repell the fury and insolence of the said Rebells :
Wherefore wee hould it of absolute necessity for the safety of the kingdome, and his Majestie's interest therein, that all the said other three provinces be forthwith in armes, as well to preserve themselves at home from
the said intended invasions, as alsoe to be ready to assist the said army
already marched into Ulster (if neede require it). Wee doe, therefore,
by this our publicke acte and proclamacion, order, comaund, and require all
the Lords, knights, gentlemen, and freehoulders, and all other persons of
what estate, degree, or quality soever within our quarters, fitt and able
to beare armes from the age of eighteene yeares to the age of three score,
forthwith to putt themselves in armes and posture of defence, and such as
wante armes and amunicion, and are able, are hereby required to provide
the same forthwith for themselves, their servants, and retinue. And for
the better effecting and regulateing of this high and important service,
wee doe hereby order, require, and comaund, all and every the Governors,
Deputy-Governors, Mayors, Sherriffs, and other head officers of the respe-
cutive counties, citties, and incorporate townes of this kingdome within
our quarters, viz., the Governor, or Deputy-Governor, in the counties
where there are Governors, calling to his assistance the High Sherriff, and
two or more of the Comissioners of the Array, and, in counties where
there are noe Governors, the High Sherriff calling to his assistance three or
more of the Commissioners of the Array, and in citties and corporate
townes, the Mayor, or other head officer, takeing to his assistance the Recorder, Sherriffs, and Bayliffs thereof, or any one or more of them, forthwith to summon all the said Lords, Knights, gentlemen, freehoulders, and
others, able and fitt to beare armes between the ages aforesaid, to appear

well armed, uppon a certaine daye, and in a certayne place within the said respective counties, cittyes, and townes respectively, and upon such appearance to inlist the names, sirnames, age, armes, and amunition of every person who will so appeare, in a booke fayrely written, and the said Governors, Deputy-Governors, Mayors, High Sherriffs, and other head officers, takeing to their assistance as aforesaid, are hereby required, and authorized to impose fines, to the double value of the armes and amunition, uppon any person or persons so summoned, that will make default, or ought to have according to the meaninge of this our proclamation, and of other our former proclamations to this effect, and to impose the single value of the armes hee should have uppon such as will appear, and not be armed as becometh.　And wee require the said Governors and other officers aforesaid, at theire perills to make due return unto the General Assembly now neere at hand, or unto us, in bookes fayrely written, of the numbers, names, sirnames, armes, amunition, defaults, and fines aforesaid, at furthest by the sixt day of the month of August next.—Given at Kilkenny, the 6th day of July, 1644.

    Mountgarret.—Fr. Thomas [Fleming, Archbishop of] Dublin.—John [Bourke, Bishop of] Clonfert.—Antrim.—Netterville.—Arthur [Magennis, Viscount] Iveaghe.—Thomas Preston.—Edmund Fitz Morice.—Richard Bellings.—Torlogh O'Neill.—Patrick Darcy.— George Commyn.

    Printed at Waterford by Thomas Bourke, Printer to the Confederate Catholicks of Ireland.

LXVII. NEGOTIATIONS BETWEEN CHARLES I. AND THE CONFEDERATION, JULY, 1644.

CHARLES I. TO ORMONDE.

CHARLES REX.—Right trusty and entirely beloved cousin and counsellour, wee greete you well : Wee beinge deeplye sensible of the miseryes and calamityes brought upon our Protestant subjects of that our kingdome of Ireland, by the Rebellion there, and findinge them likelye to growe to noe lesse than an irrepaireable ruine of all our said Protestant subjects, in case the warr should againe breake forth after the Cessation, in regard wee are utterly disabled by the unnaturall Rebellion heere in this our kingdome of England, to afford that necessary releife and support unto them, without which it is not possible that they should bee preserved from a finall and totall distruccion, have thought fitt to send you our Commission[1] under our Greate Seale of England givinge you power and authoritye to conclude either of a Peace or further Cessation there, accordinge as you shall there upon the place (out of a fuller insight into, and knowledge of the condition of that our kingdome, than wee heere can have,) judge most for the good principally of our Protestant subjects there, and generallye of that whole kingdome, as alsoe most advantagiouse unto us, in relation to the composure and settlement of the present distractions of this.

And for your better directions therein, wee have herewithall sent you the Propositions[2] made unto us, by those which were deputed from the Rebells there, to attend us heere upon the subject of a Treatye, and joyntlye with them such awnsweres[3] and concession unto them, as, by the advise of our Counsell, heere, upon a full hearinge in every particular of the same, of those of our Counsell[4] of that kingdome sent for over by us to assist heere in that businesse, and of those other fower[5] alsoe employed unto us by some of our Protestant subjects there, wee thought could not prudentlye bee denyed them, and might justlye and with honour bee graunted them in the present conjuncture of our distracted affayres, with which if you can perswade our Romaine Catholique subjects soe to rest satisfyed, as that you may conclude a Peace upon them, they givinge you thereupon securitye and assureance of such thinges as you shall judge necessary to bee demaunded, in our and in our Protestant subjects'

1. *See* p. 198.   2. For these Propositions, *see* p. 128.   3. *See* p. 175.
4 Lord Kerry, Sir Gerrard Lowther, Sir William Stewart, Justice Donellan, and Sir Philip Percival.
5. William Ridgeway, Sir Francis Hamilton, Michael Jones, and Fenton Parsons.

behalfes, for the restitution and preservation of what of right belonges both to us, and to our said Protestant subjects, and is necessarye to the future peace and good government of that our kingdome, wee shall esteeme it a happy and an acceptable service, which you are to endeavour by all meanes possible.

Notwithstandinge, although wee doe transmitt unto you our said awnsweres unto their Propositions, the better to enforme you what is thought by us, and our Counsell heere, just and honorable to be graunted, yett it is not with any intent to limitt and confine you unto those conditions or to binde you upp from streighteninge or enlargeinge the same, accordinge as, upon a right and mature consideration of the true state of that our kingdome, you shall finde necessarye for the present preservation of our Protestant subjects there, and for the future peace and happynesse of the same.

But, in case you cannot obtaine a Peace upon such termes as may bee just and honorable for us to graunt, and safe for our said Protestant subjects, it beinge unpossible for us to maintaine a warr there, or to give our said Protestant subjects any releefe whereby to protect themselves from ruine and desolation, by reason of the greate streights and pressures wee are under heere by the unnaturall Rebellion now raginge in this our kingdome of England, our will and pleasure is that you endeavour a continuance of the Cessation of armes there for such further time as you in your judgement shall finde necessary and expedient for our service, and the securitye of our Protestant subjects.

And soe, noe way doubtinge of your greate care and fidelitye in a matter of soe greate consequence and trust committed to you, wee bid you heartily farewell.

Given at our Court at Evesham, the seaventh day of July, 1644.—By his Majestie's commaund: GEORGE DIGBYE.

Addressed: To our right trusty and entirely beloved cousin and counsellour, James, Marquesse of Ormonde, our Lieutenant-Generall, and Generall Governour of our kingdome of Ireland.

LXVIII. Ormonde and the Earl of Kildare, a.d., 1644.

1. Kildare to Ormonde.

My most honoured Lord,—I am credibly informed that the Scotch are at Trim, and at Kilcocke all the people are driving away theire cattle. I desire your Excellencie's directions, and these poore English that are with me, what we shall doe. Moreover, I desire that you would send me some gunpowder, and that your Lordship would be pleased to send men to man the castle : for now it may prove a considerable place, fitt to be kept for his Majestie. If the Scotch gett into it, they will not easilybe beaten out. I have lately taken downe the spoutes of my house, which hath furnished me with great store of leade. If I had but powder proportionable, I would loose my life in the castle, before I would loose it. If I come away, the English will leave this place naked, and come all away. I expect your Excellencie's commands, which I will obay, and noe man shall be a more ready and humbler observer of you than your truly honoring kinsman,—George Kildare.

I desire to know of your Excellencye that if the gentrye of the cuntrey desire my castle, I may deliver it them, they pretending to defend it.

2. Ormonde to Earl of Kildare.

After our very harty commendacions to your Lordship : In answeare to your Lordship's letter (of this daie's date, as wee suppose, because) newly received, wee can beleeve noe such intencion in the Scotts as that they will march soe farr this way as may trouble you there, and therefore hould it not fitt, that you accidentally increase the feare (it seemes) apprehended by the people in those partes, by your Lordship's relinquishinge of that place, whither you shall not only seasonably receive powder and men to your assistance in case there bee occasion, but alsoe our further orders for your direccion as shalbee fitt. Soe, bidding your Lordship very hartily farewell, wee remaine, from his Majestie's Castle of Dublin, this 10th of July, 1644, your Lordship's affectionate kinsman and servant,— ORMONDE.

Your Lordship's servant hath warrant for twelve pounds of powder, with match and lead proportionable, in present.

Earl of Kildare.

LXIX. PROCEEDINGS RELATIVE TO OATH OF ASSOCIATION OF CONFEDERATES.

1. By the General Assembly of the Confederate Catholicks of Ireland. Kilkenny, July 26, 1644.

Upon full debate this day, in open Court Assembly, it is unanimously declared by the Lords Spiritual and Temporal, and the Knights and Burgesses of this House, That the Oath of Association, as it is already penned of record in this House, and taken by the Confederate Catholicks, is full and binding, without addition of any other words thereunto. And it is ordered, That any person or persons whatsoever, who have taken, or hereafter shall take, the said Oath of Association, and hath, or shall declare by word or actions, or by persuasions of others, that the said Oath, or any branch thereof, doth or may admit any equivocation or mental reservation (if any such person or persons be) shall be deemed a breaker of his and their Oath respectively, and adverse to the general cause, and as a delinquent or delinquents for such offence shall be punished. And it is further ordered, That the several Ordinaries shall take special care that the Parish-Priests within their respective dioceses shall publish and declare, That any person or persons who hath [taken], or shall take, the said Oath, making any such declaration, or persuasion of or concerning the said Oath, shall be taken and deemed as perjured, and accordingly for that offence punished. And it is likewise ordered, That if any particular man have heretofore delivered or uttered, or hereafter shall deliver or utter, any opinion con-

LXIX. 1, 2, 3. " Printed at Waterford by Thomas Bourke, Printer to the Confederate Catholicks of Ireland," [1644]. "History and Vindication of the Loyal Formulary or Irish Remonstrance." Appendix 1. London : 1674. In reference to the original Oath of Association, *see* vol. ii. p. 210.

trary to this declaration, that such party or parties being discovered, shall be severely punished. And all Superiors of the Secular and Regular clergy are to cause all those under their power and rule to take the said Oath of Association within three months next ensuing, and thereof make certificate to this House, or, the Assembly being adjourned or dissolved, unto the Supreme Council.

2. The Preamble to the Oath of Association.

Whereas the Roman Catholicks of this kingdom of Ireland, have been enforced to take arms for the necessary defence and preservation, as well of their religion, plotted and by many foul practices endeavoured to be quite suppressed by the Puritan faction, as likewise of their lives, liberties, and estates, and also for the defence and safeguard of His Majestie's regal power, just prerogatives, honour, state, and rights, invaded upon : and for that it is requisite, that there should be an unanimous consent and real union between all the Catholicks of this realm, to maintain the premisses and strengthen them against their adversaries : It is thought fit by them, that they and whosoever shall adhere unto their party, as a Confederate, should, for the better assurance of their adhering, fidelity, and constancy to the Publick cause, take the ensueing oath :

3. The Oath of Association.

I., A. B., do profess, swear, and protest before God, and His Saints, and Holy Angels, that I will, during life, bear true faith and allegiance to my sovereign Lord Charles, by the grace of God King of Great Britain, France, and Ireland, and to his heirs, and lawful successors ; and that I will to my power, during my life defend, uphold, and maintain all his and their just prerogatives, estates, and rights, the power and priviledge of the Parliament of this Realm, the fundamental laws of Ireland, the free exercise of the Roman Catholick Faith and Religion throughout all this land, and the lives, just liberties, possessions, estates, and rights of all those, that have taken or shall take this oath, and perform the contents thereof. And that I will obey and ratifie all the orders and decrees made, and to be made by the Supreme Council of the Confederate Catholicks of this kingdom concerning the said Public cause. And that I will not seek, directly or indirectly, any pardon or protection for any act done, or to be done, touching the general cause, without the consent of the major part of the said Council. And that I will not, directly or indirectly, do any act, or acts, that shall prejudice the said cause, but will, to the hazard of my life and estate, assist, prosecute, and maintain the same. So help me God, and His Holy Gospel.

LXX. LIST OF PEERS AND OTHER MEMBERS OF THE GENERAL ASSEMBLY OF THE IRISH CONFEDERATION, A.D., 1644.

The names, as well of the Lords Spiritual and Temporal now present as the names of the Lords of the Catholick Confederacy now absent, by reason of impediments, together with the names of the Knights, Citizens, and Burgesses, now members of the General Assembly aforesaid :

Hugo [O'Reilly] Ardmachanus.—Frater Thomas [Fleming] Archbishop of Dublin.—Thomas [Walsh] Archiepiscopus Cassellensis.—Thomas [Dease] Midensis.—David [Roth] Episcopus Ossoriensis.—Boetius [Mac Egan] Episcopus Elphin.—Patricius [Comerford] Episcopus Waterfordiensis et Lysmorensis.—Joannes [Molony] Episcopus Laonensis.— Malachias [O'Queely] Archiepiscopus Tuamensis.—Gulielmus [Tirry] Episcopus Corke et Cloine.—Joannes [Bourke] Episcopus Clonfertensis.—Edmundus [Dempsy] Episcopus Laghlin.—Emer [Mac Mahon] Episcopus Down et Connor.

Castlehaven, Audley.—Antrim.—Mountgarret.—Gormanstown.—Fingal.—Netterville.—Maurice de Rupe et Fermoy.—Muskery.—Ikereyn.—Trimleston.—Glanmaliera.—Slane.—Dunboyne.—Arthur [Magennis, Viscount] Iveagh.—Cahir Boy [Buidhe] : Upper Ossory.—Castle Connell.—Louth.—Brittas.

John Allyn.[1]—Thomas Arthur.—Walter Bagnall.—John Bagott.—

LXX. "Printed at Waterford by Thomas Bourke, Printer to the Confederate Catholicks of Ireland," [1644].

1. In the original, the names are not in the alphabetical order in which they are here given, to facilitate reference. Those to which asterisks are prefixed appear twice in the original.

Henry Barnewall.—Michael Barnewall.—Richard Barnewall.—Geoffrey Barron.—James Bath.—Barnaby Bealing.—Patrick Beetagh.—John Bellew.—Richard Bellings.—Richard Berford.—William Birmingham.—Brian Birne (or Brine).—George Blackny.—Dominick Bodkin.—Theobald Bodkyn.—Patrick Brian.—Geoffrey Brown.—*John Brown.—*Theobald Burke.—Edmund Butler.—*James Butler.—*Pierce Butler.—Richard Butler.—Theobald Butler.—Thomas Butler.

*James Callon.—John Cantwell.—*John Carroll.—Arthur Cheevers.—George Cheevers.—John Cheevers.—Terence Coghlane.—Edward Comerford.—George Commin.—Thomas Coce (sic).—James Couly.—Pierce Creagh.—Pierce Crosby.—Walter Cruise.—James Cusack.

James Daniel.—Patrick Darcy.—Thomas Darcy.—Peter Dobbyn.—Edward Dowd.—Lawrence Dowdall.—Terence Doyne.—James Duffe.—Paul Duffe.—Edward Dungan.

Thomas Esmond.—R. Everard.

Stephen Fallon.—Dominick Fanning.—Gerald Fennell.—Francis Ferraill.—Richard Ferraill.—Edmund Fitz Gerald.—Gerald Fitz Gerald.—Morice Fitz Gerald.—Pierce Fitz Gerald.—Thomas Fitz Gerald.—Garret Fitzmorice.—Florence Fitz Patrick.—James Fleming.—Lawrence Fleming.—Thomas Fleming.—Hubert Fox.—Christopher French.—James Forlong.

John Garvy.—*Patrick Goagh.—John Gould.—Robert Grace.—George Green.

John Halye.—Richard Haly.—Nicholas Halye.—Lawrence Hamon.—Robert Harpole.—Thomas Henes.—Daniel Higgin.—John Hoare.—Matth. Hoare.—*Nicholas Halliwood.

Edmund Kealy.—George King.

John Lacy.—Walter Lacy.—Richard Lawless.—James Lewis.—John Linch.—Rob : Linch.—Robert Lumbard.

Callaghan Mac Cahir.—Charles Mac Carty.—Cormuck Mac Carty.—Dermott Mac Carty.—Donogh Mac Carty.—Florence Mac Carty.—Teig Mac Carty.—James Mac Collo Mac Daniel.—James Mac Donnell.—Richard Martyn.—Owen Molloy.—Roger Moore.—Patrick Nettervill.—Richard Nettervill.

Daniel O'Brian.—Dermott O'Brian.—*Thorlogh O'Briane.—Turlogh

O'Boyle.—*Connor O'Callaghan.—Donogh O'Callaghan.—Teig O'Connor.
—Daniel O'Donovan.—Donnel O'Leary.—Art Oge O'Neill.—Phelim
O'Neill.—*Turlogh O'Neill.—Mulmore Mac Edmund O'Reilly.—Mulmore
Mac Philip O'Reilly.—Philip Mac Mulmore O'Reilly.—Daniel O'Swylle-
van.—Dermot O'Shagnussy.

Andrew Pallice.—Ambrose Plunkett.—Nicholas Plunkett.—Patrick
Plunkett.—David Power.—Edmund Power.—John Power.—James Preston.
—Thomas Preston.—James Purcell.—Philip Furcell.

Hugh Rochford.—Pierce Rowth.—Thomas Ryan.

George St. Leger.—Martin Scurlock.—Robert Shee.—Pierce Sherlock.
—Henry Slensby —James Stafford.—William Stafford.—John Stanly.—
Nicholas Sutton.

Gerald Talbott.—Gerratt Talbott.—Robert Talbott.

Christopher Veldon.

Richard Wadding.—Thomas Wadding.—Edward Wall.—John Walsh.
—Lewis Walsh.—Thomas Walsh.—Alexander Warren.—Nicholas Wogan.
—John Wise.—William Young.

LXXI. Proceedings in Munster, July, 1644.

1. Lord Broghill, etc., to the Mayor of Clonmel.

Mr. Mayor, etc.—The intelligence, which wee have received from
severall good hands of your owne party, of your bad intentions towards
us, and the new levyes of souldiers lately made in all partes of this
province, and the callinge back of part of your army, lately advanced northward against the Scotts, without the least shew of danger towards you,
giveth us just grounds to apprehend that you intend to ceaze upon our
garrizon townes, and consequently (guessing att the subsequent by your
former proceedinges[1]) to cutt us off, and distroy us, the Protestants of this
province: Wee doubt not that you will confesse it to bee most just,
before God and man, for every one to use their best endeavors for their
owne preservacion from imminent and threatninge ruine.

LXXI. 1, 2, 3. Carte Papers, xi., pp. 367, 388, 389.

1 This refers to the occupation of Clonmel and Dungarvan by the Irish, in 1641.
See vol. i., p. xliii.

This very consideracion hath prevayled with us to draw us into armes for our owne defence; nott with a purpose to offend any of the Irish quarters. Of this our resolucion wee thinke fitte to give you notice, and wee have made the same knowne to the Right Honourable the Lord Lieutenante, presuminge you will doe soe to your Supreame Councell. Wee and you may very well hope that his Lordship and they will find a way to secure us from all those jealosies and feares, which have occasioned us to putt ourselves into this posture of defence. And till wee shall understand the mind of the Lord Lieutenant and you of your Supreame Councell heerin, wee may forbeare all acts of hostillity upon both sides, and continue that quiett commerce which formerly was betwixt us: wee, by allowing you to buy in our townes such wares as you please (and wee can spare); and you, by sendinge to our markett such commodities as you think fitt, for which you shall receive ready money. If by the bearer you signifie your acceptance of this our offer, with your ingagements, upon your reputacions, to observe it punctually to us and all of our quarters, wee doe heerby undertake to performe the like unto you, and to all of your quarters. Thus, expectinge your positive answere heerin, wee remayne, your loving frends as wee find you,—BROGHILL.—W. FENTON. PERCY SMYTH.

Youghall, 26th July, 1644.

To our worthey frends, the Maior, Bailiffs, and Commonaltie of the towne of Clonmell, hast theese.

2. LETTER TO LORD INCHIQUIN FROM SUPREME COUNCIL.

Right Honnourable,—Wee received informacions that the Catholiques of Corke, Kinsaile, and Yoaghell, on Friday last were moste of them tourned out of theire howses, and despoyled of theire goodes, and the rest committed to severall prisons, upon noe other pretence, but for that they are Irish Papists, in which expression a double mallice against our nacion and religion is expressed in a tyme of Cessacion and treaty for a peace, whereby both may be preserved. And though wee have noe greate cause to lament the misfortune of those of your quarter that stood in opposicion of us to advance your designes, yett the act gives us a light of your entencions and affirmes the trueth of that resolucion of yours to extirpate our nation and religion.

Wee likewise understand that your Lordshipp and those of your partie in the countie of Corke and other adjacent partes have drawen your forces into a boddy. You cannot be ignorant how inviolably wee have observed the Articles of Cessacion in all poincts, and how kindly wee entreated those of your partie within our quarters, and how farr the raysing of any stirrs in Mounster is prejudiciall to the Kinge's service against the Rebells in Ulster. Yett wee have seene a letter[1] written by the Lorde of Broghill, Sir William Fenton, and Sir Piers Smith, of the 26th of the present [July], to the Mayor of Clonmell, thereby intimating that newe levyes were made for the raysing of more soildiours within our quarters, and parte of our army advanced towardes Ulster were comaunded backe, and that they received intelligence from some of our partie, which gave them grounde to suspect that wee had an intencion to seize upon the castles and garrisons of your partie, and consequently to destroye the Protestants thereof. Your Lordship may remember, that at such tyme as wee yssued our proclamacion[2] that those within our quarters should be in a posture of defence, a powerfull Scottish armie was advanced into Leinster and comitted therein all sortes of crueltie, and wee were informed that many Parliament shipps were to lande in the sowtherne partes, soe as it is very strange to us that in a preparacion for a service soe acceptable to his Majesty and necessary for the defence of the countrey, a construccion should bee made that wee have bad intencions and that wee had designed to seize upon your garrisons and destroye the Protestants of that province, whereas wee had noe intencion to molest or trouble any comprized within the Articles of Cessacion, nor to give any interruption to the settlement of a firme peace and quiett within the kingdome, for which his Majestie's Comission[3] is come over (as wee heere).

As for the bringing backe of our army advaunced into the north, or of any sinister intencions in us, or in any within our quarters to our know-

---

1. *See* p. 216.   2. *See* p. 205.   3. *See* p. 208.

ledge, the Lorde of Broghill and the rest were therein moste untruely and malitiously advertised.

Wee shall therefore desire your Lordship to find out, and signifie unto us, the grounde of this unexpected proceeding and the names of the authors of the saied false and scandalous reportes against us, with your further resolucions thereupon, that, as our intencions are faire and just, soe wee may approve our accions to be such as gave noe just cause of this late alteracion, and in as much as those under your comaunde have causelesly administered theise causes of distrust, you will not take it ill, nor any breach of the Cessacion, that wee shall stand on our guarde untill wee finde the groundes of our just apprehensions removed.   And soe wee remayne your Lordship's loveing friendes,—[MOUNTGARRET, ETC.]

Kilkenny, 29 July, 1644.

3. LETTER TO ORMONDE FROM VISCOUNT MOUNTGARRET, ETC.

Our very good Lord,—Wee send your Lordship here enclosed a letter[1] from the Lord of Broghill and others, directed to the Mayor of Clonmell, which, together with the coppy of our letter[2] to the Lord of Insequin, wherein wee sett forth the practices against Catholickes, will informe your Lordship of a mallicious and dangerous designe to disturb his Majestie's service and the peace of this kingdome.

Wee find likewise a correspondence betweene them and [the Fort of] Duncannon, whence a pinnace arrived at Youghill that day the Catholickes were bannished, with letters and some armes ; and wee doubt not but the enclosed letter of the Lord Esmond will in your Lordship's judgment discover very ill affeccions of his side.   For our partes, wee are resolved to observe the Articles of Cessacion, but will endeavour, both for his Majestie's service and our defence, to putt ourselves into a posture, whereof wee desire your Lordship to make no other construccion.   Thus wee rest your Lordship's humble servants,—MOUNTGARRET.

These we writt by direction of the Assembly.—N. PLUNKETT.

Kilkenny, 29 July, 1644, Lord Lieutenante.

1, 2. *See* pp. 216-17.

LXXII. Negotiations for Peace, 1644 : Letter from Ormonde to Muskerry and Supreme Council of Confederation.

After our hartie comendations : Whereas wee, the Lord Lieutenant, on the xxvith of July, 1644, received a Comission[1] from the King's most Excellent Majestie, under his Majestie's great seale of his kingdome of England, appointing us to treate concerning the settling and establishing a firme and perfect peace within this his kingdome, and authorizing us, for his Majestie and in his name, to treate, conclude, and agree with any person or persons whatsoever, deputed or to bee deputed by his Majestie's subjects of this kingdome now or late in armes, or nominated or to be nominated on their behalfe, or with any other person or persons whatsoever, as wee, the Lord Lieutenant, in our judgement shall thinck fitt for the settling and concluding of a firme and lastinge peace in this kingdome ; and to take into our serious consideration the demands and propositions which have been made to his Majestie or shalbe made or tendered to us, the Lord Lieutenant, touching or concearning the premisses or any of them ; and to compose and end all differences arrising thereuppon : And whereas by the said Commission wee, the Lord Lieutenant, are alsoe authorized, if wee thinck fitt, to conclude of a further Cessation of armes in this kingdome, wee therefore hould it fitt to acquaint you therewith, to the end you may notifie the same to his Majestie's subjects of this kingdome, now or late in armes, that soe they may depute some fitt person or persons to attend us concerning the premisses. And soe wee bid you farewell from his Majestie's Castle of Dublin, xxx Julii, 1644.—Your loving frende,—ORMONDE.

To the Lord Vice-Count Muskery, and the rest with him [who] lately attended his Majestie in England, or to any one or more of them.

LXII. Carte Papers, xi. p. 392.   1. *See* p. 208.

LXXIII. Expulsion of Irish from Cork, July, 1644.

1. Letter to Lord Muskerry from Mayor and Recorder of Cork.

Right Honorable and my very good Lord,—I would long ere this (if I durst repose confidence in any messenger) have signifyed unto your Lordship the most deplorable state and condition of this poore and of all other most unfortunate and miserable citty and Corporacion, now wholy undone, haveing all the Irish and Catholique inhabitants thereof totally banished from hence, to a very few that are alsoe driven to that exigence, as that neither rest, meat or drinke, if any they had left them, can doe them any good, the actor thereof being soe highly incensed against them without any kinde or ocasion of the least fault to be imputed unto them, if not for addresseing ourselves unto the Lord Marques [of Ormonde], when I was comitted and caryed prisoner to Donerayle, and from thence after long restraint brought back and comitted unto Shandon Castle ; all which I presume your Lordship since your arrivall hath been partly informed with the cause thereof.

And now, findeing the conveniency of this bearer, I humbly make bould by the inclosed[1] to represent unto your Lordship's view the whole passadge and maner of the extirpacion of the natives of this citty, which is now at the last period of being for ever ruined and quite extinguisht and his Majestie's interests therein perpetually lost, unlesse some speedy remedy be forthwith applyed by your Lordship's meanes, in procureing the Lord Marques and the State there [Dublin] to use some present course to alter both our Comanders, officers, and army heere in garrison, and in their roomes to send us such other as his Excellency and the State may securedly confide in for his Majestie's service, and the preservacion of theise three ports of Cork, Yeoghall, and Kinsale, and which had need to be done with all possible care and expedition, for that it is generally conceived and

LXXIII. 1, 2, 3, 4, 5. Carte Papers, xi., pp. 400, 398, 401, 402-5 ; xii. 23.
1. *See* pp. 222-230

affirmed that the Parliament forces will be heere the first easterly winde; and soe earnestly beseeching your Lordship's speciall care heerein, as you tender the preservacion of his Majestie's interests in theise parts, with my humble respects hopeing your Lordship will be pleased to excuse my tedious remonstrance, I conclude and remaine your Lordship's most humble and assured servant,—[ROBERT COPPINGER, MAYOR OF CORK.— JOHN GALLWEY, RECORDER.]

Cork, the last of July, 1644.

2. THE RELATION OF THE LORD INCHIQUIN'S CARRIAGE IN THE EXPELLING THE IRISH OUT OF CORK.

Uppon Saterday, the 27th [July], his Lordship [Inchiquin] affirmed with an oath, that, if wee weare to starve, wee should not have one bitt of any provision which should be put into the magazins, and that if any army should come to beseege the towne, and wee haveing noe provision for our-selves, wee should be presently thrust out of the gates.

Uppon Munday, Tewsday, and this present day, being the last of July, they are takeing and carying of all the provision corne of all sorts from us unto their owne magazins.

A Saterday and Monday last, they have raysed three new companies of the English and brought them into towne, where they weare all armed; and all the rest of the English inhabitants that dwelled in the suburbs and elswhere are brought within the citty, and placed in the howses of those that weare banished, and possessed themselves of all their moveables.

All the Irish and Catholiques of Yeoghall and the suburbs thereof weare used in the like nature, and twelve of the principall Irish Catholiques of Kinsale caryed into the fort and there restrayned for hostages.

Uppon Wedensday, the 24 of July, Sir Thomas Wharton and Captaine Steeres weare dispatcheed away in a vessell from Kinsale.

Uppon Fryday last, the 26th, his owne frigatt came hither from Kinsale with threescore barrells of powder and a great quantity of salt, which was no sooner landed but the frigatt was presently dispatched away.

Uppon Saturday, the 27th, the Mayor demanding what he, the Aldermen, and Sheriffs, should doe, his Lordship answeared that they might all part the towne if they pleased, but that they should not be permitted to carry anything with them.

The £4,000 payable unto his Majestie by the Corporacion by way of loane, is all payed to a matter of four or five hundred pounds, and yet his Lordship notwithstanding will force us according his owne agreement.

Alsoe, his Lordship's pinnace, uppon Saterday last, the 27th, went forth of this harbour, and was seene aloofe off with another great shipp, and a boate of some bignes, conceived to be the boate that belonged to the fort of Halbowling, severall tymes to pass from one to another. And, the same day, boath the pinnace and great shipp came in towards the harbour's mouth, as it is thought to view the harbour, and sudenly after boath went to sea together. All which, together with many other circumstances which for brevity's sake and the bearer's hast will not permitt us to insertt, wee humbly desire that your Lordship [Muskerry] will be pleased to represent those our greevances to the Lord Lieutenant, humbly desireing his Lordship that hee would be speedyly pleased to secure those places for his Majestie's service, by sending downe another garrison under the command of faithfull commanders and officers, and removeing those remayneing heere, and in the intrim to contrive it soe that the Lord of Inchiquin may not be made privy to these our greevances untill wee be secured of our lives at which tyme wee shall really and redyly affirme and prove all these particulers; and, in the mean while, wee shall and ever will remaine your Lordships most faithfull servants for his Majestie's service,—[ROBERT COPPINGER, MAYOR OF CORK.—JOHN GALLWEY, RECORDER.]

Corke, ultimo Julii, 1644.

3. INCHIQUIN'S " ORDERS FOR MAJOR BANISTER, GOVERNOR OF THE CITTY [OF CORK] TO BE OBSERVED IN PUTTING FORTH THE IRISH."

Whereas I have given leave to the severall inhabitants of the citty of Corke, uppon their departing forth of the said citty to carry with them all their goods, houshold stuffe, money, and plate, etc. It is nevertheles expected by mee that before they carry away their goods, that they leave within the said citty the full quantity of two thousand barrells of corne and meale of all sorts, and two hundred flock bedds and boulsters with cadowes [blankets]; and in case there shall be no possibility of leaving the quantity afforesaid, that then there shall be left fifteen hundred barrells of corne meale, and £200 in mony; and accordingly, if but one thousand barrells shall be found remaineing that then there shall be payed in in mony £500, in case soe much remaine unpayed of their share of £4,000 loane mony; and if there doth not soe much rest unpayd, that then £400 in mony shall bee payed, whereuppon I shall acknowledge to be fully satisfyed of £4,000 by the said inhabitants promised to be lent unto his Majestie.

And it is alsoe expected that the partyes departing the said citty shall make over their howses or goods to such of the English as they are indebted unto, in case they be not able to pay their debts in specie.

And I shall further expect, and doe require, that all persons of the Irish inhabitants within the said citty doe forthwith depart out of the same uppon payne of death, the Maior, Aldermen, and soe many other persons, to the number of one hundred men in the whole, as they shall elect, with their wives and children, and such Aldermen's widdows and such sikly persons as cannot be removed only excepted; and that all the foresaid persons shall retourne or send thither uppon Fryday next to the suburbs of the towne, and there receive their goods which shall be left behinde them, if the condition above prescribed be performed, at which tyme every person haveing goods within the said citty shall have free egresse and regresse and full liberty to pass to and fro with their said goods, provided they depart the citty the same night, uppon perrill of their lives,—INCHIQUINE.

4. A relation of the passadges betweene the Lord Inchiquin and the Mayor and Aldermen of Corke, upon his Lordship's expelling the Irish inhabitants of that citty. Subscribed by Robert Coppinger, Mayor, and John Gallwey, Sherriffe. July, 1644.

Uppon Fryday morning at six a clock, Governor Banister came to the Maior's howse, before he was out of his bed, and demanding whether the Maior was stirring, answear was made that he was, whereuppon he replyed that he must of necessity speake with him presently, uppon which the Mayor being called uppon he suddainely gott upp, and coming to him, he tould him that my Lord of Inchiquin was uppon rydeing to Downerayle that morning, and before his goeing would have both him, and all his Aldermen and Sherriffs, to come unto him with all speed to conferr with them. The Maior answeared he would, but that he conceived it was somewhat too early, and that most of the Aldermen weare as yett a-bedd or att prayers, yett that he would send to hasten them, and accordingly did soe.

And, some two howres after, all being com to the Mayor's howse, they went to my Lord's howse at Deans Court, where being come, after an hower's attendance his Lordship came downe from his chamber, and calling the Maior and Aldermen he walked with them to the garden, where, viewing of them all, he mist Mr. William Hore, and gave directions he should be presently sent for, his Lordship in the meane tyme in a discourse letting us know, and setting before our eyes the miseryes of the present state and condition wherein wee all stood for want of a present reconcilliacion or concordance of a peace between the English and the Irish, whereof his Lordship was fully resolved by severall intimations from divers partes and persons of eminence that there was little or noe hopes of any such happy agreement. To confirme which his Lordship produced a letter as he said received from my Lord of Clanricard and St. Albans, wherein he certifyed that he came then lately from Dublin, where he stayed longer than hee expected, hopeing that the Commissioners for the Irish uppon their coming thither would have produced some fruitfull hopes of a general peace, which as he then [said], he little expected, and the rather for that the Comission intended to be sent to the Lord Marques from his Majestie was not come, and that himselfe, the said Lord of St. Albans, had moved His Excellency that a letter should be sent from all the Lords unto his Majestie to declare the state of the kingdome, which letter, being accordingly drawen and signed by many, was sent unto him and the Lord of Broghill likewise to be signed; all which wee found out at last was only to detract tyme untill all the troopes weare ready to come thither, his Lordship haveing severall tymes sent to hasten their coming.

And when they came all to the church yard, his Lordship, starting forward, called to the Maior and the rest to goe see the horse, where being come betweene the troopes, and all armed a-horsback with their carabines ready spande, uppon the least notice to give fyre uppon us, his Lordship then said that they should excuse him, for untill hee had finished some service which he had to performe in the citty, wee must of force tarry there.   And thereuppon his Lordship with Sir William Courtney's troope came into the towne, where all the foote there in garrison with two companies that came from Yeoghall, being in all seaven companies, weare at a word redy with lighted matches (leaveing three troopes of horse to guard us abroad).

And, uppon his Lordship's coming into towne, hee required the Sherriffe Galwey and Mr. Hore to waite uppon him; and, presently, coming within the gates, hee comanded the said Sherriffe and Mr. Hore without any more adoe to draw forth of the citty all the Irish inhabitants, both young men and ould men, which they [not] dareing to disobey presently performed, and after weare likewise comanded to drive forth all the clergie and alsoe all the women of what quallity soever, which being alsoe done to a very small number, whereof most part hydd themselves under coverts, all the horse and foot standing still in their former posture, and all the ordinance in towne being redy fitted and charged, and presented towards the street in both the castles of the gates.

At length, late in the evening, the Mayor, Aldermen, and Sherriffs, with Mr. Hore, weare only permitted to repaire into their howses, where all night long they weare constrayned to watch themselves, and feared every hower to be their last, such streight watches and armed men running all the towne over as well in streets and lanes, as alsoe on the walls from place to place, many of the inhabitants' howses being broaken open, and all their goods plundered and conveyed away by the souldiers that night, a streight and generall search being made over all the towne for all the armes that any of the inhabitants had which they tooke to their owne coustody, leaveing them scarce their pockett knives.

The next morning, being the 27th of July, 1644, the Mayor, Aldermen, and Sherriffs, with Mr. Hore, repayred to his Lordship at the fort, where [he] lay that night, and desired to know his Lordship's pleasure and what hee intended to doe with them and the inhabitants, who answeared that they should all depart and retyre themselves where they pleased, but should cary nothing with them out of the citty ; which being answeared by the Mayor that it was something too hard measure that the poore inhabitants that for many hundred yeeres, with their predicessors, stood in a condition from tyme to tyme to doe his Majestie service, should now at last be exposed into banishment from their owne antient and native homes into the vast world without affoarding them any part of their owne goods or provision to releeve themselves and their poore children who weare for want thereof redy to starve ; unto which his Lordship answeared, that, if they weare all Lords, of necessity they must be all gone, without any other remedy. Yett, uppon some further consideracion, (a while after), adviseing with his councell of warr consisting of noe men of any ranke or quality (Sir William Courteney and Sir Andrew Barrett excepted), the rest though few being but inferior officers, [he] came unto us and said that hee thought of another course that should secure the citty with less inconveniency, and give us all better content.

Wee approved thereof, whereunto the Mayor replyed that whatsoever course his Lordship should propound for the furtherance of his Majestie's service should be by them condiscended unto, and with that he demanded hostages of them, which the Mayor and the rest presently yeelded willingly unto, demanding what number, who answeared thirty, which number they conceiveing to be somewhat too many, for avoyding of charge, which of necessity the citty must beare for their maintenance, desired his Lordship would be pleased to reduce them to a less number, whereuppon he answeared he would, soe that he should chuse whom he thought most convenient. And that being agreed unto, he thereuppon retyred with his councell, sending for severall of the English inhabitants who weare best acquainted with the townsmen for their assistance. And, after two howers' consultacion, his Lordship came and tould us that all was agreed uppon, and that he would but repaire unto his chamber and there draw a cleere lyst of the names of the hostages and deliver it us to bring them in, which being by us performed he would remove all the garrison from us, save some competent number to guard both the gates, and then permitt all the inhabitants to retourne to their owne habitacions, and leave the care and keepeing of the towne to ourselves; which much rejoyced us, being in that most deplorable and miserable condition, and accordingly there expected him for two or three howers, after which tyme he imployed unto us one Lieutenant Harcott [Harcourt], willing us to retire ourselves out of the fort unto some neere adjoyneing howse to refresh ourselves, for that his Lordship was soe earnestly imployed as that he could give noe answeare for two howers longer.

Whereuppon wee desired to be admitted to the Mayor's howse, being next the gate, which would not be graunted, and with that wee repayred unto an in-howse neere adjoyning to the fort, being conveyed thither by the Provost marshall; and there scarse remaining two howers, when there came unto us that all the troopes being a-foot and armed with their petronells redy spand in their hands, and all the souldiers with their musketts chardged and lighted matches, weare driveing all the rest of the inhabitants (that weare remaining within the towne, both men, women, and children) from out the citty, not admitting them to carry any thing with them, locking their howses and takeing all their keyes to their owne hands, soe that in lesse than two or three howers' tyme all the citty was depopulated and not one Irish inhabitant left therein.

Whereuppon the Maior, Recorder, and the rest, repayred to the fort gate, with intention to speake with his Lordship, but could have noe admittance; and after halfe an hower's attendance Major Muschampe came to the gate, and tould us that wee could not for an hower longer speake with his Lordship, and thereuppon retourned to the former in-house and there continued for an hower after, till wee had notice of his Lordship's goeing to visit the Lord Archbishop of Tuam [Richard Boyle]; and thereuppon wee waited his Lordship's retourne from thence, where meeting with him, wee renued our former complaints, desireing his Lordship to take compassion of the poore and most distressed estate of the inhabitants, haveing no other lodging but under hedges and ditches, being not able to putt one bitt into their mowths. Whereunto he replyed that there was noe possibility to remedy it, for that they must be content therewith, and that he would allow them only a hundred men with some aged and impotent persons to dwell in the towne, and they must not expect to have any part of the provision of what sort soever that then remained in the towne, but must either provide other provision for themselves or otherwise parte the towne.

And waiteing further uppon his Lordship to the fort gate, there stopping for a tyme, Sherriffe Galwey demanding of his Lordship how they should bee sure of their lives that would remaine within the towne, his Lordship made answear that hee would take his oath uppon the Holy Evangelist that whatever quarter hee would gett for himselfe he would procure the like for them, unlesse a more potent and strong army should come over whome he should have noe command; unto which the Sherriffe replyed: God defend that wee should have any other commander but your Lordship, before his Majestie should appoint a Governor to protect us. His Lordship replyed to that, that these gentlemen and officers of the army howbeit they weare under his comand that day, yett he was not sure they would observe the same to-morrow and more than formerly promised hee would not undertake. To which Sir William Courteney answeared that whilest they had life they would observe his Lordship's commands, and then, for the present, very late, he licensed the Mayor, Recorder, Aldermen, and Sherriffs, with a few other gentlemen of quality to repaire into the towne that night, where they continued (in an howerly feare) untill after evening prayer, the next day being Sunday.

Att which tyme wee repayred againe to his Lordship to know his further pleasure, and what quarter hee would affoard us. After much debate, his Lordship was pleased and fully resolved to graunt unto us no other quarter but according to the contents of the coppy sent heerewith, all received by us the 29 of this present [July] which was severall tymes proclaymed thorough the citty by sound of drum; and, alsoe, two or three tymes a day wee have proclamacions that all other persons save the afforesaid number should part the citty uppon paine of death.

Uppon Munday, the 29th, wee humbly desired that every of the inhabitants might be spared some competency out of their owne provision to manteyne them for one seven-night; which was alsoe denyed them.

And that very day and the next, being the 30th, they seized uppon all the provision that was belonging to the Irish in the citty and suburbs, and tooke the keys into their owne hands. That day Sherriffe Gallewey was imployed to his Lordship to desire that the Aldermen and gentlemen's daughters, being maydens, might be admitted to see their owne corne and provision measured and delivered into the magazine, and themselves to remaine among their frends, which request his Lordship would not graunt.—Cork, ultimo Julii, 1644.

5. ORDER BY INCHIQUIN.

It is ordered by the Right Honnourable the Lord of Inchiquine that from this day forward the marquetts be kept in the convenientest place without the North Gate. The last of July, 1644.—PEREGRINE BANASTER.

This to be proclaimed by sound of drume.

LXXIV. EXPEDITION TO ULSTER, 1644.

1. EARL OF CASTLEHAVEN TO COLONEL MATHEWS.[1]

Sir,—The berrer, my Quarter-Master, I have appointed to oversee such provision for our armie as shall come to your garrison. You wilbe pleased to let him have such libertie within your jurisdiction as his employment will require. Sir, your favours in this, being of soe great concearnement to his Majestie's servise, is not doubted by your verie loving friend,—CASTLEHAVEN AND AUDLEY.

Charlemount[2] Camp, 29 July, 1644.

Addressed : For Lieutenant-Colonel Mathew, theis.

2. COLONEL MATHEWS TO EARL OF CASTLEHAVEN.

Right Honorable,—I have received your letter by your Quarter-Master, who tells mee it is your desyre to make this a magazine, which

---

LXXIV. 1, 2, 3, Carte Papers, xii. pp. 3, 48.

1. Lieutenant-Colonel Edmond Matthews, Governor of Newry. See " Contemporary History of Affairs in Ireland, 1641-1652," Dublin: 1879, pp. 557, 593.

2. In county of Armagh. *See* p. 12.

request was formerly demanded of mee by General-Major Monro, whose awnswere was a denyall, in regard I had received no orders from my Generall to permitt any such thing without his Excellencye's knowledge. Sir, if the permission of this lay in my owne power, I should bee ready att your Lordship's command ; but in regard my speciall commands from my Lord Leuietenant are to bee directed and guided by the Articles of Cessation, and withall, considering the scandall would bee layd upon mee for actions without his Excellencye's leave, I shall desyre you will bee pleasd to excuse mee, untill my Generall say the word, as not daring of myselfe to run the hazard in so great a matter : Your Lordship knowes that what benefitt may redound to your army out of this garrison is freely granted, and if in anything wee may supply your Lordship without prejudice to ourselves, it is at your pleasure : And so I rest.

This last night, I had intelligence that the Scotts doe fortifye themselves about Dromore.

Endorsed : The Earle of Castlehaven's letter, desyring to make this a magazine : And my awnswere : on the 1 August : 1644.

3. EARL OF CASTLEHAVEN TO COLONEL MATHEWS.

Sir,—The letters I have receaved from my Lord Liuetenant and from my Lord Liuetenant and Councell, gives mee ground to proceede with the Neury, and all garrisons and holts under their comaund, with the same freedome as with any of our own : Wherefore I have directed much of my baggadge and provision to your garrison, that they may stand the more readie for my occasions. Your former favours to my people, together with your frindship in this particuler, will verie highly oblidge your frend and servant,—CASTLEHAVEN AND AUDLEY.

Tonregee[1] Camp, 9 August, 1644.

I send this berrer before to receave your licence, and prepare cellaradge, and other convenient places for certaine wines I send, and other my provisions.

1. Tanderagee, county Armagh.   *See* p. 12.

Addressed: For my worthie friend, Liuetenant-Colonell Mathews, Governor of the Newry, these. Haste, haste.

LXXV.—[LXIV. A.]—LETTER TO CARDINAL MAZARIN FROM DE LA MONNERIE, AT KILKENNY.

Monseigneur,—Depuis ma dernière escripte, les Agens de ces Messieurs sont retournés d'Angleterre, ce qui m'a occasionné de les presser de satisfaire à la parole qu'ils m'avoient donnée, et pour cet effect, suis entré ce jourd'huy au Conseil, où après qu'ils m'ont eu tesmoigné beaucoup de ressentiment des assistances qu'ils ont receues du Roy et de la Reyne Régente, sa mère: ils m'ont fait response qu'ils ne pouvoient, pour le présent, leur accorder la permission de l'entière levée, seulement de la moitié, m'asseurant que l'autre partie suivra de bien près celle qu'ils me permettent de lever présentement.

A quoy je leur ay respondu que ce n'estoit pas là correspondre aux bonnes volentez que le Roy avoit pour eulx, de ne luy accorder pas l'entière levée, après l'en avoir faict asseurer, et mesmes, pour plus grande asseurance, s'y estre obligez par escript, que je leur ay mis devant les yeux pour les convaincre : tout cela n'a de rien servy, me protestant qu'ils ne veulent pas frustrer leurs Majestez de l'autre partie, mais qu'ils les prient de patienter un peu, espérant estre en estat de lever ou accorder davantage dans deux ou trois mois.

C'est ce qui m'a obligé d'accepter ceste permission, croyant aussy que votre Eminence trouvera qu'il est plus expédient d'avoir cela que rien du tout, et que les refuser, c'eust esté donner lieu à l'Espagnol de les aliéner des bonnes volentez qu'ils ont pour la France ; joinct aussy, que je prévoy qu'ils sont en estat d'avoir plus forte guerre qu'auparavant pour le mainien de la religion Catholique, leurs Agens n'ayans rien faict avecq le Roy

LXXV. Archives des Affaires Étrangères, Paris.   Série Angleterre, vol. li., p. 99.   The date of this letter, owing to indistinctness of the manuscript, was, of late years, assumed in France to have been "1r Août, 1644."   From a minute examination recently made of the original at Paris, the correct date appears to be 1st of July, 1644, as here printed, and under which it is included in the table of contents of the present volume.

d'Angleterre, et qu'ainsy ils seront obligés de prendre la protection de quelque Prince estranger, ne pouvant pas subsister d'euxmesmes : ce qu'ils espérent du Roy et de la Reyne Régente, sa mère, ainsy que je puis cognoistre par leur discours, tesmoignant qu'ils estiment davantage la France que l'Espagne.

Je croy qu'ils feront une Assemblée Générale en forme de Parlement dans le 20eme Juillet ; si votre Eminence desire que je fasse le possible pour les destacher tout à fait des interests de l'Espagnol, elle me le fera sçavoir, et prendra, s'il luy plaist, la peyne d'en parler au Père Harthegan, [O'Hartegan] qui est tout à fait porté pour la France, et laquel a grande brigue icy, et croy mesmes que si il y estoit, il y serviroit beaucoup, tout le Conseil ayant grande croyance en luy.   Je m'en vais travailler cependant de ces mille hommes qu'ils m'ont accordés, et supplieray très humblement votre Eminence de faire en sorte que je puisse avoir passeport des Parlementaires pour le transport de ces soldats, aucun Irlandois n'osant s'aventurer de passer la mer d'autant que les Parlementaires sont de serment de les jetter tous à la mer : et en effet, ils en ont desjà jetté 50 ou 60 qui s'en alloient en Angleterre : mesmes ils n'ont pas espargné douze femmes et cinq ou six petits enfans qui estoient dans le navire.   Je croy qu'il seroit fort nécessaire, si votre Eminence le trouvoit bon, qu'il y eût quelques navires de guerre pour l'escorte de ces soldats, tant pour empescher les Espagnols de les surprendre, que pour tascher à surprendre ceux qui partiront pour l'Espagne, ne faisant point de doubte que l'Espagnol ne face ce qu'il pourra pour empescher le transport de nos soldats, en estant adverty, comme il est.

Je m'informeray dans quel port de ce pays il embarquera son monde, pour le faire sçavoir à votre Eminence.   Pour moy, je ne sçay dans lequel j'embarqueray les miens, n'ayant point encores de navires asseurez, n'en ayant point voulu arrester, que je ne fusse asseuré d'avoir du monde. Votre Eminence me pardonnera si je luy fais si longue lettre, la volonté que j'ay de luy donner advis de tout ce que je fais en est la cause, espérant qu'elle ne le trouvera pas mauvois puisque c'est, Monseigneur, votre Eminence, le très-humble, très-obeissant et très-fidèle serviteur et créature,

MONNERIE.

Quilkeny [Kilkenny], 1ᵣ Juillet, 10ᵉ (en France), 1644.

LXXVI. Payment to Thomas Preston, General of Leinster for the Confederation.

By the Commissioners of the Public Revenewe of the Confederate Catholiques of Ireland.—3 August, 1644.

May it please your Lordship,—Wee have received your Lordships' order[1] of the 22th of December last [1643], requiring us to take such immediate course for the payment of one thowsand pounds sterling unto the Lord Generall of Leinster as should seeme best; which wee were ready to doe, but that sithence the receipt of the said order noe considerable sume did com into our hands, and what small sums wee receaved, were by your Honours' orders laide out in present and necessary occasions for the publick, soe as wee could not sithence give any mony upon the said order; which, at the said Lord Generall's request, wee humbly certifie your Honours.

Geoffry Barron.—William Hore.

Endorsed : 3 August, 1644. Concerninge Generall Preston, that there was noe monyes to pay him.

LXXVII. Letter to Mathew O'Hartegan, S.J., Paris, from Supreme Council.

Wee are well satisfied of your endeavours, and the prudent course you have taken for the advancement of our common cause in that Court where you doe attend by direction from us; and as wee did, in our greatest necessityes, strive to give some testimonye of our affections to the Most Christian Kinge, and the Queene-Regent, his Majestie's mother, by givinge way to a levye of two thousand men, whereof one thousand are to be shipped at the day to be appointed by Monsieur Monnerye, Gentleman-in-

---

LXXVI. State Papers, Ireland, 1644.   No. 272, fol. 91.   Public Record Office, London.
1. *See* p. 64.

LXXVII. Ms. "Register Book of Letters" of Supreme Council of Confederation.

ordenarye of his Majestie's chamber for his Majestie's service; soe wee doe not doubt the Court will apprehend our danger, and the streights whereunto the Catholicke religion will be putt, unless wee be made able to meete with the mischevous designes of the Puritantes, who, having Scotland to their backe, and the commaund of the Parliament purse, are enemies sufficient to drawe forth the warr into some lenth, since, without assistance of meanes from abroade, wee are not able to end the warr at a blowe.

Our Commissioners are retourned, by reason the Kinge, whose inclinations wee finde favorable, was diverted, by the enemy's approache to Oxforde, from attendinge our occasions any longer.

In this Assemblye what resolutions are taken you may perceive by the enclosed declaracion[1] uppon our oath ; none can speake more plainlye what alreddye is confirmed by a two yeeres warr, and whosoever expects further testymonyes, hath some other scruple than want of beleefe of the realtye of our intentions.   Present our most humble service to their Catholick Majesties, and lett them know how firme our resolucions are to maintaine our common cause, and present unto them how theire tymely favors (for, as the matter stands, expedicion is the life of our actions) will leave to our posteritye a memorye of the zeale and good intencions of France towards our cause and nacion.—Kilkenny, 5th August, 1644.

LXXVIII. Expulsion of Irish from Cork, August, 1644.

1. Proclamation made the 5th of August, 1644, with the names of those that are admitted to remayne in [the] towne [of Cork].

By Direction from the Lord Inchiquine :

All the Irish inhabitants within the citty of Corcke are commaunded to depart the same, uppon forfeiture of all their goods and chattles, tomorrow, being Munday, the fift day of August, by nyne of the clocke in the forenoone, except the undernamed persons, who are licenced to stay; and all those that have noe considerable valew of goods are to

LXXVIII. 1-9. Carte Papers, xii., 12, 13, 19, 20, 21, 23, 35, 56, 188. 1. *See* p. 212.

expect to suffer the punishments that shalbe inflicted on them by martiall lawe if they depart not afore the said hower; and those persons soe departinge are to carry nothing with them but what apparell and household stuffe they can carry about their persons (bedding and all prohibited goods excepted), all which persons are licenced on Thursday next to returne and receive the remain[d]er of their goods, and then imediately to depart. And, for those of the Irish quarter, itt is ordered that they shall carry noe goods hince till wee have certaine knowledge that the English in their quarters have free liberty to repair hither with theire goods :

Mr. Maior.—Mr. Recorder.—David Tirry, Aldcrman.—Richard Roche, Alderman.—Thomas Martell, Alderman.—Melchior Lavallin, Alderman.— Morris Roche, Alderman.—John Roche, Alderman.—James Roche, Shee-riff.—John Gallwey, Sheeriff.

Mr. William Hore.—James Lombard.—Edmond Roche Fitz Edward — Morris Roche FitzEdward. —Phillip Martell. —Robert Thyrry Fitz Robert.— Domynicke Coppinger Fitz John.—William Tirry Fitz Oliver.— Thomas Coppinger, Esq.—William Creagh.—Edmond Mlawne, Marshall.—James Goold Fitz Nicholas.—Domynicke Thyrry Fitz Patricke.—William Cop-pinger Fitz Adame.—Thomas Goold, Vice-Admirall.—William Goold Fitz Walter.—Richard Gallwey Fitz Jefferey.—David Martell.

Alice, daughter to Alderman Martell.—Katherine Roche, wyddow, and her sonns.—Ellen Roch Fitz Edmond, wyddow.—Margaret Hore, wyddowe.

All Aldermen's wyddowes.—All impotent and sick persons.

Copia vera, exam. : Robert Coppinger,[1] Maior Corcke.—John Gallwey, Vicecomes.

---

1. A notice of Sir Robert Coppinger, Knight, will be found in the "History of the Copingers," 1884, mentioned at p. 38.

LXXVIII. 2. A PARTICULAR ACCOUNT OF MY LORD INCHIQUIN'S USAGE TO THE INHABITANTS OF CORCK, AND OF THE MANNER OF HIS PROCEEDING FROM THE 3RD OF AUGUST TILL THE EXPIRATION OF SEVEN DAYS FOLLOWING.— 1644.

First uppon Saterday, the third of this presente [August,] the Mayor, Aldermen, and Sherryves, being sent for by his Lordship, [Inchiquin] unto the fortte, where being come, after some few words past, his Lordshipe in briefe tould them that without anie more expostulatinge they must remayne there in the fortte, untill the towne were quite cleered of all the Irishe inhabitants of what ranke or quallity soever, excepting the Maior, Recorder, Aldermen, and Sherryves, consistinge onely of elleaven with a matter of 17 others of the better sorte. Uppon which the Mayor humbly beseeched his Lordship to geave way accordinge to his former conclusions and agriement, that the hundred inhabitants before condescended unto by his Lordship, might remayne within the cittie, and the rather for that all the corne and provision of all sortes, belonging as well unto the said hundred as also unto the rest of the bannished inhabitants, was already seized uppon by his Lordshipe's officers, and safely kept from any of the said inhabitants, and further wee earnestly desired in reguard as it appered by accompt of the severall Englishe surveighours that there was more corne than the twoe thowsand barrells by him expected, that his Lordship would be pleased to leave us the remayne for oure owne reliefe and maintenance untill wee further coulde speedily provide for ourselves; to which he aunswered that if wee had ten thousand barrells of all sortes of graine, besides all other kinde of provision, he would not only seize thereuppon, and have it all into the magazine, and that if wee were to starve wee should not have one bitt thereof for oure reliefe, but also sayed that he expected from us full satisfaction for all the provision by us spent from the first day that all the inhabitants were dryven oute of the towne, beinge Fryday, the 26th of July, untill that presente day, being the third of this August. Uppon which harde sentence, wee desired the benefitt of his Majestie's lettres, as well directed to his Lordship as also to this Corporacion, by which he was comaunded to take effectuall and strict care that noe souldier or others of his Majestie's army heere should offer any violence or comit

any insolency uppon any of the inhabitants of the three severall Corpo-
racions of Corcke, Youghall, and Kinsale, as by the copies heerinclosed
may appeare.   Whereunto his Lordship aunswered that his Majestie's
lettres must not be prejudiciall to himselfe in any respecte.   Wee further
acquaintinge him that the tyme of oure ellection for Magistrates was
neere at hand, and that it stoode us uppon for the furtherance of his
Majestie's service to make choise of such sufficient officers (as might conduce thereunto) according to his Majestie's gratious charter in that behaulfe
graunted to this Corporacion, the benefitt whereof wee earnestly desired,
and that the number of 28 by his Lordship admitted to remayne heere was
too few for us to proceede to performe that expectacion; therefore
beseeched him to lycense and leave us the first number of one hundred
persons first resolved uppon, assuring him that wee would with all convenient speede endeavour to bringe in such sufficient provision as should
be able to maintayne that number till God inhabled us to save oure presente harvest.   Whereunto his Lordship made speedie aunswere, notwithstanding any graunt or charter wee had, that whatever rules he had
prescribed for the worke he had in hand, he would goe thoroughe withall
(whether right or wronge) and that no more should remayne in towne but
the aforesaid number of 28, for that he did not knowe how soone he
should be besiedged, and that he was confident it should be speedily.

Aunswere being made him that if any such thinge should happen, it
could not be soe suddenly but his Lordship should have (at least) twoe
or three howers notice thereof, which haveing he then might thrust us
oute of the cittie.   Whereuppon, his Lordship (suddenly startinge from
us) required the officers of the army to goe in to towne and there performe the service by them resolved uppon; which they accordinglie
executed with all their horse and foote armed, and Proclamacion in wryting
by sounde of drumme proclaymed that all the Irishe inhabitants uppon
paine of death should departe the towne within one hower after the
shooteing of one peece of ordynance from the fortte, which was accordinglie then shott off, and wee in the meane tyme detayned in the fortte
untill all was done.

The inhabitants being thereuppon thruste oute of their howses, uppon

Saterday, late in the eavening, by the troopers and souldiers, in a most
cruell and violent manner, haveing all their carbynes readie spand, and
musketts chardged, with lighted matches goeing from howse to howse; [on]
which Saterday, and the Sunday night after, sundry and severall of their
howses were broaken upp, plundered, and all their howsehold goods, corne
provision, and other moveables taken away and imbeazelled by the common souldiers, and severall complaintes made thereof, yet no redresse.
And the same day his Lordship beinge demaunded whether he had any
directions from the Lord Lyvetenante or Councell for usinge this Corporacion as he did, his Lordship ingeniouslie[1] acknowledged that whatsoever
he did was onely by advice of the councell and comaunders heere and not
from the Lord Lyvetenante, but. that he would argue the case with his
Lordship.

Upon Munday moreninge, a second proclamacion was made and published by sounde of drumme, a copie whereof is hereinclosed,[2] and the
contents thereof accordingly observed. The same day, Munday, and the
Tuesday and Wedinsday followinge, severall persons by warrants appointed for that purpose broke open the doores of all the howses of the
banished inhabitants, and from thence tooke away with them all sortes of
provision, as wheate, maulte, meale, butter, tallowe, candles, aquavite,
wyne, beere, sault, iron, hoppes, caskes, hoopes, staves, pitch, tarr,
oakame, oares, with all kynde of fyering and fuell, beddinge, boulsters,
caddowes, brasse panns, iron and brass potts, with diverse other particulars too tedious to recite, all which they carryed away either to the magazins, or disposed of for their owne particular uses without rendering any
accompts thereof, leaving all the doores of the howses wyde oppen, and
exposed, with all the rest of the goods therein remayninge, to the insolency of the common souldiers, whoe soone founde way to consume the
remaine of all the residue of their goods and howshould stuffe, whereby
nothinge is lefte for the poore inhabitants to carry with them uppon their
returne a Thursday accordinge to the proclamacion.

The number of 28 remayninge had likewise all their provision taken

---

1. Ingenuously. 2. *See* page 235.

from them, and are not permitted to send away any parte of the remainder of their goods lefte them to relieve themselves withall, yf in case they were thruste oute, as they daily stand in feare to be.

Most of all the inhabitants' howses by warrants and tycketts [were] consigned over by his Lordship and Governor Bannister unto the Englishe whoe formerly lyved and kept their aboade as well in the suburbes as also in divers other partes of the province, whoe are dailie resortinge hether from all places, without any regard either of the inheritors or proprietors thereof, whoe were forceably thrust oute and exposed to all miseries as before.

Also severall auncient wyddowes and younge maydens, whose whole estates and fortunes consisted in what corne, maulte, aquavite, and beere they had, havinge all taken from them, yet his Lordship beinge earnestlie requested to permitt them to remayne in towne to preserve themselves from further mischiefes incidente to their kynde, his Lordship notwithstandinge absolutely refused to admitt any of them to remayne therein, also severall companies both horse and foote [are] daiely raisinge and recruetinge their former standinge companies, and daily makeinge of new bullwarkes, rampiers and fortificacions of all sydes of the towne.

Upon Sunday night, the 4th of this instant [August] being in my owne wyndowe observinge the violence of the souldiers comitted uppon the inhabitants; desiring the said souldiers to be a litle more respective, I was by one of [Hardress] Waller's companie, then guarding at the Sowth Gate, with a loude voyce cryed unto, saying, Mr. Mayor, Mr. Mayor, make hast and gett you gone, or by God, I will suddenly cutt your throate else; which complayning [of] the next morninge unto the Governour, yet nothing [was] done thereuppon.

Which, with oure former grievances, wee humbly desire you to presente unto the Right Honorable the Lord Lyvetenant, in the behaulfe of this distressed Corporacion, and most humbly to desire his Excellency to take some speedie and effectuall course as well for oure reliefe as also to prevent all future inconveniencyes that dayly may be expected to ensue thereuppon. In the meane tyme desiring you to have a speciall care of us that theise with oure former grievances may not by any meanes be made knowen to the Lord of Inchiquyne, or any of his (as comeing from us), till wee be secured of oure lyves, which refferringe to your serious care, wee conclude for the presente.—ROBERT COPPINGER, MAIOR [OF] CORCKE.—JOHN GALLWEY, VICECOMES.

Corck, 8 August, 1644.

3. The examination of Humphry Rogers, taken uppon oath before Richard Gething, Deputy-Clerk of the Council, by the command of the Lord of Inchiquin, viii Aug., 1644.

Who saith that hee having some occasion of busines to one Father Thomas Gregory, a Fryer, in Cloinmell on the xxiiii of July last, and entring into discourse with him concerning the tymes, the said fryer shewed this deponent the English Remonstrances,[1] saying that they were exceeding lofty, and of such high tearmes that in no wise they could bee graunted. Whereupon, the said Humphry Rogers demaunded what hee thought concerning the churches, who answeared, that, as for the liveings themselves, they would bee content the King should have the meanes accruing from them, and they to live as they did before; but, for the churches and the government thereof, they would never yeild, or give way for the delivery back of them, although they were constrayned to manage the warr themselves.—HUMPHRY ROGERS.

Endorsed: Copy of Humphry Rogers' examination, 8 Aug., 1644.

4. The Examinacion of Captain Peregrine Banister, Governour of the citty of Corke, taken the viiith of August, 1644.

Who saith that, on or about the 16th day of July last, hee meeting with John Archdeacon, of Monketowne, gentleman, in the citty of Corke, demaunded of him what newes in the Irish quarters, to whom the said John Archdeacon made aunswear, that one of the Fryers of eminent quallitye, named Patrick O'Donovan, lying the night before at his house, and

1. *See* p. 143.

being then come from the Supream Councell, told him that the Irish were resolved to take into their hands all the garrison townes of Corke, Kinsall, and Youghall, and that they were determined to putt forth all the English. And being demaunded whether they would cutt our throates, or give us leave to depart fairely, hee said that they would suffer such to depart as had bin moderate men; adding further, as from himselfe, that hee did believe neither Brockett, Muschamp, or Banistree, or any of the English officers, should have anything to doe with the comaund of any fort or strength in the kingdome so soone as the Irish should gett them into their hands; that the Lord Leiutenant, in regard of his great allyaunce and eminency, should bee suffred to bee at his owne dispose, if hee would not joyne with them, but that they must have the citty of Dublin; and that the Lord Clanrickard, Thomond, and all others that had not declared themselves, should bee put from their neutrality or bee imprisoned. Hee further saith that one Forrest, a priest (as he remembreth) tould him that they of the Supreame Councell were resolved not to allow us any part of the churches, but that they would have them wholy to themselves, and not them onely, but all other comaunds also.—PEREGRINE BANASTIRE.

5. The Examinacion of [Sergeant] Major Agmondisham Muschamp, taken the viii August, 1644.

Who saith that on, or about, the xxvi. of July, and at severall tymes before, hee heard John Archdeacon, of Monkestowne, gentleman, say that wee (meaneing the English) should have no peace with the Irish, unless wee joyned with them against the Scotts, and that the Irish would admit of noe neuters, and that their full intent was to enter into our garrisons, if wee joyned not with them, for that they feared wee would lett in the Parliament army.—AGMONDISHAM MUSCHAMP.

6. Proclamations made by sound of drum, at Cork, 8 August, 1644.

i. It is comaunded by the Right Honnorable the Lord of Inchiquine that all Irish shall depart this citty this night upon paine of death, except those that are lycenced to remaine here this 8th of August, 1644.—

PEREGRINE BANASTER.

This was likewise preclaymed by sound of drume.

ii. Corcke, 8 Augusti, 1644.—All houshould stuffe and wearing apparell to passe, except bedding, bedtickes, and cadoes, aquavitæ, potts, iron potts, and all other prohibited goodes.—PEREGRINE BANASTER.

Copia vera : Robert Coppinger, Maior.

7. Order from Inchiquin to Governor of Cork.

Sir,—My Lord desires you to repayre unto Mr. Mayor, and to demaunde the money undertaken by them, to lett them knowe that wee have permitted much of their goods to goe away, and that, if they pay not their money, their persons must be stayed, and that at least £200 of the money is expected this day.   In the meane tyme, you must give order that noe manner of comoditie, especiallie hydes, leather, etc., doe passe the guardes, untill the money or parte be payed.   But, uppon my Lord's expresse warrant, this much is comaunded to bee signified by your servaunt,

RICHARD GETHING.

xth August, 1644.—For Governour Banister.

Copia vera Exam. per Robert Coppinger, Maior [of] Corck.

Endorsed by the Mayor : " Order for Governour Banister to make stay of our person for non-payment of the £500 expected by his Lordship and to permitt noe goods to passe the guards. The xth of August, 1644.

8. Ormonde to the Earl of Thomond.

My Lord,—Yours of the 5th I received the 8th of this moneth, and though I have much desired the happynesse of your company to myselfe, and the advantage of your councells and assistance towards his Majestye's service in these tymes of distraction, yet I must rest satisfyed with those reasons expressed by your Lordship for your longer stay there, since they relate soe much to the necessary performance of your private affaires, and I presume to the safety of such of his Majestie's Protestant subjects as your Lordship mentions to be still there under your protection.   Something I have heard of a treacherouse design intended by the Irish in Corke to have been practised against the English there.   But if any such there were, I suppose it is prevented by my Lord of Inchiquin's foresight, to whom I have lardgly written to be more certainly informed of the truth, and of the grounds of his Lordship's turneing out of that and other places in his government many of the Irish, who till now (as it is affirmed by the Maior of Corke in a peticion to mee and the Board) have contributed lardgly to the maintenance of his Majestie's army there dureing the warr. When I am better instructed in the busynesse of that province, I shall not faile to give your Lordship such advertisments as I shall conceive may conduce to the King's service, and to your Lordship's satisfaccion and safety. In the meanetyme I rest, your Lordship's most faithfull cosin and servant,   ORMONDE.

His Majestie's Castle [of] Dublin, 10 Aug., 1644.

Endorsed : Coppy of his Excellence's lettre to the Earle of Thomond, 10 Aug., 1644.   Delivered then to Mr. Hinson, his Lordship's agent.

9. STATEMENT BY MAYOR AND SHERIFFS OF CORK.

First, uppon Saturday, the xth of August, the same day you[1] departed Governour Banaster came to us from my Lord [Inchiquin] with the inclosed note[2] or directions sent him by Captain Gethinges, with a full resolution either to have money from us or to make stay of our persons, [as] by the same you may perceive.

Uppon Tuesday after, being the 13th of this instant [August], Ensigne Synners came with twenty persons and directions from his Lordship to take away all the smale quantity of mault that was left mee, my wheat being formerly taken away, and with much intreatie prevailed with him to forbeare till I went to speak with his Lordshipe ; where being come, I staied a whole houre for his Lordshipe's comeinge, and at last desired Governour Banastir to acquainte his Lordshipe with my being there, and what my occasion was, who accordingly repaired to his Lordshipe, and suddenly comeing backe tould me there was noe remedie but that I must

1. The name of the person to whom this communication was addressed does not appear in the Ms.
2. *See* p. 243.

parte with all my corne, and that his Lordshipe could not, neither would, speake with me at all. Whereuppon, retourninge home, all my corne was taken away without leaving me any parte thereof.

Uppon the next day, being Wednesday, his Lordshipe sent for us to come to speak with him, and when we came he presently demaunded whether wee had provided for him the £500 he expected from us; to which aunswere being made that we had it not, neither could we tell how to provide it, all our estate and goodes whereof wee might make money being altogether taken from us; to which his Lordshipe replied that there were those that had it, and that he must have it, if they were forced to send to the country for it, or else that he would take such a strict course as should grieve them, by restrayninge of their persons at Bandon-bridge close prisoners, and from thence send them for London ; and then openly in the hearing of all that were in the halle tould us that he had written unto his Majestie either to send him a speedy supply, or els to give leave unto the contractors and Adventurers to come, and that he speedily expected their comeing at furthest with a good strong army [at] once before Michaelmas next. And so, with many other threathnings of us, he in a great furie parted to his chamber.

The 16th of August, his Lordshipe directed a comission to certaine Comissioners to examine uppon oath all persons then remaineing within the citty what store or quantitie of tann hydes, rawe hydes, salt, tallow, wyne, or other merchantable commodities was in their possessions, or to their knowledge any other had within the city. Uppon which there appered, as then [stated] by such persons as came before them, that there was six thousand and twoe hundred tanned and rawe hydes, besides a great many more since found out, and dayly more like to be found, out of which the owners are constrained to pay for the 6,200 twelve pence for every hyde, which accordinglie they satisfied, and paied unto his Lordshipe ; and the rest that were since or hereafter shalbe found his Lordshipe hath and is resolved to seize uppon and dispose of at his will and pleasure, without rendring the owners either any account or satisfaction therefore, to their utter undoeinge.

There was alsoe then acknowledged and found one hundred and fifty barrells of salte, threescore and twoe hogsetts, nyne great barrells, and fourteen kinderkins of tallowe, and twentie-twoe hogsetts of French wynes, which altogether was taken, and carried to his Lordship's magazine, to be disposed of for his use, neither givinge the owners any kind of satisfaction, nor accepting thereof for satisfaction of any parte of the money demaunded from this Corporation, besides all other comodities formerly taken away and imbeazilled by the souldiours. Notwithstanding all which, his Lordshipe himselfe hath made an applottment, and chardged us with his owne hand in the severall summes to oure names annexed, as by a copie here inclosed you may perceive; which severall sommes he is fully resolved to force from us or speedily to restraine oure persons (so as wee feare noe tyme wilbe allowed us for our ellection of newe magistrates), and also wee are dayly in feare that his Lordshipe (if wee were, as wee are not, hable to satisfie this) will continue in raisinge of other new taxes and impositions uppon us, and lastly restraine oure persons alsoe.

Yesterday, the 23th, there came to Youghall seaventine of the Parliament shipps, where it is reported they have landed some horses, armes, amunicion, and provision.

This very day, being the 24th, there is arrived within this harbour, though not within the comaund of Halbowlinge Forte, elleaven great Parliament shipps, and seaven more at Youghall, besides six at Kinsale. Likewise, this day proclamation was made by sound of drume that all persons (save those fewe lycensed) uppon paine of death should by sixe a-clocke parte the towne, and that all those that remained and [were] lycensed should foorthwith repaire unto Sir Roberte Travers, Knight, and enter security to provide themselves by Saturday next with sixe weekes provision, and so from tyme to tyme, for that they dayly expected a siedge, otherwise within six dayes to parte the towne as the rest; most of the twenty-eight lycensed to stay are dayly partynge for feare. So as now, 24th of August, 1644, we are confident that all men plainely discerne what course is intended to be taken, if not suddenly and speedily prevented, which prevention wee much feare will come altogether too late.   God prosper your occasions, and preserve us from future mischiefe. And soe in haste wee rest, your loving cossens,

ROBERT COPPINGER, MAIOR [OF] CORCKE.—JOHN GALLWEY, VICE-COMES.—JAMES ROCHE [VICECOMES].

Also, the 24th of this presente, being this very day, by proclamation all strangers that were Irishe Catholicques were requested uppon paine of death to parte this citty when a trumpet sounded, which for that purpose was to bee sounded at six aclocke everie eveninge till Michaelmas, and at 5 a-clocke in the eveninge from Michaelmas forth, with diverse other particulars, which yet wee know not.

Endorsed : The grievances since you parted from hence. Signed by Robert Coppinger, Mayor of Corke, and others, the 24 of August, 1644.

LXXIX. LETTERS IN RELATION TO PRISONERS AT WEXFORD, 1644.

1. ORMONDE TO BELLINGS.

Sir,—You will finde by the inclosed lettre the hard and extreame usage of those two prisoners therein mencioned, whoe are nowe prisoners at Wexford. They are persons well knowne to Doctor Siball[d] my Chaplaine, to bee well affected to his Majestie's service, otherwayes hee would not present them to bee such unto mee, as very many of that towne of Aberdeene are knowne to bee. And therefore I pray you to procure order for their present enlargement, and, if neede be, to signify to those whome you are to move therin that it is my desire. And soe I rest, your very loveing friend,—ORMONDE.

Dublin Castle, 3 August, 1644.

Endorsed : 3 August, 1644. A coppy of a lettre to Mr. Bellings, concerning the release of two Scotts men nowe prisoners at Wexford.

LXXIX. 1-2. Carte Papers, xii. pp. 11, 27.

2. BELLINGS TO ORMONDE.

My Lord,—I am commaunded to advertise your Lordship that Captaine Antonio[1] is now written unto concearneing those two prisoners at Wexford, that they may be treated civilly and their restraint made more easie, untill hee shall remitt unto the Counsell here such testimony as hee can produce to prove them disaffected to his Majestie's service and to have taken the Scotch Covenant, and upon retourne made they will be able to give your Lordship an accompt of what may be don for their enlargement.—I am, my Lord, your Lordship's humble servant,—R. BELLINGS.

Kilkenny, 6 August, 1644.

Endorsed: Mr. Bellings. Dated 6, received 8 August, 1644. Concearning prisoners with Captain Anthonio, etc.

LXXX. LETTERS TO ORMONDE FROM THE EARL OF ANTRIM AND THE DUCHESS OF BUCKINGHAM.

1. EARL OF ANTRIM TO ORMONDE.

My Lord,—If I had not a lame hand, I should not be so unmannerlie as not to returne your Lordship sooner an answere. I shall have the honor to see you shortlie, and then I shall be able to give you a cleare account of all informations given you of me, by which your Lordship will receave, I hope, so full satisfaction that you will rather incline to beleave me than what has been tould you from other hands of my beinge ill satisfied with your Lordship. I beseech you be confident of this protestation that I cannot make professions for anie ends without my hart goes allonge with it; and if your Lordship be as willinge to embrace them, as I shall be to make them good, you shall not find anie man in this kingdome in whom you shall have cause to be more confident. I have not

1. See "Contemporary History of Affairs in Ireland, 1641-1652." Dublin: 1879, vol. i. pp. 54, 585; vol. ii. 101, 118, 429 32, 470; iii. 77.

LXXX. 1, 2. Carte Papers, xii. pp. 111, 113.

The lively portraicture of the most noble
and right honourable Lady The Lady Katherin
Marchionesse of Buckingham &c.
Magdalena Passe sculpsit.

J. A. Burt. Lith.

Fac-simile of contemporary portrait.—British Museum, London.

failed to obay your commands in your letter by Jacke Barrie,[1] and I have not been able till now to give you thankes for the paket your Lordship sent me of my good weoman's.[2] I am pressed to send for the ships imployed into the Ilyes, which will grow, I confesse, to be a great charge, but I hope your Lordship will allow them to stay a litle longer till I heare of ther condition, and by them I intend to have the Ministers[3] brought, if I can find a way to send thether for them, which I can not doe for want of a shipp. If your Lordship can direct to send my letters safe, I shall not faile to writt effectivelie for ther comeinge, though the Supreme Counsell expects thay should be delivered to them, but I hope your Lordship will find a hansome way to save me, who is your Excellence's most faithfull humble servant,—Antrim.

Kilkenie, 14 August, 1644.

For his Excellence, the Marquiss of Ormond, Lord Liftenant of Irland.

Endorsed : Earl of Antrim's, [dated] 14, received 18 August, 1644.

2. The Duchess of Buckingham to Ormonde.

My Lord,—I receve great satisfaction by the honore your leter bringes me of the assurances I am made hapye by your favour, which to preserve shall be my care. I humbly aknowlege the offer of your house, but I will never ingage you in any thinge contrary to your Lordship's inclinations. My man has, I presume, given you an account of the Queen's health and condition of the west, which, I feere, will prove not much beter than the north ; I hope your Lordship has receved so full instructions from his Majestie as to give satisfaction to this kingdome as I

---

1. Colonel John Barry. *See* vol. ii. p. 390.
2. Katharine, Duchess of Buckingham, wife of the Earl of Antrim.
3. This refers to fifty clergymen commissioned from Scotland to promote the "Solemn League and Covenant" in Ulster. The ship in which they sailed was captured by vessels despatched by the Irish Confederation on the Scottish expedition. *See* Ninth Report of the Royal Commission on Historical MSS. London: 1884 pp. 342, 353.

shall se it againe setelled in a hapye peece, which is, I am sure, both the King and Quen's desiere My Lord [Antrim] has done his part to the forderancs of it, which maks him be suspexted to much the King's. I hope nether side will sufer the Bishops to be the distruction of the peece. Ther ar more Puritans at Dubline than Protestants, who desier nothing more than a breach with the Kinge, because thay are then secure ther will be non to assist his Majestie : he has litell reason to trust to a foran nation. Your Lordship's intrest is so much his as you must moderat the clergye. Pardon this freedome used from your Lordship's most humble, faithfull servant,—K[ATHARINE] BUCKINGHAM.

Waterford, [14] August [1644].

LXXXI. NEGOTIATIONS FOR PEACE.—CORRESPONDENCE, AUGUST, 1644.

1. MUSKERRY, PLUNKETT, AND BROWNE TO ORMONDE.

Our very good Lord,—Wee did receave your Lordship's letters of the 30th of July last, which were read in the Assembly of the Confederat Catholicks now sitting at Kilkenny, and by them wee are commaunded to retourne this answere, that the contents of those letters being of that weight, and meritting a longer debate than might well stand with the bearer's hast to retourne, they will within a few daies by their owne messenger send your Excellence a full and satisfactory answere to all the partes of them. Wee rest, your Lordship's humble servants,

Muskry.—N. Plunkett.—Geffr. Browne.

Kilkenny, 6 August, 1644.

For his Excellency the Marquess of Ormond, Lord Lieutennant of Ireland.

Endorsed : Lord Muskry, Mr. Plunkett, and Geffery Browne. Dated 6, received 9 Aug., 1644.—Retourne answere of the last letter by a messenger of their owne.

LXXXI. 1-7. Carte Papers, xii. pp. 29, 61, 39, 60, 68, 81, 101.

LXXXI. 2. ORMONDE TO MUSKERRY.

After our hearty comendacions: In our letter written to your Lordship and the rest who with you lately attended his Majestie in England, wee did forbeare to give our advise that none of your clergie should be deputed for the intended Treaty touching the peace of this kingdom, because wee doe well remember that the like caution being given unto you uppon the notice which was sent of the comission which was executed at Trym,[1] there weare some who tooke offence thereat, butt yett the same was soe well approved of that none of them was deputed for that service or uppon the other commission which was for the Cessation, or thought fitt to be imployed into England to his Majestie about it, which made us verry confident that you would observe the like rule in the choise of those who should be chosen for this Treaty ; which wee did likewise conceave those words in the comission which give us power to treat with such persons which wee should think fitt, purposely repeated in our said letter would put you in minde of. But now, understanding that there is a purpose to make choise of some of them, wee thought fitt to declare ourselfe that wee doe conceive this may give greate offence unto very many heare who doe wish exceeding well to this Treaty, and too much occasion unto the adverse party to asperse the same ; both which wee being desirous to avoyd, wee desire that some other choise more fitting for these tymes may be thought of, for wee having declared ourselfe in that commission executed at Trym in the like particular, wee may not admitt of any such in this, which is of the highest nature that can be, without exceeding great prejudice to his Majestie and the service in hand. And forasmuch as wee omitted in our letters to declare unto you the place which wee thought most convenient for this Treaty, as conceiving it to be understood, wee think fitt by these our letters to signify unto you that wee doe desire that this city [Dublin] may bee the place which as it will be the most comodious for those who shall repaire hither, soe wee conceive it most for his Majestie's honnor that his subjects should repaire unto us hither, being in all tymes the constant and usuall place of residence of all his Vicegerents, and the fittest place to have a negotiation of that importance transacted, and wher they may be assured to

1. *See* vol. ii., p. 154.

finde all fitting accomodation and security for which you shall have from us his Majestie's most Royall word, or any safe-conduct which you can desire. And soe wee bid you farewell from his Majestie's Castle of Dublin, 9 die Augusti, 1644.—Your loveing frend,—ORMONDE.

Addressed : To the Lord Viscount Muskry, and the rest who with him lately attended his Majestie in England, or to any one or more of them.

3. NICHOLAS PLUNKETT TO ORMONDE.

My Lord,—I am commaunded by the Assembly of the Confederat Catholicks of Ireland, now sitting at Kilkenny, to advertise your Excellence that they have made choise of the Lord Viscount Mountgarrett, Lord President of their Councell, Thomas [Fleming] Lord Archbishop of Dublin, the Earle of Antrym, the Lord Viscount Muskery, Alexander M'Donell, Sir Richard Everard, Sir Robert Talbott, Mr. Dermott O'Bryen, Mr. Patrick Darcy, Mr. Geoffery Browne, Mr. Richard Martin, Mr. John Dillon, and myselfe, to be their Commissioners to treat with your Lordship, according the authority given your Excellence by his Majestie's Comission which came into your Lordship's hands the 26th of July last, as is mencioned in your letters of the 30th of the same moneth; and they do desire a copie, attested by your Excellence, should be retourned unto them of the same commission, and that your Lordship in nominating the place of meeting, will make such election as shall well stand with the safety of the persons entrusted by them to attend your Lordship for the tyme they have resolved to be wholly directed therein as shall best suite with your Lordship's occasions. I am, my Lord, your Lordship's humble servant,— NICHOLAS PLUNKETT.

Kilkenny, the 11th of August, 1644.

For his Excellency the Marquess of Ormond, Lord Lieutennant of Ireland, Dublin.

4. ORMONDE TO NICHOLAS PLUNKETT.

After our hearty comendacions : Wee received your letter of the 11th of this month the 12th of the same, and for answeare thereunto wee doe refferr you to our lettre written unto the Lord Viscount Muskery and the rest whoe lately attended his Majesty in England about the Treaty of Peace, which came not, wee suppose, unto theyr hands after the tyme of the wryteing of your said lettre, which if it had wee are very confident that they would have altered that parte thereof which concerneth your Archbishop of Dublin [Thomas Fleming] who though a man as free from exception (as unto his person) as any wee could expect to bee treated with, for wee have heard exceeding much good of him, and wee doe beleeve noe less, soe as if wee were to admitt any of his function hee should bee the man ; yet wee may not vary from our resolucion expressed in that our lettre which, least it should miscarry or not come to theyr hands, wee thought fitt to send you herewith a coppy thereof, which wee are confident will give sufficient satisfaction in that particular, and lykewise for the place wee have appointed.

As for the coppy of the commission which you desire, wee doe send you herewith an authentique coppy thereof, and, for the tyme of meeteinge, the appointement whereof you doe leave unto us, wee not knowing your readines, doe refferr it unto you, onely wee desire that wee may have convenient notice thereof.   And soe wee rest your loveing frend,—

ORMONDE.

Dublin Castle, 13 Aug., 1644.

Mr. Plunkett.

5. NICHOLAS PLUNKETT TO ORMONDE.

MY LORD,—I am comaunded to represent unto your Excellence the unanimous sence of the Confederat Catholickes of Ireland, now sitting at Kilkenny, in answere to your Lordship's letters of the 13th of August directed unto me, and those of the 9th of the same month sent to the Lord Viscount Muskery,[1] and the rest, who with him lately attended his Majesty in England, which were receaved both at the same tyme ; which is that they may not recede from their former election grounded upon your Lordship's letters giveing them notice of a Comission,[2] whereof they have receaved an authentick copie, upon perusall whereof they do find that your Lordship is enabled to treat with any who shalbe deputed by them

1. *See* pp. 251-52.   2. *See* p. 198.

for that imployment, so as they expect the entrance into a treaty of soe great advantage to his Majesties's intrests and of soe greate concearnement to the settlement of a firme and lasting peace in this kingdome will not be shutt up because they have made a free election of such persons as they thought most trustie to agitate such weightie affaires, and in confidence of your Lordship's concurrence with them in that particular, although they might upon just grounds, be doubtful of their safe residing in the cittie of Dublin during the Treaty, yet, considering how you, his Majestie's Chiefe Governor of this kingdome have past them his royall worde for their security, and that your Lordship will send unto their Comissioners a full and free safe-conduct, which they desire may be for them, their servants and retinue, and such of what quallity soever as shall either accompany them thether, or have occasion from tyme to tyme to resorte unto them, freeing them from all suites, arrests, or molestation whatsoever in their repaire thither or their aboade there and their retourne from thence, they have, in observance of your Excellencie's desire therein, condiscended that Dublin be the place of meeting, and they are suitors to your Lordship that they be allowed a quarter, where they may be lodged in a neere distance one to the other, and such other care taken for their security as in your Lordship's judgment shalbe thought most meete.   And inasmuch as your Lordship hath putt over unto them the appointment of the tyme of meeting, they make offer of Monday the six and twentieth of this instant to be the day whereon their Comissioners (God willing) shall attend upon your Lordship at Dublin to begin that worke which they hope wilbe concluded with that blessing of a firme peace which is exceedingly desired by your Lordship's humble servant,—NICHOLAS PLUNKETT.

Kilkenny, 16 August, 1644.

6. EARL OF ANTRIM TO ORMONDE.

My Lord,—I am pressed by the Assemblie, as appeares by this en-closed order,[1] to recall the shipps imployed in the expedition of the Ilyes, his Majestie's general directions to your Lordship for shipps to attend that service does approve of his beleeveinge a necessitie of it; which was, as

1. *See* p. 256.

I conceave, your owne sence. I doe humblie begge your Lordship's orders to recall back those shipps, which is the authoritie they are to obay, and which may be for my discharge if that service therby suffer. I find this kingdome willinge to assist his Majestie in anie thinge they are able, but the charge is so great for them, haveinge an armie of ther owne to maintaine. Therefore your Lordship must be pleased to give me directions to recall them, or else to see that burden taken off the countrie. I desire your Lordship's answere by Saterday next, which is the longest time allowed me to use the best of my power for ther returne.

I cannot but acquaint your Lordship that ther will be this next mounth more occasion for the shipps than in all this time past, by reason of the heringe fishinge where manie botes will be imployed which may be easilie taken by those shipps, which, if they be taken away, that oportunitie this yeare will be lost, and without longe boats noe service can be done in that countrie beinge all ilands, which I humblie leave to your consideration, and kisse your hands, as your Excellence most humble faithfull servant,—

ANTRIM.

Kilkennie, 20 August, 1644.

7. NICHOLAS PLUNKETT TO ORMONDE.

My Lord,—Uppon readinge of your Lordship's of the 19th of this presente (directed unto me) in the full Assemblie of the Confederat Catholickes of Ireland, I am commaunded, in pursuance of theire unanimous sence expressed in theire letters of the 16th of August, subsigned by me, with the like unanimous consent, to retourne this theire answer:

That they may not varye from their former election, findinge all freedome of choise given his Catholick subjects by his Majestie's Comission (whereof they have an authentike coppie), and nothinge therein contained which should hould your Lordship from affordinge them the benefitt of that freedome, which his Majestie was gratiouslie pleased to give unto them, soe as observinge one of the persons entrusted by them omitted in the safe-conduct, and other limitacions incerted therein (whereof in his Majestie's safe-conduct uppon the like occasion noe mencion hath beene made) they have remitted it, and doe desire a full and free safe-conduct

. may be sent unto the Lord Viscount Muskerye, Mr. Alexander M'Donnell, Sir Robert Talbot, Mr. Dermot O'Brien, Mr. Geoffreye Browne, Mr. Patricke Darcye, Mr. John Dillon, and myselfe, who uppon the election were designed first to be employed, as being best acquainted with the former proceedings upon the active parte of this treatye : And if there shall be further occasion to use the assistance of any of the remaineing Commissioners, they have entrusted the Supreame Councell to call from tyme to tyme for safe-conducts for them, or any of them.

And in regarde the tyme taken upp in dispatches concerninge this matter, necessitates them to deffer the meeteinge, they desire your Lordship may doe them the favor to admitt Satterday, the last of this instant, to be the daye whereon your Lordship may expect theire said Commissioners. I take leave and rest your Lordship's humble servant,

NICHOLAS PLUNKETT.

Kilkennye, the 23th of August, 1644.

LXXXII. RECALL OF SHIPPING FROM SCOTLAND.

1. ORDER BY SUPREME COUNCIL.
19 Aug., 1644.

Wheareas the shipping appointed to wafte our souldiers to Scotland under the comaund of the Earle of Antrim are not yet retorned, which may occasion a great and vast chardge; it is ordered that the said Earle of Antrim shall forthwith write unto the Lord Lifetenante, and endevour to procure orders from his Lordshipe for recalling those shipps with theire ordinance; or, fayleing to procure the same by Satturday next, it is ordered that the said Earle of Antrim shall send his present orderes comaunding the undelayed retorne of the said shipping.

And it is further ordered that Nicholas Plunkett, Esqr., in the chayer of this Howse, shall likewise write letters to the said Lord Liftenante declaring unto his Lordshipe that the kingdome doe not conceave themselves engaged any way for the freight of those shipping.

Ex : per Philippum Kearneye, Gen. Com. Hibern. Cler.

LXXXII. 1-6. Carte Papers, xii., pp. 136, 147, 144, 177, 167, 171.

2. Nicholas Plunkett to Ormonde.

My veary good Lorde,—The shipping appointed to waft over soildiours to Scotland, under the comaunde of the Earle of Antrym, being not yett retourned, which of necessitie must occasion a greate and vast charge, and the Assembly conceiving the recalling of those shippes necessary, have comaunded me to signifie unto your Excellencie that the kingdome doe not conceive themselves any way engaged for theire freight, and if in Scotlande continued, they desire your Excellencie to take a course to satisfie the owners of those shipps, according the former agreement made with them to that purpose.   This being to noe other end, I remayne, your Lordship's humble servant,—N. Plunkett.

Killkenny, 20 Aug., 1644.

Endorsed: Nicholas Plunkett.   Dated 20, received 22 Aug., 1644. Concearning the discharge of the shipping that wafted the men to the Isles, etc.

3. The Duchess of Buckingham to Ormonde.

My Lord,—I perceve the Assembly is not willing the ships should longer atende the Iyles of Scotland, by reason, as they alege, the charge is to great for them, being thay have fuly satisfyed the muny to your Lordship due uppon the Sessation.   I beseech you give me leve to say somthing in this perticuler, being well acquainted with the King's condition in Ingland.   Thouse Scots now in the north will, I hope, be overcom by the northen forces; his Majesti feers a suplye from Scotland, but he beleevs the bisnes of the Iyles joyning with his party ther will be of so great advantage to him as ther can come no second armye into Ingland this yeere, from thence.   If these ships be recaled his Majestie's parthy, which has now declared for him, will be left in so great distrees as I feere thay may decline the servis, and joyne yet with the enimy, or becom nueters for ther o[w]ne preservation. I am sertane the Kinge looks uppon that desinge with most hopes to bringe him with honor out of his misfortuns.   He had longe sence done his worke, if Scotland had not

intred Ingland.   Your Lordship may perchance be inclined to beleeve my
Lord's intrest ther prevayls most uppon me; but truly, my Lord, it is
the lest part of my concederation.   I looke more uppon the King and the
bleeding condition of Ingland than any perticuler.   If your Lordship
pleas to desier the Assembly that the ships may yett continwe for a munth,
I beleeve thay may comply with your Lordship in it; 'tis a servis to this
cuntry, a devertion in Scotland, if thay wood rightly understand it, but I
find it hard to prevayle uppon the jugments of some, contrary to ther o[w]ne
conceptions.   My Lord is beleved here so much the King's creature as I
was tould by good hands that was the reasone thay wood not trust him.
This day a Bishope sayed it, I find it impossible to make the clergie, or
thouse which runs that way, to be satisfyed without ther churches.   I
hope the Protestant Bishope will persuayed your Lordship to consent to
it, for if the Parlement prevayl in Ingland, and in this kingdome by the
heelpe of the Scots in the north and my Lord Inchiquine, ther nam must
be blooted out by Acte of Parlement.   When my Lord goes to Dubline,
I hope your Lordship and he will understand on anouther so justly as non
shall have power to hender it.   When this is perfittly effeected I shall
beleeve myself in a very hapy condition, being infinitly your Lordship's
most faithfull, humbell servant,—K [ATHERINE] BUCKINGHAM.

Kelkeny, 20 August, [1644].

4. ORMONDE TO NICHOLAS PLUNKETT.

After our [hearty commendations] : Wee received your leter of the
20 of this month, touching the recaleing of the ships imployed into the
Isles of Scotland, which you say the Assembly conceive to bee necessary
in respect of the great and vast charge which their longer stay would
occasion ; whereunto all wee can say is, that as by his Majestie's comand,
and for the good of his service, wee used all our industry to procure those
shiping to atend the Earle of Antrim's direction, soe wee were often tould
by those exerciseing authoritie over your partie that they gave and would
give their best assistance thereunto as a service to the King, and wee
beleeve withall that they then considered of what advantage that expe-

dition would proove to themselves; but, if those ships bee now recalled, wee conceive that such inconveniencys will fall upon the King's partie in Scotland, that perhaps it had bin beter those men had not bin sent at all, and what prejudice it may draw upon your partie is more proper for the consideration of those by whose direction you writ to mee. Wherefore wee shall ofer unto them that if they will continue those ships in their pay for one month longer, wee shall not only bee content to bear such a proportion of the charge, by way of defalkeation of what remains yet due to his Majestie from your partie as shall bee held reasonable, consider-ing the advantage your partie shall reape therby, but likewise repre-sent the same to his Majestie in the best manner wee may. And soe wee bid you farewell from his Majestie's Castle of Dublin,—Your loving frend,

23 Aug., 1644.   [ORMONDE.]

Endorsed: A coppy of the letter to Mr. Plunkett, dated the 23th of Aug., 1644, concearening the shipps.

5. ORMONDE TO EARL OF ANTRIM.

My Lord,—I have written to Mr. Plunckett as earnestly as I can for the maintenance of the atendance of the shipps upon the service of the Isles for one moneth longer, with offer to abate what shall be held rea-sonable to expect from his Majestie (towards a service wherein their safty is soe much concearned) out of what is due to the King uppon the late treaty of Cessacion. If what I have now written prevaile not with those by whose direccion Mr. Plunckett writt to mee for undertaking the freight of those shipps, I cannot imagin how it will be possible to pay it out of anything the King hath; soe that if they will continue their resolution of dischardging themselves of that burden, I must desire your Lordship to give order for the returne of the shipps, least [Patrick] Archer[1] and others ingaged for their hyer at my instance should be undone for their good service. And if there come prejudice to the King's service, or danger to the kingdome, by soe unreasonable a thrift, your

1. *See* "Contemporary History of Affairs in Ireland, 1641-1652." Dublin: 1880, vol. iii , p. 403.

Lordship nor I are to answere for it,—I rest your Lordship's most faithfull, humble servant,   ORMONDE.

Dublin Castle, 23 Aug., 1644.

Endorsed : A coppy of the letter to the Earle of Antrim, dated 23 Aug. 1644, concearning the shipps.

6. THE DUCHESS OF BUCKINGHAM TO ORMONDE.

My Lord,—I confes you have reason to complain of the obstanancy of some concerning the Bishope ; my Lord's[1] appering against it has lost creditte with the most of the Bishops and Supreme Counsell. If it were not for the King's servis and good of this kingdome, he had littell reason to stay amoungst them. I hope, notwithstanding all oppositions, your Lordship will make a Peece. I am not well liked, I beleeve, by the factious pepell that I speek so much for Peece, but I vallue not oppiniones when I have right of my side. I will tell your Lordship what I perceve is ther intention, but I do most humbly bege you to burne my leter and concelle me for advertesing. The nunchy[2] promises them that within foore munths the Pope will send them three score thousand pound. Till then he desiers ther may be a Sessation or le[n]thening the Treaty. If that com not, then thay may make ther Peece, now if the penall lawes be taken away, churches given them, and outher lawes for the temperall, I am confident that ther will be a Peece ; notwithstanding all indevours to cross it.

Your Lordship has hade full proufe of my Lord's integrity to the King's servis, which will produce, I hope, a strickt kinnes betwixt you both. This is infin[i]tly desired by your Lordship's faithfull, humble servant,—K[ATHARINE] BUCKINGHAM.

Kilken[ny], the 23 of August, 1644.

1. The Earl of Antrim.   2. Nuncio.

LXXXIII. Letter to Mathew O'Hartegan, S.J., Paris, from Supreme Council.

1. Reverend Father,—Wee send you with these a duplicat of our former letters,[1] and have nothing more to add but that our wants growe uppon us dayelye, and that the tymelier wee be assisted the more cheerefull wee shall be to continue that constant course hitherto observed by us, which is to spend our whole substance, the profitts of our estates and the blood of our Confederates, in the maintenance of a cause in which his most Christian Majestie, as beinge the first child of the Churche, is highlye intrested. In what state our affaires are at this present Father Plunket will relate unto you faithfullye.—Kilkennye, the 24th of August, 1644.

2. Father Henry Plunket's Pass.

[The Supreme Council of the Confederated Catholics of Ireland request that the bearer, Father Henry Plunket, about to travel on their urgent affairs, through various countries, provinces, and kingdoms, may be accorded favour and protection by all Princes, States, Republics, Magistrates, and officials, within whose jurisdiction he may have need to come.]

Supremum Consilium Confœderatorum Catholicorum Hiberniæ Universis, ad quos presentes litteræ nos'ræ pervenerint, salutem : Cum harum lator Reverendus Pater Henricus Plunketus, negotiorum nostrorum causa in ultramarinas partes a nobis missus, pro negotiorum exigentia varias terras, provincias et regna sit obiturus rogamus Dominos, Status, Respublicas, Civitates et Magistratus, ad quos illum divertere contigerit, ut illi liberum accessum, recessum, transitum in dominiis, portubus, civitatibus ac territoriis suis terra marique præbeant, illumque favore et protectione (ubi opus erit) prosequantur. Quod ipsum mandamus et precipimus omnibus et singulis sub potestate nostra constitutis,—Datum Kilkeniæ, 25 die Augusti, 1644.

LXXXIII. 1, 2.   Ms. "Register Book of Letters" of Supreme Council.
1. *See* p. 234.

LXXXIV. Letter to Father Hugh Bourke, Flanders, from Supreme Council.

1. Reverend Father,—It is a great discouradgment to our partie that they doe discover by letters which are intercepted, directed from Amsterdam to Carriggfergus, that moneys are cheerefully brought into the committee of the Parliament of England that doe reside there by all the Protestants and Puritants of Holland, and the rest of the United Provinces, for maintenance of that which they call the Gospell against us the Catholickes of Ireland; and those who joyne with us in profession of one true faith doe give us over as if they were desirous wee should become a prey to those wolves who thirst as much to feed on them and all others that obey the Church of Rome. Wee knowe you doe not omitt what is fitt to be donn on your parte, and wee have referred the relacion of the state of our affaires to Father Plunkett, by whom you will finde how much wee stand in need of tymely assistance.—Kilkenny, the 24th of August, 1644.

2. Credentials for Father Hugh Bourke.

[To the Marquis of Castelrodrigo, Governor of the Low Countries.]

[Lord Mountgarret and his colleagues, engaged in war for their religion, have heard with pleasure of the accession of his Excellency to the chief administration of the affairs of Belgium. They are acquainted with his favourable sentiments towards their cause; and the attachment of the Irish to the house of Austria is well known. The writers trust that his Excellency will continue to favour their efforts, and beg that he will repose confidence in their delegate, Father Hugh Bourke, of the Order of

LXXXIV. 1. Ms. "Register Book of Letters" of Supreme Council.

LXXXIV. 2. Archives du Royaume, Bruxelles.—The name of the personage to whom this document was addressed has not hitherto been stated. *See* "Proceedings of the Royal Irish Academy," vol. iii. Dublin: 1847, p. 538,

St. Francis, who will inform him of the state of their affairs.—Kilkenny, 24 August, 1644.]

Excellentissime Domine,—Pergratum nobis fuit pro Catholica fide dimicantibus Belgicarum rerum summam in te, Excellentissime Domine, translatam fuisse; et cum vestri animi propensio, et studia in gentem et causam nostram satis nota sint et perspecta; et quo affectu Austriacæ Domui adhæserint Hiberni, non sit qui dubitet.   Excellentiam ergo vestram quanto potest favore res nostras prosecuturam confidimus: Quæ quo in statu sint aperiet Reverendus Pater Hugo de Burgo, Ordinis Sancti Francisci Religiosus, cui ut indubitata fides adhibeatur rogamus Excellentissimæ Dominationi vestræ addictissimi,

Mountgarett.—Thomas [Walsh] Archiepiscopus Cassilensis.—Malachias [O'Queely], Archiepiscopus Tuamensis.—Netterville.—Rob: Lynch.—Daniel O'Bryen—Dermot O'Shagnusye.—Thomas Preston.—Richard Bellings.

Kilkeniæ, 24 die Augusti, 1644.

LXXXV. LETTER TO CARDINAL MAZARIN FROM DE LA MONNERIE AT KILKENNY.

Monseigneur,—Je ne sçay si ma derniére sera tombée entre les mains de votre Eminence, par laquelle je l'informais de l'avancement de la levée des mille hommes que ces Messieurs m'ont accordez, et comme je manquois de vaisseaux pour leur transport, m'estant impossible d'en pouvoir trouvericy, quelque diligence que je puisse faire, les Parlementaires prenans tous ceux qu'ilz recontrent estre frettez pour l'Irlande; c'est ce qui m'oblige, Monseigneur, à importuner derechef votre Eminence, de commander qu'on m'en envoye pour le transport d'iceulx.

Ces Messieurs du Conseil envoyent vers leurs Majestez pour obtenir d'elles la permission de transporter des munitions de guerre, en estant en grandissime necéssité, et spéciallement, depuis que le Milord d'Insequin [Inchiquin] s'est déclaré pour le Parlement, ayant chassé tous les Catholiques qui demeuroient dans la ville de Cork, laquelle il fait fortiffier; mesmes dit on qu'il s'est mis à la campagne depuis deux jours avec 3,000 hommes en attendant six autre mille que le Parlement luy envoyera: Ce qui embarrasse fort ces Messieurs, ne sçachans où prendre des armes pour luy opposer: joinct à cela qu'ils peuvent avoir encores pour ennemis les Protestans de ce royaulme qui tiennent le party du Roy, si leurs Agens qu'ils ont envoyez vers le Marquis d'Ormond pour traitter de la paix ne la concluent: ce qui est fort incertain, d'autant que ces Messieurs icy sont résolus de maintenir la liberté de la religion Catholique: ce que l'on ne croit pas leur pouvoir estre accordé par le sieur Marquis. Que si cela est, il fauldra de nécessité qu'ils se maintiennent, tant contre l'Escossois Parlement, qu'Anglois Protestans: ce qu'ils ne sçauroient faire sans la protection d'un puissant Monarque.

Les Dunquerquois leur ont refusé des armes et autres munitions de guerre, après leur avoir promis toute sorte d'assistance: ce qui les a tellement mécontentés, qu'ils n'espérent plus rien de ce costé là et mettent toute leur espérance sur la bonté de leurs Majestez et de votre Eminence. Je crois que pour peu l'on leur accordera, cela les esloignera tout à faict du service des Espagnols. Celuy qui est icy pour l'Espagne leur a faict de grandes promesses de la part de son Maistre, et ce en pleine Assemblée: ausquelles toutesfois ils n'adjoutent aucune foy.

Pour moy, je les ay asseurés des bonnes volentez de leurs Majestez, et que j'espérois qu'ils en recepvroient plustost les effects que de l'Espagnol: à quoy ils ont tesmoigné avoir grande confiance.

C'est ce qui me fait prendre la liberté de supplier trés-humblement votre Eminence, Monseigneur, d'avoir esgard à toute cela, et de me commander ce qu'il vous plaira je fasse en toutes ces rencontres, désirant en toutes choses, tesmoigner à votre Eminence mes obeissances et tousjours en qualité, Monseigneur, de vostre Eminence, le très-humble, très-obeissant, et très-fidèle serviteur et créature,—MONNERIE.

Kilkenny, le 25 Aôut, 1644.

LXXXVI. Letter to Luke Wadding, Rome, from Supreme Council.

Reverend Father,—Although wee have fullye advertisd you by Doctor Dwyre,[1] who parted from hence six weekes since, of the state of our affaires, yet this bearer, a gentleman of neere trust to the illustrious Petrus Franciscus Scarampus, beinge employed thether by him to promote our cause, and procure us assistance, wee would not omitt to send letters by soe trusty a hand to His Holliness and the Cardinals his newphyes, and soe well wee are satisfyed with his faire carriadg amonge us, and his zeale to our cause ; that wee have remitted to his relacion many things concerning our proceedings in this war, the necessityes it hath brought us unto, and the firme resolucions wee have to remaine constant in our first undertakings.—Kilkenny, 26 August, 1644.

LXXXVII. Letters to Ormonde from Bellings.

1. My Lord,—I am commaunded by the Councell to signifie unto your Lordship, how that of late five carrs, loaden with some goods belonginge to Mr. Clement Ash, and his wife and familye, comminge from Dublin hither, have been made stay of at Catterlagh [Carlow], and are ever since detaynd by the garrison there. Besides the benefit of the Articles of Cessacion, by which free passadge could not be denyed him, he had your Lordshipp's pass, neither of which (as it should seeme) are of power with those of that garrison, who, in contempt of the one and breach of the other, refuse to restore those goods soe detained by them. And as the Councell are confident your Lordship will not give way that any under your command should discountenance your Lordship's pass, soe they expect that a speedy course will be taken to see justice donn the gentleman, in pursuance of the Articles of Cessacion.—I take leave, and rest, your Lordship's humble servant,—R. Bellings.

Kilkenny, the 24th of August, 1644.

LXXXVI. Ms. " Register Book of Letters" of Supreme Council.   1. *See* pp. 182-194.
LXXXVII. 1, 2. Carte Papers, xii. pp. 184, 194.

2. My Lord,—I acquainted the Councell with your Lordshipp's of the 10th of July last, directed to me, touchinge the payment of one hundred fiftye-foure pounds fourteene shillings and foure pence desired to be made heere unto Mr. Adrian Vanhault for twentye barrailes of powder. In answer whereof, I am commaunded to signifie unto your Lordshipp that they are confident to make it appere, the supplye [of] moneys and beeves graunted unto his Majestie, takinge into accompt the shippinge, to the payment whereof they are lyable, and the cattle taken by the garrisons in Ulster and Connaght, for which your Lordshipp is to be accomptible, are soe fully satisfyed, that nothing remaines to disengadge your Lordshipp of the money due to Mr. Vanhoult. I take leave, and rest, your Lordshipp's humble servant,—R. Bellings.

Kilkenny, the 26th of August, 1644.

LXXXVIII. Orders of the Generall Assembly of the Confederation concerning Judicature in Ireland, 1644.

Kilkenny, 30 August, 1644.

By the Commissioners of the Generall Assembly of the Confederat Catholiques of Ireland.

It is ordered and established that there shalbe a Judicatory erected, consisting of the ensueing persons : Lord Bishop of Clonfert,[1] Mr. Richard Birford, Mr. John Walsh, Mr. John Dillon, Mr. Richard Martin ; for the determynacion of all civill matters in case of appeale, bill of reversall or revewe betweene party and party, within our quarters or of our Union, and in all civill and crymynall causes, in as lardge and ample manner as the Supreame or Provinciall Councells had, or by the model[2] of government might have cognizance thereof.

And the Supreame Councell and the addicionall Comittee of Instruccions are to sett downe the pensions and fees for Judges and officers, and appointe the tymes and places of theire sittings, and order of proceedings

LXXXVIII. Carte Papers, xii. p. 217.   1. John Burke. See vol. i. p. 391.
2. See vol. i. xlix.-l. ; ii. pp. 84.

in the said Judicatory: and are likewise to provide for such Judicatory or Judicatories as shalbe necessary requisitt in the remote parts of the kingdome, by contynewance or altering of courtes already therin erected, according to the state and condicion of affaires and tymes.

And the Judicatory hereby erected are not to intermeddle in any cause under thirty pounds in originall actions, other than in such cases wherin one or all of the parties are of the province wherin they sitt; and in the same province likewise not to intermeddle with any cause under ten pounds.

And it is further ordered that all the matters betweene party and party now depending before the Supreame Councell or the Provinciall Councell of Leinster, and all informacions exhibited before the said Councell, shalbe proceeded upon and contynewed before the said Judicature in that nature and manner as such causes, matters and informacions stand before the said Supreame and Provinciall Councells.

Exam. per Philippum Kearneye, Gen. Com. Hiberniæ Cler.

LXXXIX. Negotiations relative to Cessation and Peace, 1644.

1. John Walshe to Ormonde.

May it please your Excellencie.—I have intimated your pleasure touchinge the prolonginge of the Cessation, to the Close Comittee, who are of the same opynion with your Excellencie, and will have the Instruments ready drawen for that purpose; but, as touchinge the Lord of Inchiquyne, they have referred the same to ther agents to do therin whatupon further conference had with your Excellencie they shall thinke fitt.

The enclosed I have shewed unto them, and urged the Lord Esmond's necessitie and the daunger which therby might happen. They tould me, that sithence my goinge to Dublin the souldiers of Duncannon

LXXXIX. 1, 2.   Carte Papers, xii. pp. 213, 219.

brought in from the county of Weixford eight hundred cowes and two hundred sheepe, wherefore they did not thinke fitt to take any further course for relievinge of that fort till your Excellencie's further pleasure be knowen. Upon intimation whereof, ther resolution is to comply therewith by takinge an ymediate course for sendinge parte of the wheate remayninge att Weixford. Upon consideration had of this great reliefe brought in by those souldiers, and of the resolution of the Comittee to relieve them if occasion shall require, I have directed Mr. Comerford to forbeare sendinge any monyes thither, and send what he had att the present by the bearer, Mr. Richard Shee.

Sir Brien O'Neill's[1] friends heere (who received some letters from him att my hands) give out that he is sent over to see peace concluded upon any tearmes.

Here was a letter of Fitz Gerald of Imokilly read att the Comittee late last night, importing the landinge of fourteen hundred of the Parliament forces, and that foure of ther shipps are come upp to Corcke.

The Earle of Antrim surrendered his pattent of Lieutenant-Generall,[2] and, when I went to deliver your letter to the Dutches, he complained that our close Comitee would agitate nothinge of any consequence whyle he was present, which gave him just cause (as he said) to absent himselfe. He is very desirous to repayre to Dublin, and to have a hand in the debate of the mayne businesse. He is pleased to give out heere that Ormonde's faction keepes him out of all employment.

By an order of the Assembly yesterday, he is comaunded to send his directions for recallinge of the shippes from Scotland. Our agents will not be in Dublin till Sunday night. Be sure to be carefull and wary of Sir Brien O'Neill, as you have need to be of many others. God protect you amongst us all, which none can more heartilie wish for than, my Lord, your Excellencie's ever faythfull servant,—JOHN WALSHE.

Kilkenny, 30 August, 1644.

1. See "Contemporary History of Affairs in Ireland, 1641-1652." Dublin: 1879, vol. i. pp. 571, 590, 592, 594, 798.

2 *See* p. 10.

2. Nicholas Plunkett to Ormonde.

My Lord,—I am commaunded to advertise your Lordship that the Assembly being necessitated upon very weighty occasions to stay their Comissioners from putting themselves upon their journey until to-morrow in the morning, they may not be at Dublin until Sunday at night, so as the convoy appointed for their guarde may accordingly dispose of themselves to meet them. I am, my Lord, your Excellencie's most humble servant,—N. Plunkett.

Kilkenny, 30 August, 1644.

Addressed : For his Excellencie the Marquess of Ormonde, Lord Lieutenant of Ireland.   Hast, Hast.

XC.   Commission of Delegates of the Irish Confederation to treat for peace with Charles I.

By the Supreame Councell of the Confederatt Catholicks of Ireland.

Whereas the King's most Excellent Majestie hath by his most gracious Commission[1] under the greate seale of England bearinge date the 24th of June, in the twentith yeare of his Highnes reigne, authorized his Excellency James, Lord Marquess of Ormonde, his Majestie's Lieutenant-Generall of this realme of Ireland to treate, agree, and conclude with anny person or persons, deputed, or to be deputed by his Catholicke subjects of this kingdome, or nominated or to be nominated in their behalfe for the setlinge and concludinge of a firme and lasting Peace in this kingdome, and for other matters and things thereon dependinge, mencioned in the said Commission, as hee the said, Lord Marquess, Lieutenant-Generall afforsaid, in his judgment should thincke convenient ; and, if hee found it not reasonable to consent to such Proposicions as should be made for a full Peace, then to conclude of a further Cessacion of Armes, in such manner as hee, the said Lord Marquess should thincke most behoofull for his Majestie's service, and the good of this his kingdome, as by the said Commission may more plainely appeer.

XC.   Carte Papers, xii., p. 136.   1. *See* p. 198.

And whereas likewise the Generall Assembly of the said Catholicks now held at Kilkenny hath deputed, nominated, assigned, and appointed the persons hereafter, named to be Commissioners in the behalfe of his Majestie's said Catholicke subjects of this realme, in whose integritie, wisedome, faith, and circumspection they repose much trust and confidence, to treate, agree, and conclude with the said Lord Marquess his Majestie's Lieutenant-Generall aforesaid, for the said Peace and Cessacion respectively, as afforesaid, accordinge to the tenor of the said Commission, and, to that purpose, enabled and trusted us to give Commission, for the premises, to the persons in manner as we should thincke fitt.

Wee, therefore, in pursuance thereof, and in discharge of our duetie and trust, have nominated, deputed, constituted, and appointe and by these presents doe nominatt, depute, constitute, and appointe you :

Our very good Lord, the Lord Viscount Mountgarrett, Lord President of our Councell, Thomas [Fleming] Lord Archbisshopp of Dublin ; Randle M'Donnell, Earle of Antrym ; Donnogh, Lord Viscount Muskry ; Allexander M'Donnell, Esqrs. ; Nicholas Plunckett, Esqr. ; Sir Robert Talbott, Barronett ; Sir Richard Everard, Barronett ; Dermott O'Bryen, Patricke Darcy, Geffery Browne, John Dillon, and Richard Martyn, Esqrs.,

To be Commissioners for and on the behalfe of his Majestie's said Catholicke subjects, and doe hereby give and graunte full power, warrant, and authoritie unto you, the said Commissioners, or to anny five or more of you having this our Commission for and in the behalfe of the said Catholickes to treate, agree, and conclude with the said Lord Marquess of Ormonde, Lieutenant-Generall as aforsaid, for a firme, lasting, and settled Peace within this kingdome, in such manner and forme as you, or anny five or more of you as aforsaid shall in your judgments thincke best, and most avayleable for the said Catholickes, and gennerall good of this realme.

And in case you shall not agree and conclude for such a firme Peace as afforsaid, then to treate, agree, and conclude, for and in the behalfe of the said Catholickes, with the said Lord Marquess, Lieutenant-Generall as afforsaid, of and for a further Cessacion of armes, for soe long tyme, and uppon such limitacions, and in such manner, as you in your wisedomes shall thincke expedient and most behoofefull and advantagious for the said Catholicks, and the generall good of this realme.

And lastly, for that the now Cessacion of armes in force within this kingdome may be expired before this intended Treatie of Peace may receave a full conclusion, you, or any five or more of you as afforesaid, to treate, agree, and conclude, for and in the behalfe of the said Catholickes, with the said Lord Marquess, Lieutenant-Generall, as afforesaid, of a further continuance of the said Cessacion for soe long tyme as you in your discretions shall conceive requisitt and necessary for and during that your Treatie of Peace, and attendance on the execution of his Majestie's said Commission.

Given at Kilkenny, the last daie of August, anno Domini one thousand six hundred forty and foure.

This is a true coppie of our Commission :

Muskery.—Nicholas Plunkett.—Robert Talbott.—John Dillon.—Patrick Darcy.—Dermot O'Brien.—Geffry Browne.

XCI. Letter to Queen Henrietta-Maria, from Supreme Council of Confederation.

May it please your Majestie,—Havinge understood of your Majestie's safe arrivall in France, and your happie deliverance from those dangers at sea, wherein none but such as have given over the thought of Heaven and loyaltye would attempt to engadge your Majestie, wee conceived it our duty, that as wee joyned with the rest of the Confederat Catholicks in prayseinge God for soe great a blessinge, soe we should in theire name, heereby present unto your Majestie, the testimonie of their duty and unalterable affections, hopinge in the Almighty, that although the distempers of this kingdome, and the malice of our enemyes, have for some tyme distracted us from promotinge his Majestie's intrests, in that measure which wee are ambitious to doe, yet there will be such a settlement established uppon his Majestie's Commission, enablinge the Marquess of Ormonde, Lord Liuetenant of this kingdome to conclude a Peace with his Majestie's Catholick subjects, as will be acceptable to God, usefull to his Majestie, and of advantage to this nation; that soe wee may confirme, with laying downe our lives and estates at his Majestie's feete, the solemne oath wee have taken to maintaine his Majestie's rights and prerogatives.   To facilitat the Treaty, the countenance of your Majestie's frequent intercession to our Soveraigne is the best meane, and that wee most confide in, under Heaven, which with all submissivness is implored by your Majestie's most humble suppliants.

Kilkenny, the 1st of September, 1644.

Mountgarett.—Hugo [O'Reilly] Ardmach.—Fr. Thomas [Fleming, Archbishop of] Dublin.—Thomas [Walsh, Archbishop of] Cashell.— Malachias [O'Queely] Tuamensis.—Emerus [Mac Mahon,] Dunensis Conorensis.—Nettirville.—Thomas Preston.—Daniell O'Brien.—Rob: Lynch. —Thomas Fleminge.—Richard Bellings.—Edmund Fitz Morice.—George Commyn.

Endorsed: Letter from the Supream Councell in Ireland to the Queen. 1 September, 1644.

XCII. ORMONDE TO NICHOLAS PLUNKETT.

After our hearty comendacions: Your letter of the 30th of August,[1] advertiseing the necessity of the stay of the gentlemen deputed by those by whose comand you write, were received the last of the same moneth of August, being the day by them appointed for your setting forth from Kilkenny, and the next day (being this day) by you proposed for your entrance into this citty [Dublin].   In answear to which wee thought fitt to lett you know that haveing appointed a convay for you yesterday, they went to the place where they intended to stay your coming, and that they, being uppon their returne disperst into their severall quarters, are not fitt as uppon this day to be called together againe; and therefore wee pray you to signify to the rest of your officials that it is our desire they should repose themselves this day, and that wee shall appoint a convay to meet them to-morrow.   And soe wee remaine, your loveing frend,—ORMONDE.

Dublin Castle, 1 September, 1644.

XCIII. Acquittance for money received from King of Spain.

A certificat to Fr. James Talbot, for the receipt of money, twenty thousand crownes, from Spaine :[1]

By the Supreame Councell.

Memorandum : That Father James Talbot and Father Magenis have delivered us a true and satisfactory accompt for the twenty thousand crownes given by his Catholicke Majestie to the Confederat Catholickes of Ireland. In testimony whereof wee doe subsigne these. Given at Kilkenny the 5th of September, 1644 :

Mountgarret.—Hugo [O'Reilly] Armachanus [Archiepiscopus].— Thomas [Walsh, Archbishop of] Cashill.—Malachias [O'Queely] Tuamensis [Archiepiscopus].—Emerus [Mac Mahon], Dunensis et Connorensis [Episcopus].—Thomas Flemminge.—Thomas Preston.—Rob: Lynch.— Daniell O'Brien.—Edmond Fitz Morrice.—Dermot O'Shagnussye.— George Commyn.

XCIV. Articles for Renewal of Cessation of hostilities between Charles I. and his Roman Catholic subjects in Ireland, September, 1644.

Whereas Articles of Cessation of Armes were agreed and concluded on at Sigginstowne, in the county of Kildare, the fifteenth day of September, in the nineteenth yeare of his Majestie's reigne [1643], by and between us, the Lord Lieutenant, by the name of James, Marques of Ormonde, Lieutenant-Generall of his Majestie's armie in the kingdome of Ireland, for and in the name of our gracious Soveraigne Lord, Charles, by the grace of God, King of Great Brittaine, France, and Ireland, etc., by vertue of his Majestie's Commission bearing date at Dublin the last day of August, in the said nineteenth yeare of his Majestie's

XCIII. Ms. "Register Book of Letters" of Supreme Council.
1. *See* vol. i. p.150 ; ii. pp. xxxviii. 280.
XCIV. Carte Papers, clxxvi. p. 181.

reigne, of the one parte, and Donogh Vicecount Muskry and others, authorized by his Majestie's Roman Catholicque subjects then in armes in the said kingdome, etc., of the other parte, which Cessation of armes was by the said Articles to continue for one whole yeare, beginning the fifteenth of September, one thousand six hundred fortie and three, at the houre of twelve of the clock of the said day :

And whereas by his Majestie's Commission under his Great Seale of England, dated the fowre and twentieth of June last, wee, the Lord Lieutenant, are authorized to treate concerning the settling and establishing of a firme and perfect Peace within this kingdome :

And whereas the Lord Vicecount Muskry, Nicholas Plunkett, Esquire Sir Robert Talbott, Barronett, Dermott O'Bryen, Patrick Darcy, Geffrey, Browne, and John Dillon, Esquires, deputed and authorized by his Majestie's Roman Catholicque subjectes of this kingdome, now or late in armes, to treate with us, are now heere at Dublin, attending us, the Lord Lieutenant, concerning the said Treatie of Peace :

And forasmuch as the yeare limited by the said Articles for the continuance of the present Cessation of armes in this kingdome, is soe neere an end, as the said Treatie of Peace, cannot (as is conceived) bee fully determined within that time : and for that if a Peace shall bee concluded on this Treatie, yet if it bee not concluded soe seasonably, within the said time (namely before the fifteenth of September, one thousand six hundred fortie and four) as that notice thereof may bee given to all partes of the kingdome in convenient time, before the said fifteenth of September, one thousand six hundred fortie and fowre, much mischief and inconvenience may from thence followe on both sides, to his Majestie's subjectes in this kingdome.

Wherefore, in prevencion of any such mischeefes and inconveniences to his Majestie's said subjectes, wee, the Lord Lieutenant, by vertue of his Majestie's authoritie entrusted with us as his Lieutenant-Generall and Generall Governor of this his kingdome, and by advise of the Councell, and for and in the name of his Majestie, of the one part, and wee, the said Lord Vicecount Muskery, Nicholas Plunkett, Esqr., Sir Robert Talbott, Barronett, Dermott O'Bryen, Patrick Darcy, Geffry Browne, and

John Dillon, Esquires, deputed and authorized in that behalfe by his Majestie's said subjectes now or late in armes in this kingdome, of the other parte, have concluded and accorded, and it is accordingly hereby concluded and accorded, that there bee a further Cessation of Armes, and of all actes of hostilitie in this kingdome, untill the first day of December next ensuing the date heerof, at the howre of twelve of the clock of the same day, to begin on the fifteenth of September, one thousand six hundred fortie and fowre, at the howre of twelve of the clock of the said day, uppon the like Articles and agreementes, to all intentes and purposes as are expressed in the said former Articles of Cessation concluded on at Sigginstowne on the fifteenth September, one thousand six hundred fortie and three, and as if the said Cessation first agreed on had continuance untill the said first day of December, one thousand six hundred fortie and fowre, at the houre of twelve of the clock of the same day.

In witnes wherof, the said Lord Lieutenant to that part of this agreement which remaines with the said Lord Vicecount Muskry, Nicholas Plunkett, Sir Robert Talbott, Dermott O'Bryen, Patrick Darcy, Geffry Browne, and John Dillon, hath putt his hand and seale.

And the said Lord Vicecount Muskry, Nicholas Plunkett, Sir Robert Talbott, Dermott O'Bryen, Patrick Darcie, Geffery Browne, and John Dillon, to that part of this agreement which remaines with the said Lord Lieutenant, have putt their handes and seales, the fiveth day of September, one thousand six hundred fortie and fowre, in the twentieth year of his Majestie's reigne.

MUSKRY.—NICHOLAS PLUNKETT.—ROBERT TALBOTT.—DERMOTT O'BRIEN. —PATRICK DARCY.—GEFFREY BROWNE.—JOHN DILLON.

Signed, sealed, and delivered in the presence of us : RICHARD BOLTON, C[HANCELLOR].—LAURENCE [BULKELEY, ARCHBISHOP OF] DUBLIN.—ROSCOMMON.—EDWARD BRABAZON.—ANTONY [MARTIN,] MIDENSIS.—CHARLES LAMBARTE.—JAMES WARE.

XCV. Bellings to Ormonde.

My Lord,—The express your Excelency sent with those letters directed unto me, dated the 29 of August, did deliver them in great hast at twelve of the clock yesterday ; and since that time I have not seen him. The Sheriffe of the county of Wickloe is to conveighe the powder designed for Prince Rupert from Arckloe to Bullock,[1] ther to be shipped in your Lordship's pinnace, for although a Dutch marchant mought have been contracted with to leave the powder at Hollihead, yet considering the powder might more safely be conveighed in the frigatt to Chester from whence the occasion might be sooner supplyed than from Holliheed, this was thought the fittest way. The direction to the Sherife is already sent away, and he is commaunded to use all possible speed in conveighing the powder to Bullocke, which I hoope will come oportunely to relieve the beseeged in Leverpoole against those rebels that affect our neighborhood, because they may be neer to do us a mischeife. I am, my Lord, your Excelency's most humble servant,—R. Bellings.

Kilkenny, this 5 of September [1644].

XCVI. Order in relation to "the Fourth Sheaf."

Whereas severall doubts have arrisen upon the Articles of Cessacion touchinge the fourth sheafe of this present harvest, and espetially concerninge the fourth sheafe demaunded out of some lands formerly protected within the quarters allotted to his Majestie's Romane Catholicke subjects, as alsoe concerninge a demaund of a fourth sheafe of this present harvest out of some lands within the quarters allotted to his Majestie's Protestant subjects, from such as formerly paide contribucions : For avoydeinge therefore of all such doubts, and what variances may happen thereuppon, it is agreed and accorded between his Excellencie, James, Lord Marquess of

XCV. Carte Papers, xii. p. 249.   1. In county of Dublin.
XCVI. Carte Papers, xii. p. 344.—For stipulations as to "the fourth sheaf," *see* vol. ii. pp. 369-70.

Ormonde, his Majestie's Lieutenant of Ireland, in the behalfe of his Majestie's said Protestant subjects, and Donogh, Lord Viscount Muskery, Alexander M'Donnell, and Nicholas Plunkett, Esq., Sir Robert Talbott, Barronett, Dermott O'Bryen, Patrick Darcy, Geffry Browne, and John Dillon, Esqrs., in the behalfe of his Majestie's said Roman Catholicke subjects, that, as to the fourth sheafe demaunded out of places soe formerly protected, the same is onely to bee paid out of the winter corne of this harvest, and, for the springe corne, sowen in such the said lands (soe protected) after the Cessacion, noe fourth sheafe is to bee paide thereout. And as to the said fourth sheafe demaunded from such as paide contribucion, it is agreed and accorded that noe fourth sheafe of any corne whatsoever bee paide in that case.—ORMONDE.

Dublin Castle, 16 September, 1644.

Copia vera : GEO. LANE.

XCVII. NEGOTIATIONS FOR PEACE BETWEEN ORMONDE AND COMMISSIONERS OF IRISH CONFEDERATION, SEPTEMBER, 1644.

1. PROPOSITIONS DELIVERED BY THE LORD MUSKERRY, ETC. TO THE LORD LIEUTENANT, 5 SEPTEMBER, 1644.

[These Propositions correspond with the revised "Demands of the Roman Catholics of Ireland" presented to Charles I. at Oxford, by the Commissioners of the Confederation,—for which see p. 128.

At end is the following addition, after the seventeenth Proposition :

"The severall particulars before mencioned wee humbly offerr unto your Lordshipp's consideracion, reservinge unto us the presenting of such other matters as wee conceave will tend to the further settlement of the affaires of this kingdome, and likewise reservinge unto us an explanacion of anny the Proposicions before mencioned, or the matter therein conteyned, which may be conceived generall or doubtfull."]

XCVII. 1. Carte Papers, vol. xii., p. 148.

XCVII. 2. DEBATES ON PROPOSITIONS FROM COMMISSIONERS OF CONFEDERATION.

i.—THE SUBSTANCE OF THE DEBATE BEGUN ON FRIDAY, THE SIXTH OF SEPTEMBER, 1644, BETWEENE THE LORD CHAUNCELLOR [OF IRELAND, SIR RICHARD BOLTON,] AND THOSE[1] APPOINTED BY THE LORD LIEUTENANT FOR HIS ASSISTANCE, AND THE LORD VISCOUNT MUSKERY AND THOSE[2] DEPUTED WITH HIM FOR THE TREATY, UPON THE PROPOSICIONS DELIVERED TO THE LORD LIEUTENANT, AS IT WAS REPORTED ON FRIDAIE, THE THIRTEENTH OF THE SAME MONTH:

The first daie was spent upon the second, third, and fourth Proposicions[3] (for the debate of the first Proposicion was put off to the last, according to the order prescribed by the Lord Lieutenant, though it was much urged by the other side that it might be considered in the first place), and to the end that what was urged on both sides might be the better understood, it was thought fit to reade the Proposicions, and then to summe up the chiefe matters which fell in debate.

Second Proposition: That your Majestie be pleased to cause a free Parliament in the said kingdome to be held and continued, as in the Remonstrance[4] is expressed, and that the statute of the tenth yeare of Henry VII. called Poynings Act,[5] and all Acts explayneing or inlargeing the same, be suspended dureing that Parliament for speedy settlement of the present affaires, and the repeale thereof to be further considered.

Third Proposition.[6]—That all Acts and ordinances made and passed in

XCVII. 2. Carte Papers, vol xii., pp. 173-180.

1. Sir George Shurley, Chief Justice; Thomas Dongan and Sir William Ryves, Justices of the King's Bench; Sir Maurice Eustace, Sergeant-at-Law; and some members of the Privy Council in Ireland.

2. Nicholas Plunket, Sir Robert Talbot, Dermot O'Brien, Patrick Darcy, Geoffrey Browne, and John Dillon. *See* p. 256.

3. *See* p. 128.

4, 5. *See* vol. ii. pp. 241-2. A reproduction of Poynings' Act, from the contemporary Statute Roll, appears in " Facsimiles of National MSS. of Ireland," Part iii., Plate lii. London : 1879.

6. *See* p. 128.

the now pretended Parliament in that kingdome since the seaventh day of August, 1641, be cleared, annulled, and declared voide, and taken off the file.

Fourth Proposition.[1]—That all indictments, attainders, outlaries, in the King's Bench or elsewhere sence the said seaventh day of August, 1641, and all lettres, pattents, graunts, leases, custodiams, bonds, recognizances, and all other act, or acts depending thereupon, or in prejudice of the said Catholiques, or any of them, be taken off the file, annulled, and declared voide, first by your Majestie's proclamacion, and after by Acts to be passed in the said free Parliament.

There being much affinity betweene the matter desired in the second and fourth Proposition, both looking unto a new Parliament, the consideracion of both was taken together; and in regard a free Parliament was the thinge which was so much desired, and that this Parliament should be dissolved, the Lord Viscount Muskery and the rest were asked how they could have that which they called a free Parliament, if this present Parliament were dissolved, for that many of the Peeres whoe were to sit in the House of the Lords were outlawed of High Treason, and very many of the Knights and burgesses of the House of Commons were likewise outlawed, and that most of the free-holders in the English shires whoe were to make new elections were in like sorte outlawed; soe as except these incapacities were removed by this Parliament, there was noe possibility of haveing such a Parliament as they desired. And, after much debate, it was agreed by all that neither the Peeres who were attaincted of High Treason by outlarie, nor such of the House of Commons as were in like sorte utlawed, could sit in Parliament, nor yet new elections be made in those counties where the freehoulders were outlawed before those outlaries were taken away; and, therefore, in the first place a way was to be thought of for the removeing of those incapacities, for without this nothing could be done.

The way propounded by those whoe treated for the Romane Catholicques was, that the records should be taken off the file and vacated; which some of them conceaved might be done either by directions from

---

his Majestie or by order of the House of the Lords in Parliament, in regard of the generality of the case and the necessity of doeing of it, and that the safety of the kingdome and his Majestie's service did much depende upon the hasty doing thereof, and that in such cases formalityes of law ought to be laid aside, for it was not the law but the sword that must (as they said) now doe the work.

To this the Lord Chaunncellor and those whoe assisted him made answere, that this was not to be done in the way which was propounded; and, if it were, yet that course ought to be taken which is most warrantable and just for the King to doe, and most safe for them whoe were to receive the benefit thereof, and that was by bill to passe this present Parliament.

They were further tould that the regular and ordinary way was either by plea before attainder, or by writ of error after attaincture, either in the same Courte or in Parliament, but that this being the case of very many would prove tedious and a very long worke to take this course; and therefore to proceede by bill was the speedy and safe way warranted by authority in printe advised by all the Judges of England in the like case of 1 Henry VII. fol. 5.

To this the other side agreed, but desired that if a more speedy way might be thought of that the Lord Lieutenant might be moved therein, for the business of the kingdome required it.

The second matter which fell in debate was touching the suspending of Poynings' Act.[1]

Those whoe treated for the Roman Catholicques did urge for this, that in regard of the difficultie and danger of the passage in theise tymes, and the lenght of tyme which the transmitting of every particular bill would take up, by observeing the course prescribed by Poynings' Act, and the danger that might ensue by altering the bills in England after the transmission from hence; that, therefore, there was noe safety for them, except that Poynings' Act were suspended.

To this answer was made, that it is provided by Act of Parliament

---

1. *See* p. 128.

enacted in this kingdome that no bill be certified into England for the repeale or suspending of Poynings' Act before the same bill be first agreed on, in a session of Parliament to be houlden within this realme, by the more number of the Lords assembled in Parliament, and the greater number of the Commons' House (xi Eliz. cap. 8. fol. 332) and then to be transmitted to his Majestie according to Poynings' Act, for it doth not rest in the King's power alone to doe it;[1]

That the sending of this bill into England, as it must, before Poynings' Act can be suspended, will take up as much tyme as the transmitting of all the other bills which are to be agreed upon on this Treaty;

That sithence all matters to be agreed upon on this Treaty are to be reduced into bills, and that those may be transmitted togither with the bill for the suspending of Poynings' Act, that there neede noe suspension of Poynings' Act, and that there was noe cause to suspect or feare that there would be any alteracion of the bills, which should be agreed on this treaty, in England, for that would amounte to a breach of the Articles.

After this debate the Lord Viscount Muskery and the rest withdrew, and after some consultation they returned, and Mr. [Patrick] Darcy[2] made this reporte:

1. That it was theire sence and opinion that the first thinge to be done in the free Parliament was the suspending of Poynings' Act, without which those bills to be now agreed upon could not passe in the new Parliament without a new transmission.

2. That they desired it should be only suspended as unto the ratifying of the matters to be agreed on upon the Treaty and to noe other purpose.

3. They desired that some more speedy way might be thought of for removeing the attainctures, than by bill, and that the Lord Lieutenant might be moved therein.

1. " An Act that there be no bill certified into England for the repeale or suspending of the statute past in Poynings' time, before the same bill be first agreed on, in a session of a Parliament holden in this realme, by the greater number of the Lords and Commons."—" The Statutes of Ireland." Dublin: 1621, p. 332.

2. See vol. ii., p. 394.

The second[1] and fourth[2] Proposition occasioned this debate.

The third,[3] after some dispute, was admitted by them to be qualified, for it was made apparant unto them that many good ordinances passed within the compasse of that tyme, as the letters written[4] by both Houses to Mountroe,[5] comaunding him not to take the Covenant; the joynt peticion[6] of both Houses to his Majestie, wherein they complaine of the Howses of Parliament at Westminster; and other orders of that kinde.

XCVII. 2. ii.—The substance of the debate upon Saturday, the 14th of September, 1644.

Fifth Proposition.[7]—That, inasmuch as under color of such outlaries and attainders, debts due unto the said Catholicques have been levyed and disposed of, and, of the other side, that debts due upon the said Catholicques to those of the adverse partie have been levyed, graunted, and disposed of to publicke use; that, therefore, all debts due by Act of Parliament be mutually released or to stand in statu quo.

To this it was said, in the first place, that this could not be done but by Act of Parliament, and that his Majestie could not, in justice or honnor, assent to such an Act, which should release the debts due unto his Protestant subjects, whoe had not offended.

That for those debts, which came to his Majestie by theire attaincture, which were not receaved, his Majestie, if he did see cause, might shew grace and mercy.

That if his Majestie did soe farre condiscend thereunto as to release what was forfeited unto him it was an exceeding grace and mercy, for there was not one of those debts graunted away unto any, and but one receaved to his Majestie's use, which was that debt of £1200 due to Mr. Archbould, which Mr. Carpenter was forced to pay, and that this came to noe privat hand but to the use of the army. To this much was not said, but that they desired it might be left to the debate before the Lord Lieutenant.

XCVII. 2. ii. Carte Papers, xii. pp. 173-180.

1, 2, 3, 7. *See* p. 128.   4, 6. In April, 1644.   5. "Serjeant-Major-General" in Ulster.

Sixth Proposition.[1]—That the late offices taken or founde upon fained or ould titles sence the yeare 1634, to entitle his Majestie to severall counties in Connaght, Thomonde, and the countyes of Tipperary, Limericke, and Kilkeny, and Wicklow, be vacated[2] and taken off the file, and the possessors thereof settled and secured in theire auncient estates by Act of Parliament; and that the like Act of Limitacion of his Majestie's titles, for the securitie of the estates of his Majestie's subjects in this kingdome, be passed in the said Parliament, as was enacted in the 21th yeare of his late Majestie's raigne [1623-1624].

1. *See* p. 129. 2. *See* p. 129. The following directions, in relation to these matters, are contained in a letter from Charles I., dated 24th May, 1641, addressed to Sir William Parsons, and Sir John Borlase, Lords Justices, and the Council in Ireland, touching " certain Instructions and Graces " authorised by his Majesty in 1628 :

" That for the securing of the estates of our subjects there [in Ireland], touching the limitations of our titles, not to extend above threescore years, according to the intention of the twenty-fourth article of the said Instructions ; a bill, such as did pass in this our realme of England, the one and twentieth year of the reign of our dear father of blessed memory, be by you, our said Justices and Councel, forthwith transmitted, according to Poynings' Act, to pass in Parliament there [in Ireland].

" We are graciously pleased, according to our princely promise, in the twenty-fourth and twenty-fifth articles of the said graces, and in performance of the engagements of our royal father and Queen Elizabeth, to secure the estates, or reputed estates, of the inhabitants, as well of Connaught and county of Clare, or county of Thomond, as of the counties of Limerick and Tipperary ; and to free them and their said estates, or reputed estates, from all titles accrued to us or our predecessors ; and to forego and discharge our intended Plantations therein, notwithstanding any office there found.

" And, for the better security of the said inhabitants, we are further graciously pleased, that their estates be secured in Parliament, according to the intent of the said twenty-fourth and twenty-fifth articles respectively : to which end, we will and require you, that forthwith an Act be transmitted for the settling of the said province and counties, and every part thereof, according to the tenor and intention of the said twenty-fourth and twenty-fifth articles respectively.

" And we are also graciously pleased, that the said inhabitants shall be allowed to take such other ways for the securing of their estates, as in the twenty-fourth and twenty-fifth articles are respectively expressed. And our will and pleasure is, that the offices aforesaid be vacated, upon passing such an Act."

" Journals of the House of Commons of the Kingdom of Ireland." Dublin: 1796, vol. i. p. 211.

For the laste parte, which is to have the like Act of Limitacion in this kingdom as in England, because it concerned the generall good and settlement of the kingdome, it was not opposed. But for the first parte, which was the takeing the offices off the file, it could not be don but by Act of Parliament; and that, for what concerned the county of Wickloe, it was confirmed by Act of Parliament assented unto by themselves last Parliament, and the territorie of Idough[1] past by letters pattents grounded upon his Majestie's Commission of Grace for defective titles.

Seventh Proposition.[2]—That all markes of incapacitie imposed upon the natives of this kingdome to purchase or acquire lands, leases, offices, or hereditaments, be taken away by Act of Parliament, and the same to extend to the secureing of purchases, leases, or graunts already made; and, for the education of youthes, an Act may be passed in the next Parliament for the erecting of one or more Inns of Court, Universities, free and common schooles.

The later parte of the Proposition receaved noe opposicion, onely that it might have some qualificacions; and, for the first parte, they were desired to explaine theire meaning which they did in this manner:

That, upon former settlements of Plantation, all the pattents had this provisoe in them that the pattentee nor his heires should alien to any of the meere Irish; which did argue, as they said, a suspicion of the nation, and keepe a distance betweene them and the English.

To this it was said that the end of those provisoes was for the upholding of the Plantacions, and to keepe the English there, and not for any such reason as was proposed.

That a subject might reserve such a condicion; much more the King, whoe may by law restrayne his pattentee from conveyeing his land.

---

1. An extensive territory in the county of Kilkenny, anciently styled Ui-Duach and occupied by the sept of O'Braonain or O'Brennan. The district was granted by James I., in 1617, to Francis Edgeworth, and was subsequently sold to Sir Christopher Wandesford, Master of the Rolls in Ireland, for £20,000. Letters Patent, which he took out, under the Commission for the remedy of Defective Titles, were confirmed in Parliament, as above mentioned.

2. See p. 129.

To this answere was made that such a condicion, that the pattentee might not alien to any, would give lesse offence than to leave a libertie to alien to all but the Irish.

In conclusion, the thinge left to be considered upon this Proposicion is, admitting those condicions were in those tymes of good use, whether such may not be now taken away without inconvenience.

Eighth Proposicion.[1]—That the offices and places of commaunde, honor, profit, and trust, within that kingdome be conferred upon Romane Catholicque natives, in equality and indifferency with his Majestie's other subjects.

This admitted noe dispute, in regard it was a matter which rested meerely in his Majestie's free choise; but thought fit to be left wholie to the debate before the Lord Lieutenant.

Ninth Proposition.[2]—That the insupportable oppressions of the subjects by reason of the Court of Wards, and respit of homage, be taken away, and a certaine revenue in lieu thereof settled uppon his Majestie without diminucion of his Majestie's profits.

There was not much said to the first parte of the Proposition, in regard they were not ready for the particulars, as to shew how his Majestie's tenures might be preserved, how the youth should be bred, what revenue they would make sure to his Majestie in lieu thereof, and how it should be settled; but they said they would prepare theise things to be presented to the Lord Lieutenant.

For the later parte, which is for respit of homage, they were tould it brought a good revenue to his Majestie and they were advised, (1) to informe themselves what was made of it seaven yeares before the comocion, communibus annis, and then to fix upon a medium; (2) to consider how this should be raised.

Tenth Proposition.[3]—That noe Lord not estated in this kingdom, or estated and not resident, should have vote in the Parliament by proxy or otherwise, and none admited to the House of Comons but such as should be estated and resident within this kingdome.

1, 2, 3. *See* p. 130.

The consequence of this Proposition to be presented to the Lord Lieutenant at the debate before his Lordship.

XCVII. 2. iii.—THE SUBSTANCE OF THE DEBATE ON MUNDAY, THE 16TH OF SEPTEMBER, 1644.

Eleventh Proposition.[1]—That an Act be passed in the next Parliament declaratory that the Parliament of Ireland is a free Parliament of itselfe, independant of, and not subordinate to, the Parliament of England, and that the subjects of Ireland are immediatly subjects to your Majestie as in right of your Crowne; and that the members of the said Parliament of Ireland, and all other subjects of Ireland, are independant and noe way to be ordered or concluded by the Parliament of England, and are onely to be ordered and governed within that kingdome by his said Majestie and such Governors as are or should be appointed of that kingdome, according to the lawes of the land.

1. To this it was said that a declaration of both Houses would be as effectuall as an Act, and that rested in their owne power to make.

2. That if of right it did not belonge unto them (as of all sides it was agreed it did), that an Act of Parliament passed here would not doe it, for that the Parliament in England could not be bound by an Act here.

3. That what was desired touching this was don already by two severall Acts of Parliament past in this kingdome, remembered by the Lord Chauncellor.

4. That, if the law were otherwise, this inconvenience would follow, that all the Acts past in this kingdome for the good thereof by those whoe know the state of the kingdome might be repealed there by those whoe, it may be, know little thereof.

5. That it is absurde to say that the King should be subordinate to himselfe, which must be admitted if Acts in England should bind here, for heere he is supreame in giveing the assent; and in this he must be

subordinate to himselfe in passing Acts in England, if they should binde here.

The other side did agree to all this that was said, but they did urge that there was a necessity to passe an Act; for, though it cannot gaine more right, yet, considering the late Acts which have beene don in England, as that Act which giveth away theire lands, a bare declaracion is not sufficient.

That this being a matter concerning the power of both Parliaments, his Majestie was the proper and onely judge thereof.

That his Majestie haveing given the royall assent to the Act passed in England, they by that lost ground and could not be safe except his Majestie did assent to such an Act as was desired.

To this it was said that it was to be wished that there were such an Act, but tyme was not seasonable to desire it.

That it is like the Parliament of England would desire to be heard in this, which, as the conjuncture of thinges now stand can not be; and this is the substance in brief of what was said.

Twelfth[1] Proposition.—That the assumed power or jurisdiction of the Councell board of determineing all manner of causes be limited to matters of State, and all pattents, estates, and graunts, illegally and extra-judicially avoided, there or elsewhere be left in state as before, and the parties grieved, theire heires or assignes, till legall eviction.

To the first parte of this Proposition much was not said; but against the last parte of the Proposition was said:

That some of those estates, by consent of parties, have beene confirmed by speciall Acts of Parliament, and that those were not to be touched.

Secondlie, that if way were given to the partie grieved by any of those orders to bring theire actions at Common Law, and that those orders should be noe barre in theire way, that it was a great favour; but to restore them to the possession without suite might be very prejudiciall and inconvenient to the subject.

1. Originally numbered thirteenth.—*See* p. 131.

To this it was said that by those orders many of theire deedes were taken away and cancelled, and therefore they could not be safe except they might be restored to the possessions which were taken from them.

Thirteenth[1] Proposition.—That the statutes of the eleventh, twelfth, and thirteenth yeare of Queene Elizabeth concerning staple comodities be repealed, reserveing to his Majestie lawfull and just poundage, and a book of rates to be settled by an indifferent Committee of both Houses for all comodities.

To this little was said of either side.

Fourteenth[2] Proposition.—Touching the continuance of the chiefe Governors but for three yeares, and that dureing theire government they should acquire noe mannors, etc., other than from his Majestie, his heires or successors.

Against this much was said in reason of State, as that it would be three yeares before the Governor could come to a perfect knowledge of the state of the kingdome, and to put him from the government then, when he begins to be most fit for it, would prove inconvenient;

That to restraine the Governor from purchaseing of land was a badge of slavery;

That it was better for the kingdome that he should bestow his money in it than to send it away;

That noe denizen can by law be debarred from this.

They were advised to consider better of this Proposition. But it was said by some of them that the later parte of the Proposition, which was for restrayneing from purchaseing, was of absolute necessitie.

Fifteenth Proposition[3].—That an Act may be passed in the next Parliament for the raiseing and settling of trayned-bands within the severall counties of that kingdome, as well to prevent forraigne invasions as to render them the more serviceable and ready for his Majestie's occasions, as cause shall require.

Against which it was urdged that it was neither seasonable to be propounded, nor for his Majestie to graunte.

1, 2. Originally numbered fourteenth and fifteenth.—*See* p. 131. 3. *See* p. 132.

The sixteenth Proposition,[1] which concerns the Act of Oblivion, and the seventeenth Proposition,[2] touching those to be excepted, referred to the debate before the Lord Lieutenant.

XCVII. 2. iv. THE SUBSTANCE OF THE DEBATE ON THURSDAY, THE 17TH OF SEPTEMBER,1644, WAS UPON THE FIRST PROPOSITION, WHICH FELL IN DEBATE.

First Proposition.[3]—That all Acts made against the professors of the Romane Catholicke faith, whereby any restraynte, penaltie, mulct, or incapacitie, may be laid upon any Romane Catholicke within the kingdome, of Ireland, may be repealed, and the said Catholickes to be allowed the freedome of the Romane Catholicke religion.

They, being desired to explaine what Acts they desired should be repealed, and haveing taken tyme to consider of it, expressed them thus in order:

28 Henry VIII. cap. 5, by which the King[4] is declared to be Head of the Church of Ireland, and that the King, his heires and successors, should have full power and authoritie, from tyme to tyme to visite, re-presse, redresse, reforme, order, correct, restraine, and amende all such errors, heresies, abuses, offences, contempts, and enormities whatsoever, which by any manner of spirituall authority or jurisdiction ought or may be lawfully reformed; and that the King, his heires and successors, may depute any person or persons as they shall think fitt to doe the same.

For, as they said, they could not be safe if Commissioners of a contrary religion might visit them.

To which answer was made that all were of one religion at the tyme of makeing this law, and that this was to take away the forraigne power which the Pope did usurpe, which must not by any meanes be admitted againe into the kingdome.

28 Henry VIII. cap. 6, entitled an Act of Appeales :[5] They desire that this following branche may be repealed, viz. :

XCVII. 2. iv. Carte Papers, xii. pp. 173-180.

1, 2. Originally numbered eighteenth. *See* p. 132.   3. *See* p. 128.

4. "An Act authorising the King, his heyres and successors, to be Supreme Head of the Church of Ireland."—"Statutes of Ireland." Dublin : 1621, p. 101. 5. Ib. p. 142.

That noe person or persons, subjects or resiants of this land, shall,
from the first day of this present Parliament, pursue, commence, use or
exercise any manner of provocations, appeales, or other processe to or from
[the Bishop of Rome,[1]] or from the See of Rome, or to or from any other
that clayme authoritie by reason of the same for any manner of case,
griefe, or cause, of what nature soever it be, upon paine that the offenders,
theire aiders, councellors, and abettors contrary to this Act, shall incurre
and runn into such paine, forfeitures, and penalties as be specified and
contayned in the Act of [Provision and[2]] Premunire, [made in the realme of
England, in the sixteenth yeare of King Richard the Second, sometime
King of England and Lord of Ireland, against such as procure to the
Court of Rome or elsewhere, to the derogation, or contrary to the prerogative or jurisdiction of the saide Crowne of England.[3]]

[NOTE: The order of Priesthood is not questioned by this Act, but
the matter of jurisdiction.[4]]

There is a necessity, they say, of repealing this, for that since they
are of the Romane religion they must have priests amongst them, and
these cannot be kept in order but by theire superiors, who derive authoritie from the See of Rome, before whom complainte must be many tymes
made, as, for example: two priests are in variance about dutyes in a
parish. The one sueth the other before his Ordinary. This priest, and
all such whoe shall aide him, councell or abet him, are in danger of this
statute.

[23 Henry VIII. cap. 8, and cap. 14, touching first fruits and
twentieth parts, allowed.]

[28 Henry VIII. cap. 13, which ordeyneth the refusall of taking the
Oath of Supremacy to be High Treason, repealed by the statute of 2 and
3 of Philip and Mary, as the former, and not revived.[5]]

28 Henry VIII. cap. 19, called the Act of Faculties:[6] They desire
that this followeing branch therein may be repealed:

1, 2, 3, 4, 5. The passages within brackets are from a contemporary document entitled
"Collections out of the Penall Statutes to be repealed," and commencing as follows : " In
the debate, the Acts desired by the Confederate Romanists to be repealed were," etc.—
Carte Papers, xv., pp. 447-452.   6. " Statutes of Ireland." Dublin; 1621, p. 150.

"Be it enacted that neither your Highness, your heires, or successors, Kings of this realme, nor any your subjects of this realme, nor any of any other dominions, shall from henceforth sue to the Bishop of Rome called the Pope, or to the See of Rome, or to any person or persons haveing or pretending any authoritie by the same for licences, dispensations, imposicions, faculties, graunts, rescripts, delegacies, or any other instruments or writings of what kinde, name, nature, or qualitie soever they be of, for any cause or matter for the which any licence, etc. hath beene used to be had at the See of Rome, or authoritie thereof, or by any Prelate of this realme."

This cannot stand with theire religion as they said, etc.

[33 Henry VIII. cap. 6 : That the clause therein, touching the degrees observed in marrying, be made voyde.[1]]

An Act was made, 3 et 4 Phillip and Mary which repealed all these entitled, an Act repealing all statutes, articles, and provisions made against the See Apostolick of Rome sithence the 20th yeare of King Henry the Eight.

2 Elizabeth, cap. 1, repealed[2] that Act of Phillip and Mary, and renued the Act of Appeales, the Act of Faculties, and soe much of the Act entitled an Act for Mariadges as doth touch and concerne degrees and consanguinity. And that all other lawes and statutes, and the branches and clauses of any Act or statute repealed and made voide by the saide Act of repeale made in the tyme of the said late King Phillip, Queene Mary, and not in this present Parliament renued shall stand repealed and be voide as if this statute were not made.

They urge for the repealing of this statute, and instance the pressures which, as they say, lie upon them by reason of this statute :

First, noe man shalbe admitted to have his owne lands, the inheritance whereof is by law cast upon him if held of his Majestie by knight service, before he take the Oath of Supremacy, which none of theire religion can take.

1. "Statutes of Ireland." Dublin : 1621, p. 188. 2. *See* p. 298.

Secondly, none of theire profession can have any office of honor nor trust, without takeing this oathe.

Thirdly, none of their profession can have any office to which a fee doth belong, for the like reason.

Fourthly, it doth disable theire clergy from haveing any spirituall liveing.

And, in the last place, they urge the strictness and severity of the last parte of it, which is thus:

That if any person or persons residing in this kingdome " shall, by writing, printing, teaching, preaching, expresse words, deede or act, advisedly, maliciously, and directly " maintayne the authority, "power or jurisdiction, spirituall or ecclesiasticall, of any forraigne Prince, Prelate, person, State, or Potentate whatsoever heretofore claymed, used, or usurped within this realme, or shall advisedly maliciously and directly put in use or execute any thing for the extolling, advancement, setting forth, maintenance or defence of any such pretended or usurped power," etc., that then every such person "soe doeing and offending, their abettoùrs, aydours, procurers, and councellours, being thereof lawfully convicted and attainted, according to the due order and course of the Comon Lawes" of this king-dome, shall, for the first offence, forfeite all his goods and chattles, etc. That, for the second offence, being thereof duely convict, he shall incur the danger of premunire; and that, for the third offence, being thereof lawfully convict and attainted, it shalbe adjudged High Treason.

To this it was said by the Lord Chauncellor and those whoe assisted him, that, from the tyme of makeing the said statute untill this present, none lost blood upon this statute.

It was further said, that it did not concerne religion but the suppressing of forraine jurisdiction, etc. ;[1] [that it devided itsealf into seven parts :

1. To restore the Crowne to an ancient right.—2. To abolish forreigne power.—3. To repeale the statute of Philip and Mary.—4. To revive some of the statutes repealed by the statute of Philip and Mary.—5. To repress

1. The passages within brackets are from the document mentioned at p. 290, and entitled " Collections out of the Penall Statutes to be repealed."

heresies.—6. To visitt the cleargie.—7. To punish the extolling of forraine power.]

Much more was not said to this, for it was agreed before by the Lord Chauncellor and those whoe assisted him, not to dispute this matter, but onely heare and reporte.

2 Elizabeth, cap. 2, an Act for the Uniformitie of Common Praier and Service in the Church, and Administration of the Sacrament :[1]

They desire not to be tyed to this forme of prayer, and they are content it should stand in all the other parts thereof.

This statute, as it was observed, divided itselfe into foure branches :

1. Confirmacion of the Booke of Common Prayer to be in publicke places.

2. The punishments of those whoe shall reade or use any other forme. —This goeth to the ministery and reacheth the priests.

3. Against those whoe will give any interruption in the tyme of Divine Service.—This extendeth to all.

4. Concerning absence from Church and the punishment.—This extendeth to all.

When all the particuler demaunds made on the behalfe of his Majestie, the Church, and his Majestie's Protestant subjects and their party, shall be concluded, his Majestie will be graciously pleased on his part to agree to the particulars hereafter expressed, viz. :

XCVIII. The Answeare of James, Marquess of Ormonde, his Majestie's Commissioner for the Treaty and concluding of a Peace in this Kingdome, for and in the name and behalfe of his Majestie, to the propositions of his Roman Catholique subjects of Ireland, etc.

To the first Proposition :[2] His Majestie wilbe graciously pleased, if his said Roman Catholique subjects shall by their obedience and loyaltye merritt his Majestie's favour and protection, that they shall not for the future have cause to complaine that less moderation is used towards them than hath been in the most favourable of Queene Elizabeth and King

---

1. "Statutes of Ireland." Dublin : 1621, p. 268.   2. *See* p. 128.
XCVIII. Carte Papers, vol. xii. pp. 150-157.

James his tymes; but his Majestie for divers waighty consideracions will further advise before he consent to the repeale of any of the Acts intended by the said Proposition.

To the second:[1] His Majestie will be graciously pleased to calle a new Parliament uppon condition that all particulers therein to be passed by Act of Parliament be first agreed on betweene us, his Majestie's Comissioner, and Donogh, Lord Viscount Muskery, Alexander M'Donell, and Nicholas Pluncket, Esquires, Sir Robert Talbot, Barronet, Dermot O'Brien, Patrick Darsie, Geoffrey Browne, and John Dillon, Esquires, or any five or more of them who are deputed or shall be deputed by his said Roman Catholique subjects to treat with us about the same, and the said Acts soe agreed upon be transmitted according to severall Acts of Parliament in that behalfe provided, and that there shall be noe attempt by his Majestie's Romane Catholicque subjects in that Parliament to pass any other Act than what is agreed uppon as afforesaid and first transmitted, or to bring any other prejudice to any of his Majestie's Protestant subjects in this kingdome, and if any thing shall bee attempted in the said Parliament to the contrary, that then his Majestie's Lieutenant, or other cheefe Governor or Governors before whome the said Parliament shall be houlden, shall forthwith after such attempt dissolve the said Parliament without expecting any further direction from his Majestie for the same; but his Majestie, for divers waighty consideracions, wilbe further advised before that he doe consent to the suspension of Poynings' Act.

To the third:[2] His Majestie will be graciously pleased that none of his said Roman Catholique subjects shall suffer any prejudice by any Acts or ordinances passed in this present Parliament, since the tyme in the Proposition mentioned, by reason of the present commotion; but his Majestie cannot legally declare Acts or ordinances made in Parliament which are in themselves lawfull to be voyd, nor give warrant to take them off the file.

To the fourth:[3] His Majestie cannot in course of justice by his Proclamation declare indictments, attainctures, outlawries, letters pattents,

1, 2, 3. *See* p. 128.

graunts, leases, bondes, recognisances, or any other legall record to be voyd or taken off the fyle. But his Majestie will be graciously pleased to grant a full and general pardon to all persons whatsoever, excepting such as hereafter upon this treaty shall be thought fitt to be left thereout, for all treasons, Rebellions, and other crimes whatsoever growing and ariseing for or by reason of the same, and will likewise give his consent that an Act be passed to that purpose in which his Majestie will admitt any clauses to enlarge his mercy; and his Majestie wilbe further graciously pleased to determine all custodiums which have been graunted since the 22th of October, 1641.

To the fifth Proposition:[1] His Majestie cannot in justice consent to the taking away of any debts due to his subjects who have committed noe offence which might occasion the forfeiture thereof; but for such debts as have accrued unto his Majestie by the attaineture or fugacie of any of his Majestie's Roman Catholicque subjects since the 23th of October, 1641, his Majestie wilbe graciously pleased to remitt so many of them as have not been payd unto his Majestie's Exchequer, or received otherwaies to his Majestie's use, or by his appointment.

To the sixth Proposition:[2] His Majestie wilbee graciously pleased to release and quitt his right to all such lands in the said Proposition mentioned, except within the countyes of Kilkenny and Weekloe, uppon the tearmes formerly assented unto by his Majestie in his answeare[3] to the greevances in the seventeenth yeere of his raigne [1641], and will consent to such an act of lymitation as is desired.

To the seventh:[4] His Majestie will bee graciously pleased to consent to an Act for the takeing away any incapacity as natives either to lands or offices, if any such there bee, and will willingly consent to the erecting of an Inns of Court, Universitye, or Free-schooles: Provided that they be governed by such statutes, rules, and orders as his Majestie shall approve of, and be agreeable to the customes of England.

To the eighth:[5] His Majestie wilbe graciously pleased that such of his Majestie's said subjects within this kingdome as shall manifest their

1. *See* p. 128.   2. *See* p. 129.   3. *See* p. 283.   4. *See* p. 129.   5. *See* p. 130.

duty and affection to his Majestie shall receive such markes of his Majestie's favour in offices and places of trust as shall manifest his Majestie's good acceptance and regard of them.

To the ninth Proposition:[1] His Majestie will take care that his good subjects of this kingdome shall not be opressed by his Court of Wards, and if oppressions of that kinde have been, uppon good and due informacion, his Majestie will cause justice to bee done for the tyme past, and for the future will prevent the like by instructions; but for the takeing away of that Court his Majestie can make noe answeare till the particulers for his satisfaction be sett down and presented unto him.

To the tenth Proposition :[2] His Majestie consented as farre as is fitt for him in this point, in his answeare to the 25th greevance, in the 17th yeere of his raigne, [1641], the which hee is still willing shall be enacted, looking forwards still to five yeeres to beegin after the peace concluded.

To the eleventh Proposition :[3] His Majestie conceives the substance of this Proposition, which concearneth the fundamentall rights of both kingdomes, fitt to bee referred to the free debate and expostulation of the two Parliaments, when it shall please God that they may freely and safely sitt, his Majestie being soe equally concearned in the priviledges of either that hee will take care to the uttmost of his power that they shall both conteyne themselves within their proper limitts, his Majestie being the head and equally concearned in the rights of both.

To the twelfth :[4] His Majestie hath sufficiently provided for this in his answeare to the tenth greevance, which his Majestie is content shall pass by Act of Parliament.

To the thirteenth Proposition :[5] His Majesty hath been pleased by his late Graces, that those statutes should be repealed, save only for wooles and woolfels, and is well pleased that the same bee done by Act of Parliament, and that a book of rates be settled by indifferent Commissioners.

To the fourteenth Proposition :[6] His Majestie doth not admitt or beleeve that the long continuance of the Cheefe Governors of this king-

1, 2, 3. *See* p. 130.   4, 5, 6, *See* p. 131.

dome in their places of government hath been an occasion of any tyrany or oppression, or that any tyrany or oppression hath been exercised uppon his subjects of this his kingdome.   Howsoever, his Majestie will be graciously pleased to take care that such Governors shall not continue longer in those places than hee shall find for the good of his people heere, and his Majestie is content that they shall be inhibited to make any purchase other than by lease for the provision of their houses dureing the time of their government.

To the fifteenth Proposition:[1] This Proposition is to be explayned and some particuler way to be proposed for the doeing thereof, and then consideracion beinge had of the safety and security of his Majestie's Protestant subjects, an answeare will be made thereunto.

To the sixteenth Proposition:[2] His Majestie cannot in justice consent to the forecloseing of the subject of his legall remedy for the recovery of any goods, chattells, or rents unlawfully taken or deteyned from him; but for such meane profitts, customs, prises, and rents which have accrued unto his Majestie sence the 23th of October, 1641, except the Customs[3] received at Waterford and Ross since the 15th of September, 1643, his Majestie is content to remitt the same: the rest of the Proposition is answeared in the answeare to the fourth Proposition.

To the seventeenth:[4] His Majestie will be pleased that such persons as shall be excepted out of the generall pardon shall bee tryed by the knowen lawes of this land.

The said Lord Marquess of Ormonde now declareth that albeit these Answeares are thus given by him in present to the said Propositions, yet that hee intends not to bee thereby concluded from altering the same, or adding thereunto, in any partes thereof, in such sorte as hee shall finde cause, uppon further debate.

Endorsed: Answers to the Propositions, etc., 1644.

1. *See* p. 132.   2. *See* p. 132.   3. *See* pp. 117-123.   4. *See* p. 132.

XCIX. REASONS WHICH MOVED HIS MAJESTIE'S MOST HUMBLE AND LOYALL SUBJECTS, THE CONFEDERATE ROMAN CATHOLICKS OF IRELAND, TO PRESENT CERTAIN PROPOSITIONS TO HIS EXCELLENCYE, THE MARQUESS OF ORMONDE, LORD LIEUTENANT OF IRELAND, HIS MAJESTIE'S COMMISSIONER.

I. The first Proposition,[1] that concerneth the freedome of the Catholick religion, and the repeal of all laws made against the professors of that religion, is a demaund not to introduce any innovation, but for that religion, which the inhabitants of this kingdom aunciently, and likewise the English colonies, come at first into this kingdome, and their heirs for many descents, have professed and do profess at present, and which, before the reign of King Henry the Eighth, was professed by the Kings of England and their subjects generally. It may be further added and confidently affirmed, that there are no subjects in the world of what other beliefe or perswasion soever in religion, that hold themselves so inviolably tied to the preservation of that monarchy, to whom they owe subjection, and allegiance, as the professors of the said Roman Catholick religion doe.

This Proposition consisteth of two branches : the first, for the repeale of certain acts ; the second, that the freedome of their religion may be allowed to the said Catholicks,

For the clearing of the first branch, the said Catholicks do not press the total repeal of the said statutes, their humble request being, that the great penalties, pressures, incapacities, and other unavoidable inconveniencies, [by] the said statutes imposed on them alone, may be removed as to them by Act of Parliament. By one statute[2] found among the records of Parliament of this kingdome in the second year of the raign of the late Queen Elizabeth, cap. 1 and 2, the said Catholicks are made subject to the arbitrary power of an High Commission Court, or other Commissioners to be appointed by his Majesty, or the Lord

XCIX. Carte Papers, vol. xii. p. 232.   1. *See* p. 128.

2. " An Act restoring to the Crowne the auncient jurisdiction over the State ecclesiasticall and spirituall, and abolishing all forreine power repugnant to the same."— " Statutes of Ireland." Dublin : 1621, p. 259.

Deputy for the time being, and may be questioned and punished for all offences touching religion. Irish Statutes, fol. 261, likewise fol. 270 and 271, the Archbishops, Bishops, and Ordinaries of another religion have heavily punished, and may still punish the said Catholicks for marriages [and] christenings done according to the Catholick religion; and every Catholick was driven to pay nine pence every Sunday for not repareing to church, to the great impoverishment and destruction of the said Catholicks, and no profit at all to his Majesty.

By the said statute, fol. 261, 262, not only the Catholick clergy are excluded from all dignities and benefices ecclesiastical, but likewise the Catholic layety is of all degrees and qualities, are rendered incapable of all civil offices, from the highest Judge to the petty constable, and likewise from martiall offices or employments, even to be a common souldier in his Majestie's army, where any fee or wages are due, without first taking the oath of Supremacy, and upon refusal of the said oath all dignities, offices, or wages are forfeited.

No Catholick can sue livery or ouster le maine for his estate, or any part thereof, out of his Majestie's hands, without taking the said oath. By the same statute of Elizabeth secundo, cap. primo, fol. 265: If any Catholick of what estate, degree, or quality soever within this kingdom doe by writing, printing, teaching, preaching, express words, deede, or act, affirm, hold, stand with, set forth and maintaine any other authority, preheminence, power, or jurisdiction in matters ecclesiasticall or spirituall, then the person so offending, his abettors, ayders, procurers, and counsellors, shall for the first offence forfeit their goods and leases, and suffer imprisonment for one year; for the second offence incurre the pains and forfeitures set downe by the statutes of Provision and Premunire, whereby the offender is put out of the King's protection, imprisoned during his life, and his goods and lands forfeited; for the third offence the offender is punishable as in case of High Treason. Then by consequence, if any of the Catholick layety take or procure a dispensation for marriage within the eighth degree, or any other licence or dispensation from any authorised by the See of Rome, [he] is a principall offender, and if he hears the Masse or sermon of any deriving power from thence, and keep him in his house, he is punishable as an ayder and abettor within the words of the statute, he knowing that whereof he cannot be ignorant by the rules of his profession.

As for the second branch of the said Proposition, let any man judge whether it be reason sufficient of itselfe, that the professors of the Roman Catholick religion both spirituall and temporall, being, all to a few, the natives and residents of this kingdom, should desire a freedom of their religion, and to be freed and exempted from the penalties and pressures aforesaid, whereby his Majestie never received any advantage, and [which] have been the occasion of many inconveniences in the kingdom. And it is evident, that by this freedom all his Majestie's good subjects, as well Protestants as Catholicks, will be united more than ever before, when their condition is equall, and neither party have occasion to envy or oppress the other. It will not be unworthy of consideration, that in reason of State (the constitution of his Majestie's three kingdomes, as now they stand, being duly weighed) that this freedom and exemption is most necessary for his Majestie's service and safetie.

II.[1] It is of the essence of Parliaments to be free ; the contrary was practised here. The composition of this Parliament is desired to be of men estated and interested in the kingdom, of genuine and right members, and to be retourned from proper places, and by right ministers.

The suspension of the Act for this free Parliament cannot prejudice his Majesty ; for that nothing is to passe as an Act before transmission, other than what shall be agreed upon and expressly mentioned in the Articles of Peace.

III.[2] It is conceived this pretended Parliament was determined by the death of the Lord Deputy Wandesford ;[3] most of the estated and right members thereof did not appear in it since the 7th of August, 1641. Those who now appear as members thereof, viz. of the Commons' House, are for a great part not much interested, and others wholly uninterested therein, and one order therein made to exclude the said Catholicks from the House,

1, 2, *See* p. 128. 3. Sir Christopher Wandesford, Master of the Rolls and Lord Deputy of Ireland, died at Dublin on 3 December, 1640.

other orders to their disadvantage were or might have been made in the said Commons' House. Therefore it is desired, that all the proceedings of the said pretended Parliament may be declared voyde and taken off the file.

IV.[1] When those indictments were found and outlawries promulged the said Catholicks are informed, and hope to justify, that those who governed in cheife in this kingdom, or some of them, did plott and practice the total extirpation of the said Catholicks and as much as in them lay did increase the troubles to that end, and shut up the gates of his Majestie's mercy against the said Catholicks, even against those who were undeniably innocent, as may appear by many instances, the manner of appointement of Sheriffs, who returned the jurors, and the persons appointed, the jurors' condition and affection, the infinite numbers of the persons indicted and outlawed, being never called to answer, and other circumstances, touching or depending of the said records, being so generally destructive to the said Catholicks they cannot otherwise choose than to insist on the taking them off the file, that no such marks of infamy may remain of record against them whose ancestors for the space of four hundred years and upwards faithfully served the Crowne.

V.[2] This Proposition is so just and equal in itselfe, that there needeth not any reason or proofe to be urged for it.

VI.[3] This Proposition being yeelded unto by the answer (except the late Plantations in the county of Wicklow, and Iduogh in the county of Kilkenny, and excepting the increase of rents) is referred to what shall be urged upon the sixth answer.

VII.[4] In all or most letters-patents granted of Plantation lands, and some other lands in this kingdom, since the making of the said statutes, certain clauses and conditions were inserted in them, that no land should be sold or past to any of the meere Irish, or of the Irish nation,[5] as the condition is in some patents : These clauses do and did nourish division and distinction between his Majestie's subjects; the like was never used in England, nor in any other kingdom. They extend not only to the Old Irish,

1, 2. *See* p. 128.　　　3, 4. *See* p. 129.　　　5. *See* vol. i. p. 13.

but likewise, by construction, to the Old English : For he that is born in Ireland, though his parents and all his auncestors were aliens, nay if his parents are Indians or Turks, if converted to Christianity, is an Irish-man as fully as if his auncestors were here born for thousands of years, and by the laws of England as capable of the liberties of a subject. Such marks of distinction, being the insteps to trouble and warr, are incompatible with peace and quiet.

VIII.[1] The said Roman Catholicks, being rendered incapable of any command or trust by the statutes aforesaid, may be relieved herein upon removall of the impediments mentioned in the reasons to the first Proposition and particular instances showed for the present, yet such were the characters layed upon them here, and the representations made of them from hence heretofore into England, that they apprehend they suffer thereby in his Majestie's opinion of them, which they conceave an impediment and stop to many graces and favours they expect and hope to merit from his Majestie. In all ages past, before the said statutes, their ancestors were preferred to places of eminence and trust within their native countries, and since very seldom ; three precedents since can hardly be instanced. The condition of Roman Catholicks in Ireland, where there are an hundred Catholicks to one of any other religion, differs much from that of England or Scotland, where there is scarce one Catholick to a thousand of the Protestant religion. In all the nations of Christian-dom, the natives of the place are advanced before others.

IX.[2] The Court of Wards was begun here about the fourteenth year of King James [1616-1617], and never before. It hath not the warrant of any law or statute. In England it was erected by Act of Parliament. The subject is extremely oppressed thereby, by the multitude of informations against all freeholders, from the highest to the lowest, without any limitation of time, the frequent Courts of Escheators and Feodaryes, the destruction of the tenures of mesne Lords by making many tenures to be in capite against law, by the sale of the wards from hand to hand, as of horses in a market, by the want of provisions for portions of younger children, whereby they perish or take ill courses, debts remain unsatisfied,

1. *See* p. 129.   2. *See* p. 130.

and though by the statute of Merton, cap. 5. usury doth not run upon infants, yet the collateral security either of men or land mortgaged are not relieved by that statute. The King never received one shilling advantage by this Court ultra reprisas for 20s. damage done thereby to his people;—the vast fortunes of the officers and ministers of the said Court, how suddenly raised on the ruines of many others his Majestie's subjects. And let all the wards since the erection of that Court be numbered, for one that gained civilitie and breeding during their minority, many will be found to have departed the said Court with ignorance, losse, or impayring their estates, and other great inconveniencies. No diminution of his Majestie's profit is desired, the personall service upon all occasions shall be performed. The extinction of this Court, and the tenures in capite or by knights' service, is humbly desired to be taken away, and a course for his Majestie's profit and service, and preservation of heirs and orphans, and satisfaction of creditors, shall be then humbly proposed. The respit and issues of homage, being of no considerable advantage to the Crown and an intolerable yoke to the subject, is likewise desired to be taken off, and a way of equall benefit to his Majestie shall be proposed.

X.[1] The great numbers of these Lords uninterested in the kingdom, their end in seeking for those honours, and the late introduction of the example being considered, it may be easily judged how unequall or unjust it is that the votes of men of no estate, and never resident in the kingdom, if not for design, should impose a charge, wherein they contribute nothing, or pass laws by which they are not bound themselves.

XI.[2] The independancy of the Parliament of Ireland on the Parliament of England is so cleere and manifest by law, justice, usage, necessitie, and precedents, that they humbly desire it may not be drawn into dispute; yet, inasmuch as the royal assent wrested from his Majestie to the Acts of Subscription[3] may draw a prejudice or discountenance upon our Parliament, a declaration herein and Act of Parliament is desired.

1, 2, *See* p. 130.   3. This designation was applied to the Acts passed by the Parliament at London, in 1641-2, in relation to confiscated lands in Ireland, to be allotted proportionately in return for subscriptions "for the reducing of the rebels there." *See* vol. i. p. 259.

XII.[1] This Proposition is in itselfe so reasonable, and the restraint laid on the Councell table from taking cognizance of matters determinable in the King's ordinary Courts of Justice by the Common Law, the Great Charter thirty times confirmed by Parliament, and sundry other Acts of Parliament of force in this kingdome, is so manifest and cleere, that there is no need of further reasoning or proofe for the same: Therefore it is consonant to law and justice, that the parties aggrieved should be restored to what they lost, and left in statu quo, etc., as is desired, and that no matter determinable in the ordinary courts may be determined at the Councell table.

XIII.[2] This Proposition being for free trade and commerce, so necessary for the advancement of his Majestie's service and profit, and so indifferently conducing to the weale of his people, it is conceaved that all who are interested in the kingdom ought to contribute their endeavours for the attaining of what is hereby humbly desired.

XIV.[3] The place of Chiefe Governor of this kingdom being of so great honnor and high trust, and therefore to be conferred upon such as study his Majestie's service, and the prosperity of the kingdom, without regard to particular interest, this limitation will keep the Chief Governor wary from offending any subject, or descending so low as to give occasion, even of speech, that his actions are unwarrantable, or his purchases acquired by oppression. Men are to be chosen for this place that have no need to purchase.

XV.[4] The malice and power of the Malignant party in England and Scotland, and of their adherents abroad, and threatened danger of invasion to be made by them, and the invitation thereunto of many in this kingdom who are known to have studied and plotted the ruine of this kingdom are motives sufficient for the granting of the contents of this Proposition, and that the kingdom be always in posture of defence of itselfe, and all the well affected subjects thereof.

XVI.[5] The passing of an Act of Oblivion to quiet and secure the

1, 2, 3. *See* p. 131.   4, 5. *See* 132.

minds of all his Majestie's subjects in a case so generall, wherein the most of his Majestie's subjects one way or other are involved, is so necessary, and so pursuing the precedents and examples, not only of England and Ireland, but also of other states and kingdoms, that without the passing thereof some embers of mischiefe may still remaine, which may (though God forbid) turn into greate flames; [witnesse the Barons' warres, the warres of York and Lancaster, these present troubles of England and Scotland, and other examples, even in this kingdom;] and, if there be any possibilitie, to relieve all particulars, when the generall concernment is in question.

XVII.[1] Honour, justice, equity, and reason of State plead for this Proposition.

We desire, notwithstanding those reasons, to be admitted to shew such further and other reasons and adde hereunto what we shall think fit touching the matters, in the said Propositions contained [wherein the answers are short, or not satisfactory.]

Reasons for the Propositions. Given me (Ormonde) by the Lord of Muskry, on the 28th of September, 1644.

C. [REASONS WHY THE ROMAN CATHOLICK SUBJECTS ARE NOT SATISFIED WITH THE LORD LIEUTENANT'S ANSWER[2] TO CERTAIN PROPOSITIONS PRESENTED TO HIM BY THEM ON THE 4TH OF SEPTEMBER, IN THE 20TH YEAR OF HIS MAJESTIE'S REIGN (1644)].

Inasmuch as most of the reasons, declaring how the said Answers are not satisfactory, do appear either in the said Propositions themselves, or in the Reasons[3] afterwards, in the month aforesaid, presented to your Lordship, setting forth the necessity of the said Propositions— to avoid reiteration, what is in the said Propositions or reasons expressed is herein omitted. It is therefore humbly desired, that your Lordshipp, in your consideration of the reasons now presented, will distinctly and apart reflect upon the said former Propositions and reasons.

Reasons against the first Answer : The said Catholics upon exact

1. *See* p. 132.   2. *See* p. 293.   3. *See* p. 298.   C. Carte Papers, vol. xii., p. 140.— Passages in brackets are from pp. 76, 78, vol. ix. of Ms. "Collectanea," cited at p. 312.

scrutiny and search by them made of their consciences and actions, finding nothing more desired by the one, nor aimed at by the other (next to the homage which they owe to the King of Kings) than the advancement of his Majestie's service, and the setling of a full peace and quiet in this his kingdom of Ireland, they do therefore with heavinesse of heart apprehend some expressions in the first answer (viz. If the said Roman Catholick subjects shall by their obedience and loyalty merit his Majestie's favour and protection); whereas the said Roman Catholicks are as obedient and loyall subjects to his Majesty as any other his subjects, without exception, and whereas their thoughts or actions have never deserved to put them out of his Majestie's protection. Yet the occasion of their said apprehensions they may not ascribe to your Excellency, who is intrusted by his Majesty with the acting and directing part of this great affair now in treaty, but unto some instrumental cause or other mistake.

And, as to the rest of the said first Answer,[1] viz. That when all demands made by your Lordship unto the said Catholicks in his Majestie's behalfe, or on the behalfe of the Protestant clergy, and on the behalfe of his Majestie's Protestant subjects, are concluded, and upon such merit, as is before expressed, the said Catholicks shall not have cause to complain that less moderation is used than in the most favourable of Queen Elizabeth or King James his times, and his Majesty will be further advised upon the repeale of the statutes made against the said Catholicks: Although the said Roman Catholicks are most confident of his Majestie's grace and goodnesse, yet so great is the penalty imposed by statutes of force in this kingdom, extending to the goods, estates, liberties, lives, and corruption of blood of the said Catholicks, that they must live in restlesse fears so long as those extreme punishments hang over them; and in case his Majesty by letters-patents under his great seale, or otherwise, will declare his royall pleasure against the execution of those statutes upon the said Catholicks, yet those fears will be hardly removed thereby. Such is the malice of the Malignant party who have vowed the total destruction of the said Catholicks, that their adherents here, though not known to be such, will never want will, and cannot want opportunity,

1. *See* p. 293.

sufficient to indict the said Catholicks upon the said statutes, and the Judges, before whom the said indictments are found, by their oath declared by the statute made in the 18th yeare Edward III, will not stop or suspend the proceedings of the Court for the great seale, privy seale, or his Majestie's letters, writs, or command. And your Lordship may please to observe that by long experience it is manifest, that since the making of those lawes, being 80 and odd years, the penalties or forfeitures in them expressed have not been so prevalent as to draw them, the said Catholicks, from the religion professed by them and their ancestors, and no advantage did in so long a tract of time accrue to the Crowne by those statutes. And seeing that his Majesty is content that moderation should be used towards the said Catholicks, to what purpose should the said penall lawes be continued in force, whereas the continuance thereof can produce no other effect than jealousies and fears in the minds of the people.

Reasons against the second Answere :[1] A free Parliament is propounded, and a new Parliament is mentioned in this Answer to be granted. It is true that Parliaments in their essence ought to be free, yet some examples shewing the contrary in this kingdom, and a clause in the answer, viz. that Parliament shall be dissolved upon an attempt only of propounding any other matter than shall be agreed upon by the Articles of Peace, which attempt may be purposely done by some averse to peace to dissolve a Parliament—doe induce the said Catholicks to supplicate the inserting of a free Parliament and the taking away of the said clause (attempt, etc.) And they likewise supplicate that all the Acts to be concluded on by the Treaty may not be transmitted into England, in regard the substance of that which will be passed as Acts, without transmission, are to be inserted in the Articles of Peace, which, and none other, Act of Parliament is to passe upon the suspension of Poynings' Act, without transmission, according to the usuall manner ; Wherefore the said suspension can bring no manner of prejudice upon his Majesty, or the publick service, and that by the granting thereof the peoples' judgments will be much quieted. The said Catholicks do therefore humbly desire, that the said Act be suspended, as is by them propounded.

1. *See* p. 294.

Reasons against the third Answer :[1] If the now pretended Parliament, or either of the Houses of Parliament made any orders or ordinances to the prejudice of the said Catholicks, the same Parliament may vacate them and take them off the file, and it is not to be presumed that any Member of Parliament is so little affected to the peace or quiet of the kingdom, that he will give opposition to the third Proposition, or to his Majestie's direction, or to your Lordship's request in that behalf ; and the said Catholics conceive it necessary, in point of honour and reputation, that no order or ordinance to their prejudice may remayne of record in Parliament : And if no such order or ordinance be, the Proposition can hardly be denied ; wherefore it is humbly desired, that the answer may be more full and satisfactory.

Reasons against the fourth Answer :[2] Upon consideration of the fourth Proposition, and of the reasons for the same, it is humbly desired this answer be enlarged, to the greater advantage of the said Catholicks than is expressed ; and although his Majesty cannot avoyde records of this nature by Proclamation, yet, when his Majesty is informed that those indictments and outlawries were done of design to extirpate a nation, and that in the proceedings it will appeare there was practize [and how it was practised,] his Majestie's proclamation, in a case of this generall concernment, declaring his dislike of such proceedings, will be of great consequence, and his direction to the Parliament to that effect will, no doubt, accomplish the desire of the said Catholicks contained in this Proposition ; and his royall directions to have the procurers, actors, and plotters of and in the said indictments and outlawries, and the whole proceeding, questioned ; and the design and practise being discovered and proved, then the said records, and all matters depending thereupon, ought in law and justice to be vacated and taken off the file ; and the pardon in the answer mentioned restores neither blood nor estates, as it is there set downe ; and admitting the pardon were by Parliament, it will be of absolute necessitie to avoide all grants, letters-patents, leases, and other acts, letters, or promises, made to the prejudice of the persons attainted,

1, 2. *See* p. 294.

and to restore them to their blood and estate; in which act a clause condemning the manner of the procuring of the said indictments and outlawries is thought necessary to be inserted and the exception mentioned in the said answer is humbly desired by the said Catholicks to be taken off, and the clause (viz. his Majesty will enlarge his mercy) to be made more particular.

Reason against the fifth Answer : This answer is humbly desired to be made equall to all parties one way or other, as it is propounded, and that Catholicks should pay debts due upon them, and lose the debts due unto them, is conceived not to be equall.

Reasons against the sixth Answer :[1] By his Majestie's Graces of the fourth year of his reign, all the estates in the province of Connaght, and county of Clare, in pursuance of the indentures of composition made by late Queen Elizabeth, made, for great and valuable considerations, with the Lords and gentry of the said province and county, and of the grants and promises of the late King James of happy memory, were to be confirmed and made good by Act of Parliament, the Statute of Limitation was then to be passed, which extended to all estates in the kingdom; therefore no greater rent ought to be reserved upon the lands in the said province or countie, nor upon the lands in the counties of Tipperary and Limerick, than was answered to his Majesty in the said fourth yeare of his Majestie's reign. And the great offices entitling his Majestie unto the before mentioned lands, and to many men's estates in the county of Wicklow, and to the territory of Idough[1] in the county of Kilkenny, were enforced by an high hand, the freeholders thereof being in possession of their respective estates then and for many ages before without interruption or question. It is therefore humbly desired, that those offices be vacated and taken off the file by his Majestie's gracious directions, his Highnesse, or his patentees, being therein only concerned as to the title found by the said offices ; and that the Statute of Limitation may be here enacted, with a retrospect to the fourth yeare of his Majestie's reign, at which time it was promised by his Majesty to have been passed as an Act in this

1. *See* p. 295.

kingdom, and if it had been so done, the said offices had not been found; and that the case of the county of Wicklowe and county of Kilkennie meriting equall justice and favour with the rest, ought not to be distinguished from them.

Reasons against part of the seventh Answer :[1] The clause in the said answer concerning Inns of Court, and Free-schooles, as it is expressed in the answer, will debarre Roman Catholicks, so long as they are of that religion, from attaining to the knowledge of the lawes of the land, or any other learning within this kingdom.

Reason against the eighth Answer:[2] This answer is conceived not to be satisfactory and too generall, and particular instances of the marks of his Majestie's favour towards the said Catholicks are humbly desired.

To the ninth Answer :[3] The reasons against this answer : all the parts thereof are the same that are urged for the ninth Proposition, and, upon consideration of these reasons, the answer is humbly desired to be enlarged.

To the tenth Answer:[4] His Majestie's Answer made to the 25th Grievance, in the 17th yeare of his Majestie's reign [1641] gives five yeares time to the unestated Lords to acquire estates in this kingdom. It is therefore humbly desired, that the Answer may be more satisfactory on consideration of the Reasons for the tenth Proposition, and the state of affairs is so altered since that time, that upon the now intended generall settlement more circumspection and wariness is to be used than at any time before.

To the eleventh Answer :[5] The said Catholicks do conceive and affirm in all cleerness, that the Parliament of Ireland is independent of the Parliament of England, without which independancy this realme could be no kingdom nor any Parliaments here necessary, nor any subject of this kingdom sure of his estate, life, or liberty, other than at the will and pleasure of a Parliament, wherein neither Lords, Knights, nor burgessess of this kingdom have place or vote, and which vowed the destruction of all or most of this nation, and unwarrantably assumed the power to dispose of their estates, by the Statutes of Subscription, to Malignants and Hollanders.[1] To draw this into any debate or question might prove of most dangerous consequence to this nation, and yet a declaration of the Parliament here, and an act as in the Proposition is set down is humbly desired, in regard his Majesty was drawn to give the royall assent to the Acts of subscription.

To the twelfth Answer : [2] This answer is humbly desired to be enlarged according to the reasons for the twelfth Proposition.

To the thirteenth Answer : [3] The rates of staple commodities are humbly desired to be moderated by Commissioners to be appointed by both Houses of Parliament.

To the fourteenth Answer : [4] The reasons for the not continuance of the Chief Governor above three years are the same urged for the fourteenth Proposition.

To the fifteenth Answer : [5] The reasons for the erecting and continuance of trained bands are the same that are urged for the fifteenth Proposition.

To the sixteenth Answer : [5] This answer is humbly desired to be enlarged, and the Act of Oblivion to extend to goods taken of either side, although the Roman Catholicks suffered much more than all others in this warr, and your Lordship will consider the reasons for the sixteenth Proposition.

To the seventeenth Answer : [7] It is of necessitie the triall of the persons propounded by us to be tried be by Parliament ; otherwise the triall cannot be indifferent in this case.

We desire, notwithstanding those reasons, to be admitted to shew such further and other reasons, and to add hereunto what we shall think fit, touching the matters wherein the answers are short, or not satisfactory.

Endorsed : Reasons to the Answeres.   Given mee [Ormonde] by the Lord of Muskry on the 28th of September, 1644.

1. *See* vol. i. p. 265.   2, 3, 4. *See* p. 296.   5, 6, 7. *See* p. 297.

CI. Demands [made by Ormonde] in the behalf of all his Majestie's Protestant subjects, and their party.

I. That present restitution be made unto them of all their castles, lordships, mannors, and all other hereditaments and chattles real, of what kind soever, whereof they were seized and possessed by themselves or their servants on the 22th of October, 1641, and which remaine within the quarters allotted by the Articles of Cessation to the said Confederate Roman Catholick party.

II. That, where any of the goods, evidences, or writings of the Protestant subjects, and such as adhere unto them, have been delivered in trust to any that are or have been of the said Confederate Roman Catholick party, to be kept by any of them, that such goods, evidences, and writings be restored to those that so delivered them in trust, as aforesaid, or to their heirs, executors, administrators, or assigns.

III. That all goods which have been pillaged and taken away by any of the said Confederate Roman Catholick party, which may be had in specie, and the property whereof was not altered by sale in market before the 24th of June, 1644 (being the day of the date of his Majestie's commission warranting this Treaty), be restored, or otherwise the proprietor may be left to his remedy at Common Law for the recovery thereof; and that any sale in market, since the said 24th of June, shall be no hindrance or barre thereunto.

IV. That, where any of that party have pillaged or taken away any goods from any of his Majestie's Protestant subjects, or any adhering to them, between the 21th of October, 1641, and the 21th of January, 1641[2], that the party so pillaged may be left to take his remedy at law for recovery of his goods, or damages for the same, against such as did so pillage them.

V. That all castles and houses, which were surrendered upon quarter,

CI. Ms. " Collectanea de rebus Hibernicis," vol. ix. p. 79. National Library of Ireland, Dublin.

upon articles under hands, wherein it was undertaken that the said castles or houses should be preserved from being destroyed or demolished, that the said Confederates, who have so articled, may rebuild the said castles or houses in as good estate as they were at the surrendering up of the same upon articles, as aforesaid.

VI. That, where any lands belonging to his Majestie's Protestant subjects, or their tenants or adherents, have been possessed by any of the said Confederate Roman Catholick party, and corne sown therein by any of that party, since the 15th of September, 1643, that the Protestant subjects, or their adherents, who by themselves or their tenants were possessed of the said lands on the 22th of October, 1641, or their heirs, executors, administrators, or assigns, may respectively receive the fourth sheafe[1] of all the said corne this present harvest, 1644, or the value thereof.

Those propositions, thus made in present, are not in exclusion of any other propositions, which we shall adjudge necessary to be propounded or insisted on, for the glory of God, the honor of his Majesty, the interests of his good subjects, and the safety of the kingdom, nor in exclusion of sundry other particulars which may be necessary for us to insist on, as conducing to the formerly mentioned ends, and which may arise upon the present Treaty.

CII. Ormonde's Explanation of his Answers[2] to Propositions of Commissioners of the Confederation.

As the Lord Lieutenant in his Answeare gave the proposers noe occasion to use any unfitting expressions : soe he may not but declare the comparison and some other expressions in their preamble[3] to be very unnecessary and unseasonable, and such as hee may not admitt.   However, he now offereth,—

An explanation of some of the Answears given by James, Marquess of Ormonde, his Majestie's Comissioner for the concluding of a Peace in this kingdome, to the Propositions of his Majestie's Roman Catholique subjects of Ireland, with some further concessions.

First Answer:[1] For the exception taken to the answer to the first Proposition: Although neither the statute of 2 Eliz. cap. primo, nor any other statute of force in this kingdome, doe impose any mulct or penalty for saying, singing, or hearing of mass, or keeping a Roman Catholique priest in their houses, yett his Majestie, for the further satisfaction of his said Roman Catholique subjects in any doubt or scruple that may arise uppon the construction of any of the said statutes which may disquiett their mindes, is graciously pleased that a declaracion of the lawe as unto that point be prepared and published; and his Majestie is likewise graciously pleased to suspend the High Commission Court; and that as the Oath of Supremacy hath not been imposed uppon any of them of late tymes uppon the sueing of liveryes, soe they shall for the tyme to come bee admitted to sue their liveries uppon taking the oath by his Majestie's directions now in that case provided. Which being added to the Answear[2] to the eighth Proposition (by which his Majestie hath declared that they shall receive such markes of his favour in offices and places of trust as shall manifest his Majestie's good acceptance and regard of them), may for the present abundantly satisfy his said subjects; and for the repeale of any of the Acts intended by the said Proposition his Majestie will further advise.

Second Answeare:[3] For the exception taken to the word new Parliament in the Answeare to the second Proposition,—" Whereas a free Parliament was propounded,"—the said Lord Marquess declares that the said new Parliament is to be as free as by the lawes and statutes of this kingdome any Parliament to be held in this kingdome ought to bee, yet soe as noe interpretacion bee from thence made that there should bee any proceeding in the said Parliament in any particular contrary to the agreement on this Treaty.

As to the exception taken to the clause in the Answear,[4] viz., " That

<hr>

1. *See* p. 305.   2. *See* p. 295.   3, 4. *See* p. 307.

the Parliament shall be dissolved uppon an attempt only of propounding any other matter than shall bee agreed uppon by the Articles of Peace ; albeit the clause is not soe as it is recited, yett the Lord Marquess, for their further satisfaction, is pleased that the word "attempt" be left out of the clause wherein it is, and it be expressed in manner following, viz., And that nothing be concluded by both or either of the said Houses cf Parliament which may bring prejudice to any of his Majestie's Protestant party or theire adhearents.

And for their desire to have Poynings' Act suspended,[1] forasmuch as it is assented unto that noe Act of Parliament is to pass, uppon the suspention of Poynings' Act, without transmission, according to the usuall manner, but what shall be provided for in the Articles of Peace, and that it is enacted by Act of Parliament of force in this kingdome that Poynings' Act cannot be suspended but by bill to bee first agreed uppon by both Houses of Parliament in this kingdome, which is likewise to bee transmitted, according to the usuall manner, which will take upp as much tyme as the transmitting of the bills which are to bee agreed on this Treaty ; and seeing the benefits which shall bee held fitt to be derived to the proposers may bee as effectually and with more speed done without suspending of Poynings' Act, as by suspending thereof his Majestie doth not see cause why the same should bee desired. But hee is very apprehensive of the prejudice the suspension thereof may bring uppon himselfe and the publick service by disquieting the minds of his Protestant subjects in both kingdomes, if that hee should admitt such innovation att this tyme, there being noe necessity thereof. And therefore his Majesty, as well for that as other waighty consideracions, may not vary as unto that particular from his former answear.

3. If both or either of the Houses of Parliament have made any orders wherein his Majestie's concurrence hath not been, it doth rest only in the power of the House or Houses, and not in his Majestie, to vacate such orders, except they doe appear in themselves to be illegall ; and in such

1. *See* p. 307.

cases his Majestie will declare such to be voyd, and give direcions for the vacating of them, as in the particuler whereof instance is made, for excluding members duly elected and retourned according to the established lawes of this kingdome out of the House of Commons who should refuse to take the oath of Supremacy, which, without an Act of Parliament to warrant it cannot be in such case imposed. But his Majestie may not admitt the present Parliament to be voyd, nor declare all that hath been done therein since the 7th of August, 1641, to be voyd, for that many orders much tending to his Majestie's honor, and the safety of this kingdome, wherein both Houses did joyne, have been made since that tyme, as the prohibiting the taking of the Covenant, soe destructive to monarchy and the Church, which had been condemned by both the said Houses, their joynt approbacion of the late Cessacion, the peticion wherein both Houses joyned to his Majestie, and others of that kinde.

4. Touching the exception taken to that part of the answear to the fourth Proposition concerning the generall pardon, the Lord Marquess declares that it is meant thereby that the said generall pardon shall extend to restore them, excepting such as shalbee on this Treatie agreed to bee excepted, to their blood and estate by Act of Parliament, whereby all graunts, letters patents, acts, letters, or promises shall be avoyded.

But his Majestie cannot, in justice, publish any such proclamacion, or give any such direction to the Parliament as is desired, before the persons intended to be charged be heard, and the matters suggested proved, which if they shall, his Majesty will then doe therein what shall bee just, and in the meane tyme cannot think ill of his Ministers of State imployed in this kingdome, nor of the proceedings of any of his Majestie's Courts of Justice. And for their desire that there should be no exception in the pardon, his Majestie may not assent thereunto.

5. His Majestie will bee pleased that debts doe stand in statu quo: saving as unto such who shall bee agreed in this Treaty to bee excepted out of the generall pardon, and excepting one particular summe which hath been payd into his Majestie's Exchequer.

6. His Majestie may not agree to the avoydeing of the Plantations in

the county of Wickloe and territory of Iduough[1] in the county of Kilkenny, part of the lands in the county of Wickloe, viz. the Ranelagh, being confirmed by Act of Parliament, and soe much of the rest of the lands in the said county as fell to his Majestie upon the division, and the territory of Iduogh being passed by letters-pattents under the great seale uppon the Commission of Grace for Remedie of Defective Titles, strengthened likewise by Act of Parliament, which his Majestie may not in honor avoide. And his Majestie doth conceive it weare unsafe for divers of his Majestie's subjects, who have purchased estates grounded uppon his Majestie's title, that the Statute of Limitacions should have such a retrospect as is desired, which in tyme would overthrow the estates of many of his Majestie's subjects who acquired estates for valuable considerations; and therefore his Majestie may not assent thereunto. But for takeinge off or abateing of rents contracted or agreed for, his Majestie is pleased that the course presented in his Answeare[2] to the twelfth Additional Proposition be observed.

7. His Majestie may not admitt that the governing of the Inns of Court, University, and Free Schooles, by such statutes, rules, and orders as his Majestie shall approve of and be agreeable to the customes of England, will debarr Roman Catholiques, so long as they are of that religion, from attayneing to the knowledge of the lawes of the land, or any other learning within the kingdome; for those of that religion in England, and who goe from hence, doe attaine the knowledge of both in the Universityes and Inns of Court there in an eminent manner, and may doe the like heere.

8. There being noe office or place excepted in the former answear, the proposers may rest satisfyed therewith, it being in his Majestie's power to dispose of such places and offices by his letters-patents as occasion shall be offered, and thereby to remove all impediments mentioned by the proposers.

9. His Majestie doth not admitt such abuses to have been in his Court of Wards, and the ministers thereof, as are sett forth in the reasons[3] for the ninth Proposition, untill proofe be made thereof. And his Majestie

1. *See* p. 284.   2. *See* p. 328.   3. *See* p. 302.

doth beleeve that exceeding great benefitt may redound to the kingdome by the continuance and right orderinge thereof, and therefore conceiveth his former answer to be reasonable. And it seemeth not equall, which is propounded, that there should be first an extinguishing of the Court, and the tenures in capite taken away, and that then a course for his Majestie's proffit and service should be proposed, that being offered in the first place before his Majestie part with the other, and the like is to be done for the respitt of homage.

10. His Majestie may not recead from the former answear, with which the proposers may rest satisfied.

11. As his Majestie may not vary from his former answear, soe hee may not foreclose the Houses of Parliament from making any declaracion agreeable to the lawes of the land.

12. The proposers may rest satisfyed with the former answeare, considering that all partyes greeved may have the benefitt of the lawes of the land, and that by consent of the partyes interested many matters determined att Councell Board are confirmed by Act of Parliament.

13. His Majestie will be pleased that indifferent persons be agreed in this Treaty who shall be authorised by Commission to moderate and settle the booke of rates in such sort as they shall think fitt.

14. His Majestie may not assent any further to this Proposition than hee hath already done, without apparant prejudice to his service.

15. His Majestie may not receade from his former answear.

16. His Majestie thinkes not fitt to give any further answeare to this Proposition than hee hath done already untill the proposers make answeare to the Propositions made and delivered unto them in the behalfe of his Majestie's Protestant subjects[1] and their adherents, and then uppon further debate his Majestie will give such answeare as shall be thought fitt.

17. It may not be admitted that tryalls by the knowen lawes of the land, assented unto by the former answear, should not be indifferent, and therefore his Majestie may not recead from his former answeare.

The said Lord Marquess of Ormonde now declares that albeit these answers are thus given by him in present to the said Propositions, yet

1. *See* p. 312.

that hee intends not to bee therby concluded from altering the same or adding thereunto in any parts therof, in such sorte as hee shall finde cause uppon further debate.

CIII. Demands made by Ormonde on behalf of Charles I.

I. That present restitution be made by the Confederate Roman Catholick party of the command, rule, and government of the cities of Limerick, Waterford, Kilkenny, and Cashell, the townes of Galway, Clonmell, Weixford, and Rosse, and of all other cities, townes, counties, and territories, of right belonging to his Majestie, and now in the possession or under the command of the Confederate Roman Catholick party ; and that restitution likewise be made by them of all his Majestie's castles, forts, lands, tenements, and hereditaments, and of all his Majestie's ordinance, artillerie, arms, and ammunition, which have been seized on or taken by the said Confederate Roman Catholick party since the 21th of October, 1641, in the cities of Limerick, Waterford, Galway, the castle and towne of Newry, Charlemount, and other places within the kingdom: and that all such power, jurisdiction or government as hath been assumed by the said Confederate Roman Catholick party over their party since the 22th of October, 1641, be from henceforth abrogated, deserted, and deemed voyde: and that all his Majestie's subjects, as well the Roman Catholicks as others within the kingdom, shall be from henceforth ameanable to the laws of force in this kingdom, and obedient to his Majestie's government and Courts of Justice.

II. That all the armies raysed by the said Confederate Roman Catholick party, with their armes and munition, and such forts, garrisons, and wardes, as are now kept by them, shall from henceforth be under the command of his Majesty and his Majestie's Lieutenant, or other his Majestie's Chief Governor or Governors of this kingdom for the time being, and such others as his Majesty from time to time shall appoint.

III. That his Majesty may be answered such certain rents, composi-

CIII. Ms. " Collectanea de rebus Hibernicis," vol. ix. p. 78.   National Library of Ireland, Dublin.

tions and casual profits, and subsidies, and all customs and subsidies for merchandize, as were accrued and grown due before and on the 23th of October, 1641, and which shall from henceforth grow due.

IV. That all the remaine of the £30,000 appearing to be payable to his Majesty, by the instrument[1] signed by the Lord Muskery and others, dated the 16th of September, 1643, which hath not yet been paid in money or cattle, in manner as in the said instrument is expressed, be paid to his Majestie's Vice-Treasurer and Treasurer-at-Warres, or to his Deputy, or to such other person or persons, as the Lord Lieutenant, or other Chiefe Governor or Governors of this kingdom for the time being shall appoint, to his Majestie's use, by the said Confederate Roman Catholick party, at, by, or before the [blank] day of [blank].

V. That the said Confederate Roman Catholick party doe make a true account and present payment of his Majestie's Customs and impositions of Waterford and Rosse,[2] according to the Booke of rates for all such commodities as have been exported out of or imported into the said harbours since the 15th of September, 1643.

VI. That the grant of the licensing of retayling wine and aquavitæ, and of transportation of linnen yarne, at [blank] per packe, in Ireland, towards the support of the charge of this kingdom, may be settled by Act of Parliament upon the Crowne according to the resolution of his Majestie's late Graces in the year 1641, with some apt proviso that they may be kept and continued as a revenue of the Crowne.

VII. That [blank] on the pound of tobacco be setled by Act of Parliament unto his Majestie's use, as a custom upon that commoditie, whereupon the emption of tobacco to be free, and the monopoly[3] wholly taken away.

Demands made by the Lord Lieutenant on the behalf of his Majesty.

1. *See* p. 266; vol. i., p. 163; vol. ii. p. 379.　　2. *See* pp. 117-120.
3. *See* vol. i. p. 4.

CIV. Demands made [by Ormonde] in behalf of the Protestant Clergy.

I. That the Archbishops, Bishops, and all other ecclesiastical persons be presently restored to theire respective churches, jurisdiction, and possessions, both spiritual and temporall, and to the free exercise of their several and respective functions; and that they enjoy the same without any interruption to be given them thereunto by the said Confederate Roman Catholick party, in such manner as they have enjoyed the same before and on the 23rd of October, 1641.

II. That all Cathedral and Parish churches, and all Archbishops and Bishop's mansion-houses, which have been any way demolished or defaced by any of the said Confederate Roman Catholick party, shall be, with all convenient speede, by the Confederate Roman Catholick party repaired and put in as good condition as they were on the 23rd of October, 1641.

III. That, for the present subsistance of the Protestant clergy, they may be allowed the one halfe of all the tyth-corne, belonging to their benefices respectively, arising out of this present harvest, 1644, within the quarters allotted by the Articles of Cessation to the said Confederate Roman Catholick party, or the value thereof.

CV. Answers of Commissioners of Confederation to the Demands made by Ormonde on behalf of Charles I.

I. To the first demand, his Majestie's faithfull subjects, the Confederate Catholicks of his kingdom of Ireland, do answer, that the cities and townes in the said demand mentioned are, and always have been, ruled and governed according to his Majestie's laws, and the charters unto them respectively granted by his Majesty and his royal progenitors and predecessors, Kings and Queenes of England and Ireland, and are preserved

CIV. Ms. "Collectanea de rebus Hibernicis," vol. ix. p. 79. National Library of Ireland, Dublin. CV. Carte Papers, vol. xii. pp. 194-5.

VOL. III. 22

and kept by the said Confederate Catholicks for his use and service against
the Malignant partie and their adherents ; and as for his Majestie's forts,
castles, territories, hereditaments, ordnance and artillery, in the said
demand mentioned, the same are likewise kept and maintained for his
Majestie's use and service, and the safetie of the kingdom, and his
Majestie's interest therein, against such as are joined in a rebellious Covenant, and are actually in armes against his royal person ;
and they know of no considerable ammunition taken by the said Catholicks, and such as was so taken, and much more, was by them imployed in his Majestie's service.   And as to the power and jurisdiction
mentioned to be assumed by the said Confederate Catholicks, they say
they were necessitated to rule and govern their party, to avoyde the
extirpation of their religion and nation, plotted and contrived by the said
Malignant party, and to preserve his Majestie's rights ; and their proceedings were and are as near and consonant to the laws of the kingdom
as the state and condition of the times did or can permit ; and they will
be ready to relinquish the said rule and government upon a full settlement of the affairs of the kingdome.

II. To the second they answer, that the armies raised by the said
Confederate Catholicks were raised, and the said armies, forts, garrisons,
and wardes in the demand mentioned are maintained for the safety of the
kingdom, and to preserve his Majestie's interest ; and the said armies
always were and are in actual service accordingly, and that upon a full
settlement the same are to be disposed of as his Majesty will direct.

III. To the third they say, that so much of the profits therein mentioned as grew due since the 7th day of August, 1641 (on which day happened that inforced and fatall adjournment of the Parliament[1] from whence
all the distractions of this kingdom did spring) as was received by the
said Confederate Catholicks, and many an hundred times more, was by
them employed and expended in his Majestie's service for the defence
of the kingdom.   And the said profits for the time to come, after a full
settlement, are to be disposed by such hands as his Majesty will think fit.

IV. To the fourth they say, that the free gift granted to his Majesty

---

1. *See* vol. ii. pp. 232-3,—" Remonstrance of Grievances."

by the said Confederate Catholicks is already overpayed,[1] as shall be made appear upon account by the Supreme Council of the said Confederate Catholicks, to whom that affair is intrusted.

V. To the fifth they say, that the ports of Waterford and Rosse, being within the quarters of the said Confederate Catholicks by the Articles of Cessation, they have, according [to] the said Articles, received the profits accruing out of the customes of those ports, and imployed the same in his Majestie's service and defence of the kingdom.

VI., VII. The matters contained in the sixth and seventh demands are properly to be determined in such manner as shall be agreed upon in the conclusion of this Treaty ; and what further concerns the said demands, or the matters in them or any of them, contained, we conceive proper for a debate, and to be determined upon conclusion of the Treaty.

The said Confederate Catholicks do referr their answers to the demands made on the behalf of the Protestant clergy to the first of the Propositions[2] presented by them, and to the debate,[3] and the determination thereof.

CVI. Answers of Commissioners of Confederation to the Demands made by Ormonde on behalf of his Majesty's Protestant subjects.

1. To the first, the said Confederate Catholicques doe answeare that after a full settlement of affaires, reciprocall restitucion is to bee made, as well to the said Confederate Catholicques, and every of them, as allsoe to his Majestie's said Protestant subjects, and to every of them, other than such of the said Protestants as are or shalbee joyned in a rebellious Covenant against his Majestie, or adhere to the Malignant partie, of theire respective castles, lordshipps, mannors, hereditaments, and chattells reall, whereof they were respectively seised or possessed on the 22th of October, 1641, within the quarters allotted to either partie by the Articles of Cessation ; and other than the castles, lordshipps, mannors, and hereditaments in the county of Wickloe, and in the territorie of Idough, out of

1. *See* p. 320.   2. *See* p. 128.   3. *See* p. 289.
CVI. Carte Papers, xii. pp. 194-5.

which the natives thereof were by an high and injurious hand, or extra-judiciall and arbitrarie proceeding's, expulsed, since the yeare of our Lord God, 1633.

2, 3, 4. To the second, third, and fourth, they say that the said Confederate Catholickes are much more damnified therein than the said Protestants; and yet, in regard the same may begett many endlesse suites and troubles, they conceave they are fitt to bee seriouslie debated, and finallie ended upon the settlement.

5. To the fifth, they answeare that they knowe of noe forte or castle that was demolished contrarie to Articles; and when the particulars shall appear, they will give particular answeares.

6. To the sixth, they say that the Confederate Catholicques doe re-ceave noe profitt of theire estates detained from them; wherefore they conceave it not equall that the Protestants should receave the profitts of theire estates untill after settlement, and then the profitts of both estates are to bee reciprocally received by all parties respectively in such manner as shalbee agreed uppon.

Endorsed: A coppie of the Answers made to the demands of the Lord Lieutenant. On the originall (whereof this is a coppie) there is an in-dorsement as followeth, and written by Mr. [George] Lane: "Answer to the Propositions of demands on his Majestie's behalf, etc." Given mee [Ormonde] the 9 of September, 1644.

CVII. ADDITIONAL PROPOSITIONS FROM COMMISSIONERS OF CONFEDERATION.

I. That an Act be passed this next Parliament, prohibiting that neither the Lord Deputy, Lord Chancellor, Lord High-Treasurer, Vice-Treasurer, Chancellor, or any of the Barons of the Exchequer, Privy-Councill, or Judges of the Four Courts, be farmers of his Majesty's customs.

II. That an Act of Parliament may pass in this kingdome against all

CVII. Carte Papers, vol. xii. pp. 208-9. This document is endorsed: "Received 19 September, 1644. Additional Propositions." The answer will be found at p. 327. Ormonde, as will be seen at p. 317, referred to a section of the "Additional Proposi-tions" in the "Explanation of his Answers," but he made no special mention of them in his letter to Digby, pp. 329-333.

monopolies, such as was enacted in England, 21 Jacobi, with a further clause for repealing of all grants of monopolies in this kingdom.

III. That the Court of Castle-Chamber in this kingdom, having been an oppression to the subject, and there being other remedies for the offences questioned in that Court by the Common Law and statutes of the realme, be taken away, or otherwise limited, as both Houses of Parliament shall think fit.

IV. That two Acts lately past in this kingdom, one prohibiting the plowing of horses by the taile, and the other prohibiting the burning of oats in straw, may be repealed.

V. That, upon presenting the names of three persons of qualitie in each county by us to your Lordship, patents be passed to such of those so to be presented, respectively to be Sherives in each county, as your Lordship shall see meet to make choice of for that purpose.

VI. That one or more agents from this kingdom may be admitted still to attend his Majesty for his better information of the affairs of this kingdom; and that, as a testimony of his Majestie's favour, some of the nobles and others of qualitie of this kingdom may be employed about his Majestie's person.

VIII. Forasmuch as divers of the Scottish nation, and others in this kingdom, doe not obey the present Cessation, and many of them having of late taken the Covenant proposed by the members of Parliament at Westminster, now in arms against his Majesty, it is therefore humbly desired that such as disobey the said Cessation, or have taken the said Covenant, be proclaimed Traitors and prosecuted accordingly by his Majestie's authority; and that such counties or Corporations as have not submitted to the now Cessation of arms in this kingdom, according [to] his Majestie's Commission, be not admitted to make any returne to the Parliament.

VIII. Forasmuch as sundry persons estated in this kingdom have either actually raised arms in England against his Majestie, or have otherwise adhered to the Malignant Party now in arms against his Majesty, that, therefore, it may please his Majesty to give way to the impeachment and attainders of those, and such others whose names we shall heere represent to your Lordship by way of bill in Parliament, whereby they may receive condign punishment for their offences, and his Majesty take advantage of the forfeiture of their estates, and in the interim the possessions to remaine in the hands wherein they are at present.

IX. Forasmuch as, upon application of agents from this kingdom to his Majestie in the fourth yeare of his reign,[1] and lately, upon humble suite made to his Majesty by a committee of both Houses of the Parliament in this kingdom, order[2] was given by his Majestie for redresse of severall grievances ; it is, therefore, humbly desired that for so many of those as are not expressed in the now Propositions presented to your Lordship, whereof both Houses in the next ensuing Parliament shall desire the benefit of his Majestie's said former directions for redresses, that the same be afforded them.

X. That the office of Admiralty in this kingdom be settled independent of none but his Majesty, whereby maritime causes may be determined here without driving merchants or others to appeal or seek justice elsewhere in those causes.

XI. That a course may be taken for all such as owe debts in this kingdom ; for that, by reason of the general devastation of the kingdom, the land is not like in some years to come to be of any considerable value, being the only means that many of the nobility, gentry, and others of this kingdom had to satisfie their debts, and therefore a competent time be given, by Act to be passed in the next Parliament, for payment thereof, and the uses or rents moderated.

XII. That the subjects of this kingdom may be eased of the increase of rent lately raised and imposed on them upon the late Commission of Defective Titles in the Earl of Strafford's time.

XIII. That if any of your Lordship's party during these troubles have by fines, recoveries, or otherwise, disinherited those who were next to succeed them of our partie as heirs, or in reversion or remainder, without

1. This refers to " the Graces " from Charles I., under date of 24th May, 1628.
2. Letter of Charles I., dated 3rd April, 1641, " touching the Graces promised in the fourth year of his Majesty's reign."—"Journals of House of Commons of the Kingdom of Ireland." Dublin : 1796, vol. i. p. 211.

reall and full consideration, but for being of our partie, that all acts so done be avoided in Parliament.

XIV. That such of our partie whose estates are in the hands of the Scottish and Parliament party, either in this kingdom or in England, be recompensed out of the estates of those Malignants in this kingdom.

CVIII. THE ANSWER OF JAMES, MARQUESS OF ORMONDE, HIS MAJESTIE'S COMMISSIONER FOR THE TREATIE AND CONCLUDING OF A PEACE IN THIS KING-DOME, FOR AND IN THE NAME AND BEHALFE OF HIS MAJESTIE, TO THE ADDITIONAL PROPOSITIONS OF HIS ROMAN CATHOLICQUE SUBJECTS OF IRELAND, ETC.

When all the particular demands made on the behalf of his Majesty,[1] the Church,[2] and his Majestie's Protestant subjects,[3] and their partie, shall be concluded, his Majestie will be graciously pleased, on his part, to agree to the particulars hereafter expressed, viz. :

I. To the first Proposition : His Majesty hath declared his pleasure in this point (excepting in that part which concerns Privy Councellors) in his answer to the ninth grievance in the seventeenth year of his Majestie's reign [1641] which his Majesty will be graciously pleased may stand as a rule in this case ; and, as to that part which concerns Privy Councillors, the same shall be humbly represented to his Majesty, and his royall pleasure therein expected.

II. To the second Proposition : His Majesty will be graciously pleased to assent to this Proposition, yet so as first there be care taken to secure his Majesty in the particulars proposed in the sixth and seventh articles of the demands in the behalf of his Majesty delivered by the Lord Lieutenant on this Treaty to the Lord Muskery, etc.

III. To the third Proposition : The particulars, wherein it is desired that the Court of Castle-Chamber may be limited, are to be proposed, and

CVIII. Carte Papers, vol. xii., p. 205.
1. *See* p. 319.   2. *See* p. 321.   3. *See* p. 312.

then such consideration shall be had of this Proposition as shall be thought fit.

IV. To the fourth Proposition: His Majesty will be graciously pleased that the two Acts in this proposition mentioned be suspended for such time as on this treaty shall be agreed on.

V. To the fifth Proposition: The laws have already provided for the manner of appointing Sheriffs, from which course his Majesty thinks not fit to vary.

VI. To the sixth Proposition: After a Peace shall be fully settled, application may be had herein to his Majesty, who in his high wisdom best knows how to extend his royal favour in this particular.

VII. To the seventh Proposition: For the first part of this Proposition, the Lord Lieutenant declareth that his Majestie's Commission[1] to him, warranting this Treaty, gives him authority to conclude a Peace, but gives him no authority for publishing such a proclamation, or for such a prosecution, as in this Proposition is proposed: and, for the latter part of this Proposition, the granting thereof is inconsistent with the condition of a Free Parliament.

VIII. To the eighth Proposition: When the proposers shall present to the Lord Lieutenant the names of the persons in this Proposition intended to be impeached and attainted, such consideration shall be had of this Proposition as shall be fit.

IX. To the ninth Proposition: The proposers setting down the particulars of the things contained in this Proposition, such consideration shall be had thereof as shall be fit.

X. To the tenth Proposition: His Majesty will be pleased to advise concerning this Proposition.

XI. To the eleventh Proposition: This is left to further consideration on debate.

XII. To the twelfth Proposition: This is not held fit for his Majesty to be assented to on this Treaty; yet the case of remittals or abatements we intend humbly to represent to his Majesty, who will be graciously pleased in fit time to set downe such a course herein, by commission or

1. *See* p. 198.

otherwise, as may still further magnifie his goodness and indulgence to all his subjects.

XIII. To the thirteenth Proposition: His Majesty may not assent to this, it being against the liberty of the subject, and the laws of the land.

XIV. To the fourteenth Proposition: Such of the estates in this Proposition mentioned, as shall accrue to his Majesty, are to be left to his Majesty to be disposed of as in his high wisdom he shall think fit.

Endorsed: Answere to the Additional Propositions, 1644.

CIX. Treaty for Peace : Ormonde's Account of Negotiations with Commissioners of Confederation.

Ormonde to Lord George Digby.[1]

Our very good Lord,—Uppon the 26th of July last, I, the Lieutenant, received his Majestie's commission,[2] authorising mee to proceed to a Treaty with his Majesty's Roman Catholique subjects, now or late in arms, for settling a firm peace in this kingdome, which I communicated to the Councell [at Dublin], and, by their advise, did, by letters[3] dated the 30th of the same, acquaint the Viscount Muskry, and the rest who latelie attended his Majesty in England, therewith, to the end that they might notifie the same to his Majesty's said subjects that soe they might depute

CIX. Carte Papers, vol. xv., pp. 468, 474.

1. Endorsed: " A coppy of a letter to the Lord Digby [sent] by Lord Brabazon etc." Lord Brabazon was, with Sir Henry Tichburne, and Sir James Ware, sent by Ormonde " to give his Majesty an account of all the proceedings in the Treaty, and to know his pleasure in the particulars which remained to be adjusted." To allow time for their return, the Treaty was adjourned to January 10 [1644-5].—" Life of James, Duke of Ormonde." 1736, vol. i., p. 520. The above letter, which is undated, appears to have been written in October, 1644. In another letter to Digby, on the 19th of that month, Ormonde wrote : " The Lord Brabazon, having some occasion of his own to attend his Majestie at this time, it was held fit to add him to Sir Henry Tichburne and Sir James Ware, but he is not made acquainted with the inwards of the business."— Carte Papers, vol. xii., p. 305.

2. *See* p. 198.   3. *See* p. 220.

som fitt person or persons to attende us concerning the same. But the choice which they made gave such occasion of dispute, by reason of their joyning of one of their clergy[1] with those which they had chosen, which I, the Lieutenant, would by noe meanes admit, as your Lordship may perceive by the copies of the severall letters[2] which did pass betweene us, that it was the [blank] of September before the said Viscount Muskry, and the rest who were trusted with him for the Treaty, came to Dublin. Upon whose coming, by advise of the Councell, it was held expedient for his Majestie's service, seeing that the former Cessacion of Armes drew very neere to an end, to continue the same unto the first of December next, uppon the like articles and agreements, to all intents and purposes, as are expressed in the said former Articles of Cessacion,[3] as by the Proclamation and instrument heerewith sent appeareth.

On the [blank] of September, I, the Lieutenant, being then attended by the Councell, received from the said Viscount Muskry and the rest, the Propositions, which weare in effect the same tendered by Agents of the Roman Catholicks to his Majestie at Oxford.[4] And in regard the said Propositions did offer diverse matters in law to be considered of, it was thought fit by mee, by advise of the Councell, whose assistance I tooke in the whole course of this Treaty, that a Special Committee should be appointed to debate the matters arising upon the severall Propositions with those deputed as aforesaid by the Roman Catholick party. And to that purpose, the Lord Chancellor [Sir Richard Bolton], some of the Councell, his Majestie's Judges of the King's Bench, and his Majestie's Serjeant-at-Law, were appointed[5] for the debate ; and there being five dayes spent therin, a report[6] thereof was made by his Majestie's said Serjeant at the Councell Board, the substance whereof wee have thought fit to send unto your Lordship. After the making of this report, severall days were spent at the Councell Table in preparing the Answeres[7] which should be given unto the Propositions, which, after much debate, weare

1. *See* p. 251.   2. *See* pp. 252-3.   3. *See* p. 273 and vol. ii., pp. 65-81.   4. *See* p. 277.
     5. *See* p. 278.   6. *See* pp. 278-293.   7. *See* p. 293.

agreed to be in substance the same with those they received at Oxford.

Uppon the [28th] of September, the Viscount Muskry and the rest, not being satisfyed with the Answeares, delivered in their Reasons[1] for their Propositions, together with their exceptions[2] to the Answeares agreed on by the Board. Whereupon, by advise of the Councell, the Explanacions[3] of the former Answeares, with some other concessions, weare thought fitt to be delivered, coppyes of all which proceedings you will heerwith receive. It was alsoe thought fitt, by advise of the Councell, to make certaine Propositions unto the said Viscount Muskry, etc., some of them on the behalfe of his Majestie,[4] some on the behalfe of the clergie[5] and others on the behalfe of his Majestie's Protestant subjects,[6] a coppy whereof you will heerwith receive. But those Propositions resting still in debate, and noe determinate answeare given thereunto, wee doe not thinke fitt to trouble your Lordship therewith.

Upon all which your Lordship will finde that the mayne matters likely to be insisted upon are the repeale of the Penall Lawes in force in this kingdome against recusants, what persons or crimes should be excepted out of the Act for the General Pardon, the suspending of Poynings' Act, and the triall of offendors in their new Parliament. In three whereof they have received from me, the Lieutenant, by advise of the Councell, a negative answere; and the 4th, which concerneth the exception out of the Pardon, wherein there is like to be exceeding great opposition, hath not as yet received much debate. And in regard that, without his Majestie's direction, noe satisfaction is likely to be given unto them, especially in the first, it was thought fitt to adjourne the Treaty until the 4th of the next moneth, by which time wee doe humbly desire that his Majestie's royall pleasure may be signified unto us.

And now, having given your Lordship this particular accompt, wee cannot but observe unto you the many advantages which his Majestie's Roman Catholique subjects had uppon the Treaty.

1. *See* p. 298. 2. *See* p. 305. 3. *See* p. 313. 4. *See* p. 319.
5. *See* p. 321. 6. *See* p. 312.

First, they had a considerable army in the field, both before the Treaty and since, which was a very great convenance unto them in their proceedings.

Secondly, divers officers of their party, who have been bred in the German warres, arrived att Dungarvan with great store of powder and amunition dureing the Treaty, and many more are said to bee in a redynes to come over for their ayd, in case there be a breach.

Thirdly, the Fort of Duncannon then likewise revolted to the Parliament, which was a great weakenes and discountenance to our party.

Fourthly, the Lord of Inchiquin and his adhearents did in the tyme of Treatie fall from us, by which we lost the citty of Corke, and the townes of Kinsale and Yoghall, and all other considerable places which wee had in the province of Mounster. And [add] unto this the great rent and separacion, which the late Covenant sett upp in this kingdome hath made, whereby wee can make noe use either by the Lord of Inchiquin or of the forces of the north, in case a breach happen, except wee should involve ourselves with them in the same Covenant, against which wee have long since declared. And as these unhappy devisions have made us the less formidable to the Roman Catholique party, soe they, apprehending our weakness, thereby doe conceive the greater hopes of gaineing their own ends, and doe accordingly worke uppon us. But that which exceedeth all this is those pressing wants, which wee have soe often represented to his Majestie, under which wee doe still lye, which hath enforced many of our common souldiers to forsake us, and seek as well to the Roman Catholique party as to the Scotts for releefe, and may in tyme work uppon many of our officers, if some tymely provision be not made. And although wee have used our utmost endeavours towards the support of that small remaine of his Majestie's forces which have not yett submitted to the Covenant, yett there is now wanting £240 weekly to the necessary chardge of the common souldiers, besides that the Captens and other officers of the horse and foot have received noe pay for these [blank] weekes last past. Wee have also just cause to feare that not only the small supply which wee have out of the adjacent country, but likewise our chiefest help towards this chardge, which is the weekly contribution and excise raised uppon the city of Dublin, will in short time fayle us.   For the city, by reason of this chardge, is soe wasted that at this tyme there are therein [*blank*] hundred howses without inhabitants, and the excise itselfe is already fallen neere halfe what it was when it was first raysed, and will infallibly come to little or nothing if the free commerce and intercourse which wee now enjoy be taken away.   And then in what extremityes wee shall be sudainely involved, considering our generall wants of almost all other necessaryes requisite for warr, is too apparant.

Wee doe, therefore, earnestly desire you to take a fitt opertunity to acquaint his sacred Majestie with our present condition, as alsoe with the severall passadges of this Treaty, that soe his Majestie, best knowing what may sute with the state of his affaires in England, and the preservation of this his kingdome, may by his excellent judgment give us tymely direction to guide our further proceedings, whose commands heerein shall be by us most willingly obeyed.—[ORMONDE.]

ADDENDA.

1. Engagement at Julianstown, November, 1641.

Letter to Ormonde from Sir Patrick Wemys.

[The following, in connexion with the engagement at Julianstown, near Drogheda, in November, 1641, is the letter mentioned by Ormonde in his communication to Charles I., dated 1st December in that year, and printed at p. 232 of vol. i.]

My Lord and patron,—I most now tell your Lordshipp of our ill fortoun this day for the foote companyes which I cam along with, the officers not haveing power to mak them marche yisternight to Drogheda, we lodgid last night at Balrudrye, wher we wer informed that the enemie wes befoir us, and did intend to fall uponn us that night, but did not. This morning, we cam soe far as Gormonstoun, wher my Lord send me woird that he did heir thair wes twe thousand foote and fyve hundreth horse at the bridge thrie myles from Drogheda. Uponn this report, I sent severall scouttis towards the bridge, but all returned thair wes no enemie thair at all; and being confident that Sir Henry Titchburne wald have bene thair befoir us, marched on towards the bridge, wher no enemie did appeir. But we haid not past the bridge a quarter of a mylle when I discovered sum ten horse, I sent on to sie what they wer, whoe broght me word they wer the Rebells, and within a litill whyill I sie them marching towards us in very goode order as ever I sie any men. I wewid them all, and to my conjecture thair wes no less then thrie thousand men, horse and foote. They had thrie troupis of lanceirs, and twoe troupis that haid pistolls, and tw[o] feild peicis. I advysid the foote Captanes to draw thair men within the feild just opposite wher they wer ; for when

<hr />

1. Carte Papers, vol. ii. p. 124.

we did first sie them we wer marching within a durtie lane, and a hie ditch on everie side of us, soe that my perswasionn prevaild with them that to my thinking they drew upe themselves handsumlie. I drew upe the troup in thair front and told the Capitanes that we wer ingadged in honor to charge them, and that I wald charge them first with thoise horse I haid. They promeist faithfuly to second me, but when I maid the trumpit sound, the Rebells advancit towards us in fyve gret bodyes of foote, the horse being on bothe thair wingis, a litill advancit befoir the foote. But just as I wes going to charge, the troup cryid unto me, and told me the foote haid left thair officers, throwin doun thair armes and twok themselves to running. I most confess I haid thorssmen with me that willingly and bravele wald have deid thair, but it wes to noe purpose. I wes abill to doe noe goode uponn them, but to have cast ourselves in thair hands. I bethoght myself how I might fairlie bring them and myselff fairlie aff, the rest being gon ; wiche I did with very much adoe, all the cuntry being inclosed grounds. Yet I maid a fair retrait and broght all my men to Drogheda except Patrik Pursell and Curse ; thair horses haveing fallin lame. But I heir they ar saiff with the loss of thair clothes, being stript of thair clothes not by the Rebells but by the cuntry people as they past throw the villages. This is all our loss, the Rebells haithe gott all the armes and amonitioun. I conceave it is the gritist on loss that we have haid. It wes not weill done to trust so many armes with such men. If they could have bene perswadit to have cum hither yisternight, this had bene preventtit ; but I could not prevaill to mak them doe it. But, to be breiff, we wer a waik counsell. Thus, my Lord, I have sent your Lord-shipp the trew relatioun of this unfortunat rancounter, yit not blodie, for I cannot heir above fyve men kild. I beleive thair is sum of the Captanes takin. I can heir noe accounpt of them as yit. They might have kild everie one of the foote companyes if they haid pleasid. We ar now heir at Drogheda : we can nather gett meat for ourselves nor our horses. Soe wishing us a better fortoun the nixt tyme, I humbly tak leive, and am, my Lord, your Honor's indeard, faithful servantt till death, —P. WEMYS.

Drogheda, this Monday at night.

My Lord, for fear they thinke we ar kild in the cuntry, I pray you send this lettre to my lady, that hir Honor may acquent my wyiff that we ar weill.—I doe perceave heir they doe too muche underwalew the Rebells; but, beleive it my Lord, they will fynd them no suche contemptable men, I am much effaird, when they medle with them.

Thair marched uponn evirie devisionn of the Rebells' foote a frier or a preist.

Endorsed: From Sir Patrick Wems.   Dated 29, received 30, November, 1641.

2. French Manifesto from Irish Confederates.

Manifeste et Articles que les Catholiques Confederez d'Hibernie demandent en toute humilité, au Serenissime Charles, leur Roy, pour trouver une bonne voye d'accord.

Avec Permission.

Nous, les Catholiques sujets de sa Majesté en ce royaume d'Hibernie, requerrons, que les mesmes conditions et articles, que les Esossois pareillement sujets ont demandez et impetrez par leur nouvelle irruption en Angleterre, nous soyent aussi accordez et comfirmez, confessant franchement, qu' à leur exemple, esmeus de la façon de proceder du Parlement d'Angleterre, nous avons justement prins les armes, non contre sa Majesté, de laquelle nous nous reconnoissons les humble sujets, ains seulement pour nostre juste defense contre ceux qui nous accable tres-injustement.

Car, ayant apprins leur insolens et violens desseins contre les Catholiques d'Angleterre, la rigueur desquels surpassoit encore les ordonnances tres-severes promulgées pour d'autres occasions, et en autre temps, par l'oppression des Catholiques seculiers, et la tres-cruelle boucherie des ecclesiastiques, la faction des Puritains estant la plus forte; et seduisant la plus puissante, plus moderée, et plus judicieuse partie des nobles et gentil-hommes, et des autres representans les provinces qui les envoient

2. The original, printed in small quarto, without date, name of printer or of place of publication, is preserved in the Archives of Franciscans of the Irish Province.

pour leur deputez et agens ; defendant aussi par une usurpation d'une puissance souveraine, que nos soldats Hibernois ne prennent parti soûs le Roy d'Espagne,[1] comme ils desiroient, qui est un attentat tout contraire à la puissance et prerogative Royale ; sçachans toutes ces violences, nous avons raisonablement et justement apprehendés que, par la mesme usurpation sur l'authorité souveraine de sa Majesté, ils ne unissent a introduire en ce royaume leur nouvelle reforme Calvinistique, et leur Puritanisme comme ils ont fait en Ecosse, avec la perte entiere de la religion Catholique, qui a fleuri tant de siecles en tous les royaumes d'Angleterre, d'Ecosse et d'Hibernie : ne doutans nullement que nous n'ayons beaucoup meilleure raison de demander l'exercice libre de nostre sainte religion, qui s'est tousjours publiquement conservé des les temps des Apostres jusques à maintenant, sans interruption, que les Ecossois n'ont pour leur secte, si nouvelle qu'il conte qu'il n'y a environ que cent ans qu'elle a commencé sous Luther ; si que nous pouvons à bon droit dire ce que jadis Tertullien : *Nous sommes les premiers en possession.* Pour ces causes nous declarons nos articles par ces points suivans.

1.—Nous demandons, en premier lieu, la liberté de conscience et l'exercice public de nostre religion, comme les Ecossois l'ont de la leur, en sorte que cette innovation et pretendue reformation, qui s'est faite en Ecosse, ne se glisse dans nostre royaume, et ne s'y establisse ; mais que la religion Catholique, la Hierarchie ecclesiastique, et les ordres des religions y soyent derechef reçus, sans qu'aucune secte ou heresie si tolere, que celle des Protestans, qui a vogue en Angleterre, en Allemagne, et en quelques autres provinces : qu'il n'y ait aucun Evesque que Catholique ; que les prestres jouyssent des benefices ecclesiastiques, et des revenus anciennement fondez; et que les ministres Protestans jouyssent seulement des eveschez ou benefices que ceux de leur secte leur procureront et assigneront pour vivre.

2.—Nous demandons en second lieu, que pour la police temporelle nous soyons gouvernez par un President, Conseil, et Officiers Catholiques, et que les Governeurs de chasteaux, forteresses, et des villes soyent

1. *See* vol. i., p. 224.

23

pareillement Catholiques et du pays, le tout neantmoins avec la deuë subordination à sa Majestè, des mains de laquelle nous recevrons les Officiers susdits.

3.—Nous demandons, en troisiesme lieu, que les terres et seigneuries des Catholiques, qui ont esté confisquées pour la Religion, tant du temps de la Reyne Elizabeth que du depuis, soyent exactement restituées ou au moins la juste valeur d'icelles.

4.—Nous demandons, en quatriesme lieu, que d'oresenavant on n'envoye aucuns Anglois ou Ecossois pour peupler ce Royaume, s'ils ne sont Catholiques, ou bien Protestans bien moderez, et que les seules colonies, qui ont esté establis de l'authorité publique, soient tolerées et permises sans l'interest ny le prejudice de la nation Hibernoise.

5.—Nous demandons, en cinquiesme lieu, que nostre commerce avec l'Angleterre, l'Escosse, et les autres provinces soit continué comme du temps passé.

6.—Enfin, nous demandons humblement, que ces articles soyent, pour nostre soulagement et nostre asseurance, distinctement confirmez par sa Majesté, et par nostre Parlement d'Hibernie, ne reconnoissans aucune subjection ou subordination à aucun autre Parlement, soit d'Angleterre, soit d'Escosse, comme l'Escosse ne recognoit point celuy d'Angleterre, ains seulement à sa Majesté, à son Conseil privé, et à nostre Parlement procedant juridiquement et selon nos coustumes, et enfin, à nos Conseils d'Hibernie. Protestans, avec toute humilité, que le Roy Charles presentement regnant est nostre seul souverain Prince et Gouverneur ès affaires, nuëment temporelles, également en Hibernie, en Angleterre, et en Ecosse, nous offrans d'estre tousjours prests à faire de bon cœur la mesme protestation, et de l'assurer et confirmer par serment, qui sera jugé et trouvé conforme à nos consciences, et à la Religion Catholique, au jugement de nos Theologiens, et de nos Evesques, notamment du Pape de Rome, nostre souverain Pasteur et directeur és choses spirituelles, auquel appartient proprement l'approbation des sermens, en tant qu'ils touchent les consciences.

Nous asseurons de plus et promettons tout ensemble de defendre jusques au dernier effort de nostre puissance, la souveraineté et prerogative de sa Majesté sur le Parlement, condamnans serieusement et sincerement comme proposition seditieuse, et derogeante à la puissance Monarchique, et à la souveraineté, celle qui avance que les Parlemens sont pardessus leurs souverains, et non pas les Princes souverains sur leurs Parlemens, asseurons pareillement que nous ruinerons de toutes nos forces ces factieux Catisimes, lesquels degenerans de la premiere erection des Parlemens, maintiennent avec opiniastrise, que les mesmes Parlemens ont, non seulement droit de consulter et de deliberer, et proposer, ains encore d'ordonner, et de transiger des affaires de la souveraineté de leur Prince, contre son jugement et sa volonté; ou, si d'aventure leur perfide et malheureuse presomption en vient jusques à là, de dire: *Nous ne voulons pas que celuy cy regne sur nous,* ou s'ils tachent par quelque moyen que ce soit, de prejudicier à sa Majesté, à sa personne, ou à sa couronne, et de diminuer, ou oster son authorité souveraine et Monarchique, soit pour establir et affermir leur reformation Calvinistique, soit pour quelque autre pretexte que ce soit, qui garde la Religion, ou le manquement au gouvernement temporel.

Cependant nous protestons solemnellement et asseurons, que nous ne procederons pas comme severes vangeurs de nostre oppression (de laquelle nous sçavons que nostre debonnaire et bon Roy n'est pas cause, ains ses Officiers turbulens et factieux), mais comme supplians aupres de sa Majesté, pour obtenir d'elle nostre soulagement juste et raisonnable, promettans en bonne foy que nous poserons les armes, lors que sa Majesté nous aura promis en foy de Roy, qu'elle nous accordera nos demandes. Finalement, nous souhaitons passionnement que cette guerre se termine en obtenant la satisfaction que nous demandons, et non pas avec epanchement du sang humain, et que sa Majesté par sa clemence pourra faire si elle veut, avec beaucoup moindres frais, que le Parlement d'Angleterre n'a racheté les troubles et les soulevemens d'Ecosse, que la faction Puritaine à approuvez et sostenus avec tant d'applaudissemens.—Fin.[1]

1. On the title-page is the following entry in a contemporary hand: " Printed at Lille, 26 of Ja[nuary] 1642 [-3]. James Dempsey." James Dempsey, for many years Vicar-Apostolic of Kildare, was among those suggested in 1646 as Bishop for that see, to which, however, no appointment was then made. Dempsey was subsequently Vicar-Apostolic of Dublin.

3.—Catalogue[1] of persons outlawed in Ireland for High Treason, a.d. 1641-43.

i.—Memorandum: That all the undernamed Lords[2] are indicted and outlawed in the King's Bench, as it appears now on record, for High Treason on account of the Rebellion begun in this kingdome [Ireland], the twenty-third of October, 1641 :

> James [Touchet], Earle of Castlehaven [and Audley].
> Christopher [Plunkett], Earle of Fingall.
> Donogh McCarthy, Lord Viscount Muskry.
> Maurice [Roch], Lord Viscount Roch of Fermoy.
> Nicholas [Preston], Lord Viscount Gormanstowne.
> Pierce [Butler], Lord Viscount Ikerin.[3]
> Arthur [Magenis], Lord Viscount Magenis of Iveagh.
> Richard [Butler], Lord Viscount Mountgarrett.
> Nicholas [Nettervill], Lord Viscount Nettervill of Dowth.
> James [Butler], Lord Baron of Dunboyne.
> Connor [Maguire], Lord Baron of Inniskillin.[4]
> Oliver [Plunkett], Lord Baron of Lowth.
> William [Fleming], Lord Baron of Slane.
> Mathias [Barnewall], Lord Baron of Trimleston.
> William [Burke], Lord Baron of Castleconnell.

ii.—Persons indicted and outlawed of Treason in the King's Bench, in Hillary Terme, anno decimo septimo Caroli Regis, 1641 :

KILDARE :—Archbold,[5] Christopher, of Tymolin, gent.—Archbold William, of the same, Esq.—Archbold, Richard, of Flemingstowne,

---

1. Add. MS. No. 4,772.—British Museum, London. *See* Preface, p. x.

2. Notices of these peers will be found in the present volume, and in vols. i. and ii. *See also* " Contemporary History of Affairs in Ireland, 1641-52." Dublin : 1879-81.

3. In margin : " Corke." 4. In margin : " C[ounty of] C[ity of] D[ublin]."

5. Some names appear more than once in the manuscript, and the orthography throughout is irregular.

gent.—Allen, John, of Rewe, gent.—Allen, Edward, of Bishopcourt, gent.—Archbold, James, of Crookestowne, gent.—Allen, Edward, of Oughterard, gent.—Allen, Richard, of the same, gent.—Aysh, Thomas, of Naas, gent.—Aysh, Henry, of the same, gent.—Aysh, Thomas, of Moyvalley, gent.—Aysh, Walter, of Naas, merchant.—M'Aulaghny, Connor, of the same, clerke.—Aylmer, Robert, of Killeighterhery, gent.— Aylmer, Anthony, of Cockranstowne, gent.

WICKLOE :—Archbold, Theobald, of Rathbran, in the county of Wickloe, yeoman.—Archbold, Edward, of Frayne, gent.—Archbold Robert, of Puckmyn, gent.—Archbold, Henry, of the same, gent.— Archbold, Thomas, of Wickloe, gent.—Archbold, George, of Glancorn-incke, gent.—Archbold, Edward Owne, of Kilmurry, gent.—Archbold, Theobald, of Templecargie, gent.—Archbold, Gerrald, of Brea, gent.

DUBLIN :—Aulen, James, of Rathenny, in the county of ·Dublin, yeoman.—Ayshpoole, Robert, of the same, yeoman.—Archbold, William, of Cloghran-Swords, gent —Archbold, William, of Cloghran-Swords, idem.—Archbold, Rowland, of the same, gent.—Archbold, Edward, of the same, gent.—Archbold, Robert, of Tuckmyn, in the county of Wickloe, gent.—Archbold, James, of the same, gent.—Archbold, Henry, of the same, gent.—Archbold, Rowland, of Cloghran Swords, in county Dublin, yeoman.—Archbold, Henry, of Lysk, yeoman.—Archbold, Christopher, of Skedowe.—Armstrong, Jenkin, late of Burgage in county Wickloe, gent.

KILDARE :—Archbold, Richard, of Flemingstowne, gent.

MEATH :—Aylmer, James, of Dullardstowne, Esq.

DUBLIN :—Aylmer, Alexander, of Killanstowne, gent.—Ashley, Anthony, of Corbally, gent.—Archbold, Christopher, of Skidowe, gent.— Archbold, William, of Cloghran-Swords, gent.—Archbold, Rowland, of the same, gent.

WICKLOE :—Archbold, James, of Ballyrea, gent.—Archbold, Edward, of Pollocapple, gent.

DUBLIN :—Archbold, Nicholas, of Carrowkill, yeoman—Arthur, Nicholas, of Hacketstowne, yeoman.

CORKE :—M'Awliffe, Fynnyne, of Carriggycashell, gent.—M'Awliffe, alias Teige Ivegher, of the same, gent.—M'Awliffe, Donogh M'Owen, of Lismalconyne, gent.—M'Awliffe, Cornelius, of the same, gent.—Arundell, Garrett, of Aghidullane, gent.—Arundell, Garrett, of Darrirg, gent.— Arundell, Garrett Oge, of Aghidullane, gent.—Agherin, Maurice M'Shane, of Cregg, gent.[1]

MEATH :—Bath, James, of Athcarne, Esq.—Barnewall, Mathew, of Breamore, in county Dublin, armiger.—Bellewe, John, of Stamine, gent.— Bermingham, Richard, of Dorhamstowne, Esq.—Betagh, junior, Edward, of Moynaltie, gent.—Berford, Adam, of Scarlockstowne, gent.—Barnewall, Christopher, of Crackanstowne, gent.—Balfe, James, of Kells, merchant.

KILDARE :—Bealing, Richard, of Killussy, in county Kildare, armiger. Byrne, Bryan, of Downings, clerke.—Beary, William, of Kildare, clerke. —Bretton,[2] Beverly, of Lyons, Esq.—Barnsley, Henry, of Leixlipp, clerke. —Baterne, Edmond, of Rahinkeigh, gent.—Brock, Henry, of Castlemichell, gent.—Barnewall, William, of Stephenstowne, gent.—Bermingham, William, of Ballynemallough, gent.—Bermingham, John, of Rahin, Esq. —Byrne, David, of Killemean, gent.—Bermingham, Pierce, of Ballynekill, gent.—Bermingham, Gerald, of the same, gent.—Bermingham, Luke, of Parsonstowne, gent.—Barnesley, Henry, of Leixlipp, clerke.—Browne, Nicholas, of the same, yeoman.—Bermingham, Gerald, of Donfert, clerke. —Bermingham, Edward, of Naas, clerke.—Bermingham, Thomas, of Carricke, gent.—Bermingham, Thomas, of Fues, clerke.—Bermingham, Edward, of Ardkill, clerke.—Bermingham, Edward, of Fues, clerke.— Bermingham, John, of Micklard, gent.—Byrne, Hugh M'Phelim, of Rossaltan, in county Wickloe, gent.—Baggot, Thomas, of Castlemartin, gent.— Bardan, Barnaby, of Kilcullenbridge, yeoman.—Byrne, Walter, of Russellstowne, in county Catherlagh, gent.—Byrne, Patrick, of Ballaghmone, yeoman.

WICKLOE :—Byrne, John M'Donogh, of Ballynecroe, gent.—Byrne, Edmond M'Art, of Monduffe, gent.—Byrne, Tirlagh M'Phelim, de Killcashell, gent.—Byrne, Donnoll Oge M'Donnell, of Ballinderry, gent.— Byrne, M'Dowlin Tirlagh, of Wickloe, haberdasher.—Byrne, Shane, [son] of Redmond, of Killmacoo, gent.—Basnett, Thomas, of Ballyknockar,

---

1. The names connected with Cork in this catalogue will also be found in the " Council book of the Corporation of Kinsale," edited by R. Caulfield, LL.D., 1879.

2 *See* vol. i. p. 132; ii. p. 260.

gent.—Byrne, Bryan M'Gallogh, of Knockadrite, gent.—Byrne, Walter Boy, of Garrygsan, gent.—Byrne, Gerald, of Wickloe, gent.—Byrne, Lucas M'Teige, of Crowroe, gent.—Byrne, Garrett M'Feagh, of Tintowne, gent.—Byrne, Luke M'Redmond, of Killcloghran, gent.—Byrne, Phelim M'Redmond, of Killvane, gent.—Byrne, Hugh M'Laghlin, of Ballyteige, gent.—Bermingham, Peter, late of Dromyn, clerke.—Byrne, Donnagh Carragh M'Teige, of Cloone, gent.—Byrne, John M'Bryan M'Phelim, of Ballynecorr, gent.—Byrne, Caher M'Phelim, of Laragh, gent.—Byrne, Art M'Phelim, of Ballyhughduffe, gent.—Byrne, Richard M'Melaghlin, of Castle M'Adam, gent.—Byrne, Tirlagh M'Gill-Patricke, of Garrymore, gent.—Byrne, George, of Ardnary, gent.—Byrne, James M'Phelim, of Tygronane, gent.—Burne, Edmond, of Killroade, gent.—Byrne, Phelim M'Tirlogh, of Ballymorhin, gent.—Byrne, Richard M'Bryan, of Downe, gent.—Byrne, Garrett Oge, of Dromyn, gent.—Byrne, Edmond M'Bryen, of Tommore, gent.—Byrne, Morrogh M'Teige, of Leighbegg, gent.— Byrne, Patrick, of Glyn, gent.—Byrne, Teige Oge, of Ballinvalley, gent.— Byrne, Teige Oge, of Morrogh of Cowlywony, gent.—Byrne, Dowlin M'Shane, of Rossenagh, gent.—Byrne, Edmond M'Caher, of Cowlemore, gent.—Byrne, Walter, of Newry, gent.—Byrne, John, of Ballynecurrogh, gent.—Byrne, Thomas, of the same, gent.—Byrne, Teige, of Bridesfoote, gent.—Byrne, Bryan M'Tirlagh, of Kellymanagh, gent.—Byrne, Tirlogh Oge, of Ballynepark, gent.—Byrne, Tirlagh M'Alexander, of Monitagh, gent.—Byrne, Dennis M'Alexander, of the same, gent.—Byrne, James, of Wickloe, cooper.—Byrne, Callogh, of Bannickmurrogh, gent.—Byrne, Nicholas M'Art, of Ballynevarn, gent.—Byrne, Bran M'Teige, of Ballinvalla, gent.—Byrne, Thady Oge, of Ballinvalla, gent.—Byrne, Dowlin M'Caher, of Toberbiller, gent.—Byrne, James M'Caher, of Polenekally, gent.—Byrne, Walter Boy, of Garrygolan, gent.—Byrne, Bryan M'Icallowe, of Knockdrite, gent.—Byrne, Edmond Duffe, of Killoughter, gent.— Byrne, Caher M'Bryen, of Tommore, gent.—Byrne, James, of Wickloe, cooper.—Byrne, Thady M'Murrogh, of Coolevonny, gent.—Byrne, Bryan M'Cahir, of Moony, gent.—Byrne, Gerald M'Cahir, of Knockloe, gent.—Byrne, Art M'Garrett, of Knockfadda, gent.—Byrne, Edmond, of Downe, gent.—Byrne, Charles M'Bryen, of Tommore, gent.—

Byrne, Charles M'Art, of Ballyronane, gent.—Byrne, Richard M·Art, of the same, gent.—Byrne, Edmond M'Melaghlin, of Killoghter, gent.—Byrne, Phelim M'Art, of Ballynestry, gent.—Byrne, Walter Boy, of Newrugh, gent. - Byrne, Luke M'Redmond, of Killclogh- ran, gent.—Byrne, Thady Oge, of Ballinvalla, gent.—Byrne, James M'Phelim, of Tygronan, gent.—Byrne, Bryan M'Tirlagh, of Killemanagh, gent.—Byrne, Dermott M'Phelim, of Toberlawnaght, gent.—Byrne, Thady M'Dowlin, of Mongflugh, gent.—Byrne, Tirlagh M'Gerald, of Ballymac Icarragh, gent.—Byrne, Tirlagh, of Cooledrosse, gent. —Bermegan, Murtagh, of Kelloge, gent.—Byrne, Gerald Oge, of Ballyhenrygowe, gent.—Byrne, Thady M'Murrogh, of Coolevonery, gent.—Byrne, James, M'Cahir, of Timvollen, gent.—Byrne, Bran, of Killboy, gent.—Byrne, Richard M'Melaghlin, of Castlemacadam, gent.—Byrne, Edmond, of Kill- more, gent.—Byrne, Gerrald, of Oghill, gent.—Byrne, Edward Oge, of Ballynegilloge, gent.—Byrne, Edmond M'Teige, of Ballintlea, gent.— Byrne, Donnogh Carragh, of Clone, gent.—Byrne, Edmond M'Dowlin, of Carraneaslan, gent.—Byrne, Gerald, of Knockloe, gent.—Byrne, Walter Boy, of Garrygolan, gent.—Byrne, Gerald M'Phelim, of Ballycreene, gent.—Byrne, Hugh, of Killkeele in county Wexford, clerke —Byrne, James M'Gerald, of Seskin, gent.

DUBLIN :—Butterly, Nicholas, of Jordentowne, yeoman.—Byrne, Hugh, of Ballinteskin, in the county of Wickloe, gent.—Blakeny, George, of Rickenhoare, Esq.—Byrne, Symon, late of Booterstowne, yeoman.— Bourke, William, late of Templeoge, yeoman.—Byrne, Symon, late of Templeoge, yeoman.—Barnewall, Richard, of Lispople, Esq.—Begge, senior, Mathew, de Boranstowne, gent.—Boyling, John, of Killbarrock, yeoman.—Browne, James, of Ballydoyle, yeoman.—Bee, Nicholas, of Howth, yeoman.—Blakeny, George, of Rickenhoare, Esq.—Bret, Richard, of Tul- loge, in county Meath, gent.—Bret, George, of the same, gent.—Bering- ham, Edward, of Coolemyne, gent.—Barnewall, Francis, of Lispople, gent.—Bowen, Robert, of Mabestowne, yeoman.—Belling, Lawrence, of Bellingstowne, gent.—Barnewall, Andrew, of Luske, gent.—Bellings, John, Bellingston, gent. —Bermingham, James, of Ballogh, Esq.—Bellew, Nicholas, of Ballruddery, chyrurgeon.

WICKLOE : — Byrne, Hugh, of Ballinteskin, in county Wickloe, gent.—Barnewall, George, of Sprikletowne. —Byrd, John, of Gracedeue, yeoman.—Ball, John, of Dunnine, yeoman.—Barnewall. Mathew, of Bremore, Esq.—Belling, Marke, of Ardlawe, gent.—Basnet, Michael, of Burgage, gent.—Barnewall, Andrew, of Luske, gent.—Betagh, jun., Edmond, of Moynaltagh, in county Meath, gent.—Brett, George, of Tulloge, in the same county, gent.—Berryes, Thomas, of Luske, yeoman.—Beaghan, John, of the same, yeoman. —Byrne, Hugh M'Phelim, of Ballinteskin, in county Wickloe, gent.

Persons indicted of Treason in the King's Bench, in Easter terme, anno Decimo octavo Caroli Regis, 1642 :

KILDARE :—Bermingham, Luke, of Parsonstowne, gent.—Bermingham, Edward, of Carricke, gent. —Bealing, Christopher, of Killussey, gent. Bath, Robert, of Killussy, gent. —Bryan, Michael, of the same, yeoman.—Bealing, Sir Henry, of the same, Knight.—Barnewall, William, of Stephenstowne, gent. — Bery, William, of Feighcullen, clerke.—Buggill, Gillpatricke, of Killdrought, yeoman.

MEATH :—Barnewall, Sir Richard, of Crickstowne, Barronet.[1]—Bath, James, of Athcarne, Esq.—Barnewall, Andrew, of Kilbrewe, gent.—Barnewall, James, of Athroneane, gent.—Berford, Richard, of Ballybyn, Esq.—Bath, Robert, of Clonturke, gent.—Balfe, Richard, of Fidalfe, gent.—Bath, Robert, late of Dublin, gent.—Bath, James, of Athcarne, Esq.—Byrne, Hugh, of Ballinteskin, in county Wickloe, Esq.—Byrford, Richard, of Ballybin, Esq.—Barnewall, Richard, of Trimblestowne, Esq.—Bellew, Patrick, of Athboy, gent.—Browne, Richard, of the same, merchant.—Balfe, Oliver, of Galmolstowne, gent.—Burnell, Christopher, of Castleknok, gent. — Barnewall, Simon, of Cooledary, gent.—Bermingham, Patrick, of Corballis, Esq.—Bermingham, Garrett, late of Dublin, gent.—Barnewall, Richard, of Rosse, gent.—Barnewall, Robert, of Rossetowne, Esq.—Brady, Thomas, of Beanstowne, yeoman.—Brady, Shane, of Brittonsland, yeoman.—Brady, Shane Oge, of the same,

---

1. See vol. i, p. 389.

yeoman.—M'Brereto, Shane, of the Grange, yeoman.—Boyland, Patrick, of Garistowne, yeoman.—Bardon, Thomas, of the same, yeoman.—Betagh, Edward, of Moynalty, Esq.—Betagh, Robert Moyle, of Mullagheh, gent.—M'Bryan, Owen Crosseigh, of Moynalty, yeoman.

COUNTY DUBLIN :—Boylan, Rose, of the Kill, spinster.—Berming-ham, James, of Ballagh, Esq.—Ball, John, of Balldromin, gent.—Ball, John, of Pennycomequick, gent.—Ball, John, of the Naall, gent.—Ball, Richard, of the same, gent.—Barnewall, Andrew, of Luske, gent.—Barnewall, Richard, of Lispople, Esq.—Belling, John, of Belling-stown, gent.—Bealing, Marcus, of Ardlaw, gent.—Brett, George, of Tulloge, gent.—Bowen, Robert, of Mabestowne, gent.—Byrne, Hugh M'Phelim, of Ballinteskin, in county Wickloe, Esq.—Blackney, George, of Rickenhore, Esq.—Bermingham, Edward, of Coolemyne, gent.—Barnewall, Christopher, of Crakenstowne, in county Meath, gent.—Barnewall, James, of Rathregan, eodem comitatu, gent.—Barne-wall, Andrew, of Kilbrew, in the same county, gent.--Byrford, Robert, of Ratoath, in the same county, gent.—Balfe, Richard, of Fidorth, in the same county, gent.—Bath, William, of Clonturke, in the same county, gent.—Bath, Robert, of the same, gent.—Barnewall, George, of Crickes-towne, gent.—Belling, Lawrence, of Bealingstowne, gent.—Bowen, Robert, of Mapestowne, gent.—Barnewall, Richard, of Lispople, Esq.--Baggott, Robert, of the parish of St. Audoen's, Dublin, gent.—Bermingham, Richard, of Derhamstowne, in the county of Meath, Esq.—Bath, Peter, of the parish of St. Audoen's, in the county of the city of Dublin, mer-chant.—Boran, David, of the parish of St. Michael the Archangel, Dublin, merchant.

WICKLOE :—Byrne, Teige M'Shane, of Ballynebary, gent.—Byrne, Murtagh M'Gillpatricke, of Kilvenny, gent.—M'Bryan, Maurice, of Acki-keogh, gent.—Byrne, Edward Duffe M'Shane, of Ballynecare, gent.—Byrne, Lawrence, of Wickloe, gent.—Byrne, Art, of Ballaghelengeare, gent.—Byrne, Tirlagh Duffe, of Ballygaughan, gent.—Byrne, Edmond Duffe, of Ballinmony, gent.—Byrne, Donogh Oge, of Ballyrichard, gent.—Byrne, William Murry, of Ballynegeelay, gent.—Byrne, John M'Cahir, of

Scratternagh, gent.—Byrne, alias Bullagh Garrett, of Cronekipp, gent.—
Byrne, John, of Killmartin, gent. Byrne, Gerald, of Ballyncorre, gent. –
Byrne, Edmond M'Teige Oge, of Ballykeene, gent.—Byrne, James, of
Ballynerny, gent.—Byrne, John, late of the same, clerke.—Byrne, Edmond,
late of the same, gent.—Bealing, Richard, of Parke, Esq.—Byrne, Red-
mond M'Feagh, of Kilveane, Esq.—Byrne, Bryan M'Icallowe, of Kill-
toner, Esq.—Byrne, James M'Edmond, of Comery, gent.—Byrne, Dermott
M'Gillpatricke, of Killmanurry, gent.—Byrne, Donnogh M'Melaghlin, of
Ballintlen, gent.—Byrne, Tirlagh M'Edmond, of Coolebane, gent.—Byrne,
Patrick M'Icallowe, of Clorogh, gent.—Byrne, Bryan M'Edmond, of
Downe, gent.—Byrne, Shane M'Imere, of Tommore, gent.—Byrne, Tirlagh
M'Donogh, of Downe, gent.—Byrne, Art M'Cahir, of Baliduffe, gent.—
Byrne, Cahir M'Tirlagh, of Ballyedocke, gent.—Byrne, John M'Daniel,
of Ballimurre, gent.—Byrne, Symon M'Shane, of Ballimergin, gent.—
Byrne, Dowlin M'Edmond, of Aghoole, gent.—Byrne, Donogh M'Me-
leighlin Oge, of Killmurry, gent.—Byrne, Gerald M'Gillpatrick, of the
same, gent.—Byrne, Edmond Oge, of Ballynegeeloge, gent.—Byrne, Shane
Duffe M'Donogh, of Chappell, gent.—Byrne, Rory M'Patrick, of Cullencra,
gent.—Byrne, Murrogh M'Tiege, of Ballykeene, gent.—Byrne, Murrogh
M'Melaghlin, of the same, gent.—Byrne, Nicholas M'Teige Boy [buidhe],
of Oghie, gent.—Byrne, Hugh Ballogh, of the same, gent.—Byrne, Teige
M'Murrogh, of Coolenerly, gent.—Byrne, Bran M'Gerald, of Coolene-
killy, gent.—Byrne, Calue M'Donogh, of the same, gent.—Byrne, Patrick
M'Shane, of Oghill, gent.—Byrne, Edmond M'Bryan, of Ballyteigecar-
ragh, gent.—Byrne, Donnell M'Murtagh, of Ballymurrogh, gent.—Byrne,
Hugh, of Ballynearbeg, gent.—Byrne, Bran M'Dowlin, of Parksbewne-
logh, gent.—Byrne, Alexander M'Tirlogh, of Ballyneparke, gent.—Byrne,
Phelim M'Tirlogh, of Tomcovile, gent.—Byrne, Edmond M'Phillip, of
Cloghleagh, gent.—Byrne, Donogh M'Edmond, of Ballyissa, gent.—Byrne,
Donagh M'Murrogh; Byrne, Phelim M'Art; Byrne, Hugh M'Art, of
the same, gents.—Byrne, Daniel Reagh M'Edmond, of Mongduffe,
gent.—Byrne, Hugh M'Shane, of Kilmacra, gent.—Byrne, Bryan M'Tirlagh, of Brolagh, gent.—Byrne, Meleghlin M'Art, of the same, gent.—

Byrne, Teige M'Murrogh, of Ballyteigecarragh, gent —Byrne, Murrogh M'Murtogh, of Ballinhorreh, gent.—Byrne, Tirlagh M'Hugh, of the same, gent.—Byrne, Shane M'Gerald, of Ballyteigecurragh, gent.

Persons indicted of Treason in the King's Bench, in Trinity Terme, anno decimo octavo Caroli Regis, 1641, and outlawed thereupon :

DUBLIN:—Bert, Richard, of Tullocke, in county Meath, gent —Barnewall, Robert, of Terrynore, gent.—Barnewall, Francis, of Lispople, Esq.—Bealing, Lawrence, of Bealingstowne, gent.—Byrne, Hugh, of Ballyne corre, in county Wickloe, gent.—Byrne, Phelim, of the same, gent.

MEATH :—Burnell, Henry, of Castlerickard, gent.— Bath, James, of Athcarne, Esq.—Bermingham, Patrick, of Corballis, Esq.— Barnewall, Gerald, of Robertstowne, Esq.   Beetagh, of New towne, gent.   Barnewall, Richard, of Trimleston, Esq.—Bath, Robert, of Grange and of Dunsaghlin, gent.—Boylan, alias M'Morie, John, of Killeene, yeoman.—Bath, Robert, of Dublin, gent.—Bath, William, of Dublin, sadler. - Barnewall, James, of Rathrigan, gent.

Persons indicted of Treason in the county of Corke, att the sessions holden att Youghall, the second of August, 1642, and outlawed in the King's Bench for the same :

CORKE :—Baggott, John, of Downemanus, Esq.—Baggott, Thomas, of same, gent.—Barry, Redmond, of Lisgriffin, gent.—Barry, Phillip, Drinagh, gent.—Barry, Gerald, of Lisgriffin, gent.—Barry, Nicholas, of Drinagh, gent.—Barry, John, of the same, gent.—Barry, Phillip Oge, of Rynearrane, Esq.—Barry, Richard, of Thomastowne, gent.—Barry, Phillip, of Corryvayhell, gent.—Barry, John, of Donboigg, gent.—Barry, David, Barry, Phillipp, Barry, John, of Donboigge, gent[n].—Barry, James, of Rathshinigane, gent.—Barry, David, of Ballygumine, gent.—Balding, Walter, of Garancomy, gent.—Balding, Henry, of Meucrompe, gent. -Barry, John, of Ballyfeate, gent.—Barry, William, of the same, gent.—Barrett, Richard, of Ballycohina, gent.—Barrett, William, of Ballyally, gent.—Barrett, Edmond, of Ballymackow, gent.—Barrett, John, of Pluckans, gent.— Barrett, Redmond Fitzjames, of Ballyshonynn East, gent.—Burden, Thomas, of Knockmebardenagh. gent.—Barrett, James Oge, of Carryleagh, gent.—Barrett, James, of Gurtine, gent.—Barry, alias Haraman, Wm. M'Shane, of Birne, gent.—

Barrett, William, of Pluckane, gent.—Barry, Richard, of Curryleagh, gent.—Barrett, Richard, of Fagha, gent.—Barrett, Robert, of Lissing, gent.—Barrett, John, of Ballyshonyne,West, gent.—Barrett, William, of Knockanetindery, gent.—Barrett, Fitzwilliam John, of Ballencolly, gent.— Barrett, John, of Ballyally, gent.—Brennagh, James, of Faghy, gent. yeoman.—Brennagh, Edmond, of the same, yeoman.—Barry, John, of Newcastle, gent.—Barry, David, of the same, gent,—Barry, William, of Lishly, gent.—Barry, Edmond, of Derryluorne, gent.—Barry, John, of Downarlug, gent.—Barry, James; Barry, William; Barry, John Oge; Barry, Richard, of same, gent.—Barry, John Oge; Barry, William; Barry, Richard, of Downededy, gent^n.—Barry Garrett, alias General Barry, of Blarny, gent.[1]

Persons indicted of Treason in the King's Bench, in Hillary Terme, anno Regis Caroli decimo octavo, 1642, and outlawed thereupon:

DUBLIN:—Birt, Richard, of Tullocke, in county Meath, gent.—Bowen, Walter, of Leistowne, yeoman.—Butterly, Robert, late of Wyamstown, gent.—Burley, John, of Westpellstowne, miller.—Bealing, John, of Bealingstowne, gent.—Bourke, John, of the parish of St. Nicholas without the walls, gent.—Byrne, Thomas, of the same, gent.

Persons indicted of Treason in the King's Bench, in Hillary Terme, anno decimo septimo Caroli Regis, 1641, and outlawed thereupon:

MEATH:—Cusacke, Christopher, of Mullevat, gent.—Cusack, George, of Trimleston, gent.—Cusack, Patrick, of Gerardstowne, Esq.

KILDARE:—Cardiffe, Edward, of Naas, clerke.—Cavenagh, Dionisius, of Clane, gent.—Crosby, Sir John, of Waterstowne, Baronet.—Garran, William, of Killrush, clerke.—M'Cahell, John, of Carbry, clerke.

WICKLOE:—Comerford, Peirce, of Manger, gent.—Cullen, John, of Frayne, gent.—Cusack, Adam, of Monomkell, gent.—Cusack, Henry, of Corresullagh, gent.—Cullon, Patrick, of Wickloe.—Cullon, Morgan, of Ballydonnoghreogh, gent.—Cavenagh, Shane Roe, of Killydrenyn, gent.—Cavenagh, Phelim, of Ballyrone, gent.—Cahir, James, of Ballymegaroge, gent.—Cullen, Connor, of Ballyarther, gent.—Cullane, Donnell, of Wickloe, chirurgeon.—Cullane, Farrell, of Moony, gent.—

1. *See* vol. ii., p. 390.

Cullon, Connor M'Farrell, of the same gent.—Cullane, Farrell, of Moony, gent.—Cullon, Con., of Ballydonnoghreogh, gent.

DUBLIN :—Corbally, Thomas, of Moortowne, yeoman.—Cruise, Peter, of the Naall, gent.—Chamberlen, John, of Ouldtowne Clonmethan, gent.— M'Connell, Nicholas, of Mooretowne, yeoman.—Cheevers, Walter, of Monketon, gent.—Cheevers, Thomas, of the same, gent.—Cruise, Peter, of the Naall, gent.—Coman, Richard, of Rathenny, yeoman.—Cooke, Thomas of Balldoyle, yeoman.—Caddell, Patrick, of Lissenhall, gent.—Chamberlan, John, of Oldtowne Clonmethan, gent.—Caddle, Mathew, of Mooretowne, gent.—Caddle, William, of Mooretowne, gent.—Clinch, Richard, of Cappocke, yeoman.—Cannan, Richard, of Rathenny, yeoman.—Coleman, John, of Tartane, yeoman.—Clarke, John, of Bay, gent.—Casie, Thomas, of Courtduffe, yeoman.—Casie, William, of the same, yeoman.—Connor, Dennis, of Killmainham, near Dublin, gent.—Caddell, Richard, of Harberston, in county Meath, gent.—Cardiffe, Henry, of Stephenstowne, gent.—Casie, Richard, late of Knighston, yeoman—Caddell, John, of the Naal, in county Meath, gent.—Caddell, Thomas, of Harbertston, in the same county, gent.—Corkran, Walter, of Lyske, yeoman.—Corbally, Richard, of the same, yeoman.

Persons indicted of Treason in the King's Bench [Dublin], in Easter Terme, anno decimo octavo Caroli Regis, 1642, and outlawed thereupon :

KILDARE[1] :—Castlehaven, James, Earle of.—Cavenagh, Sir Morgan, of Clonmullen, in county Catherlogh, Knight.—Cavenagh, Art M'Bryen, of Ballinloghare, in the same county, gent.

MEATH :—Caddle, Richard, of Harbertstowne, gent.—Cusacke, Patrick, of Gerardstowne, Esq.—Caddell, Richard, of Harbertstowne, gent.— Cusack, James, of Clonemeghand, gent.—Cusack, George, of Trym, gent.—Corkeran, Edmond, of St. Michan's parish, Dublin, yeoman.— Cusack, George, of Boyardstowne, gent.—Cusack, Christopher, of Ardsulagh, gent.—Conrane, Thomas, of Wyanstowne, Esq.—Conrane, George, of the same, gent.—Casy, Michael, of Athboy, merchant.—Cusack, Adam,

---

1. In margin : " Utlagati in comitatu civitatis Dublin."

of Trevet, Esq.—Cruise, Walter, of Cruisetowne, Esq.—Cusack, George, of Trim, gent.

COUNTY DUBLIN :—Cusack, Adam, of Trevett, in county Meath, Esq.—Coleman, Patrick, of the Kill, butcher, [and] Anne, his wife.—Clinch, Henry, of the same, yeoman, [and] Anne his wife.—Cadle, Mathew, of Mooretowne, gent.—Cadle, William, of the same, gent.—Cruise, Peter, of the Naall, gent.—Cusack, Patrick, of Gerardstowne, Esq.—Cardiffe, Christopher, of Ratouth, gent.—Conran, George, of Wyanstowne, gent.—Conran, Patrick, late of the Curragh, gent.—Clarke, John, of the Bay, gent.—Chamberlen, Robert, of Killreske, gent.—Clarke, John, of Roans, in county Meath, gent.—Crumpe, Patrick, late of Dublin, merchant.—Conran, Thomas, of Wyanstowne, Esq.—Conran, Phillip ; Conran, Patrick ; of the same, gents.—Clarke, Francis, of the Bay, gent.—Corkeran, Edmond, of the parish of St. Michan, Dublin, yeoman.—Connor, Donnagh, of the parish of St. Michael the Archangel, Dublin, gent.

WICKLOE :—Coghlan, John, of Wickloe, gent.—Coniam, Eny, alias Edmond, of Kilcandricke, gent.—Coniam, Dionisius, of Glanely, gent.—Cullen, Cale, of Ballywoum, gent.

Persons indicted of Treason in the King's Bench, in Trinity Terme, anno decimo octavo Caroli Regis, 1642, and outlawed thereupon :

DUBLIN :—Conran, Patrick, of Wyanston, gent., in county Meath.—Couran, Phillip, of the same, gent.

MEATH :—Cusack, Patrick, of Gerardstowne, Esq.—Cruice, Walter, of Arlonan, Esq.—Cusacke, Christopher, of Ardreagh, gent.—Cadle, Richard, of Herbertstowne, gent.

Persons indicted of Treason in the county of Corke, att the Sessions holden att Youghall, and returned in the King's Bench the second of August, 1642, and outlawed in the King's Bench for the same :

CORKE :—McCarthy, Dermott, of Ballyhea, gent.—Carthy, Donnell M'Teige, of the same, gent.—Carthy, Fynnyn M'Cormuck, of Gluneverrune, gent.—Carthy, Fynnyn M'Cormuck, of Corrcwrane, gent.—Carthy, Donnell M'Teige, alias M'Teige, of Gortegowlane, gent.—Carthy, Donnell, of Dyrry, gent.—O'Carthy, Phelim M'Donnogh, of Regrellagh, gent.—

Carthy, Donnell M'Owen, of Carrynodybegg, gent.—O'Carthy, Owen M'Phelim, of Rathgrillagh, gent.—Carthy, Donnogh M'Donnell, of Dissert, gent.—O'Carthy, Cormuck M'Owen, of Birne, gent.—O'Carthy, jun., Donogh, M'Phelim, of Regrelagh, gent.—O'Carthy, Owen M'Donnell, of Curnody, gent.—Carthy, Cormuck M'Donnell, of the same, gent.—O'Carthy, Donell M·Owen, of Regrellagh, gent.—O'Carthy, Donogh M'Donnell, of Disert, gent.—M'Carthy, Dermott Oge, of Courtcullenane, gent.—Coppinger, Robert, of Newcastle, gent.—M'Carthy, Dermott, of Cawlarke, Esq.—M'Carthy, Donogh, of the same, gent.—O'Callaghane, Cahir, of Dromenyne, gent.—O'Callaghane, Donogh, of Clonemyne, gent.—O'Callaghane, Dermott, of Gortroe, gent.—O'Callaghane, Cahir, of Killpadder, gent.—O'Coylane, Phillip, of Knockeneglaste, gent.—O'Connellane, Edmond, of Killgibbane, gent.—Carthy, Teige Oge, of Killballyvorilur, gent.—M'Carthy, Florence, of Gallygorte, gent.—O'Cartane, Cornelius, of Dromenyne, gent—O'Callaghane, Owen M'Donnogh, of Kilbramty, gent.—O'Callaghane, Teige Rore, of Dromenyne, gent.—O'Callaghane, Callaghane; O'Callaghane, Cornelius, of the same, gent^n.—O'Callaghane, Dermod M'Donogh, of Killbramitty, gent.—O'Callaghane, Cornelius Reigh, of Coolegeile, gent.—O'Curtaine, Cornelius, of Clonmyne, gent.—O'Callaghane, Ireleagh, of the same, gent—O'Callaghane, Teige, of Kilpadder, gent.—O'Callaghane, Donogh, of the same, gent.—O'Conlane, Cornelius, of Scarhough, gent.—O'Conlane, William, of Killnecronine, gent.—Conlane, James, of Rathduffe, gent.—M'Carthy, Teige, of Killevarry, gent.—O'Carthy, Cormuck M'Donogh, of Curragh, gent.—O'Connell, Phillip, of Knockrobbin, gent.—O'Callaghane, John, of Coolemoty, gent.—O'Callaghane, Cahir, late of Icarrowe, gent.—O'Callaghane, Teige, of Roans, gent.—Condon, James, of Aaghalike, gent.—Condon, John, of Carrigmoury, gent.—Condon, Richard, of Ballydergan, gent.—Condon, Edmond, of Torbeghy, gent.—Condon, Edmond, of Carriggune, gent.—Condon, John, of Currehine, gent.—Condon, Edmond, of Ballybeg, gent.—Condon, John, of Ballyragh, gent.—Condon, John, of Ballymacpatrick, gent.—Condon, Richard, of same, gent.—Condon, John, of Ballydergan, gent.—Condon, Maurice, of Killbarry, gent.—Condon, David, Condon,

John, of the same, gent[n].—Condon, Patricke, of Carigynoury, gent.—Condon, John M'Edmond Gaucagh, of Ballymacpatrick, gent.—Condon, Redmond, of Ballyvudocke, gent.—Condon, Maurice, of the same, gent.—Condon, Maurice, of Ballyarthure, gent.—Condon, Thomas, of Aghelinske, gent.—Condon, James, of Killdrony, gent.—O'Crowly, Teige, of Maulein Redmond, gent.—Carthy, Donogh Oge, of Ballyhand, gent.—Courcy, David, of Downemacpatricke, gent.—Coppinger, Stephen, of Grange, gent.—O'Crowly, John M'Teige, of Ardhane, gent.—M'Carthy, Cormuck, alias M'Carthy Reigh, of Killbrittane, Esq.—M'Carthy, Florence, of Castle Downevane, Esq.—M'Carthy, Donogh, of Killbrittane, gent.—M'Carthy, Teige, alias Idowny, of Downemeanvy, gent.—M'Carthy, Teige, alias Eversy, of Togher, gent.—Carthy, Dermott M'Teige, of Downemeanvy, gent.—Carthy, Florence M'Daniell, of Banduffe, gent.—Carthy, Donell M'Fynnyn, of the same, gent.—Carthy, Florence M'Owen, of Brahellis, gent.—Carthy, Teige M'Fynnyn; M'Carthy, Florence Oge, of the same, gent[n].—Coppinger, Fitzwalter Thomas, of Manures, Esq.—M'Carthy, Dermott, alias M'Glacke, of Downleskane, gent.—Carthy, Callaghane M'Donogh, of Addergoole, gent.—M'Carthy, Florence, of Derry, gent.—M'Carthy, Florence M'Donell, of Dirrivilline, gent.—Carthy, Florence M'Dermody, of Maddaine, gent.—M'Carthy, Dermott, of Killdire, gent.—Carthy, Florence M'Dermody, of the same, gent.—Carthy, Owen M'Callaghane, of Dromlegagh, gent.—Carthy, Callaghan M'Owen, of the same, gent.—O'Cullane, Donell, of Coule Kelloure, gent.—O'Cullane, Cnogher, of the same, gent.—O'Crowly, Teige, of Dromfeagh, gent.—O'Crowly, Teige Oge, of the same, gent.—M'Carthy, Donell, of Ballyvillane, gent.—O'Crowly, Dermott, alias Dermott Backagh O'Crowly, of Beghcullane, gent.—M'Carthy, Donogh, of Carriganevoy, gent.—Carthy, Donogh M'Donell, of the same, gent.—Carthy, John M'Donell, of Beailymore, gent.—M'Carthy, Donogh, of Killroe, gent.—Carthy, Donogh M'Donell, of Lishane, gent.—M'Carthy, Florence, of Starke, gent.—Carthy, Teige M'Donell, of Baregownie, gent.—Coppinger, Richard, of Ringuaogie, gent.—Coppinger, Walter, of the same, gent.—O'Crowly, Teige M'Fynnyn, of Aghiduffe, gent.—M'Carthy, Owen, of Croghane, gent.—O'Crowly,

Teige M'David, of Dromclogh, gent.—O'Crowly, David, of Dromfeagh, gent.—M'Carthy, Cormuck, of Manchy, gent.—M'Carthy, Cormuck Oge; M'Carthy, Donell, of the same, gent^{n}.—Carthy, Owen M'Donogh, of Cahirkirky, gent.—Carthy, Donell M'Owen, of the same, gent.—O'Crowly, Awliffe, of Drome Irike, gent.—Crowly, Donell M'Teige Oge, of Skeaffe, gent.—O'Crowly, John M'Teige; O'Crowley, Redmond M'Teige, of the same, gent^{n}.—M'Carthy, Florence, of Ardeguluna, gent.—M'Carthy, Donogh, of Smurrane, gent.—M'Carthy, Owen, of Ballyorane, gent.—Carthy, John M'Dermody, of Barraghivilly, gent.—Canily, William, of Carrowalder, gent.—Canilie, Teige; Canily, Dermod; Canily, Cnogher; of the same, gents.—O'Crowly, Cormuck M'Cnogher, of Lishineleagh, gent.—O'Cullenane, Thomas, of Courci his country, gent.—Carthy, Dermod M'Donogh, of Hacketstowne, gent.—M'Carthy, Donell, of Clonecallybegg, gent.—O'Crowly, David, of Shynagh, gent.—M'Carthy, Florence, of Lishinlyne, gent.—Carthy, Dermod M'Fynnyne, of Knockicullen, gent.—O'Crowly, Fynyn M'David, of Kynneglibegg, gent.—Carthy, Donogh M'Fynyn, of Maulebracke, gent.—Carthy, Cormuck M'Fynnyn, of Buoltinagh, gent.—Carthy, Owen M'Donogh, of Fyall, gent.—O'Crowly, Teige, of Skeaffe, gent.—O'Crowly, Donogh M'Teige, of Annaherlicke, gent.—O'Crowly, David M'Teige, of Boikerres, gent.—M'Carthy, Donogh, alias Sassinagh, of Knockskeagh, gent.—Carthy, Connor M'Daniell, of Croghane, gent.—Carthy, Cnogher M'Dermody, of Knockycullen, gent. [and] Shily, his wife.—O'Crowly, Donogh M'Teige, of Skeaffe, gent.—Carthy, Teige M'Fynnyn, of Carrycrowly, gent.—Coghlan, Dermod M'Teige, of Long Iland, gent.—O'Coghlan, Donogh M'Teige, of the same, gent.—O'Crowly, Teige M'Dermody Backagh, of Coheragh, gent.—Carthy, Cormuck M'Fynnyn M'Owen, of Lishinhane, gent.—O'Cullane, Dermod, of Castlelyon, gent.—O'Crowly, Cormuck M'Cnogher, of Lishunelegh, gent.—O'Carthy, Donogh M'Donogh, alias Sassenagh, of Knockshenagh, gent.—Carthy, Cnogher M'Dermody, of Garranure, gent.—M'Cahir, Teige, of Dromekeile, gent.—Carthy, Teige M'Dermody, of Aghicloghelly, gent.—O'Carthy, Dermod M'Donogh, of Maulebracke, gent.—Carthy, Donogh M'Owen M'Dermody, of Moulmore, gent.—O'Crowly, Donell M'Teige, of Bowdrune, gent. O'Crowly, Cnogher Oge, of the same, gent.—Carthy, Donnell M'Dermody, of Dirry, gent.—Carthy, Cnogher Dermody, of Maddame, gent.—O'Coghlan, Phillipp, of Iniskeene, gent.—O'Crowly, Humfry Oge, of the same, yeoman.—O'Coghlan, Donogh, of Boddermyne, yeoman.—O'Callaghane, Cahir, of Dromlegagh, gent.—O'Crowly, Cnogher, of Dromfeagh, gent.—M'Carthy, Cnogher, of Killroe, gent.—M'Carthy, Owen, of the same, gent.—O'Crowly, Cormuck M'Teige, of Aghiduffe, gent.—O'Crowly, Awliffe, of Kilvarnowe, gent.—O'Connery, Manus, of Agherin, gent.—Cush, Garrett, of Faruhye, gent.—M'Carthy, Donogh, of Blarny, Lord Viscount Muscry.—M'Carthy, Charles, of Castlemore, Esq.—Carthy, Teige M'Cormuck, of Aglish, gent.—M'Carthy, Dermott, of Inchyrahelly, gent.—Carthy, Cormuck M'Donogh, of Courtbracke, gent.—Carthy, Cormuck M'Callaghane, of Carrigmucke, gent.—M'Carthy, Donogh, of Cahirbeenagh, gent.—M'Carthy, Donell, of Carrignevar, gent.—M'Carthy, Donogh, of Drishane, gent.—M'Carthy, Tiege, of Ouldcastle, gent.—M'Carthy, Dermod, of Gortveghy, gent.—M'Carthy, Cormuck, of Killvidy, gent.—M'Carthy, Owen, of Gort neglogh, gent.— M'Carthy, Dermod, of Downederericke, gent.—M'Carthy, Owen, of Lisbuy, gent.—Carthy, Teige M'Donell, of Licke, gent.—M'Carthy, Callaghane, of Carehowe, gent.—Carthy, Dermod M'Donogh, of Downye, gent.—Carthy, Teige M'Fynnyn, of Knocksarraren, gent.—Carthy, Teige M'Donogh, of Prihus, gent.—Carthy, Teige M'Phelimy, of Drislanebegg, gent.—Carthy, Cormuck M'Callaghane, of Comeyugillagh, gent.—Carthy, Fynnyn M'Dermody, of Inchinebrakane, gent.—Carthy, Callaghane M'Owen, of Drishane, gent.—Cronyne, Cornelius, of Blarny, gent.— M'Cahir, Cowne, of Killcrea, gent.—Creagh, Patrick, of the same, gent.— Carthy, Teige M'Cormuck, of Carrignemucke, gent.—Carthy, Phelim M'Owen, of Castlemore, gent.—Cloddagh, Cormuck, of Misshanghlasse, gent.—Cloddagh, Owen, of the same, gent.—Carthy, Callaghane M'Teige, of Oldcastle, gent.—Carthy, Teige M'Dermody, of Gortiveghy, gent.— Carthy, Cormuck M'Dermody, of the same, gent.—Cronyne, Andrewe, late of Corke, merchant.—Castleconnell, William [Burke], Lord Baron of.—O'Connell, Charles Oge, of Knockrobbin, gent.

Persons indicted of treason in the King's Bench, Michaelmas Terme, anno Regis [Caroli I.] decimo octavo, 1642, and outlawed thereupon:

Castlehaven, James, Earle of.[1]

Persons indicted of treason in the King's Bench, in Hilary Terme, anno Regis Caroli decimo octavo, 1642, and outlawed thereupon:

DUBLIN :—Corbally, Thomas, of Jordanstowne, gent.—Corbally, Ellis, of the same, gent.—Clinton, Thomas, of Feildstowne, gent.—Caddell, John, of Naall, gent.—Coman, Patrick, of Mallahowe, gent.—Conran, Walter, of Curragh, gent.—Casie, William, of Newtowne, of Westpalstowne, gent.—Chamberlen, John, of Oldtowne, yeoman.—Canvan, Patricke, of Mooreside, gent.

Persons indicted of treason in the King's Bench, in Hilary Terme, anno Regis decimo septimo, 1641 :

MEATH :—Darcy, Nicholas, of Plattin, Esq.—Draycott, John, of Mornantowne, Esq.—Dowdall, Nicholas, of Tymole, gent.—Dowdall, Lawrence, of Athlumney, Esq.—Dillon, Andrew, of Riverstowne, Esq.—Drake, William, of Drakerath, gent.—Dowling, John, of Angistowne, gent.—Doyle, James, of Grange, yeoman.

KILDARE :—Dowlin, Maurice, of Narraghmore, clerke.—Denne, Mathew, of Sallons, clerke.—Dormer, John, of the same, clerke.—Dowlin, Morgan, of Kilcocke, clerke.—Deise, William, of Leixlipp, clerke.—Dempsie, Lewis, of Barbetstowne, gent.—Dun, jun., John, of Athye, yeoman.—Deereing, William, of the same, yeoman.—Dormer, Luke, of Sallons, gent.—Dongan, jun., Thomas, of Cartowne, Esq.—Dongan, Edward, of Blackwood, Esq.—Darcy, Francis, of Ballymond, gent.—Dongan, Oliver, of Castletowne, gent.—Dillon, Dermott, of Longtowne, gent.—Dempsie, Robert, of Ballybegg, gent.—Duffe, John, of the same, yeoman.—Dempsie, James, of Tully, clerke—Dempsie, Dominick, of the same, clerke.—Dempsie, Henry, of Ballybrittas, gent.—Duffe, Donnogh, of Naas, clerke.—M'Donough, Daniel, of Ardkill, clerke.—O'Douley, Daniel, of Pitchfordstowne, yeoman.—M'Donnell, Maurice, of Rahin-

1. This is the only name under the above heading. In margin is the entry : " Ut lagatus Civit. Dublin."

sillagh, gent.—Dolane, John, of Castlemartin, yeoman —Dormer, Luke, of Sallaghane, gent.

WICKLOE:—Dowes, Shane, of Ballaghmoone, yeoman.—M'Donnell, Edmond, of Knockericke, gent.—M'Donnell, Alexander, of Wickloe, gent.—Duffe, Donnell M'Hugh, of Ballindery, yeoman.—Doyle, John, of Carrick, Esq.—Doyle, Mullmurry M'Walter, of Ballinrush, gent.— M'Davy, Dermott, of Killogh, gent.—Duffe, Bryan, of Powerscourt, yeoman.—M'Donogh, Hugh Boy, of Koolekenny, gent.—Doyle,[1] William, of Fortchichester, in county Wexford, gent.—M'Donnell, David, of Ballyshaneduffe, gent.—Doyle, Mullmurry, of Ballinrush, gent.— Doyle, John, of Carrick, Esq.—Doyle, alias Gowre, Murtagh, of Monallyne, gent.

DUBLIN:—Duffe, Henry. late of the Ward, yeoman.—Dolan, John, of Castlemartin, yeoman.—Davis, John, of Rathenny, yeoman.—Dungan, Oliver, of Castletowne, in county Kildare, gent.—Duffe, Richard, of Luske, yeoman.—Daly, Laghlin, of Litle Clonsogh, yeoman.—Donnell, Richard, of Palmerstowne, yeoman.—Dongan, Thomas, of Tonregee, ... yeoman.—Devenish,[2] George, Ballgriffin, gent.—Daniel, Anthony, of Toolefairyes, in county Wickloe, gent.—Daniel, Dudley, of the same, gent.— Dowlin, Edmond, of the same.—Donell, Clement, of Swords, yeoman.— Deane, Patrick, of Luske, yeoman.—Duffe, Cahell, of the same, yeoman.—Dermott, William, of the same, yeoman.—Duffe, Thomas, of Rush, yeoman.—Duregan, John, of Ballyrea, yeoman.—Daniel, Jacobus M'Walter, of Toolefarryes, in county Wickloe, gent.—Duffe, Richard, of Luske, yeoman.—Dermott, William, of the same, yeoman.

KILDARE:—Dunboyne, James [Butler], Lord Baron of.—Dempsie, Edmond, of Kildare, gent.—Duffe, James, of Clane, yeoman.

MEATH:—Darcy, Nicholas, of Platten, Esq.—Dillon, William, of Flinestowne, gent.—Dowdall, Laurence, of Athlumny, Esq.—Darcy, Christopher, of Platten, gent.—Dillon, Henry, of Beetaghstowne, gent.—

1. In margin : "Non utlagat."
2. In margin : "Non utlagat."

Dowdall, Walter, of Athboy, gent.—Dillon, Andrew, of Riverston, Esq.—
Daly, Donnogh, of Roeston, yeoman.—Daly, Hugh Boy, of the same,
yeoman.—Dardize, Walter, of Harbetstowne, yeoman.—Drake, William,
of Drakerath, yeoman.—Duffe, Richard, of Oristowne, yeoman.—Doyne,
John, of Dunboyne, yeoman.

COUNTY DUBLIN :—Dowdall, L'·urence, of Athlumny, in county Meath,
Esq.—M'Donnell, Dudley, of Toolefarryes, in county Wickloe, gent.—
Dongane, Oliver, of Castletowne, in county Kildare, gent.—Dillon, Thomas,
of Ratoath, in county Meath, gent.—Dillon, Michael, of the same, gent.—
Dillon, Thomas, of Flinestowne, in the same county, gent.—Delahide,
Frauncis, late of Pheposton, gent.—Dun, James, of Trym, in county
Meath, gent.—Dillon, Lucas, of Killeagh, gent.

WICKLOE :—Dongane, Peter, of Ballincury, gent.—Dillon, Francis,
of Ballymorris, gent.

MEATH :—O'Doyne, Phelim, late of Killeeine, yeoman.

Persons indicted of treason in the county of Corke, att the Sessions
holden att Youghall, the second of August, 1642, and outlawed in the
King's Bench for the same :

CORKE :—Donnevane, Hugh Oge, of Dellygymera, gent.—M'David,
Maurice, of Ballyvilloge, gent.—M'David, James ; M'David, John ;
M'David, Oge ; of the same, gentⁿ —M'Donnogh, Cormuck, of Knockecawly,
gent.—M'Daniel, Murtagh, of Ryne, gent.—Daly, Eneas, of Nughvally,
gent.—O'Dowgane, Donnell, of Castlecurry, gent.—M'Dermody, Teige,
of Gortaghmuse, gent.—M'Donoghoe, Melaghlin, of Lismubronyne.—
O'Dorney, Owen, of Clonedalane, gent.—O'Donnevane, alias O'Donevane,
Donell, of Castledonovane, Esq.—O'Donevane, Donell Oge, of the same,
gent.—O'Driscoll, Teige, of Ballymacrawne, gent.—O'Driscoll, Donogh,
of Downelong, gent.—O'Driscoll, Cornelius, of the same, gent.—O'Driscoll, Donogh, of Glanemonfoyne, gent.—O'Driscoll, Florence, alias
Fynnyn, of Ballymacrawne, gent.—O'Donevane, Murtagh M'Donell, of
Cloghihadbally, gent.—O'Donevane, Richard, of Ballingorneagh, gent.
—O'Donevane, Murrogh, of Carrowgarriffe, gent.—O'Daly, Eneas,
of Ballyrowne, gent.—O'Driscoll, Dermott, of Ouldcourt, gent.—M'Dermody, Fynnyn M'Fynnyn M'Cnogher, of Knockicullen, gent.—

M'Dermody, John M'Teige, of Long Island, gent.—M'Dermody, Teige, of the same, gent.—M'Dermody, Owen, of Knockcurroe, gent.—O'Driscoll, Fynnyn M'Enysle, of Ballyn Iteragh.—M'Dermody, Donnogh, of Knockistoky, gent.—M'Donogh, Dermod M'Teige Oge, of Kilbrunie, gent. —O'Donovane, Donnell, of Dirriviline, gent.—O'Donovane, Donnell Oge, of the same, gent.—M'Donoghoe, Teige, of Westmauchy, gent.—Dennan, John, of Ballynaultybeg, gent.—Dennane, Redmond, of Dennanstowne, gent.—M'Donnell, Owen, of Annaghally, gent.—M'Donnell, Owen; M'Donnell, Donogh; of the same, gent[n].—O'Doogane, William, of Moshanglasse, yeoman.—Dunboyne, James [Butler], Lord Baron of.

Persons indicted of treason in the King's Bench, in Hilary Terme, anno Regis Caroli decimo octavo, 1642, and outlawed thereupon:

DUBLIN:—Duffe, Caher, late of Ballykea.—Duffe, Patricke, of Wespelstowne, gent.

Persons indicted of treason in the King's Bench, in Hillary Terme, anno decimo septimo Caroli Regis, 1641, and outlawed thereupon:

MEATH:—Evers, James, late of Rathtaine, gent.—Enos, Thady, of Outerard, clerke.

KILDARE:—Eustace, John Fitzchristopher, of Balltrasny, gent.— Eustace, Maurice, of Castlemartin, Esq.—Eustace, of Mullagheath, gent.— East, Samuel, of Caucort, Esq.—Eustace, Rowland, of Blackhall, gent.— Eustace, John, of Clane, gent.—Eustace, Walter, of Mullaghcash, gent.— Eustace, Thomas, of the same, gent.—Eustace, Richard, of the same, gent.—Eustace, Richard, of Blackreith, gent.—Eustace, Christopher, of Ballycullen, gent.—Eustace, Christopher, of Newland, Esq.—Eustace, John, of the same, gent.—Eustace, William, of the same, gent.—Eustace, William, of Craddockstowne, gent.—Eustace, Rowland, of Moone, gent.— Eustace, Oliver, of Donfert, clerke.—Eustace, Robert, of the same, clerke.—Eustace, Thomas, of Collinstowne, gent.—Eustace, Rowland, of the same, gent.—Eustace, Maurice, of Castlemartin, Esq.—Eustace, Edmond, of Castlemartin, gent.—Eustace, Rowland, of Ballybrin, gent.

DUBLIN:—Eustace, Maurice, of Castlemartin, in county Kildare, armiger.—Eustace, Edward, of Whitstowne, in county Wickloe, gent.—Eustace, James, of Damalstowne, gent.—Engle, Richard, of the Bridge of Colemyne, yeoman.—Eustace, Nicholas, of Pelletstowne, yeoman.—Eustace, Walter, of Elverston, gent.—Eustace, Thomas, of Burgage, in the county of Wicklow, gent —Ethredge, Adam, of Donabate, gent.

Persons indicted of treason in the King's Bench, in Easter Terme, anno decimo octavo Caroli Regis, 1642, and outlawed thereupon :

KILDARE :—Eustace, Maurice, of Castlemartin, Esq.—Eustace, John, of Newland, gent.—M'Evally, John, of Killedowan, yeoman.—Ennos, James, of Groninagh, county Wickloe, gent.—Enos, Mullinurry, of the same, yeoman.—Enos, James, of Clane, blacksmith.—Eustace, John, of the same, yeoman.

MEATH :—M'Evally, William, of Clonee, gent.—M'Evoy, Francis, of Ballyneskeogh, Esq.—Evers, Patricke, of Betterdane.—Evers, Edward, of Pessingstowne, gent.—Evers, Patricke, of Ardanstowne, gent.—Evers, Alexander, of Rathaine, gent.

WICKLOE :—Edmond, Stephen, of Ballyniskiduffe, gent.—East, Samuell, of Laurencetown, Esq.

Persons indicted of treason in the King's Bench, in Trinity Terme, anno decimo octavo Caroli Regis, 1642 :

DUBLIN :—Eustace, James, of Damalstowne, gent.—Enos, Walter, of Hacketstowne, clerke.

MEATH :—M'Evoy, Francis, of Ballynekeigh, Esq.

Persons indicted of treason in the county of Corke, att the sessions holden att Youghall, and returned in the King's Bench, the second of August, 1642, and outlawed in the King's Bench for the same :

CORKE :—M'Enislis, Donell, of Glearhy, gent—M'Eagan, Owen, of Aghinnagh, gent.—M'Edmond, Mulmurry, of Mohollagh, gent.—M'Eagan, John, of Aghinagh, gent.

Persons indicted of treason in the King's Bench, in Hilary Terme, anno decimo septimo Caroli Regis, 1641, and outlawed thereupon :

MEATH :—Fingall, Christopher [Plunkett], Earl of.—Fleming, James, of Stahalmocke, Esq.—Fluddy, Cornelius Oge, of Augistowne, gent.— Fluddy, Mauras, of the same, gent.—Fluddy, John, of the same, gent.— Farrily, Daniell, of the same, gent.—Farrell, William, of the same, gent.—Fluddy, Patricius, of the same, gent.

KILDARE:—Flatsbury, Phillip, of Brogeston, clerke.—Flatsbury, James, of Drinan, Esq.—Farrell, Gerald, late of Kill, clerke.—Farrell, Dionisius, of Killdrought, clerke.—Foord, Edward, of Leixlipp, clerke.— Fennell, Patrick, of Kilrush, yeoman.—Flatsbury, Phillip, of Drinanstowne, gent.—Flatsbury, Robert, of Palmerstowne, gent.—Flood, William, of the Naas, merchant.—Fay, Oliver, of Ballaghmoone, gent.— Foord, Edward, of Leixlipp, clerke.—Fyan, Robert, of the same, gent.— Flannegan, James, of Tully, clerke.—Firris, Henry, of Castlemartin, yeoman.

DUBLIN:—Firris, Henry, of Castlemartin, in county Kildare, yeoman.—Fottrell, Richard, of Swords, clerke.—Fleming, James, of Slane, in county Meath, Esq.—Freind, Richard, of Dunsink, yeoman.—Freind, Henry, of the same, gent.—Fleming, George, of Blakestowne, gent.— Fullam, Patricke, of Luske, yeoman.—Finglas, John, of Westpelstowne, gent.—Farran, Patrick, of Dublin, yeoman.

Persons indicted of treason in the King's Bench, in Easter Terme, anno decimo octavo Caroli Regis, 1642, and outlawed thereupon:

KILDARE:—Flattsbury, James, of Drinanstowne, Esq.—Flattsbury, Phillip, of the same, gent.—Flattsbury, Phillip of Kildare, clerke.— Flattsbury, John, of the same, clerke.

MEATH:—Fingall, Christopher, Earle of.—Fox, Arthur, late of Cromlyn, in county Dublin, Esq.—Flemming, James, of Stahalmocke, Esq.— Fleming, Christopher, of Clonelean, Esq.—Flemming, James, of Stahalmocke, Esq.—Fury, Terence, of Forsterstowne, gent.—Fagan, James, of Athboy, merchant.

CIVIT: DUBLIN:—Arthur Fox, late of Cromlyn, in county Dublin, Esq.—Fleming, James, of Stahalmocke, in county Meath, Esq.—Fleming, Thomas, of Crevagh, in the same county, Esq.

DUBLIN:—Farrell, Nicholas, of the Kill, butcher.—Finglas, John, of

Porterane, gent.—Finglas, John, of Westpalstowne, gent.—Fleming, James, of Slane, in county Meath, armiger.—Finglas, John, of Portrane, in eodem comitatu, gent.—Fotrell, James, of Feildstowne, gent.—Fulsagh, Patrick, of Ratouth, gent.

Persons indicted of treason in the King's Bench, in Trinity Terme, anno decimo octavo, Caroli Regis, 1642, and outlawed thereupon :

DUBLIN :—Finglas, John, of Westpelstowne, gent.—Finglas, Redmond, of the same, gent.—Finglas, Roger, late of Morrogh, gent.—Fotrell, John, of Fieldston, yeoman.

MEATH :—Flanegane, Tiege, of Dunshaghlin, yeoman.

Persons indicted of treason in the county of Corke, att the Sessions holden att Youghall, and returned in the King's Bench, the second of August, 1642, and outlawed in the King's bench for the same :

CORKE:—Faggrane, John, of Parkstowne, gent.—M'Falleigh, Donnogh, of Ballynea, gent.—Fermoy, Maurice [Roch], Lord Viscount Roch of.—O'Feighy, Donnell, late of Corke, barber.

Persons indicted of treason in the King's Bench, in Hillary Terme anno Regis Caroli decimo octavo, 1642, and outlawed thereupon :

DUBLIN :—Finglase, John, of Westpelstowne, gent.—Fotrell, John, of Fieldstowne, gent.—Fotrell, Peter, of Westerbealingstowne, gent.— Finglas, James, of Fieldstowne, gent.—Finglas, Redmond, of Newtowne, of Westpalstowne, gent.—Fotrell, Richard, of Westerbealingstowne, gent.

Persons indicted of treason in the King's Bench, in Hilary Terme, anno decimo septimo Caroli Regis, 1641, and outlawed thereupon :

MEATH :—Gormanstowne, Nicholas, Viscount.—Gillsonan, William, of Augistowne, gent.

KILDARE :—Fitz Gerald, James, late of Tymolyn, gent.—Fitz Gerald, Maurice, of Allon, Esq.—Fitz Gerald, Edward, of Athy, Esq.—M'Geran, William, of Ballysonan, clerke.—Geoghegan, Anthony, of Kildare, clerke. —Geoghegan, Rosse, of the same, clerke.—Fitz Gerald, Maurice, of Osbaldston, Esq.—Fitz Gerald, Oliver, of Blackhall, clerke.—Fitz Gerald, Edward, of Glassely, clerke.—Fitz Gerald, Maurice, of the same, gent.—

Fitz Gerald, William, of Glassely, gent.—Fitz Gerald, Paul, of Killon, near Narraghmore, gent.—Fitz Gerald, Gerald, of Castleroe, gent.—Fitz Gerald, Gerald Fitz James, of Bealan, gent.—Goulding, Henry, of Killdroughd [Celbridge], yeoman.—Fitz Gerald, Richard, of Oldtowne, gent. —Fitz Gerald, Richard, of Killmurry, gent.—Fitz Gerald, Pierce, of Ballysonan, Esq.—Fitz Gerald, William, of Blackhall, Esq.—Fitz Gerald, James, of Norraghbegg, Esq.—Fitz Gerald, Gerald, of Brownestowne, gent.—Fitz Gerald, Henry, of Kildare, gent.—Fitz Gerald, John, of Walshestowne, gent.—Fitz Gerald, Edward, of Timahoe, gent.—Fitz Gerald, William, late of Donowre, gent.—Fitz Gerald, James, of Blackhall, gent.—Fitz Gerald, John, of the same, gent.—Fitz Gerald, Edward, of Pluckerdstowne, gent.—Fitz Gerald, William, of Hartwell, gent.— Fitz Gerald, Thomas, of Welshestowne, gent.—Fitz Gerald, James, of Killrush, gent.—Fitz Gerald, George, of Christianstowne, gent.—Grace, Robert, of Carnalwy, gent.—Fitz Gerald, John, of Mullaghmoyne, gent.— Grace, John, of Gigginstowne, gent.—Gerald, Maurice, of Graiges, gent. —Fitz Gerald, Thomas, of Ellistowne, Esq.—Fitz Gerald, Redmond, of the same, gent.—Fitz Gerald, Oliver, of Doneany, gent.—Geoghegan, Lawrence, of Erbertun, gent.—Fitz Walter, of Grangemore, gent.—Fitz Gerald, Thomas, of Littlebealan, gent.—O'Gormooll, Brian, of Tully, clerk.— Fitz Gerald, Oliver, of Donfert, clerke.—Gibbons, Henry, of Naas, clerke.—M'Grady, Mahond, of the same, clerke.—Fitz Gerald, Thomas, of Lisscrosselaghan, gent.—Geoghegan, Dermott, of Cardiffstowne, clerke. —Fitz Gerald, Pierce, of Ballyrone, in comitatu Regis [King's County], gent.—Fitz Gerald, John, of Rathwheat, in county Catherlagh, gent.— Fitz Gerald, Garrett Fitz Maurice, of Lackagh, gent.—Fitz Gerald, Nicholas, of Killcock, gent.—Fitz Gerald, James M'Walter, of Castlemartin, Esq.—Gowe, Brian, of Rathbran, in county Wickloe, yeoman.— Grace, Gerald, of the same, gent.—Fitz Gerald, James, of Blackhall, gent.—Fitz Gerald, William, late of Hartwell, gent.—Fitz Gerald, William, of Blackhall, Esq.—Fitz Gerald, William, of Blackhall, Esq.—Fitz Gerald, John, of the same, gent.—Fitz Gerald, Richard, of Landstowne,

gent.—Fitz Gerald, William Fitz Edward, late of Hartwell, gent.—
Garaght, James M'Hugh, of Span, gent.

WICKLOE:—Grace, Redmond, of Knockbane, gent.—Gormogan, John,
of Ballynecarrige, gent.—Goodman, James, of Cronroe, gent.—Gowe,
Dermott M'Shane, of Ballynornan, gent.—M'Gerald, Brian, of Ballyne-
cola, gent.

DUBLIN:—Golding, Richard, of Kinsaley, gent.—Goodman, senior,
James, of Loghnanstowne, gent.—Goodman, junior, James, of the same, gent.
—Goodman, Rowland, of Ballinthea, gent.—Goodman, James, of Ballinthea,
gent.—Goodman, senior, James, of Loghnanstowne, gent.—Goodman,
junior, James, of the same, gent.—Gormanston, Nicholas [Preston], Vis-
count] of.—Golding, Richard, of Kinsaley, gent.—Fitz Gerald, Pierce, of
Ballysonan, in county Kildare, gent.—Garvy, William, of Dublin, yeoman.—Geogh, Richard, of Luske, yeoman.—Gall, Peter, of Ballykea,
yeoman.—Geogh, John, of Heathton, yeoman.—Fitz Gerald, Pierce, of
Ballysonan, in county Kildare, armiger.

Persons indicted of treason in the King's Bench, in Easter Terme,
anno decimo octavo Domini Caroli Regis, 1642, and outlawed thereupon :

KILDARE:—Fitz Gerald, Gerald, of Brownestowne, gent.—Fitz
Gerald, Richard, of Ouldtowne, gent.—Fitz Gerald, Pierce, of Ballysonan,
Esq.—Golding, Walter, of Killdrought, yeoman.—Grig, Lawrence, of
Ardengrosse, gent.—Geydon, John, of Irishtowne, Esq.—Fitz Gerald,
James, of Lackagh, gent.

MEATH:—Gormanstowne, Nicholas [Preston], Viscount.—Garrett,
James, of Dunboyne, gent.—FitzGerald, Sir Luke, of Tecroghan, Knight.—
Geoghegan, Thomas, of Bealfeaghan, gent.—Fitz Gerald, Richard, of Rath-
roan, gent.—Gernon, George, of Agherpallice, gent.—Fitz Gerald, James,
of Dunboyne, gent.—Garvy, Richard, of Painstowne, yeoman.—M'Ginne,
Farsey ; M'Gownagh, John, of Oristowne, yeomen.—M'Garre, Shane ;
M'Garre, Pharsey, of Ladyrath, yeomen.—Garvy, Edward ; Garvy, Francis;
Garvy, Christopher, of the Grange, gent[n].

CIVIT: DUBLIN :—Gormanstowne, Nicholas [Preston], Viscount.

DUBLIN :—Fitz Gerald, John, of Walshestowne, in county Kildare, gent.—Fitz Gerald, Thomas, of the same, gent.—Goodman, senior, James, of Loughlinstowne, gent.—Golding, Richard, of Kinsaley, gent.—Viscount Gormanstowne, Nicholas [Preston].—Fitz Gerald, Pierce, of Ballysonan, in county Kildare, Esq.—Fitz Gerald, Clement, of Kilcoskan, gent.—Fitz Gerald, Bartholomew, of the same, gent.—Fitz Gerald, James, of Dunboyne, in county Meath.

WICKLOE :—Gough, William, of Ballyeanuir, Esq.—Gough, Patrick, of Arckloe, gent.—Glasse, Donell, of Tomcoill, gent.

DUBLIN :—Griffin, Walter, of Hacketstowne, gent.—Goodman, James, of Loghnanstowne, gent.

MEATH :—Fitz Gerald, Sir Luke, of Tecroghan, Knight.—Fitz Gerald, Richard, of Rathroane, gent.

Persons indicted of treason in the county of Corke, att the Sessions held att Youghal, and returned in the King's Bench, the second of August, 1642, and outlawed in the King's Bench for the same :

CORKE :—Gallway, Sir Jeffery, of Tyssaxenbeg, Baronett.—Gibbon, William, Fitz Richard, of Killtoagh, gent.—Fitz Gibbon, William, of Milltowne, gent.—Fitz Gibbon, Maurice, of Ballynegrenogg, gent.—Fitz Gibbon, Gerald, of Colecemmine, gent.—Fitz Gerald, Maurice, Castellyshyne, Esq.—Goggane, Peter, of Ballynecourty, gent.—Goggane, William, of Bearnehely, gent.—Goggane, Phillip, of Knockanevarody, gent.—Goggane, James, of the same, gent.—Goggane, Edmond, of Ringarrime, gent.—Goggane, James, of Ballenaboy, gent.—Goggane, Edmond, of Bearnehealy, gent.—O'Garvane, Donnogh, of Clonmyne, gent.—M'Grugh, Thomas, of Dromleigh, gent.—Fitz Gibbon, Garret, of Killmagneary, gent.—Gerald, Thomas Fitz Edmond Fitz Richard, of Ballybane, gent.—Fitz Gerald, Garrett Fitz James, of Dromkale, gent.—Gold, Garrett, of Castletowne, gent.—Gerrald, Richard Fitz Edmond, of Rosteallane, Esq.—Gerrald, Garrett Fitz Edmond, of the same, gent.—Goold, John Fitz Richard, of Towerbridge, merchant.—Goold, James, Fitz Richard, of the same, merchant.—Gallway, John Fitz Christopher, of Blarny, gent.—Gallway, William ; Gallway, David ; of the same, gent[n].

Persons indicted of treason in the King's Bench, in Hilary Terme, anno decimo septimo Caroli Regis, 1641, and outlawed for the same:

MEATH :—Hill, Sir William, of Ballybegg, Knight.—Hussey, Hugh, of Rathkenny, gent.—Houlder, John, of Ballymoghan, gent.—Hussey, Patrick, of Galltrim, Esq.—Halpenny, Cornelius, of Augistowne, gent.

KILDARE :—Higgin, Petrus, of Naas, clerke.—Hussey, Matheus, of Rathcoffy, clerke.—Hussey, Alexander, of Timoghoe, clerke.—Harrold, Gerald, of Kildrought [Celbridge], gent.—Harrold, Richard, of Killheele, gent.—Houlder, John, of Kill, gent.—Hanly, Connor, of Naas, clerke.— Hanly, Donagh, of the same, clerke.—Hussey, Lucas, of Ouldtowne, in county Meath, gent.—Hickie, Cornelius, of Rathbran, in county Wickloe, yeoman.—M'Hugh, Donnell, of Ballaghmoone, yeoman.

WICKLOE :—Harrold, Thomas, of Coolnehorne, gent.—M'Hugh, Melaghlin, of Ballyvane, gent.—Hill, Phillipp, of Dromyn, gent.

DUBLIN :—Hore, Phillip, of Killsalaghan, Esq.—Hollywood, Nicholas, of Tartane [Artane], Esq.—Hore, James, of Killsalaghan, gent.—Hackett, George, of Ballinehinsy, in county Wickloe, gent.—Heyward, John, of Rathenny, gent.—Horish, John, of Ballylaghall, gent.—Harne, Richard, of Stacoole, gent.—Hayward, John, of Rathenny, yeoman.—Hetherington, Charles, of Rathcoole, gent.—Hart, Patrick, of Fosterstowne, yeoman.— Hurlston, William, of Skerries, yeoman.—Hurlston, Jasper, of Drogheda, merchant.—Hurlston, Thomas, of Skerries, gent.—Hamilton, Thomas, of Luske, yeoman.—Halpenny, John Ogie, of the same, yeoman.—Hetherington, Edward, of Rathcoole, gent.—Howard, John, of Rathenny, yeoman.

Persons indicted of treason in the King's Bench, in Easter Terme, anno decimo octavo Caroli Regis, 1642, and outlawed thereupon :

MEATH :—Hussey, Edward, of Moylehussey, Esq.—Hill, Sir William, of Ballybegg, Knight.—Hussey, John, of Radanstown, gent.—Hussey, Marcus, of the same, gent.—Hussey, Walter, of Rath, gent.—Hussey, Nicholas, of Gallowe, gent.—Hussey, Oliver, of Togher, gent.—Hussey, Hugh, of Rathenny, gent.—Halpenny, Terrence, of Roeston, yeoman.

COUNTY DUBLIN :—Hollywood, Christopher, of Tartaine [Artane], gent.—Hore, Phillipp, of Killsalaghan, Esq.—Hussey, Edward, of Mulhussey, in county Meath, Esq.—Hollywood, Nicholas, of Tartaine, Esq.

WICKLOE :—Hill, Patrick, of Dromin, Esq.—Heyden, Richard, of Aghoole, gent.

Persons indicted of treason, in the King's Bench, in Trinity Terme, anno decimo octavo Caroli Regis, 1642, and outlawed thereupon :

DUBLIN :—Heyward, John, of Rathenny, yeoman.—Horish, John, Ballyboughall, yeoman.

MEATH :—Hussey, Hugh, of Galtrym, gent.

Persons indicted of treason in the county of Corke, att the sessions holden att Youghall, and returned in the King's Bench, the second of August, 1642, and outlawed in the King's Bench for the same :

CORKE :—O'Hallyhy, John, of Ballyburden.—O'Hallyhy, Donogh, of the same, Doctor in Physick.—Hutchcocke, John, of Killmurry, gent.—Hodnett, Edmund, of Court M'Sheary, gent.—O'Hea, Thomas, of Aghermilly, gent.—O'Hea, Thomas, of Pallice, gent.—O'Hart, John, of Tullyneiskine, gent.—O'Hea, Teige, of Corbully, gent.—O'Hea, John Oge, of Carogroe, gent.—O'Hea, Donogh, of the same, gent.—O'Hea, Donogh, of Shannacoole, gent.—Hodnett, Richard, of Barrireagh, gent.—O'Hea, William Oge, of Pallice, gent.—O'Hart, Teige, of Knock, gent.—Hodnett, James Fitz Edmond, of Court M'Sheary, gent.—O'Hea, Mahoone, of Kilberrane, gent.—Hurly, Randle, of Beallenecarrigy, gent.—Hurly, Randall Oge, of the same, gent.—Hurly, William, of Ballinvarde, gent.—Hurly, William, of Lisgubby, gent.—O'Hannifare, Teige, of Agheleuane, gent.—Hurly, Donogh M'Donnell, of Bunnumugiry, gent.—Hurly, Ellen, of Grillagh Ighteragh, widowe.—Hurly, Donell Oge, of Killbrittaine, gent.—O'Haughlin, Dermod M'Fynnyne, of Rathdrought, gent.—Hurly, James, of Ballinvurde, gent.—Hurly, James, of Grillagh, gent.—Hennesy, William, of Ballynustealy, gent.—O'Highlaghy, William, of Bullyvorny, gent.—O'Hiallighy, Oliver, of Fornaght, gent.—O'Hiallighly, Donell, of Killcullen, gent.—O'Hiallighly, Thomas, of Gowlane, gent.—O'Hierlighy, Thomas, of Kippagh, gent.—O'Hiallighy, Donogh, of Monitagirta, gent.—O'Hiallighy, Thomas M'Meater, of Barrecarhine, gent.—O'Hierlighy,

Donogh Oge, of Kippagh, gent.—O'Hiallighy, Maurice, of Killinterane, gent.—O'Hanylyn, Fynnyn, of Castlemore, gent.—O'Hiallighy, John, of the same, gent.—O'Hiallighy, Thomas, of Moshanglasse, gent.—O'Hierlihy, John, of Ballyvorny, gent.—O'Haly, David, of Killcrea, gent.

Persons indicted of treason in the King's Bench, in Hillary Terme, anno decimo octavo Caroli Regis, 1642, and thereupon outlawed :

DUBLIN :—Hunter, George, late of Wyanstowne, gent.—Horish, John, of Ballyboghall, gent.—Horish, Richard, of the same, gent.—Horish, Christopher, of the same, gent.—Horish, Valentine, of the same, gent.— Horish, Richard, of Grange, gent.—Horish, James, of the same, gent.— Harford, Patrick, of Cottrellstowne, gent.

Persons indicted of treason in his Majestie's Court of King's Bench, in Hillary terme, anno decimo septimo Caroli Regis, 1641, and outlawed thereupon :

MEATH :—Jellowes, John, of Jellowestowne, gent.

DUBLIN :—Jones, James, of the Ward, gent.—Jordan, Symon, of Darbiston, gent.—Jones, Thomas, of Swords, yeoman.—Jordan, Richard, of the Raglas of Luske, yeoman.—Jordan, Patrick, of Luske, yeoman.— Jordan, Patrick, of the same, yeoman.

Persons indicted of treason in the King's Bench, in Easter Terme, anno decimo octavo Caroli Regis, and thereupon outlawed, 1642 :

KILDARE :—Ikerryn, Pierce [Butler], Viscount of.

MEATH :—Joanes, Patrick, of Kells, gent.—Joanes, Thomas, of Slane, gent.—Joanes, Robert, of Painstowne, yeoman.—Joanes, Martin, of Oristowne, yeoman.—Joanes, Luke, of the same, yeoman.

CIVIT: DUBLIN :—Iniskillin, Connor [Maguire], Lord Baron of.

DUBLIN :—Jordan, James, of Ballinagwire, gent.—Jordan, Richard, of Swords, yeoman.—Jans, James, of The Ward, gent.—Jordan, Ralph, of the parish of St. Michael the Archangel, Dublin, merchant.

DOWNE :—Iveagh, Arthur, Viscount Magenis.

Persons indicted of treason in the county of Corke, att the sessions holden att Youghall, and returned in the King's Bench, the second of August, 1642, and outlawed in the King's Bench for the same :

CORKE :—Fitz Gibbon, John, of Killmagneary, gent.—Ilotane, Donnell M'Teige ; Ilotane, Dermod M'Teige ; Ilotane, Mahowne M'Teige, of Killmolody, gentⁿ.—Iloghy, Donnell Oge, Meneshaneglasse, gent.— Iloghy, Owen Oge, of the same, gent.—Ikerryn, Peirce [Butler], Lord Viscount.

Persons indicted of treason in the King's Bench, in Hillary Terme, anno decimo septimo Caroli Regis, 1641[-2], and outlawed thereupon :

MEATH :—Kelly, John, of Falrath, gent.

KILDARE :—Kildare, Elizabeth, Countess Dowager of.[1]—Kavanagh, Gerald, of Killdrought [Celbridge], clerke.—Kerdiffe, Oliver, of Kerdiffstowne, gent.—Kerdiffe, John, of the same, gent.—Kerdiffe, James, of the same, gent.—Killan, Barnaby, of Downings, gent.—Kent, Christopher, of Danestowne, in county Meath, gent.—O'Kelly, William, of Caddamstowne, gent.—M'Keoghoe, Thomas M'Mullmirry, of Knockandarragh, in county Wickloe, gent.—M'Keoghoe, William M'Shane M'Farrell, of the same, gent.—Kerdiffe, John, of Kerdiffestowne, gent.—Kerdiffe, James, of the same, gent.—Kerin, Morrogh, of Ballaghmoone, yeoman.—Kinsellagh, Dermott, of the same, yeoman.—O'Kelly, Shane, of the same, yeoman.

WICKLOE :—Kerovane, Connor, of Knockbane, yeoman.—Kerny, William, of Wickloe, tanner.

DUBLIN :—Kellie, Richard, late of Pasloeston, yeoman.—Kent, Christopher, of Gortstowne, gent.—King, George, of Clantarfe, gent.—Kelly, James, of Luske, yeoman.—Kelly, James, of Luske, yeoman.—Kelly, James, of the same, yeoman.—Kelly, Bartholomew, of the same, yeoman.—Kelly, Thomas, of Ballyowen, yeoman.—Kelly, Mathew, of Luske, yeoman.—Kelly, Richard, of Johnston, yeoman.—Keiegan, John, of the same, yeoman.—Kernan, Phillip, of Luske, yeoman.—Kelly, James, of same, yeoman.

Persons indicted of treason in the King's Bench, in Easter terme, anno decimo octavo Caroli Regis, 1642, and outlawed thereupon :

---

1. Relict of Gerald, fourteenth Earl of Kildare, and daughter of Christopher Nugent, Lord Delvin. *See, also,* vol. ii. p. lxiv.

27

MEATH :—King, George, of Galtrim, gent.—Kelly, William, of Allenstowne, turner.—Kittagh, William, of Isakstowne, yeoman.—Knavagh, Patrick ; Knavagh, Hugh, of Cristowne, yeomen.

COUNTY DUBLIN :—Kegane, Donogh, of Ballyowen, yeoman.—Kelly, John, Wimbleton, gent.—Kilsagh, Patrick, of Ratouth, in county Meath, gent.

Persons indicted of treason in the county of Corke, att the sessions holden att Youghall, the second of August, 1642 (and returned in the King's Bench), and outlawed in the King's Bench for the same :

CORKE :—O'Keiffe, Donell, of Dromagh, gent.—O'Keiffe, Cornelius Oge, of Culleine, gent.—O'Keiffe, Keiffe, of Killcollman, gent.— O'Keiffe, Donogh, M'Donell, of Droumagh, gent.—O'Keiffe, Donnogh Oge, of the same, gent.

Persons indicted of treason in the King's Bench, in Hillary Terme, anno Regis Caroli decimo octavo, 1642[-3], and outlawed thereupon :

DUBLIN :—Kelly, William, of the parish of St. Nicholas Without the Walls, gent.

Persons indicted of treason in his Majestie's Court of King's Bench, in Hillary Terme, anno xvii. Caroli Regis, 1641[-2], and outlawed thereupon :

MEATH :—Leynes, Gerald, of Knock, Esq.—Lyneam, Richard, of Adamstowne.—Lowth, Oliver [Plunkett], Lord Baron of.—Leynes, Lawrence, of Donowre.

KILDARE :—Long, Thomas, of Castledillon, gent.—Lattin, John, of Morrishtowne, gent.—Ley, John, of Rathbridge, Esq.—Ley, Andrew, of Calveston, gent.—Lea, David, of Ballynekilly, in county Catherlagh, gent.—Lyen, Owen, of Pitchfordstowne, yeoman.—Linch, Miles, of Clomorry, in county Meath.

WICKLOE :—Linchie, Brian, of Powerscourt, gent.

DUBLIN :—Lyneham, Bartholomew, of Swords, yeoman.—Lemon, Richard, of Rathenny, yeoman.—St. Lawrence, Walter, of Carchagh, gent.—Long, James, of Abbotstowne, gent.—Long, John, of the same, gent.—Leyne, C.lus, of Ballynure, in county Wickloe, gent.—Lock,

Henry, of Terrellstowne, yeoman.—Long, Richard, of Abbottstowne, gent.
—St. Lawrence, Walter, of Carchagh, gent.—St. Lawrence, Francis, of
Drogheda, merchant.

Persons indicted of treason in the King's Bench, in Easter Terme,
anno decimo octavo Caroli Regis, 1642, and outlawed thereupon :

KILDARE:—Lee, John, of Rathbride, Esq.—Lyons, Christopher, of
Ardrusse, yeoman.

MEATH:—Lyneham, Richard, of Adamstowne, gent.—Lowth, Oliver,
Lord Baron of.—Lynes, Garrett, of Knock, Esq.—Lyneham, Richard, of
Adamstowne, gent.—Lynch, Oliver, of Dublin, merchant.—Lynch, Law-
rence, of Croganstowne, gent.—Ledwich, Richard, of Coppogh, in county
Westmeath, gent.—Lynehy, Bryan ; Lynehy, Daniell ; Luttrell, Robert, of
Cristowne, yeomen.—Luttrell, Oliver, of Tankardstowne, Esq.

DUBLIN:—Lyneham, James, of the parish of St. Michael the Archangel, Dublin, merchant.—Lynch, Oliver, of Dublin, merchant.

Persons indicted of treason in the King's Bench, in Trinity Terme,
anno decimo octavo, Caroli Regis, 1642, and outlawed thereupon :

MEATH:—Leynes, Gerald, of Knock, Esq.—Lyneham, Richard, of
Adamstowne, gent.

Persons indicted of treason in the county of Corke att the Sessions
holden att Youghall, and returned in the King's Bench, the second of
August, 1642, and outlawed in the King's Bench for the same :

CORKE:—Long, John, of Mountlong, Esq.—Long, James, of Pully-
moghelly, gent.—O'Leyne, Melaghlin, of Jordanstowne, gent.—Long,
John, Jun., of Mountlong, gent.—Long, James Fitz-John, of the same,
gent.—O'Loaghly, John, of Robertstowne, gent.—O'Lemy, Dermott, of
Killcaskane, gent.—O'Leary, Connor, of Carrignycorry, gent.—Long,
John, of Cannawey, gent.—O'Leary, Awliffe, of Currowhy, gent.—
O'Leary, Cnogher, of Gortivachy, gent.—O'Leary, Art, of Tynegeagh,
gent.—O'Leary, Dermod Oge, of Tyraneasye, gent.—O'Leary, Cnogher,
of Gortinechonebully, gent.—O'Leary, Cornelius M'Donagh, of Grange,
gent.—O'Leary, Lisagh, of Inshuorane, gent.—O'Leary, Teige, of Tir-
remspiddogy, gent.—O'Leary, Teige M'Dermody, of Comenyhabelly,

gent.—O'Leary, Art, of Mullinevarrodigy, gent.—O'Leary, Donnell, of Grange, gent.—O'Leary, Teige, of Carrignecorry, gent.—O'Leary, Donnell; O'Leary, Dermod, of the same, gent[n].—O'Leary, Art, of Carrignegillagh, gent.

DUBLIN :—St. Lawrence, George, late of Wyanstowne, gent.

Persons indicted of treason in the King's Bench, in Hillary Terme, anno decimo septimo Caroli Regis, 1641[-2], and outlawed thereupon :

MEATH :—Might, Thomas, of Trym, gent.—Magennis, of Iveagh, Arthur, Viscount.—Moore, Roger, of Ballyna, in county Kildare, Esq.— Moore, Bartholomew, of Gawlestone, gent.—Mape, Garrett, of Maprath, gent.—Mape, Edward, of the same, gent.—Moole, John, of Gormanstowne, gent.—Moole, Walter, of the same, gent.—Magennold, Cahell, of Augistowne, gent.—Magarre, Murrogh, of the same, gent.—Magarre, Thomas, of the same, gent.—Mulpatrick, John, of the same, gent.—Mulpatrick, Patrick, of the same, gent.—Magenis, Daniell, of the same, gent.—Magennold, Patrick, of the same, gent.

KILDARE :—St. Michael, Christopher, of Terrelston, gent.—Moore, Roger, of Ballyna, Esq.—[1]Moore, Lysagh, of the same, gent.[2]—St. Michael, Peter, of Terrillstowne, gent.—Missett, James, of Castlemartin, gent.— Missett, George, of Kilcullenbridge, yeoman.—Maguire, Donogh, of Castlemartin, yeoman.—Missett, Lawrence, of the same, gent.

WICKLOE :—Melaghlin, William Duffe, of Ballshanteriffe, gent.— Moore, Lisagh, of Ballyna, in the county of Kildare, Esq.—Magie, John, of Rathenny, yeoman.—Marly, George, of Feltrym, yeoman.—Murfie, Michael, of Balruddery, yeoman.—Moore, Roger, of Ballyna, in county Kildare, Esq.—Moore, Lysagh, of the same, gent.—Mulkeran, Thomas, of Rathbray, in county Wickloe, clerk.—Manwaring, Randall, of Baltinglass, in comitatu predicto, gent.—Moore, Richard, of Coolock, yeoman.—Murghoe, Thady, of Dunganstowne, yeoman.—Murtagh, Laghlin, of the same, yeoman.—Mongan, Mathew, of Swords, yeoman.—Malone, John, late of Skerries, clerke.—Malone, Christopher, of Drogheda, merchant.—Murfie,

1, 2. *See* vol ii. p. 403.

Michael, of Balruddery, yeoman.—Morgan, Thomas, of Luske, yeoman.—Meyler, Christopher, of the same, yeoman.—M'Mahowne, John, of Rush, yeoman.

KILDARE :—Mountgarrett, Richard [Butler], Viscount.—Mangan, Teige, of Killussy, yeoman.—Murphy, alias Murchoe, Donogh, of Clane, clerke.—Mulchael, Nicholas, of Athy, merchant.—Might, Henry, of Trym, gent.—Malone, William, of Lissemullen, Esq.—Moore, Bartholomew, of Dowanstowne, gent.—Morgan, Richard, of Kelles, gent.—Mullsacke, Walter, of Oristowne, yeoman.—Mullbredy, Patrick Bane, of Ballinreske, yeoman.—M'Manneghan, John, of the Grange, yeoman.—Magrath, Richard, of Fyanstowne, yeoman.—Magrath, Patrick, of the same, yeoman.

COUNTY DUBLIN :—Murry, William, of the Kill, yeoman, [and] Owny, his wife.—Murphy, George, late of the parish of St. Michael, Dublin, merchant.—Murphy, Michael, of Balruddery, gent.—Moore, Lisagh, of Ballyna, in county Kildare, gent.—Miles, John, of Carkagh, gent.—Might, Henry, of Trym, gent.—Mapas, Christopher, late of the parish of St. Michael the Archangel, merchant.—Mapas, Nicholas, late of the same parish, gent.—Meara, Dermott, of the parish of St. Warboroughes, Dublin, Doctor in Physicke, [and] Katherin, his wife.

WICKLOE :—Mainwaring, William, of Feddencoile, gent.—Moor, Thomas, of Walterstowne, gent.—Moyle, William, of Ackikeagh, gent.

Persons indicted of Treason in the county of Corke att the sessions holden att Youghall the second of August, 1642, and returned in the King's Bench, and outlawed in the King's Bench for the same.

CORKE :—Magner, Robert, of Castlemagner, gent.—Malefont, James, of Arlandstowne, gent.—Mahowny, Keane, of Geary, gent.—Malefont, Robert, of Watersland, gent.—Malefont, William ; Malefont, Gerald, of the same, gentⁿ.—Malefont, Phillipp, of Faghineteskane, gent.—Malefont, William, of Knockleigh, gent.—Murphy, Donogh, of Brinny, gent.—Miagh, John, of Longhurle, gent.—O'Mahowny, Dermott, alias Muskrigh, of Shaghenore, gent.—O'Melaghlin, Donogh Oge, of Kilbarry, gent.—O'Mahowny, Connor, of Leamcon, gent.—O'Mahowny, Florence, alias Fynnyn, of Ardavingy, gent.—O'Mahowny, Keane, alias Mahowny, of

Ballyneskeagh, gent.—O'Mahowny, Donell, of the same, gent.—O'Mahowny, Donell, alias Mahowny Foune, of Carrigynaghy, gent.—O'Mahowny, Cnogher M'Fynnyn, of Gortranully, gent.—O'Mahowny, Dermod,
of Fernane, gent.—M'Mullmurry, Edmond, of Mohellagh, gent.—Murphy,
Connor, of Blarny, gent.—M'Murrogh, Donell M'Owen, of Annaghally,
gent.—Mathew, David, of Castlemore, gent.—Mountgarrett, Richard
[Butler], Lord Viscount of.—O'Mahowny, Connor, . alias M'Idwylia, of
Ballyrisad, gent.

Persons indicted of treason in the King's Bench, in Hillary Terme,
anno Regis Caroli decimo octavo, 1642[-3], and outlawed thereupon :

DUBLIN :—Magill, John, of Naptowne, gent.

WICKLOE :—Megagh, alias Conry, Maurice, of Donard, clerke.—
Mannering, Randall, of Dunbouke, gent.—Mannering, Charles, of the
same, gent.—Mannering, Edward, of the same, gent.—Moore, Manus, of
the same, gent.—M'Manus, Owen, of the same, gent.—M'Melaughlin,
Edmond, of Ballyshane Duffe, gent.—M'Morish, Nicholas, of Maghery-
more, gent.

Persons indicted of treason in the King's Bench, in Hillary Terme,
anno decimo septimo Caroli Regis, 1641[-2], and outlawed thereupon :

MEATH :—Nettervill, of Dowth, Nicholas [Nettervill], Viscount.—
Nettervill, Luke, of Corballies, in the county of Dublin, Esq.

KILDARE :—Nugent, Richard, of Crockett, gent.—Nugent, Edward,
of the same, gent.—Nangle, Rowland, of Ardrasse, gent.—Nolan, John, of
Killcool, gent.—Neall, Thomas, of Athy, yeoman.—Nangle, Mathew, of
Ballysax, gent.—Nangle, Robert, of the same, gent.—Norreis, Maurice, of
Kilbegge, gent.—Nugent, Robert, of Killika, gent.—Nangle, Peter, of
Naas, clerke.

WICKLOE :—Norris, Thomas, of Rathmeloige, gent.

DUBLIN :—Nettervill, Luke, of Corballies, Esq.—Nolan, Nicholas, of
Rathenny, yeoman.—Nettervill, Luke, of Corballies, Esq.—Neall, James,
of Feltrim.

Persons indicted of treason in the King's Bench, in Easter Terme,
anno decimo octavo Caroli Regis, 1642, and outlawed thereupon :

KILDARE :—Nangle, Robert, of Ballysaxe, gent.—Norries, James, of Killdroght, yeoman.

MEATH :—Nettervill, Nicholas [Nettervill], Viscount of Dowth.— Nangle, Thomas, of the Navan, called Baron of the Navan.—Nettervill, Thomas, of Blackcastle, gent.—Nugent, Christopher, of Halton, gent.— Nugent, Sir Thomas, of Moyrath, Barronet.—Nangle, Joselyn, of Kildalky, gent.—Nugent, James, of Dromcree, in the county of Westmeath, Esq.—Neyle, Patrick, of Roeston, yeoman.—Neyle, Thomas, of the same, yeoman.

DUBLIN :—Nettervill, Luke, of Corballies, Esq.—Nugent, Christopher, of Halton, in county Meath, Esq.

MEATH :—Nangle, Mathew, of Rathmore, gent.

Persons indicted of treason in the county of Corke att the sessions holden at Youghall, and returned in the King's Bench, and outlawed in the King's Bench for the same :

CORKE :—Nugent, James, of Aghemarten, gent.—Nugent, Garrett, of Commyne, gent.—Nugent, Richard, of Carrybehagh, gent.—Nugent, Patrick, of Aghasollus, gent.—Nash, James ; Nash, Phillipp, of Coolegeile, gent[n].—Nugent, Patricke, of Agherlasse, gent.—Nagle, Richard, of Moneannyenny, gent.—Nagle, James, of Glannor, gent.—Nugent, Redmond, of Castletowne, gent.—Nugent, Christopher, of the same, gent.—Nagle, John, of Moneannimy, gent.—Nugent, Fitz Garrett, Thomas, Tracteny, gent.

MEATH : Nettervill, Robert, of Knockomber, gent.

Persons indicted of treason in the King's Bench, in Hillary Terme, anno decimo octavo Caroli Regis, 1642[-3].

KILDARE :—Owgan, Oliver, of Downings, gent.—Orde, Edward, of Killcullenbridge, innkeeper.

Persons indicted of Treason in the King's Bench, in Easter Terme, anno decimo octavo Caroli Regis, 1642 :

KILDARE :—Owgan [Wogan], Nicholas, of Rathcoffy, Esq.

WICKLOE :—Garrett Oge, of the parish of Wickloe, gent.

Persons indicted of treason in the county of Corke att the sessions houlden att Youghall (and returned in the King's Bench) the second of August, 1642 :

CORKE:—M'Owen, Boy, Donnell, of Leytrim, gent.—M'Owen, Teige, of Parhoe, gent.—M'Owen, Dermod, of Knockanroe, gent.

Persons indicted in the King's Bench of treason, in Hillary Terme, anno decimo septimo Caroli Regis, 1641[-2], and outlawed thereupon :

MEATH:—Preston [*blank*], of Rogerstowne, gent.—Plunket, James, of Killeene, Esq.—Plunkett, Michael, of Telltowne, gent.

KILDARE:—Plunkett, John, of Darre, clerke.—Peppard, Walter, of Killkae, gent.—Preston, James, of Grangemore, gent.—Pilsworth, John, of Bert, gent.—Plunkett, Gerald, of Garvoge, gent.—Pilsworth, Thomas, of Bealashanna, gent.—Pilsworth, Edward, of Toberogan, gent.

WICKLOE :—M'Patrick, John, of Ballynecarige, yeoman.—Peirse, John, of Wickloe, gent.—Pluck, William, of Ballyeres, gent.—Phelim, Cahir, of Knockbrandon, gent.—Plack, William, of Ballyissa, gent.

DUBLIN:—Parker, Edward, late of Templeoge, yeoman.—Plunkett, Robert, of the Grange of Portmarnocke, gent.—Pasmere, senior, John, of Ballruddery, yeoman.

Persons indicted of treason in the King's Bench, in Easter Terme, anno decimo octavo Caroli Regis, 1642, and outlawed thereupon :

KILDARE:—Purcell, William, of Irishtowne, clerk.

MEATH :—Plunkett, George, of Killeene, Esq.—Plunkett, Nicholas, of Killallon, Esq.—Penteny, Richard, of the Knock, gent.—Plunkett, Nicholas, of Balrath, Esq.—Preston, Richard, of Kellelan, gent.—Pallys, William, late of Dublin, gent.—Plunkett, Robert, of Athboy, merchant.— Preston, Robert, of Gormanstowne, Esq.—Plunkett, Christopher, of Girly, Esq.—Plunkett, Thomas, of Clonecatt, gent.—Plunkett, Thomas, of Girly, gent.—Plunkett, Christopher, of the same, gent.—Phepoe, Robert, of Dunboyne, gent.—Plunkett, George, of Roddenstowne, gent.—Plunkett, Alexander, of Isackstowne, gent.—Plunkett, Patrick, of the Grange, gent. —Plunkett, Henry, of the same, gent.—Plunkett, Richard, late of Dunsaghlin, in county Dublin, Esq.[1]—Porter, Richard, of Oldbridge, in county

1. In margin : "Civitat: Dublin."

Meath, gent.[1]—Plunkett, James, of Killeene, in the same county, Esq.—
Preston, Robert, of Ballmadun, Esq.—Pallys, Andrewe, of Collatrath,
gent.—Proctor, Thomas, of Coolemullen, in county Meath, Esq.—Penteny,
Richard, of Knock, gent.

Wickloe :—Pasmere, Nicholas, of Milltowne, gent.—Ponten, Lodo-
vicke, of Newtowne, gent.

Persons indicted of treason in the King's Bench, in Trinity Terme,
anno decimo octavo Caroli Regis, 1642, and outlawed thereupon :

Dublin :—Pasmore, Robert, of Ballruddery, clerke.

Meath :—Plunkett, Thomas, of Girlee, gent.—Plunkett, Patrick,
of Crossekeile, gent.—Plunkett, Robert, of Rathmore, Esq.

Persons indicted of treason in the county of Corke, att the sessions
houlden att Youghall, and returned into the King's Bench, the second of
August, 1642, and outlawed in the King's Bench for the same :

Corke :—Power, David Fitz John Fitz William, of Rohwus, gent.—
Patrick, Edmond, alias Naghter, of Dromenyne, gent.—Pounch, Richard,
of Longharte, gent.—M'Phelim, Haleigh, of Ballynoe, gent.—Power, Robert,
of Castletowne, gent.

Persons indicted of treason in the King's Bench, in Michaelmas
terme, anno Regis Caroli decimo octavo, 1642 :

Meath :—Plunkett, Henry, of Liskerrivan, gent.

Persons indicted of treason, in Hillary Terme, in the King's Bench,
anno decimo septimo Caroli Regis, 1641[-2], and outlawed thereupon :

Wickloe :—Quyn, Richard, of Ballyhoicke, gent.—Quyn, Loghlon, of
the same, gent.—Quaytrott, Francis, of Newcastle, gent.—Quyn, Edmond,
of Ballinteskin, clerke.—Quinn, Richard, of Ballyhoicke, gent.

Persons indicted of treason in the King's Bench, in Easter Terme,
anno decimo octavo Caroli Regis, 1642, and outlawed thereupon :

County Dublin :—M'Quy, Donnell, of the Kill, yeoman, [and] Mary,
his wife.—Quyn, Christopher, late of the parish of St. Michael the Archangel, Dublin, merchant.

1. In margin : " Dublin."

Persons indicted of treason in the county of Corke, att the sessions houlden att Youghall, and returned into the King's Bench, the second of August, 1642, and outlawed in the King's Bench for the same:—

CORKE:—M'Quirke, Teige, of Bally M'Quirke, gent.—M'Quirke, Donnell M'Teige, of the same, gent.—M'Quirke, Cornelius M'Teige, of the same, gent.

Persons indicted of treason in Hilary Terme, in the King's Bench, anno decimo septimo Caroli Regis, 1641[-2], and outlawed thereupon:

MEATH:—Reade, Martin, of Scurlockstowne, gent.—Rely, Philipp, of Augistowne, gent.

KILDARE:—Rooth, Thomas, of Castledermott, gent.—Rooth, Michael, of the same, clerke.—Rooth, Andrew, of Tymolin, clerke.—Rochford, Walter, of Mullaghcash, clerke.—Rochford, James, of Clane, gent.—Ryan, Robert, of Killcullenbridge, yeoman.

DUBLIN:—Rochford, Alexander, of Ballincarige, gent.—Rowen, Laurence, of Finglas, clerke.—Russell, Thomas Roe, of Rush, gent.—Roe, John, of Kilbarrocke, yeoman.—Russell, Christopher, of Seaton, gent.—Russell, Andrewe, of Swords, yeoman.—Russell, Patricke, of Brownstowne, gent.—Russell, Nicholas, of Collinstowne, gent.—Russell, Thomas, of Dreynham, gent.—Richards, John, of Cappocke, yeoman.—Russell, Andrewe, of Swords, yeoman.—Rely, James, of Clantarfe, yeoman.—Rely, Owen, of Pelletstowne, yeoman.—Rely, Gerrald, of the same, yeoman.—Ratty, John, of Courtduffe, yeoman.—Rochford, Robert, of Killbridge, in county Meath, gent.—Russell, Francis, of Killrush, gent.—Ratty, Thomas, of Newtowne, yeoman.—M'Rory, Patrick, of Luske, yeoman.—Ratty, John, of the same, yeoman.—Reynolds, Patrick, of Newcastle, gent.[1]—Rely, James, of Killmurry, yeoman.

Persons indicted of treason in the King's Bench, in Easter Terme, anno decimo octavo Caroli Regis, 1642, and outlawed thereupon:

MEATH:—Read, John, of Plattin, Esq.—Rochford, Michael, of Kerans-

---

1. The following are here entered in the Ms. : " Rely, Richard, of Clantarfe, yeoman ; Rely, James, of the same, yeoman, [for] felony and burglary."

towne, gent.—Rochford, Jenico, of Killbride, gent.—Rochford, late of Wyanstowne, gent.—Russell, Patrick, of Roddenstowne, gent.—Rispin, Patrick ; Rely, Thomas, of Oristowne, yeomen.

KILDARE :—Rely, Garrett, of Symonstowne, yeoman.—O'Ronane, Owen, of Bolybegge, yeoman.—Rochford, Oliver, of Clane, yeoman.

COUNTY DUBLIN :—Russell, George, late of the parish of St. Michael the Archangel, Dublin, vintner.—Russell, Nicholas, of Collinstowne, gent. —Rely, Connor, of Luske, yeoman.—Russell, Thomas, of Drynan, in county Meath, gent.—Russell, Andrewe, of Swords, yeoman.—Russell, Thomas, of Dryneham, in county Meath, gent.—Russell, Patricke, of Brownestowne, gent.—Rowen, Lawrence, late of Finglas, clerke.—Russell, Thomas, of Lyske. gent.—Russell, Christopher, of Seaton, yeoman.

WICKLOE :—Redmond, John, of the parish of Wickloe, gent.

Persons indicted of treason in the county of the Corke, att the sessions holden att Youghall, and returned into the King's Bench, the second of August, 1642, and outlawed in the King's Bench for the same :

CORKE:—Roch, Patricke, of Powlenelong, gent.—Roch, Richard, of Glvny, gent.—Roch, David, of Ballyneloghy, gent.—Roch, David, of the Island, gent.—Roch, Richard, of Knockinhingin, gent.—Roch, James, of Kinure, gent.—Roch, John, of Ballenvallagh, gent.—Roch, William, of Ringarrane, gent.—Roch, Adam, of the same, gent.—Roch, M'Edmond ; Roch, Rory M'James, of Birne, gent[n].—Roch, David, of Gartmecouroe, gent.— Royse, Robert, of Clekeyle, gent.—Royse, Jerome, of the same, gent.— Roch, Thomas, of Aghelenane, gent.—Roch, Ullicke, of Ballindangin, gent.—Roch, John, of Castlekevine, gent.—Roch, Edmond, of Ballenlegune, gent.—Roch, James, of Kippagh, gent.—Roch, Theobald, of Killagh, gent.—Roch, Thomas, of Ballincargeagh, gent.—Roch, Redmond, of Garranadrolane, gent.—Roch, Thomas, of Castoigge, gent.—Roch, William, of Killeigh, gent.—Roch, John, of Castletowne, gent.—Roch, Miles, of the same, gent.—Roch, John, of Ballynemony, gent.—Roch, Edward, of Castletowne, gent.—Roch, Fitz John Theobald, of the same, gent.—Roch, John, of Ballendargin, gent.—Roch, Fitz John Ullicke, of Castlekine, gent.—Roch, William, of Ballinlergane, gent. —Roch, William Fitz

Thomas, of Clostoige, gent.—Roch, James, of Ballymackonikine, gent.—
Roch, David, of Killeigh, gent.—O'Ryerdane, John M'William, of Blarny,
gent.—O'Ryerdane, of Cloghendae, gent.—O'Ryerdane, John M'Donnell,
of Cooleviddane, gent.

Persons indicted of treason, in Hillary Terme, in the King's Bench,
anno decimo septimo Caroli Regis, 1641[-2], and outlawed thereupon:

MEATH:—Slane, William [Fleming], Lord Baron of.—M'Symon,
Patricke, of Galtrim, merchant.—Scurlocke, Barnabie, of Scurlockestowne,
gent.—Staples, Patricke, of Augistowne, gent.

KILDARE:—Sherlocke, Edward, of Blackhall, clerke.—Sutton, Law-
rence, of Tipper, clerke.—Sutton, Gerald, of Richardston, gent.—Sutton,
Nicholas, of Tipper, Esq.—Sherlocke, Thomas, of Naas, gent.—Scurlocke,
Thomas, of Rathcredan, in county Dublin, gent.—Sherlocke, Edward, of
Blackhall, clerke.—Smyth, Richard, of Maddenston, clerke—Sutton,
Nicholas, of Tipper, Esq.—Scurlocke, Patrick, of Rathcreadan, in county
Dublin, Esq.

DUBLIN:—Fitz Simons, Marke, of Surgolstowne, gent.—Fitz Simons,
Luke, of the same, gent.—Sutton, Nicholas, of Tipper, in county Kildare,
gent.—Scurlocke, Patrick, of Rathcreadan, Esq.—Scurlocke, Thomas, of
the same, gent.—Stronge, George, of Grange, Ballycoolan, gent.—Stany-
hurst, Thomas, late of Dublin, gent.—Sever, Richard, of Dunganstowne,
yeoman.—Savage, William, of Luske, yeoman.—Scurlocke, Martin, of
Rathcreadan, gent.—Scurlocke, Patricke, of the same, Esq.—Scurlocke,
Thomas, of the same, gent.

WICKLOE:—Shane, Art, of Wickloe, yeoman.—Sherlocke, George, of
the same, merchant.—Story, George, of Milltowne, yeoman.—Shorthall,
Richard, of Limericke, in county Wexford, gent.

Persons indicted of treason in the King's Bench, in Easter Terme,
anno decimo octavo Caroli Regis, 1642, and outlawed thereupon:

KILDARE:—Sutton, Nicholas, of Tipper, Esq.—Sarsfeild, Peter, of
Tully, Esq.

MEATH:—Slane, William [Fleming], Lord Baron of.—Streete,
Richard, of Platten, yeoman.—Sedgrave, Patricke, of Killeglan, Esq.—

Scurlock, Barnaby, of Scurlockstown, gent.—Scurlocke, Edward, of Fraines, gent.—Fitz Simons, Edward, of Allenstowne, gent.—Segard, William, of Fyanstowne, yeoman.—Slewnan, Donogh, of Martery, yeoman. COUNTY DUBLIN :—Fitz Simons, Thomas, of Grange, Baldoyle, gent.— Shervan, Christopher, of Ballyowen, yeoman.—Sweetman, Richard, of Tirrelstowne, yeoman.—Stanihurst, Thomas, late of Courtduffe, gent.— Stokes, Nicholas, of Ballhary, gent.—Sedgrave, Patricke, of Killeglan, in county Meath, Esq.—Stokes, Nicholas, of Ballhary, gent.—Scurlocke, Barnaby, of Scurlockstowne, gent.—Sparke, Peter, of Ratouth, in county Meath, gent.—Scurlocke, Patricke, late of Dublin, gent.

WICKLOE :—Sherlocke, George, of Wickloe, gent.—Sexton, Pierce, of Ballyneclogh, Esq.—Sexton, Robert, Ballygilleroe, gent.

Persons indicted of treason in the King's Bench, in Trinity Terme, anno decimo octavo Caroli Regis, 1642, and outlawed thereupon :

DUBLIN :—Sneezing, Donogh, of Portmarnocke, yeoman.

MEATH :—Scurlocke, Edward, of Fraine, gent.

Persons indicted of Treason in the county of Corke, att the Sessions holden att Youghall, and returned into the King's Bench the second of August, 1642, and outlawed in the King's Bench for the same :

CORKE :—O'Sullivane Beer, Donnell, of Beerehaven, Esq.—O'Sullivane, Phillipp, of Loghanbeg, gent.—O'Sullivane, Owen, of Inchiclogh, gent.—O'Sullivane, Owen, of Dromduvane, gent.—O'Sullivane, Donogh M'Owen, of Dromgarvane, gent.—O'Sullivane, John M'Dermody, of Derryne, gent.—O'Sullivane, Gillicody, of Trughprasky, gent.—O'Sullivane, Connor, of Loghane, gent.—O'Sullivane, Owen Reagh, of Dromgowlane, gent.—O'Sheyne, Teige, of the parish of Clonferte, gent.—O'Shelly, James, of Donnoghmore, gent.—M'Swyny, Mullmurry, of Artaghrugh, gent.—M'Shyhy, Murrogh, of Knocknemaddery, gent—Shynnane, William, of Castletowne, gent.—M'Swyny, Owen, of Moshanglasse, gent.

DUBLIN :—Sweetman, James, of Ilighstowne, gent.

Persons indicted of Treason in the King's Bench, in Hillary Terme, anno decimo septimo Caroli Regis, 1641[-2], and outlawed thereupon :

MEATH :—Trimleston, Mathias [Barnewall], Lord Baron of.

KILDARE :—Talbott, John, of Castletowne, clerke.—Talbott, Gerald, of Naas, gent.—Talbott, Gilbert, of Carton, gent.—Talbott, Garrett, of the same, gent.—Toole, Daniell M'Tirlagh, of Penvote, in county Wickloe, gent.—O'Toole, Hugh Carragh, of Brittas, in the same county, gent.

DUBLIN :—Talbott, Mathewe, of Templeoge, gent.—Taylor, John, of Swords, Esq.—Talbott, George, of Mallahyde, clerke.—Talbott, William, of Mallahyde, gent.—Toole, Luke, of the same, yeoman.—Tirrell, Patrick, of Rathenny, yeoman.—Travers, Robert, of Ballykea, gent.— Taylor, Robert, of Swords, gent.—Travers, William, of Ballykea, gent.— Thunder, Alexander, late of Colcott, gent.—Talbott, Thomas, of Poerston, gent.—Taylor, Thomas, of Swords, gent.—Talbott, John, of Mallahyde, Esq.—Travers, Luke, of Ballykea, gent.—Toole, Luke, of Castlekevin, in county Wickloe, gent.—Talbott, Gerald, of Cartan, in county Kildare, gent.

WICKLOE :—Toole, Luke, of Castlekevin, Esq.—Toole, Barnabie, of the same, gent.—Toole, Donnogh, of the same, gent.—Toole, Tirlagh, of the same gent.—Tirlagh, Farrell, of Curtletowne, yeoman.—Toole, Cahir M'James, of Killcrony, gent.—Toole, TeigeM'Cahir, of Killmakenocke, gent.—Toole, Edmond M'Loghlin, of the same, gent.—Toole, Art M'Edmond, of the same, gent —Toole, Hobart M'Davy, of the same, gent.—Toole, Davy M'Hobart, of the same, gent.—Toole, James M'Shane Glasse, of Callarogh, gent.—Toole, Brian M'Alexander, of the same, gent.—Toole, Donnogh M'Art, of Killmurry, gent.—M'Teige, Art, of Ballyronan, gent. —Toole, Barnabie, of Castlekevin, Esq.—Toole, Francis, of the same, sonne of Luke Toole, gent.—Toole, Luke, of Castlekevin, Esq.— Toole, Barnabie, of the same, gent., sonne of the said Luke.—Tynane, Barnabie, of Wickloe, gent.

Persons indicted of Treason in the King's Bench, in Easter terme, anno decimo octavo Caroli Regis, 1642, and outlawed for the same :

KILDARE:—Talbott, Garrett, of Caretown, gent.—Tirrell, Henry, of Killussy, cooke.—O'Toole, of Rathangan, clerke.

MEATH :—Trimlestowne, Mathias [Barnewall], Lord Baron of.— Talbott, James, of Robertstowne, clerke.—Talbott, William, of Mallahyde, gent.—Taylor, John, of Swords, gent.—Tirrell, Peter; Tirrell, Thomas; Talbott, James, of Athboy, merchants.—Tewland, Patricke, of Oristowne, yeoman.—O'Termcry, Cnogher, of the same, yeoman.

COUNTY DUBLIN:—Travers, Patrick, of Ballykea, clerke.—Travers, William, of the same, gent.—Thunder, Richard, of Ballyally, gent.— Travers, Richard, of Ballykea, clerke.—Travers, Robert, of the same, gent.—Taylor, Robert, of Swords, gent.—Thunder, Alexander, late of Collcott, gent.—Taylor, John, of Naall, Esq.—Talbott, Garrett, of Carton, in county Kildare, gent.

WICKLOE:—Toole, Coole, of Ballygullen, Esq.—Toole, Charles, alias Cahir, of Roshduffe, gent.—Toole, John, of Donnoghmore, gent.—Toole, Bryan, of Ballycullen, gent.—Toole, Murtagh M'Hugh Carragh, of Fidancoile, gent.

Persons indicted of Treason in the King's Bench, in Trinity Terme, anno decimo octavo Caroli Regis, 1642, and outlawed thereupon :

DUBLIN:—Talbott, Thomas, of Poerston, gent.—Talbott, William, of the same, gent.—Talbott, William, of Robertstowne, in county Meath, gent —Travers, Robert, of Ballykea, gent.—Toole, Luke, of Farty, in county Wickloe, gent.

MEATH:—Talbott, James, of Dunsaghlin, yeoman.—Taaffe, Lawrence, of Killeene, gent.

Persons indicted of Treason in the county of Corke, att the sessions holden att Youghall, and returned into the King's Bench, the second of August, 1642, and outlawed in the King's Bench for the same :

CORKE:—Teige, boy Donnell, of Ruscagh, gent.—O'Touny, Dermod, of Birne, gent.—O'Torny, William, of Disert, gent.—Tyrry, Fitz Dominicke William, of Ballymacperry, gent.—Tyrry, Fitz Dominicke, Dominicke, of Clonturke, gent.—Tyrry, Edmond, of Ballymacquirke, gent.— M'Tirlagh, John, Ballymacpatricke, gent—M'Teige, Donogh, of Prihus, gent.

Persons indicted of Treason in the King's Bench, in Hillary Terme, anno decimo octavo Caroli Regis, 1642[-3], and outlawed thereupon :

DUBLIN :—Travers, Robert, of Ballykea, gent.—Taylor, John, of Swords, Esq.

Persons indicted of Treason in the King's Bench, in Hillary Terme, anno decimo septimo Caroli Regis, 1641[-2], and outlawed thereupon :

MEATH :—Verdon, John, of Clonmore, in the county of Lowth, Esq. —Usher, Richard, late of Falrath, gent.

DUBLIN :—Veldon, Christopher, of Tulloge, in county Meath, yeoman.

Persons indicted of treason in the county of Corke, att the sessions holden att Corke, and returned into the King's Bench, the second of August, 1642, and outlawed in the King's Bench for the same :

CORKE :—Vaughan, John, of Callibegge, gent.—Vaughan, Cormuck ; Vaughan, Connor, of the same, gent[n].

Persons indicted of Treason in the King's Bench, in Easter Terme, anno decimo septimo Caroli Regis, 1641, and outlawed thereupon : de prodicione.

MEATH :—Wellesly, Valerian, of Dangen, Esq.—Ware, John, of Castletowne Moylagh, Esq.—Withers, Edmond, of Galtrim, gent.—Walsh, William, of Augistowne, gent.

KILDARE :—Wogan, Nicholas, of Rathcoffy, Esq.—White, James, of Carbry, clerke.—Walsh, Oliver, of Mooretowne, clerke.—Walsh, Lawrence, of the same, clerke.—Wolfe, Edmond, of Athy, gent.—Wogan, Thomas, of Downings, gent.—Wogan, William, of Downings, gent.— Walshe, Christopher, of Mooretowne, gent.—Walshe, Nicholas, of Kil-drought [Celbridge], gent.—Wesly, James, of Norraghmore, Esq.—Wolfe, Nicholas, late of Killcollman, gent.—Walsh, John, of Castledermott, clerke.—Walsh, George, of Painstowne, gent.—Wogan, William, of Dun-boine, gent.—Wesly, George, of Ballenebarny, gent.—Walker, Jun., George, of Ratheard, gent.—Wolfe, Gerald, of Moate, gent.—Wesly, Edward, of Allasty, gent.—Wesly, Jasper, of the same, gent.—Walsh, Richard, of Killcullenbridge, gent.—Wellesly, Walter, of Piercetowne, gent.—White, James, of Carricke, clerke.—Walsh, Peirce, of Logglas, in county Wickloe, gent.—Wolverstowne, James, of Frainstowne, in the same county, gent.

DUBLIN :—White, Ambrose, of Killcullen, in county Kildare, yeoman.—Walsh, Theobald, of Carrickmayne, gent.—Walsh, Edmond, of Clonmanen, in county Wickloe, gent.—Walsh, Henry, of the same, gent.—Walsh, Edmond, of the same, gent.—Warren, Edmond, of Swords, gent.—Walsh, William, of Ballmadrought, gent.—Fitz William, Thomas, of Balldungan, gent.—Wolverston, James, of Rathbram, in county Wickloe, gent.—Ward, Patricke, of Terrolstowne, yeoman.—Walsh, John, of Newtowne, Coolock, yeoman.—Wale, Richard, of Polegige, in Courtduffe, gent.—Wade, John, of the same, yeoman.—Warren, Thomas, of Silloge, gent.—Wotton, John, of Tankardston, yeoman.—Wade, Thomas, of Courtduffe, yeoman.—Ward, Patricke, of Luske, yeoman.—Wogan, Oliver, of Downings, gent.—Wolverston, James, of Rathbran, gent.—Wolverston, Paull, of the same, gent.—M'William, Teige, of Knockliane, gent.—Wolfe, Robert, of Glins, gent.—Walsh, Michaell, of Parke, gent.—Walsh, William, of the same, gent.—M'William, John, of Ballimargan, gent.—M'William, Patricke, of the same, gent.—Walsh, John, of Killincargie, gent.—Wolverston, Christopher, of Newcastle, gent.

Persons indicted of treason in the King's Bench, in Easter Terme, anno decimo octavo Caroli Regis, 1642, and outlawed thereupon :

MEATH :—Wolgar, Arthur, of Dowth, yeoman.—Wesly, Wellesley, Valerian, of Dangen, Esq.—Warren, John, of Churchtowne, gent.—Wafer, Francis, of Gianstowne, gent.—Walsh, William, of Ballynawly, yeoman.—White, Patricke, of Roddenstowne, gent.—Warren, John, of Churchtowne, gent.—White, James, of Clonegell, gent.—White, Nicholas, of the same, yeoman.

COUNTY DUBLIN :—Warren, Thomas, late of Dublin, gent.—Walsh, Tibbott, of Carrickmaine, gent.—Wade, Thomas, late of Courtduffe, yeoman.—Warren, Edward, of Swords, gent.—Walsh, William, of Ballinadrought, gent.—Warren, Alexander, late of Ballybyn, gent., in county Meath.—Wellesley, Valerian, of Dangan, in county Meath, armiger.—

Fitz William, Thomas, of Baldongan, gent.—Warren, John, late of Castleknock, yeoman.—Wade, Thomas, of Newhaggard, yeoman.

WICKLOE:—Wicombe, Marcus, of Barndery, gent.—Wicombe, Christopher, of Butlerswood, gent.—Walsh, Edward, of Clonmanen, Esq.—Wicombe, Peter, of Butlerswood, Esq.

Persons indicted of treason in the King's Bench, in Trinity Terme, anno decimo octavo Caroli Regis, 1642, and outlawed thereupon:

MEATH:—Wesly, Valerian, of Dangan, Esq.—Wesly, Walter, of Blackhall, gent.—Warren, Patrick, of Churchtowne, gent.

Persons indicted of treason in the county of Corke, att the sessions holden att Youghall, and returned into the King's Bench, the second of August, 1642, and outlawed in the King's Bench for the same:

CORKE:—Wale, James, of Clamolte, gent.—Fitz William, James, of Ballyburden, gent.—Wooden, Thomas, of Killchiagh, gent.

END OF VOLUME III.

A
REMONSTRANCE
OF GRIEVANCES PRESEN-
ted to his moſt Excellent Maieſtie, in
the behalfe of the Catholicks
of IRELAND.

Printed at *VVaterford* by *Thomas Bourke*, Printer
to the Confederate Catholicks of *Ireland*.
Anno Dom. 1643.

Forster & Cº Dublin.

FACSIMILE OF TITLE PAGE.
[See vol. ii., pp. 226-242.]

[See Back]

THis remonſtrance was delivered, by the Lord Viſcount Gormonſtowne, Sir Lucas Dillon Knight, Sir Robert Talbot Barronnet, & Iohn VValſh Eſquire, thereunto authoriſed, by the Confederate Catholicks of Ireland, to his Majeſties Commiſsioners, at the Towne of Trim, in the County of Meath, on the 17. of March 1642. to be preſented to his moſt Excellent Majeſtie.

Forster & Cº Dublin.

FACSIMILE OF BACK OF TITLE PAGE, 1643.
[See vol. ii, pp. 226-42.]

P1